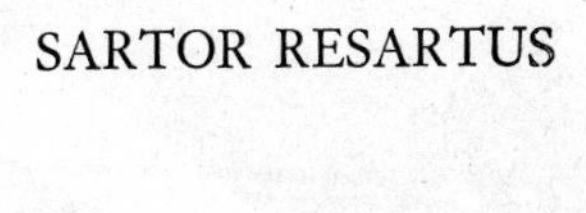

SARTOR RESARTUS

THOMAS CARLYLE
(From a photograph taken about 1860 by Messrs. Elliott and Fry, and reproduced with their permission.)

CARLYLE

SARTOR RESARTUS

The Life and Opinions of Herr Teufelsdröckh

Mein Vermächtniss, wie herrlich weit und breit!
Die Zeit ist mein Vermächtniss, mein Acker ist die Zeit.

GOETHE

Edited by CHARLES FREDERICK HARROLD

THE ODYSSEY PRESS

New York

PRINTED IN THE UNITED STATES

B 0 9 8 7 6 5 4 3 2 1

To

KARL YOUNG

in appreciation of

wise counsel,

unfailing encouragement,

and illuminating insights

into the mind, character, and work of

Thomas Carlyle.

PREFACE

Sartor Resartus has been one of the most frequently edited of the great Victorian classics. Its constant allusiveness, its involved style, its unfamiliar transcendentalism have all justified the attempts of editors to make the book intelligible to the ordinary reader. No recent edition, however, has presented the text in the light of a thorough re-examination of its literary and philosophical foundations. The last edition to attempt this, in a limited way, was that of P. C. Parr, published posthumously in 1913, without the benefit of the editor's final revision. The pioneer labours in the editing of *Sartor* had been undertaken by the late Archibald MacMechan, and had resulted, in 1896, in an edition to which all subsequent editors of the book have been heavily indebted. Independently of MacMechan, Mr. James A. S. Barrett, of Peebles, Scotland, published in 1897 an edition of *Sartor* which was the first to include, in its Introduction, an extensive consideration of Carlyle's use of German ideas. This edition, which has not been so well known in America as it has deserved, was revised in 1901 and in 1905. In 1882 there had appeared a German translation of *Sartor* (rev. ed. 1903), with helpful notes, by the ardent German Carlylean, Thomas A. Fischer. Since the publication of these editions, *Sartor* has appeared in many forms, with or without editorial apparatus. The present edition attempts to make the book intelligible not only by compact yet adequate annotation, but also by an Introduction which levies upon the results of scholarly research in Carlyle which has developed in recent years.

In the Introduction, a number of special emphases will be noted. In addition to the usual, and necessary, account of the composition of *Sartor,* there are sections devoted to the nature of the age in which it was written, to the plan of the work, to its meaning, and to its character as a work of literature. In discussing the meaning of *Sartor,* the editor has outlined the Calvinistic pattern which lies beneath the more modern, "German" design; and has indicated, as thoroughly as space permitted, the metaphysical, ethical, and social doctrines expressed in the work. The "modernity" of *Sartor* is but briefly suggested, the treatment of this theme making no claim to completeness. In the footnotes to the text, two kinds of material are presented: explanations of allusions, generally pointed out by previous editors of *Sartor,* but verified and usually condensed, and expository comments on Carlyle's meaning, especially as indicated by his German sources, and by the conclusions of scholars in Carlyle. In the notes it is possible for the reader to observe Carlyle's immense debt to Milton and Jean Paul for his phrasing, as well as to the Bible, to the Greek and Latin classics, and to the eighteenth-century English humourists. The notes reveal the vast reading, in literature, philosophy, science, history, and religion, which formed the background of *Sartor;* Carlyle was an omnivorous reader, and in *Sartor* he produced one of the most allusive books in the language. The present edition is also equipped with an adequate, annotated, selected bibliography, and with five Appendixes. Carlyle's chapter outlines, which are usually printed as a list of summaries in the back of the book, have been lifted to the place of analytical sub-titles for the respective chapters, in the hope that they will prove helpful to the reader.

It need hardly be said that the editor owes a heavy debt to his predecessors, especially to Archibald MacMechan, P. C. Parr, Thomas A. Fischer, and Mr. James A. S. Barrett. To Mr. Barrett in particular is he grateful for aid and suggestion through correspondence, and for certain very pleasant hours at Redbraes, in the valley of the Tweed, where Carlyle and his beloved Germans were discussed. Gratitude is due also to Mr. Isaac Watson Dyer, a mellow student and collector of Carlyle, whose *Carlyle Bibliography* is a monument of erudition in Carlyle, in his works, and in his reputation. Permission has kindly been granted to use, in Appendix I, material originally published in Mr. Dyer's bibliography. Finally, in all matters, the editor has benefited by the aid of his wife, Elizabeth Hebblewhite Harrold.

C. F. H.

Ypsilanti,
Michigan.

CONTENTS

SARTOR RESARTUS

BOOK I

INTRODUCTION

I. ON THE READING OF *SARTOR*

Sartor Resartus is not one of the easy and transparent masterpieces of literature. It belongs in the category of those unclassifiable and dynamic works which are to certain kinds of readers a perpetual delight, though to others either a stumbling block or the merest foolishness. As a half-mystical rhapsody, strangely composed by turns of fragments of biography, philosophic fantasies, and apocalyptic prose-poetry, it has been read with despair, indignation, rapture, or bewilderment, but probably never with mere indifference. As an elaborate literary hoax, it puzzled its own age; and as an eccentrically written work of literature, it still leaves many readers with mixed feelings of admiration and dismay. Several considerations are therefore necessary to place the book in its proper perspective and to reveal its essential nature.

More than most masterpieces of the early Victorians, *Sartor* requires of the reader of today an understanding of the circumstances and the point of view which conditioned its composition. In the first place, Carlyle in 1830 was still living in an age in which the great problems of philosophy, religion, and ethics could, for many thinking men, be validly approached by a method similar to that of the Old Testament prophets, by moral intuition, and by a challenging exhortation, illuminated by a vividly imaginative conception of the universe and its overwhelming significance to the prophetic mind. It was not yet the practice to subject all problems to severe scientific scrutiny. Though dogmatic theology had long since lost its grip on many minds, men still sought a religious and moral explanation of the world. Men like Carlyle believed that through some adjustment of the human will to the total scheme of things, life might be made not only better but more intelligible. Knowledge would wait upon will. In Carlyle's time, the adjustment of that will to reality was not yet, as it has since tended to become, strongly secular. Indeed Carlyle is one of the last great thinkers who sought a solution which should be at once non-theological and non-secular. To him no consideration of ultimate human problems could be satisfying which failed to be, in the deepest and broadest sense, religious. Thus *Sartor Resartus,* in its original purpose, as in its actual nature, was largely "prophetic." Its appeal was primarily to the moral will, not to the understanding; it sought to convince by challenging and affirming, not, as in present-day scientific methods, merely by explaining.

In 1830, Carlyle had developed that character of the "seer" which was only to harden and deepen as he lived on into the century. He was indeed in search of disciples, profoundly convinced that he had for the world a message which should be nothing short of a moral deliverance. He had reached the age—he was thirty-five—when the religious man's convictions may fuse and flame up into a prophetic passion. When Crabb Robinson met him in the winter of 1831–32, while Carlyle was seeking a publisher for *Sartor,* he observed that the young Scotchman, by "his voice and manner, and even the style of his conversation," appeared to be a "religious zealot," given to rhetorical "declamations against the anti-religious." Though the god of his idolatry was Goethe, it was as a "priest and prophet" of the *religion* of Goethe that Carlyle "spoke like an enthusiast [or zealot]."[1] That he believed the age to be in need of a moral deliverance is clear from his own words: "In my own heterodox heart," he wrote to his brother John, "there is yearly growing up the strangest crabbed one-sided persuasion, that all Art is but a reminiscence now, that for us in these days *Prophecy* (well understood) not Poetry is the thing

[1]*Diary, Reminiscences, and Correspondence of Henry Crabb Robinson,* ed. Thomas Sadler, 2 vols., Boston, 1871, II, 168–69.

wanted; how can we *sing* and *paint* when we do not yet *believe* and *see?*"[1] *Sartor Resartus* is therefore, by its author's own intentions, a book of prophecy. Parts of its "message" have been rendered somewhat difficult of apprehension by the passage of time: it is no longer easy to put oneself back into the intellectual climate of 1831, when the spirit of Calvinism, Evangelicalism, and other fervid religious faiths supplied a living background and a vital vocabulary for one's approach to *Sartor.* It is becoming increasingly difficult for younger readers to grasp the original meaning of "Prophecy," the "Moral Will," or "Imagination" and "Reason" as Carlyle used these terms. Since the days of Carlyle and the German romanticists, man's scale of values has shifted, its outlines have to some extent become blurred, and some values have virtually disappeared. It is only with effort that certain readers understand Teufelsdröckh to be, like Spinoza, and Novalis after him, a "God-intoxicated man." The world, especially the American world, is rapidly investing its capital in the logical understanding, in an objective and utilitarian faith in the laws of nature. The old tradition of the mystics, of the life of the soul as more important than any possible manipulation of matter, no longer enters so intimately, as it once did through the church, the daily conduct of life. Carlyle's overwhelming sense of a divine presence in all objects and actions—his intoxication with deity—finds a much less vital tradition than it once did. Indeed, "all that is American, or modern," as Santayana has said, "is the absence of any tradition in which the . . . God-intoxicated man could take root."[2] Yet a true understanding of *Sartor* demands at least an imaginative grasp of what that tradition means. And it is one of the great services of the book that it keeps alive an ideal and a discipline which mankind cannot wholly ignore. Throughout one's reading of *Sartor,* therefore, it is necessary to remember that Carlyle writes as a lay prophet, whose ideas, while sometimes

---

[1]*Letters of Thomas Carlyle: 1826–1836,* ed. Charles Eliot Norton, London, 1889, p. 378.

[2]See *The Saturday Review of Literature,* March 7, 1936, p. 9.

clothed in the language of another day, have yet their own vitality, and their own peculiar value for the minds of any age.

Another consideration which may enable us to approach *Sartor* with intelligence has to do with its style. We shall examine that style in detail on a later page. It is worth noting here, however, that the obscurity, the erratic syntax, and the riot of allusion in the book are all owing, in some degree, to Carlyle's sense of frustration during his apprenticeship, both in Edinburgh and at Craigenputtock. John Stuart Mill asked him in 1833 whether he thought the partly ironic and partly earnest style of *Sartor* and the essay on Cagliostro deserved such honour as his frequent use of it implied. Carlyle's reply is extremely illuminating: "You are right about my style . . . I think often of the matter myself; and *see* only that I cannot yet see. Irony is a sharp instrument . . . I cannot justify, yet can too well explain what sets me so often on it of late: it is my singularly anomalous position to the world,—and, if you will, my own singularly unreasonable temper. I never know or can even guess what or who my audience is, or whether I have any audience: thus too naturally I adjust myself on the Devil-may-care principle. Besides I have under all my gloom a genuine feeling of the ludicrous; and could have been the merriest of men, *had I not* been the sickliest and saddest."[1] It is evident that Carlyle wrote *Sartor Resartus* partly in a spirit of ironic despair. Uncertain whether it would be seen in print, he wrote largely to please himself, freeing all his impulses to indulge in wild humours, fantastic speculations, recondite allusions. It is, indeed, preëminently a sincere book, straight from his inmost convictions, expressed in his heartiest style, though exaggerated by the bitter humour of a man desperate with frustration and failure.

It will be instructive to turn now to the two major factors in the genesis of *Sartor:* the character of the age for which it was designed; and the personal problems of Carlyle out of which the strange lineaments of the book emerged.

---

[1]*Letters of Thomas Carlyle to John Stuart Mill, John Sterling and Robert Browning,* ed. Alexander Carlyle, London, 1923, p. 74.

II. THE AGE

To Carlyle the early decades of the century were the "Whirlwind of a departing Era."[1] The "old spiritual highways and recognised paths" were being torn up and then submerged under "oceans of Hypocrisy and Unbelievability."[2] The post-Napoleonic world was a world of cynicism, sentimentality, scepticism, reactionary dread of change, utilitarianism. The age of Reason, culminating in the French Revolution, had left all institutions, all dogmas, all expressions of man's spirit, virtually in shreds and tatters. Everywhere there was a crying need of creative change, of constructive channelling of the new economic and social forces; and everywhere, in Church and State, there was refusal to face the realities of crisis. Carlyle, like Jean Paul before him, had fallen into "the fermenting vat" of a time when all the elements of society were passing into solution, dissolving and "foaming through each other."[3] The century stood before him "in all its contradiction and perplexity, barren, mean and baleful."[4] The world was to him "an extinct world, deserted of God, and incapable of welldoing till it changed its heart and spirit."[5]

When Carlyle began the writing of "Thoughts on Clothes," England was reaching the end of a Tory régime which, except for one unimportant interval, had existed since 1783. The "old Tory orthodoxy," once the living thought of Burke, but now ossified into a scheme of barren dogma as a bulwark against reform, or "Jacobinism," was nearing its collapse, as economic misery, pauperism, starvation, and class injustice brought society to the verge of revolution. Rickburning kept the south in terror; while in the industrial north, workmen were drilling and preparing for social war. The middle class

---

[1]Carlyle, *Critical and Miscellaneous Essays,* III, 30.

[2]Carlyle, *Life of Sterling,* p. 96.

[3]*Ess.,* I, 145.

[4]*Id.,* I, 66.

[5]*Life of Sterling,* p. 58.

clamoured for reform, equally to appease the menacing lower classes, and to secure its own rights against an aristocracy it no longer trusted. That aristocracy was bent mainly on enjoying its privileges without fulfilling its obligations to the country. Preserving its game, it made the woods resound at night with gun-shots, as gentlemen and their servants grappled with poachers, while the "mantrap" and the "spring-gun" lurked in the undergrowth. For more than thirty years, economic unrest had warned the rulers of England of an approaching crisis.[1] "The stern Avatar of Democracy, hymning its world-thrilling birth- and battle-song,"[2] had raised its head in such portentous happenings as the Luddite riots of 1811–17, the Peterloo Massacre of 1819, the anti-Corn-Law agitation of the late twenties, and the Chartist movement culminating in the late thirties. The industrial revolution had come upon a nation still thinking in terms of the old domestic economy of semi-feudal England. As yet "a fatal ineptitude clogged the imagination of public men."[3] The vast potentialities of a new social order awaited the hand of true leadership. In the meantime Carlyle noted that in spite of "labour's thousand arms, of sinew and metal," nine-tenths of mankind struggled in the lowest battle against famine. He saw the age as the "stertorous last fever-sleep" of a sick world.[4]

Yet the age was capable of incredible levity and gaiety. It was still the age of the dandy. Beau Brummel was no longer in the ascendancy; but Count D'Orsay reigned at Gore House, and Byron, adding the wizardry of the poet to the glitter of the beau, had epitomized all the mockery and brilliant despair of an epoch which saw the hopes of the Revolution trampled

[1]G. M. Trevelyan, *British History in the Nineteenth Century: 1782–1901*, London, 1925, pp. 150–51, 230, *etc.;* D. C. Somervell, *English Thought in the Nineteenth Century*, New York, 1929, pp. 3, 11, *etc.; Early Victorian England: 1830–1865*, 2 vols., London, 1934, II, 413, 417, *etc.*

[2]Carlyle, *Ess.*, III, 270.

[3]Richard Hill, *Toryism and the People: 1832–1846*, London, 1929, p. 203.

[4]Carlyle, *Ess.*, III, 271.

under by the dictatorship of Napoleon. It became fashionable to bewail the unattainable, rather than to project the possible. Beneath the bitter levity, however, a "nameless Unrest, the blind struggle of a soul in bondage, a high, sad, longing Discontent,"[1] which had found a voice in Goethe's *Werther,* now cried in seductive power through the verses of Byron. To the poetic despairs of Byronism, there was added the factitious charm of sentimentality, through the discovery of what Carlyle satirically called "the extremely ornamental nature of high feeling."[2] And where sentimentality was barred, the last survivals of Augustan wit gathered at Holland House or at the breakfasts of the banker-poet, Rogers. The age also presented that characteristic social phenomenon, the "rout," or fashionable evening party, which was to prove so trying to Carlyle's nerves and digestion. Everywhere, on the "thin film above catastrophe," entrenched privilege ate and quipped its way to the edge of social conflagration.

In the sphere of leadership, intellectual or moral, little was being done which could satisfy Carlyle. Philosophy and religion seemed virtually dead. The Established Church had become known as "the praying section of the Tory party";[3] its clergy were content to follow the advice of the first Lord Shaftesbury, "to be gentlemen and to believe that God is a gentleman who would hardly send one to hell for a few gentlemanly sins."[4] Many of the clergy were espousing the new ideals of "liberalism," which was to stir the fine fury of John Henry Newman, and which dismissed such spiritual values as reverence and awe as "the rubbish of superstition." Religion had become, for many, a mere "sanction to civil morality . . . a help to the Constable and Hangman."[5] The age of Deism had produced a religion which operated, through persuasion

[1]Carlyle, *Ess.,* I, 217.

[2]*Id.,* III, 9.

[3]Somervell, p. 16.

[4]E. A. Knox, *The Tractarian Movement: 1833–1845,* rev. ed., London, 1934, p. 28.

[5]Carlyle, *Ess.,* I, 216.

or coercion, chiefly in public. "No one," said Lord Melbourne in a famous *mot,* "has more respect for the Christian religion than I have; but really, when it comes to intruding it into private life——"[1] By 1832, Dr. Arnold was forced to declare that "The Church, as it now stands, no human power can save."[2] To that conviction Carlyle had long since come. He had seen the bishops as a whole vote with the Tory Lords against the Reform Bill, and had understood why the mob at Bristol had burnt the palace of Bishop Gray.

While the Established Church was slumbering in easy livings, or riding gaily to hounds, a great movement of thought was going on in the country, gaining hold on a number of powerful minds, and threatening to become the dominant popular philosophy. It was now making a vigorous attempt to take possession of the whole province of morals, as it had already claimed the domains of psychology and political economy. This was Utilitarianism. The great names of this movement are well known. It was one of many varieties of radicalism flourishing virulently in the first third of the century. The revolutionary rationalism of Paine, the philosophical anarchism of Godwin, the disturbing theories of Malthus about population and the food supply, the radical economic individualism of Adam Smith, all poured themselves out of the last years of the eighteenth century into the "fermenting vat" of the new age. The Utilitarians, led by Jeremy Bentham and James Mill, erected upon the physiological psychology of David Hartley, and the associationist doctrines of Hume a "mechanic of pleasure and pain" to displace the old ethical concepts of duty and obligation. According to the new "hedonistic calculus," the sovereign masters of man's conduct, pleasure and pain, may be quantitatively measured, and they alone determine the moral quality of an act. The

[1] G. K. Chesterton, *The Victorian Age in Literature,* New York, 1913, p. 42.

[2] A. P. Stanley, *Life of Thomas Arnold, D.D.,* London, 1904, p. 278; S. L. Ollard, *A Short History of the Oxford Movement,* London, 1915, pp. 4–12.

criterion of the goodness of a law or act is the principle of Utility, the measure in which it subserves the happiness of the individual, which is the proper aim of life. The motive of our acts is always self-interest; and the welfare of society may best be promoted by permitting the free-play and mechanical adjustment of social individuals in their pursuit of happiness. What Carlyle called the "mysterious Self-impulse of the whole man," or the dynamic unity of the self, prompted by duty, was fast disappearing from current discussions of human nature. And in the same fashion, what Carlyle had regarded as the "mystic miraculous unfathomable Union"[1] of man in society, now became a mechanical, quite fathomable aggregate of social atoms, or individuals, each seeking his own separate end. As the individual had lost his inner unity in a mechanism of association—his mind or soul being now but the sum of sensations and ideas received from external nature—so now society was losing its inner spiritual unity in a mechanism of "sanctions," "motives," "rewards," and "punishments." Instead of religion, and the old ideals of reverence, obedience, obligation, and pious labour, as the cement of society, he now found a system of checks and balances, reforms, suffrages, and organizations, as the means by which society was to be held together, and even re-fashioned.

The business of government was to promote the greatest happiness for the greatest number, by rewarding and punishing. In the sphere of economics, it was to observe the principle of laissez-faire, by which the people were theoretically to be the judges and determinants of their own interests. In practice, this resulted in the refusal, by responsible authority, through indifference or timidity, to intervene on behalf of the weak, in the cause of social justice. Both theory and practice soon became an irresistible pattern: the laws of economics increasingly took on the semblance of natural law, even of divine ordinance. Malthus had shown that the poor increase faster than the food supply; the enthusiasts for laissez-faire

[1]Carlyle, *Ess.,* III, 11.

had shown that industry can flourish only when its laws are permitted to operate without interference; and economic practice had shown an unparalleled production of wealth. All classes except the poor benefited by these conclusions. And while the Tories, within or without the Church, found in such doctrines merely the proof of what they already regarded as axiomatic, the middle-class Evangelicals, with their fortunes to make, or well in the making, could see nothing in the doctrines incompatible with their religious zeal. But Carlyle could easily see the curious alliance between many of them, even in their most religious moments, and the followers of Bentham and Mill. The Tories believed in the defence of property, the Benthamites in free competition; and any religious sect could apparently agree with both, and evidently did. For there rose at this time that phenomenon which Carlyle unweariedly satirized: "respectability," the compromise between precept and practice, between the pursuit of success and the profession of Christian virtues. "Respectability with her thousand gigs" became the symbol of the hollowness and concealed brutality of a mechanical age.

Indeed, from Carlyle's point of view, the evil of the age was summed up in the overwhelmingly mechanistic character of its standards. All problems were to be solved by "machinery," physical or intellectual. As an age of mechanistic rather than moral reform, the first third of the century had repealed the Test Act in 1828, had enacted Catholic Emancipation in 1829, and had passed the Reform Bill of 1832. In industry, the application of machinery had begun to transform the land which Cobbett loved into the blackened England which Ruskin was to grieve over. The rise of new problems in industry, society, religion, and thought was met by purely external treatment. Carlyle could find little tendency to penetrate into the inner, dynamic, and vital sources of those problems. And he observed that the peculiarly modern habit is to patch up the old or invent new and mechanical methods without examining the reality beneath, to believe that all problems are material, that the "garment" is the man. This was the purport of mechanism, whether in Utilitarianism or in Whig political reform or in the universal belief in the "march of mind." "We have machines for Education . . . Religious machines, the Bible Society," he mournfully noted, machines even in art and literature, in "Royal Academies . . . Paternoster-row mechanisms"; and, at last, metaphysics itself is reduced to a mechanical level, in the sterile doctrines of Reid and Dugald Stewart.[1]

Such was the period to which *Sartor Resartus* was addressed. In the violent language of indignation, Carlyle attacked the "old hidebound Toryism . . . [as] an overgrown Imposture, supporting itself not by human reason, but by flunky blustering and brazen lying."[2] He saw that "all Science had become mechanical . . . Churches themselves had died away . . . Men's souls were blinded, hebetated; and sunk under the influence of Atheism and Materialism, and Hume and Voltaire."[3] In the midst of crisis, the sin of the age was dilettantism: "the Whigs, and all 'moderate Tories' [were] the grand Dilettanti . . . this [was] no world where a man should stand trimming his whiskers, looking on at work, or touching it with the point of a gloved finger."[4] Instead of rising heroically to its challenge, in practical work towards a humane civilization, the England of Bulwer's *Pelham* "lay all puking and sprawling in Werterism, Byronism, and other Sentimentalism,"[5] or putting its trust in political economy, that "dismal science" which had arisen on the doctrines of Bentham. How far Carlyle exaggerated or misrepresented the conditions of English society it is not our present purpose to inquire. There was enough truth in what he said to justify him in presenting, in *Sartor,* such doctrines as the sacredness of labour; the need of heroes, or leaders; the transcendent values of reverence and obedience;

---

[1]Carlyle, *Ess.,* II, 61–62.

[2]Carlyle, *Life of Sterling,* p. 51.

[3]*Life of Sterling,* p. 58.

[4]D. A. Wilson, *Carlyle to "The French Revolution,"* London, 1924, p. 176.

[5]Carlyle, *Ess.,* IV, 39.

the spiritual unity of society; the infinite nature of duty; the function of matter as symbol, dress, and instrument; the reality of spirit; the need of finding new expressions for man's soul, new garments for his ideas and ideals.

If *Sartor* owed its content to the age for which it was written, it also owed a debt to the times for its form and style. We must not forget that *Sartor Resartus* is a product of the age of Pickwick, an age peculiarly tender towards individuality, quaintness, or eccentricity. The harsh buffooneries of contemporary journalism, as exemplified in *Fraser's Magazine,* gave Carlyle a wide freedom in delineating Teufelsdröckh and his strange universe. The times were sick and out of joint, it is true; but the contemporaries of Alfred Jingle knew how to laugh. The reader who fails to smile even through all the sublimities, the prophetic fury, the pathos, and the fantasy of *Sartor,* has failed to understand a man who, in spite of his sadness and dyspepsia, was, if not among the "merriest of men," at least among the greatest of English humorists.

III. THE GENESIS OF *SARTOR*

The story of the composition of *Sartor* has been told many times. In its original form it was a "strange piece 'On Clothes,' "[1] intended for a review article, which later developed into a longer work of two essays, and which grew out of Carlyle's meditations on the philosophical and ethical foundations of society, as he conceived them during his early Craigenputtock period. Settling down in his "Dunscore Patmos," he thought his way to clear convictions about the world which he confronted. As early as August, 1830, he wrote to Goethe that he felt within him a "wonderful Chaos . . . full of natural Supernaturalism, and all manner of Antediluvian fragments."[2] In his journals and in his letters throughout 1830

[1]J. A. Froude, *Carlyle: First Forty Years,* etc., New York, 1882, II, 53.

[2]*Correspondence between Goethe and Carlyle,* ed. C. E. Norton, London, 1887, pp. 210–11.

and 1831, there are frequent references, direct or indirect, to the growth of *Sartor,* called as yet either "Thoughts on Clothes" or *Teufelsdreck*.[1] In his Journal for September 18[?], 1830, he writes, "I am going to write—Nonsense. It is on 'Clothes.' Heaven be my comforter!"[2] Throughout October he is uncertain whether he is writing a book or a "string of Magazine Articles," but is certain that it is "a very singular piece," which "glances from Heaven to Earth and back again in a strange satirical frenzy, whether *fine* or not remains to be seen."[3] Early in November, this "singular piece," in the form of two articles (which now form Book I of *Sartor*) was sent to Fraser under the title of "Thoughts on Clothes." To Carlyle's great disappointment, the work was rejected, and in January, 1831, he asked his brother John, who was then in London, to get the manuscript and return it home for revision and elaboration. "I can devise some more biography for *Teufelsdreck;* give a second deeper part, in the same vein, leading through Religion and the nature of Society, and Lord knows what . . . I have taken a notion that I can make rather a good *Book,* and one, above all, likely to produce some desirable impression on the world even now."[4] From January to late in July, 1831, Carlyle laboured over his book, unable at times to view it as "the right thing yet," but always sure that "there is a kind of life in it."[5] By the end of July, his work was finished. The original paper, in two parts, became, as we have noted, Book I of *Sartor;* the "biography for *Teufelsdreck*" evidently formed Book II; and the "deeper part, in the same vein, leading through Religion and the nature of Society," became Book III.

Borrowing fifty pounds from Jeffrey, of the *Edinburgh Re-*

---

[1]So spelled in the early versions of the work; the change to *Teufelsdröckh* was made by February, 1833. (*Letters,* etc., ed. C. E. Norton, p. 365, *n.*)

[2]Wilson, *Carlyle to "The French Revolution,"* p. 182.

[3]*Letters, etc.,* ed. C. E. Norton, p. 174.

[4]*Id.,* p. 183.

[5]*Letters,* pp. 179–99; Wilson, *Carlyle,* II, 190–220.

view, he started on August 4 for London to find a publisher. He was now thirty-six, yet relatively unknown. Though he had been writing for almost a decade, he was far from success. Besides his hack-work articles for *Brewster's Encyclopaedia,* his *Life of Schiller,* and his article on "The Signs of the Times" for the *Edinburgh Review,* in 1829, his published work had been confined to translations and reviews. The moment was, in some respects, a moment of crisis in Carlyle's life. Craigenputtock was no longer the seed ground of his genius; his apprenticeship was over. In *Sartor* he had gathered up all of the best that his mind had produced in the silence and solitude of Dunscore. Moreover, his income had shrunk, as review articles were less and less in demand; at the same time his brothers, John and Alick, were dependent on him for support. Carlyle offered his work, not yet called *Sartor Resartus,* to several publishers, but all markets, literary or otherwise, were in suspension owing to the Reform Bill agitation, which had created a great public sense of insecurity. While in London, however, he corrected proof-sheets of "Characteristics," his most recent article for Jeffrey, in which many of the themes of *Sartor* appeared without benefit of booksellers. Finally, concluding in despair that "British Literature [was] a mud-ocean, and boundless 'mother of dead dogs,'"[1] Carlyle returned with his manuscript to Craigenputtock, in April, 1832.[2] Attempts to publish the book in Edinburgh proved futile. At last, a year later, on May 27, 1833, he sent off a letter to James Fraser, announcing his determination to "slit [the book] up into strips, and send it forth in the Periodical way."[3] Fraser accepted the work for serial publication, and it appeared, under the title of *Sartor Resartus,* in *Fraser's Magazine* from November, 1833, to August, 1834.

The reception of *Sartor* by the public, the "unqualified disapprobation" which it met on all hands, is now a part of the

---

[1]*Letters,* p. 287.

[2]Wilson, pp. 283–84.

[3]*Letters,* pp. 364–66; see Appendix II.

very legend of Carlyle. How it received enthusiastic attention in America, and its *editio princeps* there in 1836, under the loving supervision of Emerson, who wrote an unsigned preface for it, is also a part of that legend, as well as a highly creditable chapter in American literary insight. Mrs. Carlyle had pronounced it a "work of genius," but Carlyle had to write *The French Revolution* (1837) and to take London by storm before Fraser would follow the American publisher of *Sartor* and bring out an English edition in 1838.

IV. THE PLAN OF *SARTOR*

To understand the nature of *Sartor Resartus,* it is necessary to remember that it was the culmination, as we have noted, of a long period of agonizing apprenticeship. The years following his studies at the University of Edinburgh were the most wretched in Carlyle's life: his slow uncertain intellectual development, the beginnings of dyspepsia, the increasingly confused state of his religious beliefs, all added to the already heavy burden of finding some suitable life-work. From 1816 to 1823, he took up and abandoned school teaching, the law, divinity studies, literary hack-work, tutoring. In 1818 he read Gibbon's *Decline and Fall of the Roman Empire,* and saw at once that he could no longer believe in the religion of his fathers. Throughout this troublous period, he read widely in philosophy and science, groping for an intelligible and coherent view of the world. Whether from a desire to read Werner's *Mineralogy* in the original German, or from a hope that German literature and thought would bring order into his belief,[1] it is noteworthy that in 1819 he began the study of the German language. The first crisis of his life was now approach-

[1]*Corresp. between Goethe and Carlyle,* pp. 156–57; Wilson, *Carlyle till Marriage,* pp. 165–67, 173–78; Froude, *Carlyle: First Forty Years, II,* p. 209. Carlyle told Emerson that "he had learned German by the advice of a man who told him he would find in that language what he wanted"—presumably ethical and philosophical enlightenment. See Emerson's *English Traits,* Boston, 1856, p. 22.

ing: by 1821, he had met Jane Welsh and he had begun to read Goethe and Schiller.

The world of German literature and philosophy came to Carlyle like a revelation. From 1821 to 1831, he unceasingly occupied himself in exploring and expounding German ideas. By 1826, when his long and troublous courtship ended in marriage, and he and Jane Carlyle settled at Comley Bank, Edinburgh, he had begun the composition of a number of essays on German writers, which were eventually to become a kind of reservoir of ideas from which to fashion the intellectual structure of *Sartor Resartus.* By that time, also, he had had his own "Everlasting No," his "conversion" in Leith Walk, in 1822, and his final calm in the translation of Goethe's *Wilhelm Meisters Wanderjahre,* at Hoddam Hill in 1825–26. Between June, 1827, and the publication of *Sartor* by Fraser, in November, 1833, Carlyle published review articles—long expository and critical essays—on Richter, Werner, Goethe, Novalis, Schiller, and "The State of German Literature." His mind became steeped in German thought; his style was soon affected by German sentence-patterns; his beliefs were coloured by German mysticism and idealism. *Sartor Resartus* was but the logical result of an intensive study of German character and of the German mind.

Another source of materials for incorporation into the work on "Clothes" was an unfinished novel, *Wotton Reinfred,*[1] begun at Comley Bank in January, 1827, and thrown aside early in June of the same year. His venture into fiction, like his previous attempts at verse, ended in failure. Only seven chapters were written. Their contents, however, prefigure *Sartor* in several striking details. Like Teufelsdröckh, the hero is young and moody, and crossed in love. Like Blumine, the heroine, Jane Montagu, is won from him by a friend. Young Wotton, like young Carlyle, had been bullied at school, had lost a sister by death, had learnt little at the university, had

[1]Reprinted, with "Excursion (Futile Enough) to Paris" and some letters to Varnhagen von Ense, in *Last Words of Thomas Carlyle,* London, 1892, pp. 1–148.

found strength in a deeply religious mother, and had drifted into desperate unbelief. The plot, however, promises to be little more than a shadow of much in current popular fiction: the mysterious locket containing a portrait with an unmistakable likeness to himself; the mysterious stranger; the House on the Wold; the journey through romantic mountain scenery —these elements conspire with others to produce a very conventional effect. But in the House on the Wold, which resembles in character the symbolical castle in *Wilhelm Meister,* Wotton meets a strange company of philosophical speculators who, around a dinner table, discuss the merits and shortcomings of the Kantian philosophy, in speeches frequently foreshadowing the transcendental passages in *Sartor.* A later meeting of Wotton and Jane Montagu is the occasion for a lengthy explanation of the latter's conduct, and the uncompleted novel ends. As in the *Life of Schiller* (1823–24), the style of *Wotton Reinfred* is curiously unprophetic of the later Carlyle; it is conventionally smooth, undistinguished, at times long-winded. But the novel shows Carlyle dealing tentatively with a hero susceptible to "German" treatment, handling philosophical ideas, and attempting a love-theme which will provide Teufelsdröckh with the impetus towards the "Everlasting No."

The plan which emerged from these sources[1] was eminently fitted to Carlyle and his times. In an age of anonymity, broad humour, and love of eccentricity, Carlyle was able to capitalize the then popular conception of the Germans, their curious

[1]Three other sources should be mentioned: (i) the folk-tale, *Reinecke Fuchs,* from which Carlyle said he drew "perhaps [his] whole speculation about 'Clothes'" (Wilson, II, 184). Little can be determined as to just what this source contributed, except, as Barrett notes, a vivid life-vision of human passions, of the beast-godhood, divine infernal pageant of existence, in the guise of animals; (ii) the journal which Carlyle kept at Craigenputtock from 1828 to 1830 (see appropriate chapters in Froude and in Wilson, and *Two Note Books of Thomas Carlyle from 23d March 1822 to 16th May 1832,* ed. C. E. Norton, New York [Grolier Club], 1898); (iii) the fund of undogmatic Calvinism which provided a structure for all the ideas, images, and beliefs which in *Sartor* appear to be of German origin. This source is discussed in Section V, a, of the present Introduction.

scholarship, their mysticism and humour, their metaphysical discussions, beer gardens, simple manners, their learned and eccentric professors. In order to give the "Clothes Philosophy" a wide appeal, he decided to trace its development in the mind of the author, revealing the spiritual struggle of which it was the result. He therefore devised the figure of Professor Diogenes Teufelsdröckh, the author of a number of philosophic fragments which Carlyle ostensibly edits for the British public. From these fragments Carlyle pretends to derive both a philosophy and a biography. For several reasons, this method was of great value. It enabled him to transform a weakness into a virtue: his genius was too discontinuous and philosophical for the production of a novel; the very lack of organization became one of the sources of *Sartor's* humour and eccentric power. The method had other merits: it took full advantage of the derivative nature of Carlyle's philosophy; it enabled him to present a very unpopular and misunderstood subject, German transcendentalism, without the formidable apparatus and the appearance of metaphysical inquiry; it gave him an opportunity for objective evaluation of—and occasional raillery at—his own ideas; it provided a screen behind which he might hide when his doctrines threatened to arouse the indignation or contempt of the reader; it united the didactic aim of the philosophic discourse with the human interest of the biographical novel; and finally it permitted him to indulge the wayward, boisterously ironic freedom of his genius. Much of it is undoubtedly indebted to Jean Paul, who made the humorous theme of disorder the ground-plan for many a strange and rhapsodical work.

On the surface, then, *Sartor Resartus* is a collection of philosophic fragments, biographical narrative, and editorial comment. The work as a whole falls into three Books. The first Book introduces and defines the subject of "clothes," and delineates the personality of Teufelsdröckh, as pieced together from the notes sent by Teufelsdröckh's friend, Heuschrecke, in six paper bags under labels inscribed with the signs of the zodiac. Fragments of the professor's volume, dealing with

the "history" of clothes, appear between the fifth and eighth chapters. The theoretical part of *Sartor* begins, however, in Chapter VIII, with a discussion of the world of spirit, *i.e.,* of the world *out of* clothes, or the world of reality behind the "living visible Garment" commonly called Nature. The rest of Book I elaborates this theme, showing Teufelsdröckh to be almost a new "Adamite" in his preference for the real man (the soul) rather than the clothing (the body), and dwelling on the necessity of employing "pure Reason" (the equivalent to imaginative insight, or moral intuition) in looking upon all material forms as merely raiment or emblems of a spiritual, creative reality beneath (Chapters X, XI). Book II appears at first sight to be an interruption. But it is really the development, from the angle of moral biography, of the implications of the earlier chapters, and a foreshadowing of many ideas in Book III. Instead of committing the error of tiring the reader with a whole work on the plan of either Book I or Book III, Carlyle hit upon the happy thought of inserting into the middle of his book a narrative which should secure at once his reader's interest in Teufelsdröckh himself, in his heroic inner struggle, and in the universal significance of his final experience. Book II contains some of the most eloquent and penetrating passages in the whole of Carlyle's works. Skilfully avoiding the problems of the novelist—effective dialogue, organic plot, the interplay of characters—Carlyle gives himself the freedom of piecing together the life of Teufelsdröckh from the notes sent by Heuschrecke, commenting on them, leisurely analysing the professor's character, pointing out the moral or philosophical significance of various facts, indeed making the biographical data the occasion for a "criticism of life." Teufelsdröckh is seen first as a foundling, then is followed through his schooling, his attempts to establish himself in his profession, his romantic love of Blumine, his rejection, his sorrows and wanderings, and his final triumph through a great inner experience. Book II gains much by being more autobiographical than any other part of *Sartor*. Though Carlyle later wrote that the close of the Book was "symbolical myth all,"[1] he excepted the experience in the Rue de l'Enfer. He might have added, however, that while much of the external character of Teufelsdröckh had little in common with himself, the whole story of the inner struggle and victory was essentially his own. Book III returns to the "Clothes Philosophy," with emphasis on the application of Teufelsdröckh's ideas to religion, politics, wage-slavery ("Helotage"), dilettantism (symbolised by the dandy, in Chapter X), the outlook for social regeneration (Chapter V, "The Phoenix"), and the new attitude towards nature and the supernatural as suggested by German transcendentalism, namely "natural supernaturalism" (Chapter VIII).

The obscurity of *Sartor,* in style and structure and meaning, has long been a major charge against Carlyle as writer and thinker. There is much to be said in defence of this charge. Certainly few great literary works have had a more unfortunate opening paragraph. And Carlyle's frequent references to the chaos of Teufelsdröckh's papers and methods may be taken as roughly descriptive of the actual jumble which is *Sartor Resartus.* Yet there is more order than is apparent to the timid reader; and the very disorder is, as has been said, a part of the humour of the design, and also an evidence of how little value Carlyle placed on systematic and logically impeccable presentations of the "truth." In reality, Carlyle has employed every art of arrangement in the general structure: the three great divisions, the short chapters, with relevant though often cryptic titles, and the helpful summaries. Wherever he aims to reach the reader with important ideas, he drops his wayward rhetoric, and speaks in clear if highly metaphorical language. In all important passages it is not the style but the message which may confuse the reader—the transcendentalism which has not yet filtered down into common thought as has the Cartesian rationalism of the seventeenth century. It should be noted, also, that reading *Sartor* would be far less difficult than is generally assumed, if many

[1]Froude, *Carlyle: First Forty Years, etc.,* I, 58.

of the passages on the "history" of clothes, much of the biographical material, and almost all the orgy of allusion in the book were taken for only what they are worth, which is sometimes very little, except as a part of the curious humour of a Scotchman writing for the readers of *Fraser's Magazine*. Like *The Anatomy of Melancholy,* or *Tristram Shandy,* or *Gargantua,* Carlyle's book is best read in appropriate moods, a little at a time, not continuously from beginning to end. This is the historical and proper way of reading works which either preach a gospel or please a palate, and *Sartor* does both, for different groups of readers. It may be read either as a kind of "Scripture" or as a work of art, so many-sided, so alive, so attractive in its very repulsion, that the reader, once he catches the idiom, returns again and again to his favourite passages for an imaginative experience which no other book can quite give.

V. THE MEANING OF *SARTOR*

a. The Calvinistic Sub-Pattern

The informing theme of *Sartor Resartus* is suggested by the meaning of its Latin title.[1] "The Tailor Re-tailored" deals with a conception of the world which is as old as Oriental thought, and as familiar as the Biblical saying: "As a vesture shalt thou change them, and they shall be changed."[2] Swift had written of "worshippers who held that the universe was a suit of clothes which invests everything";[3] and Pascal had written of nature as the "symbolical" dress of the Invisible.[4] With Carlyle, it was the *use* of the figure, not its adoption, which proved to be original. It permitted him to retain the

[1]On the title, see Appendix I.

[2]Psalms, cii, 26. See also Job, xxxviii, 9; Isaiah, l, 9, li, 6; Hebrews, i, 11, 12.

[3]Swift, *Tale of a Tub,* Section II.

[4]Pascal, *Œuvres complètes,* ed. F. Strowski, Paris, 1931, III, 187, 202–03.

dualism ingrained in him by a deep heritage of Calvinism, to find modern expression for his consciousness of a transcendent world of values behind the world of flux, or of physical nature. "He saw all that he looked on *sub specie aeternitatis*—and eternity never ceased to excite him."[1]

As a Calvinist without Calvin's theology, he developed a transcendentalism, more realistic than subjective, on the thought-patterns of his native faith.[2] *Sartor Resartus* is thus a brilliant metaphorical adaptation of German idealism, in its terms and concepts, to the surviving intellectual design bequeathed by Calvinism when shorn of its dogmas. It will be worth while to state briefly the chief elements in the Calvinist faith which enabled Carlyle to transform into prophecy and into materials of great literary beauty a number of German ideas on man, the world, history, heroes, symbols, knowledge, ethics, and social relations.

Of Calvinism it has been said that "where the sense of divine providential government is deep and strong, where the eye of faith sees God sitting at the loom of time weaving the web of individual lives, where the mystical in human nature is given proper recognition and due rights, where men live life under a profound sense of responsibility and a keen realisation of its incalculable issues in eternity, there Calvinism lives."[3] It is noteworthy that Calvinism is not identical with its system of doctrine. It is enough if one regards all the world and all its history as the carrying-out of one divine plan, conceived in the eternal reason of the Godhead, and executed in time; if one further believes that, in any generation of mankind, only a few individuals are born "elected" to righteousness and leadership, and that all others are born "in darkness," to be followers; and if one believes that life is made real only through obedient *action,* through faith rather than through intellectual knowledge, and through rigorous self-renunciation,

---

[1]Mary Agnes Hamilton, *Carlyle,* 1926, p. 99.

[2]See C. F. Harrold, "The Nature of Carlyle's Calvinism," *Studies in Philology,* XXXIII (1936), pp. 475–86.

[3]A. M. Hunter, *The Teaching of Calvin,* Glasgow, 1920, p. 297.

acceptance of duty and sorrow, rather than through the pursuit of "grace" or happiness. The Calvinist's God is divinely irrational: He has predestined the greater mass of mankind to error; yet He commands that *all* must labour as if "elected," that men's righteousness may show in their work. Man's reason is only a tool for action; it never comprehends or solves any final problem. Salvation lies only in action, in playing one's part in the eternal plan, to help promote the "sanctification," or spiritualization, of the whole world. Though man is to renounce the world as a value in itself, he is yet to engage in "moralizing" it through his worldly calling, through honest, pious labour, performed with little thought of wages but with great thoroughness. There is here no "world-joyousness," as in Lutheranism; the universe is completely reduced to the status of *means,* though consecrated to eternal ends. The social implications of this faith are, of course, extremely significant. In the first place, despite its "fatalism," Calvinism sets the strongest personal value on the individual, gives him an immeasurable responsibility, endows him with an enormous individualism and self-dependence. This is not because of any "modern" pre-conception of the democratic individual. Only the "elect" are divinely given such superb individuality; but all must act as if so endowed. Paradoxically this system of faith, with its predestinarian basis, has spurred men to great activity; and with its exaltation of the individual, it has led to doctrines suggestive of socialism. Indeed, Calvinism implies a socialism without democracy and without communism, in which every man is to stand for himself, yet allied with his fellows through obligation and compassion. In the great Calvinist society, every man would have his honour, his maintenance, his right, safeguarded by Church and State. His life would be an integral part of a vast socialism of mutual responsibility, administered in a patriarchal, theocratic rule of the best men (Carlyle's "heroes") in an all-inclusive effort to spiritualize, turn to ethical ends, the entire fabric of the world.

Stated thus briefly, Calvinism may be seen to be susceptible, in the hands of Carlyle, to translation into German terms. Carlyle's translation was, of course, neither critical nor philosophically sophisticated, but it was a striking feat of imagination and literary art. In Goethe, Schiller, Kant, Fichte, Novalis, and Schelling, he found all that he needed to build up a coherent philosophy sufficient for what he considered to be the needs of his age. The Calvinist sense of "election" was satisfied in Fichte's doctrine of the *Gelehrt* (scholar, or great man). Indeed Fichte's ethical idealism supplied Carlyle with a whole series of idea-patterns suitable for a general rehabilitation of the Calvinistic view of the world. Predestination became Fichte's doctrine of the progressive and inevitable realization of the Divine Idea in the world's history; Calvin's exaltation of action appeared, in new dress, in Fichte's emphasis on the moral deed, rather than on the pretensions of the Understanding; the Calvinist's conviction that the world is a snare and a delusion, now gained new meaning in the Fichtean conception of time, space, and matter as unreal if taken as self-existent, yet real if regarded as manifestations and instruments of the Idea, or spirit. From Goethe, Carlyle took such phrases as would give this new world a vivid pictorial dress, and from *Wilhelm Meister,* especially, such passages as would give new and richer expression to the Calvinist doctrines of fulfilment through labour, of self-renunciation, and of the "worship of sorrow" rather than the pursuit of happiness. Novalis and Schelling, each in his own way, further developed certain ideas of Fichte, and thus provided Carlyle with still other sources. We shall see on later pages more specifically how these German doctrines contributed to Carlyle's system. It is enough here if we note the extent to which Calvinism formed the sub-pattern beneath the obvious pattern of German ideas which gives *Sartor* its individual character. What struck Carlyle was that his newly discovered German thinkers, whether philosophers like Kant or literary men like Goethe, were all opposing the mechanism of the eighteenth century, and were conceiving all things in terms of the dynamic, of the inner as real and of the outer as merely the vesture or tool.

They were indeed "re-tailoring" the world for modern man.[1] With their aid, Carlyle fashioned a metaphysic, an ethic, and a theory of social relations.

b. The Universe of *Sartor*

The world of Teufelsdröckh is no static or drab-coloured world for the unimaginative utilitarian. It is an apocalyptic, boundless phantasmagoria, with "thousand-figured, thousand-voiced, harmonious Nature" mysteriously weaving itself into a "living visible Garment of God." Within and behind this cosmic raiment, however, is the divine reality, called by various non-theological names—the Eternities, the Immensities, the Superior Powers—yet frequently reminding us of the earlier, more anthropomorphic God of Puritanism. The world, and all of man's history, is a part of an eternal plan—at times identified with Fichte's "Divine Idea"—which is to be realized in the realm of matter, time, and space, which, in turn, "exist only spiritually, and to represent [the] Idea, and *body* it forth." Space and time, "deepest of all illusory Appearances," are considered by Teufelsdröckh partly in the manner of Kant, as forms of our sense-perception, and partly in the manner of Fichte and Novalis, as the "vesture of the Eternal." All nature, then, is emblematic, the evidence of spirit, or life, at work. Indeed, in a moment of pantheistic adoration, Teufelsdröckh is impelled to cry: "Why do I not name thee God?" The universe is the "star-domed City of God"; in "every grass-blade, and most through every Living Soul, the glory of a present God still beams." And this universe, at once so solid-seeming and yet so evanescent, is organically one: there is a continuity of essence, and an "immeasurable, universal World-tissue," running through all things; so that any "smithy-fire was (primarily) kindled at the Sun, [and] is [now] fed by air that circulates from before Noah's Deluge,

[1]On Carlyle's debt to German ideas, see C. F. Harrold, *Carlyle and German Thought: 1819–1834,* New Haven, 1934.

from beyond the Dogstar." One, likewise, is the *moral* universe: "Not a red Indian," says Teufelsdröckh, "hunting by Lake Winnipic, can quarrel with his squaw, but the whole world must smart for it . . . Nature is one, and a living indivisible whole."[1]

Yet the world of Teufelsdröckh is ever changing, ever being destroyed and created anew: "Death and Birth are the vesper and the matin bells . . . nothing is completed, but ever completing." In various forms, as in the doctrine of *Palingenesia* or the "Phoenix doctrine" (*cf.* Bk. III, Ch. v), we meet in *Sartor Resartus* the notion of "universal becoming," that dynamic conception of reality which was the peculiar gift bestowed on modern thought by the German mind. In Herder's theory of the movement of humanity; in Goethe's speculations on the progression of vegetable forms and of higher species; in Fichte's conception of the world as the progressive expression of the Divine Ego; above all, in Wilhelm Meister's moral development as an individual—in all these, Carlyle found the idea of "Eternal Growth" (*das Werdende*). And that idea brought order into his speculations on permanence and change, on time and eternity. As a Calvinist he now saw change as potential for good; and behind all transiency he saw the unchanging Ideal, the God behind the Garment, at once the Judge and the Fulfilment. In *Sartor,* time is the world's vast "seedfield"; and change and death are but evidences of the undying, indwelling force which works out an infinite and eternal design.

Knowledge about that design is withheld from man. His intelligence is properly the servant of his act. Evidences of infinite significance, however, are scattered everywhere throughout Teufelsdröckh's universe: these evidences are symbols. The universe of *Sartor* is a vast hieroglyph, "one vast Symbol of God," but intelligible only to those who "well know the Alphabet" of the mysterious "Volume of Nature." To read that volume aright, and to apprehend the reality which

[1]See, respectively, pp. 55, 72, 73, 188, 264, 245, 71, 246.

transcends it, it is necessary to employ *Reason,* as understood by such post-Kantians as Fichte and Novalis. *Reason* in *Sartor* is equivalent to mystical intuition, to imaginative or moral insight. It is opposite and superior to *Understanding.* "Not our Logical, Mensurative faculty, but our Imaginative one is King over us." Exclusive attention to the products of the Understanding leads to materialism and mechanism. To the eye of "vulgar Logic," what is man but "an omnivorous Biped that wears Breeches," or the universe anything other than a "huge, dead, immeasurable" machine? To the eye of "Pure Reason," however, man is "a Soul, a Spirit, and divine Apparition"; the universe is the "living Garment of God"; and "Man's history . . . a perpetual Evangel." At times, Teufelsdröckh is not wholly satisfied with Reason; in one place he quotes Friedrich von Schlegel's remark that *"Fantasy* [is] the organ of the Godlike." In the end, he seems to have concluded that it is through Reason, Imagination, Fantasy—transcendental intuition under other names—that man may be said, "through *Symbols* . . . consciously or unconsciously" to live, work, and have his being. His logical Understanding, far from penetrating to the deepest truth, merely combines, separates, and re-arranges the mysterious symbolic data of his experience.[1]

The universe of *Sartor,* though at bottom Calvinistic, is strangely Teutonic. To one acquainted with the philosophy of German romanticism, it suggests at once a number of debts. It is indebted to Goethe, of course, for its metaphorical grandeur as the "Garment of God"; to Fichte for its character as Divine Idea in the act of being embodied in nature and in man's history; to Schelling, as well as to Fichte and Goethe, for its organic unity, its mysterious union of process and permanency; to Kant, Fichte, and Novalis, for the "grand enveloping illusions" of Time and Space, and for the distinction between Reason, Understanding, and Imagination; to Goethe, Schelling, and Schiller for the symbolical, *hieroglyphical* char-

---

[1]See pp. 217–26.

acter of nature; and to Jean Paul for innumerable phrases expressive of its sublimity and mystery. It is in many respects the world of the mystic: it is a world of oneness, of immediate and perpetual contact with the divine, of dazzling flashes of insight; it is a dynamic unfolding of the eternal Godhead; and its beauty and terror are for Teufelsdröckh, as for all mystics, ineffable, expressible only in symbols, actions, or ecstatic affirmations.[1]

As an expression of imaginative metaphysics, Carlyle's universe, as found in *Sartor,* is an extremely interesting fusion of transcendental idealism and Puritan mysticism. It does justice to the Calvinist's emphasis on the transcendence of God, and on the instrumental role of nature and history as carrying out an infinite plan in the "seedfield of Time." More than any other part of *Sartor,* the "metaphysical" passages show Carlyle's visionary power, his ability to strip off the sheath of things, to reveal in one dazzling moment their mysterious heart. It is no doubt concerning these passages that it has been said: "There are pages of ecstasy in *Sartor Resartus;* and in its ecstasy, in its intellectual intoxication, is the great strength and the great beauty of the book."[2]

c. The Ethic of *Sartor*

Teufelsdröckh's struggle with the problem of conduct is conditioned by the dualistic character of his world, and by the paradoxical nature of its physical realm as at once illusion and instrument. It will be helpful to consider his final ethical doctrine from the point of view of his convictions as to (i) the enigma of *time,* (ii) the nature of the *self,* and (iii) the stages by which he arrives at the "Everlasting Yea."

With an intensity curiously in advance of his day, Carlyle was haunted all his life by the mystery of time. Above all, he was fascinated by the *paradox* of time. From one standpoint,

---

[1]On Carlyle's mysticism, see C. F. Harrold, "The Mystical Element in Carlyle," *Modern Philology,* XXIX (1932), 459–75.

[2]L. Cazamian. *Carlyle,* tr. E. K. Brown, New York, 1932, p. 110.

it was a mere veil hiding the splendours of eternity; from another view it was the arena and the means of personal evolution. For Teufelsdröckh, who, in spite of his name, is a Calvinist, life is a warfare, a battle, a conquest. It is also a labour in "Time's seedfield." But while time is thus an opportunity, it is also a grievous limitation. Teufelsdröckh is indeed a "son of Time," imprisoned in the "troublous dim Time-element," wherein, nevertheless, he is to "produce" in the interests of infinite and mysterious ends, divine values. Time often appears to him as the very principle of evil, the Devil himself; that is, as the force which opposes the very principle of one's soul in its outward thrusting towards the Infinite, yet which is indispensable to the soul's development, as *bad* is a condition without which *good* would be impossible. Time, as Fichte had said, is an arresting and hemming-in (*anhaltend und hemmend*) of the life of the spirit, yet the sphere of activity for the realization of that life. The whole realm of matter, time, and space is thus a "not-me," the Non-Ego (*Nicht-Ich*) of Fichte and Novalis, on which we seize in order to work out our inner potentialities, our "Me."[1]

The "Me" or ego of Teufelsdröckh is just as dual as is his universe. It is made up of a "divine Me," and the mere practical "self." Carlyle seems to derive these from Fichte's doctrine of the "pure ego" (*das reine Ich*) and the "empirical [practical] ego" (*das empirische Ich*), respectively. The former or "divine" self is that part of Teufelsdröckh which is transcendental, a part of the Divine Ego, or God; it is indicated in the name Diogenes ("God-born"). His practical, or worldly self is the "descendental" part of him, belonging to the realm of time, space, matter, necessity, and death; it is indicated by the name Teufelsdröckh ("devil's dung"). The latter self is to the former as the garment to the man, the instrument to the purpose, the body to the soul. Teufelsdröckh's vocation, as a son of time, is to subdue as an illusion or obstruction, and to apply as an instrument, his

---

[1]See pp. 112, 121; and Fichte, *Ueber das Wesen des Gelehrten,* Berlin, 1806, p. 30 (see *Popular Works,* tr. W. Smith, London, 1873, p. 149).

worldly self (manifested by his body), and to play his part in subduing and applying the body or garment of God (namely, Nature) to the realization of divine ends or values. Teufelsdröckh's complete "ego" is held in tension by a polarity of contradictory thrusts, one "upward" and one "downward," like Faust's *zwei Seelen.*[1] And this polarity is dynamic, resting in unstable equilibrium, providing a constant temptation to grovel in the lusts of matter, and to aspire to the heights of spiritual achievement. To hold with Hume, Bentham, and other mechanists, that the lower self is alone real is to deny the dynamic, vital element in human experience. The mechanistic account of the self appeals to our love of logic. It is a product of the *Understanding.* A quite different account is delivered by the *Reason,* though it leaves the logical intelligence unsatisfied, since it is akin to faith, and thus appeals to imagination and the will to act. The reality of the "divine self," its origin and its destiny, are in fact enshrouded in mystery; the true ego of man is "an authentic ghost," poised mysteriously "in the centre of Immensities, in the conflux of Eternities." The most "authentic" knowledge we have of that ghost, says Teufelsdröckh, comes through the performance of duty, *i.e.,* through the deepest realization of the self. Logical analysis, when dealing with such a subject, "is by nature endless, formless, a vortex amid vortices," issuing finally in contradiction and denial. It is "only by a felt indubitable certainty of Experience," through action, that we arrive at certitude.[2]

Now by the time the hero of *Sartor* had fallen in love with Blumine (Bk. II, Ch. v), he had gradually and unconsciously lost the sense of the duality in the world and in himself.

---

[1]See *Faust, I,* lines 1112–17:

> "Zwei Seelen wohnen, ach! in meiner Brust,
> Die eine will sich von der andern trennen," *etc.*
>
> Two souls, alas; reside within my breast,
> And each withdraws from, and repels, its brother.
> (Bayard Taylor's translation)

[2]See pp. 66, 195–96.

His "logical, mensurative faculty," the Understanding, had developed at the expense of the instinctive, spiritual immediacy surviving from childhood. Thus when he loses Blumine, he has no internal support but his logical reason, which had caught up the "Profit-and-Loss Philosophy" of the Utilitarians, conceived of the world as a mechanism, and had "yielded up [all] moral questions in despair."[1] In his sorrow, his Understanding reels and stumbles through the "vain interminable controversy" on the "Origin of Evil." Throughout his being the "Everlasting No" peals authoritatively, denying any moral or purposive quality to existence; the world is mechanical, morally neutral, at last *hostile*. Teufelsdröckh passes from mere "passivity" to "the painfullest feeling [of] Feebleness (*Unkraft*)," then to a "continual, indefinite, pining fear." Not conscious that "Unbelief is unbelief in yourself," he cowers and trembles before the world, as if "in its dead indifference," it would "grind [him] limb from limb." Resentful and self-pitying, he momentarily indulges in Byronic moods, or like Werther, contemplates suicide. Disdainfully he comments: "How beautiful to die of broken heart, on Paper! Quite another thing in practice." Finally, in the *Rue Saint-Thomas de l'Enfer,* he confronts himself with the sudden question: "What *art* thou afraid of?" Whereupon he discovers, to his surprise, that in his wrath at the "hostile" scheme of things, he absolutely defies it, defies even Death. Then he notices that his defiance is launched, not by his ordinary self, by his logical reason, but by a power in him (the "native God-created" Me) that *affirms* its status as above mere nature, above "the iron ring of Necessity," and *asserts* its freedom and moral autonomy. This discovery seems to send "a stream of fire over [his] whole soul," to give him a kind of "fire-baptism." Base fear leaves him; he knows himself as a "Me"; and "perhaps directly thereupon begins to be a man."[2]

---

[1]As did Wordsworth under the influence of the rationalism of William Godwin. See *The Prelude (1805)*, ed. E. de Selincourt, London, 1933, x, 901.

[2]See pp. 157–68.

But he has not yet been "converted" to a new way of life, nor has he achieved a new philosophy. The Everlasting No had said: "The world is a blind complex of forces; you are alone and defenseless"; to which Teufelsdröckh had replied by asserting his own freedom to *hate* those forces; he had not yet, of course, had time to re-interpret them in terms of the same inner freedom, to see Nature at heart as spiritual as himself. At present, in the Centre of Indifference, in a state of torpor, insensibility, and resigned sadness, he has only a sense of release and freedom; he is still in an alien universe. Yet he does turn away from his former habit of introspection, "and [he] clutches round him outwardly on the Not-Me for wholesomer food." Into the alien universe, which now stirs his interest in a new way, he sets forth, like other romantics of his time, to begin his *Wanderjahre,* and carries through the world, like Byron, "the pageant of his bleeding heart." Like the poet in Shelley's *Alastor,* he visits the deserts, the ruins, the ancient places of the earth; like Meister he wanders through romantic mountain scenery; like Childe Harold, he visits famous or remote cities and places, and there speculates upon the mystery of human experience, upon government, social institutions, war, literature, great men, history. He has reached the "dead centre," midway between the opposite poles of unimaginative mechanistic realism, and inspired dynamic idealism. After a period of exploration in the Not-Me, he is ready for the next step in his evolution.[1]

This next step, however, is in reality three steps. It involves first the act of renunciation, then the acceptance of suffering and duty rather than happiness as our aim, and finally the will to act. In the Everlasting Yea, Teufelsdröckh matches his positive inner state with the affirmations of a new ethic and a new metaphysic. In clutching at the Not-Me, he has discerned within it the ground for his own autonomy; the universe ceases to be "alien" and becomes now his Mother, alive as he is, but godlike. Teufelsdröckh has now passed

---

[1]See pp. 169–82.

through his "temptation in the wilderness," *i.e.,* in "the wide World in an Atheistic Century." He has been tempted especially by two things: the hope of knowledge, and the hope of happiness. Now, however, he has decided "to renounce utterly," to cease chasing "false shadows of Hope," and fleeing from "haggard spectres of Fear." The result is as sudden and illuminating as was the result of his defiance in the Everlasting No: he awakens "to a new Heaven and a new Earth." Self-annihilation (*Selbsttödtung*), or renunciation (*Entsagen*) —terms borrowed from Novalis and Goethe, respectively— serve to describe the "preliminary moral act" by which Teufelsdröckh enters into a new life. He has renounced the hope of ever *understanding* the mystery of existence, and of ever being entirely *happy*. This renunciation produces in him "an infinite Love, an infinite Pity," both for "poor, wandering, wayward man," and for "the poor Earth, with her poor joys." And it leads naturally to the second step in the Everlasting Yea: his own solution of the problem of suffering.[1]

Each age, he declares, must solve the problem in its own way. As for himself, the "origin of evil" and of suffering lies, not in man's weakness and littleness, but in his greatness: "it is because there is an Infinite in him, which . . . he cannot quite bury under the Finite." This "infinite," however, leads to evil when it becomes an appetite for happiness or pleasure. It leads to good when it is made the dynamic, creative power of action or duty, regardless of reward, or even comfort. Teufelsdröckh therefore accepts sorrow as holy; he can love the Earth even while it injures him. The *Worship of Sorrow,* involving, as it does, renunciation and labour, is for Teufelsdröckh the new faith, indeed the answer to Voltaire, who had demonstrated "that the Mythus of the Christian Religion looks not in the eighteenth century as it did in the eighth." It is the new non-creedal religion, preserving the essence of Christianity.[2]

---

[1]See pp. 183–89.

[2]See pp. 189–91.

The final step in the Everlasting Yea comes when Teufelsdröckh decides to "close [his] Byron," and to "open [his] Goethe." This means that he will relinquish his futile self-analysis and morbid brooding on the mystery of things, and will follow the practical ethics of *Wilhelm Meisters Wanderjahre.* For the poetic futility of Byron, he will substitute the prosaic but creative aims of Goethe's hero. Now that happiness is no longer the end of living, now that "blessedness," or the deep fulfilment of man's true self, is the true aim, Teufelsdröckh finds salvation in practical labour, in doing the "duty which lies nearest." The ambitious hopes of the Byronic generation outsoared the actual, were indeed the Ideal untethered to the Real, and were thus doomed to frustration. Teufelsdröckh sees that "here, in this poor, miserable, hampered, despicable Actual [the prosaic daily environment] . . . here or nowhere is thy Ideal . . . The Ideal is in thyself, the impediment too is in thyself." Like Lothario in *Wilhelm Meister,* he discovers that "here [in the immediate task] or nowhere is America." Thus that "strangest Dualism," which Carlyle the "editor" found in Teufelsdröckh, is at last sublimated into a higher, dynamic harmony. Both Teufelsdröckh and his universe are now un-mechanized; both are seen as partly free and partly determined; both are spirit, yet both are clothed, and the "clothing" or the "actual" is but the instrument for the realization of more and more *life.*

The ethic of *Sartor* becomes in the end very much like the Christian ethic. Carlyle's Calvinistic needs had been amply met by German ideas. From Goethe there had come, though profoundly altered and redirected, the conceptions of the "worship of sorrow" (religious acceptance of humility and pain), "renunciation" (in Goethe, a temporary self-denial for the sake of larger ends), and self-realization through work (Goethe's doctrine of "capabilities"). Novalis's idea of *Selbsttödtung,* originally a *philosophical* act, became in *Sartor* synonymous with Puritan self-denial. Fichte contributed occasionally a more conceptualized form of Goethe's ethic of *Bildung,* or harmonious personal evolution, through activity in the "seedfield of Time." In the end, these German thinkers utter in *Sartor* the old Scriptural commandments: "Whatsoever thy hand findeth to do, do it with thy whole might. Work while it is called Today; for the Night cometh, wherein no man can work."[1]

d. The Social Doctrines in *Sartor*

"If Nature is one, and a living indivisible whole," writes Professor Teufelsdröckh, "much more is Mankind, the Image that reflects and creates Nature."[2] In this sentence we have the basis of Teufelsdröckh's sociology. In the first place, as Goethe had said, "All men make up mankind"; humanity is a unity, according to *Sartor,* a "mystic Union . . . a mysterious brotherhood."[3] As profoundly as Fichte, Carlyle believed that "the great mystery of the invisible world, and its fundamental law [is] the union, and direct reciprocal action, of many separate and independent wills."[4] Society is to Teufelsdröckh the "standing wonder of our existence." In it, men are united by the homogeneous soul-stuff of their higher egos, especially through religion, "the inmost Pericardial and Nervous Tissue" of society. Yet their garment of flesh, though "contextured in the Loom of Heaven," forces men to dwell both "in Union and Division": in union because of similar necessities and obligations; in division because the flesh-garment prevents any man from wholly knowing or sympathetically identifying himself with another. Indeed, society is possible only because of man's dual-functioning flesh-garment: without it he would cease to be a visible entity; with it, he needs to unite himself with his fellows, and thus

---

[1]See pp. 191–97.

[2]See p. 246.

[3]See p. 214; also Carlyle's tr. of *Wilhelm Meister,* II, 131; and *Ess.*, III, 10–13.

[4]Fichte, *Popular Works,* tr. W. Smith, p. 361 (*Vocation of Man,* Bk. iii).

create social relationships. Society, if it is to be vital, must combine these two opposing forces, the centripetal and the centrifugal, the self-preserving and the self-giving. Here the garment is a social instrument. Furthermore, man's whole social existence is, to a surprising extent, "founded upon Cloth," on men's willingness to accept uniforms, insignia, and other symbolic dress, as equivalent to power. All garments, in fact—metaphorical or literal—are the instruments of spiritual force, or life. Whether with symbols, or with actual clothes, or with institutional means, mind is ever expressing itself, imposing its law. And in its operation in society, we see, says Teufelsdröckh, an epitome of Nature: a oneness, a whole, which manifests itself in a processal and physical multiplicity, while remaining at heart a dynamic and spiritual unity. This is "that wonder of wonders, Society."[1]

But "Teufelsdröckh is one of those who consider Society, properly so called, to be as good as extinct." Its collective faith, its religion, "where lies the Life-essence of Society," appears to be dead. Government, which is the "outward *skin* of the Body Politic," has shrunken; the Church "has gone sorrowfully out-at-elbows." Men are "no longer Social, but Gregarious," no longer united by fellowship, but merely herding together for protection or gain. Teufelsdröckh knows whom to name as the pall-bearers of "extinct Society": they are the "Liberals, Economists, Utilitarians . . . our European Mechanisers." They see society no longer as a spiritual whole, mysterious and dynamic, but as a physical aggregate, wholly intelligible and mechanical, as the epitome of a universe equally intelligible and mechanical. Not for them does "Society become possible by Religion," but by "contract," organization, laissez-faire legislation, reform, the ballot-box. Teufelsdröckh is forced therefore to protest against the "boundless 'Armament of Mechanisers' and Unbelievers [who] threaten to strip us bare!"[2]

---

[1]See p. 214.

[2]See Chapters ii, v, and vii of Book III.

Black as is the prospect, however, the Professor nevertheless cries: "Society is not dead: that Carcass, which you call dead Society, is but her mortal coil which she has shuffled-off, to assume a nobler." Applying the German doctrine of "becoming," under the figure of the fabled Phoenix, he prophesies the re-birth of Society. "As the ashes of the Old are blown about . . . organic filaments of the New mysteriously spin themselves" into a new organism. Tradition, opinion, inherited ways, "as preserved in Institutions, Polities, Churches, above all in Books," live on and create new forms; "beautiful it is," says Teufelsdröckh in one of his mystical moments, "to understand and know that a Thought did never yet die." The whole past and future are one; and men are spiritually embraced by a "living, literal *Communion of Saints," i.e.,* the wisest of mankind, dead or living, who, by their thought and deeds, lead man on to newer and more living forms. Teufelsdröckh—or rather the young, idealistic Carlyle—now considers the practical aspect of the future. As a "radical" in the sense accepted in 1830, Carlyle was opposed to the *status quo;* thus Teufelsdröckh is given "a deep, silent, slow-burning, inextinguishable Radicalism," which breaks out in iconoclastic satire, and demands of the proprietary classes something more than "preserving their game." Looking into the future, he expects representative government to survive; in addition, political reforms, extended trade with the colonies, education, and emigration will all be preliminary steps in a vast reconstruction of society. He hopes, however, that men will not stop at mechanical reform, but will proceed to a rediscovery of the ancient wisdom, to the ideals of obedience and loyalty to true leaders, in that "Hero-worship" which is the "cornerstone of living rock, whereon all Polities for the remotest time may stand secure." In spite of Teufelsdröckh's "radicalism"—which reflects Carlyle's indignation at the economic injustice he saw in Annandale—there is at the heart of *Sartor* a profound conservatism. Its social doctrine is *étatiste;* its collectivistic implications point towards the super-state. Though it may at times suggest socialism, it expresses only the socialism of responsibility, hierarchically administered, which Carlyle inherited from Calvin.[1]

In the "Phoenix Death-Birth" of society, new powers will arise, or rather old powers with new and greater functions. Two powers, especially, will assume leadership: labour and literature. "Two men I honour, and no third," says Teufelsdröckh in a famous passage: "first the toilworn Craftsman . . . second the Artist, . . . the inspired Thinker." The new world is to be a world of labour, and the new Church is to be found in the Church of Letters. Carlyle was among the first of his time to foresee the immense power and influence of the press. He knew that, whether or not it proved worthy of its power, the press—the newspaper, the magazine, and the book—would mirror the aspirations of the people; it would guide, instruct, and set up ideals. Time has given a bitter irony to his predictions. The new "church" has sadly betrayed its champion. Carlyle was of course considering literature in terms of thinkers like Goethe, Schiller, and Fichte, for whom the literary man was, ideally, a moral leader and teacher. Carlyle's exaltation of the poet as inspired thinker is prompted by his conviction that the imaginative faculty is the mother of the moral faculty; dogmas and creeds may perish, *should* grow old and tattered as garments, but the creative force beneath remains to be imaged forth by the artist, the poet, the thinker, in newer and more vital forms. The new religion of letters, therefore, is not far from what Arnold had in mind when he spoke of the future of poetry as being "immense."[2] Literature as a moral discipline, as an opener of new vistas, as the originator of ideals, would gradually assume the functions formerly monopolized by dogmatic religion. The literary man as a kind of priest or sage for the modern mind appeared not only in Carlyle himself, and in

---

[1]See pp. xxxiii–xxxv, 236–37, 244 ff.

[2]Matthew Arnold, "The Study of Poetry," *Essays in Criticism: Second Series,* London, 1888. See the opening paragraph, where poetry—and literature—is said to be a sure stay in an age when "our religion has materialised itself in fact," and every creed is shaken.

Emerson, but also, later, in Tolstoy, Nietzsche, and Romain Rolland. Such men, in league with the powers of labour, would re-mould the world. In Carlyle's thought, such men would make a dynamic return to the essence beneath the attributes. To be sure, Carlyle expected and hoped that they would preach the gospel which he found in Goethe and the transcendentalists; that they did not, has little relevance to the pattern which Carlyle outlined. He saw that the old garments of men's thoughts and aspirations had worn out, that the old institutions, and beliefs, and methods were no longer adequate. The human spirit had outgrown them. Two forces were necessary in the coming reconstruction: thinkers with sound inspiration, and labourers willing to build a new world.

The social message of *Sartor* is arrived at by a penetration through "those outmost vulgar, palpable Woollen Hulls of Man, through his wondrous Flesh-Garments, and his wondrous Social Garnitures, inwards to the Garments of his very Soul's Soul, to Time and Space themselves."[1] Teufelsdröckh has sought the truth physically, psychologically, and socially. He has, from the start, demanded new forms, new concepts, new institutions, "clothes" for the modern mind. He has prophesied man re-clothed, the tailor re-tailored, *sartor resartus.*

e. The Continuing Vitality of *Sartor*

Independently of the literary qualities which give it permanence among other imaginative works, *Sartor Resartus* contains much which commends it as a work of philosophical insight. It expresses, in a highly metaphorical way, some of the elements of a philosophy as perennially attractive to men as that of Plato, regardless of what the contemporary data of knowledge happen to be: namely, idealism, as opposed to

[1]See p. 267.

naturalism. To be sure, its idealism is a strange mixture of Calvinism, German romanticism, and Puritan mysticism. But for vivid statements of the idealistic interpretation of reality, certain passages in *Sartor* are of great suggestive value. Carlyle's metaphysic, uncritical and pictorial as it is, exerts a great attraction upon those who see "this so solid-seeming World [as], after all . . . an air image, our Me the only reality, and Nature . . . but the reflex of our own inward Force."[1] This is merely Carlyle's figurative way of summing up, with more emphasis on the subjective than is usual with him, the very essence of philosophical idealism, namely, that in reality "only minds and their contents exist."[2] *Sartor* is thus a brilliant imaginative delineation of the world as an embodiment of mind, as essentially psychical. In its treatment of the mysteries of time and space, of the limitations of our knowledge, of the fundamental intangibility of matter, of the mysterious and powerful supremacy of spirit (or mind, life, reason), *Sartor* is Carlyle's answer—and, in part, the essential answer of all idealists—to the claims of materialism and naturalism. Carlyle's idealism, like Fichte's, makes a permanent appeal in its moral challenge to regard nature, the realm of the sensuous or material in experience, as the great arena for man's conquest and utilization of all forces to bring humanity into richer self-consciousness. It expresses a religious and ethical outlook in an undogmatic form, and replaces the supernaturalism of orthodox faith with the *natural* supernaturalism (or essential mystery) of the everyday world before our eyes. It continues to do for the imaginative reader what it has always done: it affirms, in the language of poetry, the reality of those ethical, religious, and social ideals which have been threatened by the weakening of institutional religion, and which all idealisms have been peculiarly concerned in supporting and justifying.

On its mystical side, Carlyle's idealism expresses something

[1]See p. 55.

[2]*Cf.* J. A. Leighton, *The Field of Philosophy,* Columbus, O., 1919, Chap. XVIII.

which persists in much modern thought in spite of the domination of the analytical and pragmatic spirit: that is, the concepts of continuity, organism, and unity in the world, especially as apprehended through "intuition," as in Bergson,[1] rather than through an act of logic. Carlyle's mystical "irrationalism" has a long and impressive pedigree, that of the sages from the earliest stirrings of Oriental thought to the meditations of Goethe as expressed in some of the quasi-mystical utterances of his last years. It represents the age-old faith which the reason cannot know. Its methods are those of the imagination, the emotions, the impassioned will; it is always the way of the creative artist as well as the saint, for whom what is completely explainable is utterly trivial. Artistic unity, like moral unity, transcends the logical understanding, and Carlyle as a literary man and as a moralist never tired of stating the supremacy of imaginative and moral insight over analytical reasoning. This emphasis is found, in greater or less degree, in all idealisms, ancient or modern. Carlyle stresses the moral and teleological question *why,* for the purposes of right action, rather than the scientific question *how,* for the purposes of analytical knowledge. He sees the world as a living, flowering, unfathomable mystery, a dynamic whole, achieving its highest level in the development of man in society. His metaphysical universe is a coherent and harmonious order, reconciling all opposites—good and evil, happiness and suffering, the passing and the permanent—in a transcendent Unity. From the standpoint of the whole it is an unchanging process; from the standpoint of any finite part, it is an eternal whole. In glorifying the imaginative will, *Sartor* appeals to the poetic and the religious mind; in preaching the deep unity of men in society, it appeals to all minds alive to the need of social solidarity, of a growing sense of shared responsibility and achievement. This is especially true in the light of modern consciousness of change.

---

[1]See Henri Bergson, *The Two Sources of Morality and Religion,* tr. R. Ashley Audra and Cloudesley Brereton, New York, 1935, p. 238, and *passim.*

By conceiving of the world as in a constant state of *dynamic flux,* Carlyle, in following Fichte, expressed an idea of great potential significance for the nineteenth and twentieth centuries, especially as it involved the principle of organism, for which Carlyle may have been indebted to Schelling. *Sartor* brilliantly expresses, at times, the modern concept of "growth," or development, which has its basis in the *Entwicklung* of the post-Kantians. It is not, to be sure, the evolutionism of Darwin; for Carlyle's world, the world of Teufelsdröckh in 1830, could of course have no place for evolution in the biological sense; its evolution at best approximates the Fichtean concept of the realization of an *idea,* the unfolding or actualization of a plan. The gospel of labour involves a belief in order, and in the possibility of fulfilling a purpose. Evolution occurs in Teufelsdröckh's world in the sense that an inherent design becomes more and more explicit. Yet even while Teufelsdröckh has no place for biological evolution, he does perceive that *Entwicklung* requires an *organic* world in which to occur. Carlyle's mystical sense of the "continuity of essence," of the oneness and unity of all things, demanded that the total be mirrored in the part, and the part aspire to the total. He thus arrives at virtually the position which is expressed, abstractly, in the following: "An individual entity, whose own life-history is a part within the life-history of some larger, deeper, more complete pattern, is [likely] to have aspects of that larger pattern dominating its own being, and to experience modifications of that larger pattern reflected in itself as modifications of its own being."[1] It is no doubt a far cry from Carlyle's mysticism to Whitehead's "theory of organic mechanism"; yet it is noteworthy that he perceived, far more than the generation of Mill and Huxley, the organic relations between the patterns of the individual and those of the universe. The Carlyle of *Sartor*—the young idealist, and contemporary of Romanticism—bore witness to the fact that

---

[1]Alfred N. Whitehead, *Science and the Modern World,* New York, 1925, p. 156. *Cf.* Mary Agnes Hamilton, *Carlyle,* New York, 1926, p. 112 ff.

nature cannot be divorced from its moral and aesthetic values, and that these values arise from the cumulation, in some sense, of the brooding presence of the whole on its various parts. Carlyle began his career as a part of that protest on behalf of the organic view of nature which found its greatest expression in the poetry of Wordsworth. In his doctrines of "becoming" and of "organism" he not only gave voice to theories emanating from Germany, and sometimes embodied in English Romantic poetry, but also anticipated the conclusions of a number of twentieth-century minds. He saw that "while the harmony of logic lies upon the universe as an iron necessity, the aesthetic harmony stands before it as a living ideal moulding the general flux in its broken progress towards finer, subtler issues."[1]

Sartor's enduring vitality is seen, further, in some of its social and ethical teachings. The importance and dignity of labour, the necessity of the individual to discover his "capability" and to find his happiness in creative work; the importance of the man of thought, and his responsibility to society; the use of history as a text for the guidance of humanity in the future; the need of rulers who will be truly "kingly" by serving others before themselves; the demand that government not only rule but also assume responsibility for the physical and moral welfare of the people; the need of vast social and economic readjustments in the interest of comprehensive social justice; the conception of nature as an instrument for the realization of a greater and more abundant life; and the exaltation of the human spirit above all material and mechanical forces—all these conceptions underly the continuing significance of *Sartor Resartus*. Carlyle's attack on the anarchic individualism of the Utilitarians, on the brutal "do-nothingism" of the ruling class, and on the elegant sentimentalism of the dilettanti led naturally to his powerful statement of a brotherhood of men more real than that celebrated in the religious cant of the day. All that was later

[1]Whitehead, *op. cit.*, p. 28.

called "social conscience" appears in condensed statement in *Sartor Resartus.*

This emphasis on the natural interdependence among men leads Carlyle to a concept of the state which has never fully naturalized itself among Anglo-Saxon peoples, but which has long since commended itself to Germany: the *corporate* state, the totalitarian ideal of statehood recommended by Fichte in *Der geschlossene Handelsstaat* (1800). In the Calvinistic collectivism which lies beneath the Fichtean gospel of social organism in *Sartor,* there is a pattern which, with different materials and different terms, coincides with the non-democratic, non-Liberal interpretation of man's social nature. It has, from certain angles, the appearance of socialism, and has indeed led many an unwary socialist to claim Carlyle as a great socialist John-the-Baptist. But Teufelsdröckh's socialism, as we have seen, is not one of equality, of rational analysis concerning final political decisions, but of organic inequality, of inter-locking responsibilities ranging from the least privileged up to the "hero" or "leader" whose acts are beyond the judgement of the multitude. Teufelsdröckh, like Napoleon, believed in *La carrière ouverte aux talens* (The tools to him that can handle them). In the Professor's "great society," all would labour, each according to his "capabilities," in service to the Whole; and each would be accorded his degree of reward and privilege. All would labour reverently, obediently, unquestioningly, in a society where privileges would be limited and unequal, and the responsibilities equal and unlimited. The "leader" would be under obligation to serve, and merit the allegiance by which men implement the grand designs of society. The *corporate* and organic state is thus implied in all the social utterances of Teufelsdröckh. Carlyle's political ideas, as they appear in *Sartor,* are but the evidence in the field of social thought of that "irrationalism" which so fundamentally marks his metaphysics. Totalitarianism makes its appeal to will, imagination, and passion, rather than to dispassionate reasoning and discussion. It demands the subordination of popular debate to mass-obedience and loyalty. Wherever in the world democracy has failed to take firm root, or wherever it has grown moribund, there the anti-intellectualism, the faith in will and symbols and exciting leaders, which Carlyle exalted, is a natural and inevitable phenomenon.

The ethic of *Sartor,* like its mysticism, retains its vitality inasmuch as it is both old and new. One notes that Teufelsdröckh's discoveries about himself as a moral being are all *re*-discoveries, are new in the sense that the old, as essential truth, may reappear in new dress. Teufelsdröckh's discovery of the principle of *Entsagen* is his recognition of the "negative path" which all mystics, in all times and places, have found to be the proper introduction to positive moral action. And his experience in doubt and faith, as delineated in the last four chapters of Book II of *Sartor,* constitutes one of the classic accounts of what William James called "the twice-born soul,"[1] and is an often-quoted contribution to the literature of the psychology of religious conversion.[2] On its positive side, Teufelsdröckh's moral ideal is akin to the ethical ideal of "self-realization": we are to find our work, and in doing that work we shall find the happiness which comes from a self completely realizing its potentialities. Such activity will release the self from morbid brooding, from the lust for pleasure, from endless and futile intellectual speculations. The appeal which Carlyle's gospel of work has made upon modern minds has been enormous. The nineteenth and twentieth centuries have done more than justice to his challenge to "produce," to use the forces of nature for human purposes, and to exalt labour as both a means and an end. Indeed, the uncritical acceptance of *Sartor's* message is no doubt responsible for much blind exploitation of human and natural resources in the hundred years following its appearance.

---

[1]The phrase is really F. W. Newman's (in *The Soul; its Sorrows and its Aspirations*); but see William James, *Varieties of Religious Experience,* London, 1902, pp. 80 ff.

[2]See J. H. Leuba, *The Psychology of Religious Mysticism,* London, 1925, pp. 220–21.

Carlyle's original ideal, however, remains valuable in its insistence upon the importance of work in the dynamic and creative development of personality.

VI. *SARTOR* AS A WORK OF LITERATURE

The beauty and power of *Sartor,* considered solely as a literary work, is the beauty and power of great philosophical poetry, of Dante, Milton, Goethe, Hugo, Nietzsche, Whitman. The intellectual content of such poetry may or may not be intellectually accepted; it is offered not merely as a proposition to the mind, but also as the material and structure for an aesthetic effect. One may read *Sartor* as one reads the ode on *Intimations of Immortality,* with imaginative assent to its ideas as they are used in an artistic pattern. Metaphysical ideas, and certain ethical ideas, have lost their relevance for many minds. Yet they represent something in man which goes beyond exact science. The modern mind casts them off reluctantly. It goes back with comfort, at times with excitement, to the *Divina Commedia,* to *De Rerum Natura,* to *Paradise Lost.* The metaphysics and theology in such works now belong to the domain of poetic truth. They symbolize the subtler psychological facts which escape the "mensurative faculty" and which make up the fundamental powers of the human soul. The interplay of these symbolized facts reconciles for the modern mind the existence and development of myth with the knowledge that it is only myth and not objective reality. For such a mind, an aesthetic design may work out a number of universal themes in human experience with the aid of ancient formulae, dogmas, myths, or creeds.[1] The result, as in *Faust,* may be the re-utterance of deep-lying truths through the re-vitalization of an ancient legend, leading to a peculiarly modern solution of an age-old problem, in a work of art valuable for its own sake. *Sartor Resartus,* in so far as it

[1] *Cf.* Denis Saurat, "The Function of Philosophical Poetry," *Literature and Occult Tradition: Studies in Philosophical Poetry,* New York, 1930, pp. 157–62.

may be called a "prose poem," belongs in the category of philosophical poetry, and offers to certain kinds of readers the same sort of pleasure as the masterpieces of Goethe, Milton, or Lucretius.

The style alone would explain a great deal of such pleasure in *Sartor*. It is a magnificent style, with many degrees of light and shade, of harmony and cacophony. It is full of contrasts: rolling like thunder or flashing with lurid lightning, it descends momentarily to strangely idyllic tones and the tenderest pathos. It rises to the tremendous rhythms of the Old Testament prophets, then colloquially satirizes a contemporary foible; it sweeps the heavens with an abstraction, then evokes a host of vivid images to exemplify it. It is bewilderingly allusive, brilliantly metaphorical, picturesque, full of movement. It delights in disconcerting and illuminating the reader by leaping from the sublime to the ridiculous. Its humour is gigantic, cosmic; and its dramatic power embraces the world, as in the thrilling Wagnerian finale of the chapter on "Natural Supernaturalism." It is, of course, a highly rhetorical style. In such stock devices as the pluralizing of proper nouns, the repeated coördination of words and phrases, the use of exclamations and apostrophes and interrogations, the hyphenating of words, the employment of alliteration and rhyme and assonance—in all these Carlyle, like an impassioned orator, is appealing to the ear and the imagination. Yet delicacy is also within his range, as may be seen if one turns to the fine pathos in the chapter entitled "Pedagogy."[1] On the whole, however, it is a violent style, and a striking example, in rhythm and imagery, of the grotesque in the art of prose.

The sources of Carlyle's style are well known. It owes something to the great English divines of the seventeenth century, and to Sterne, *Hudibras,* and Swift. It owes even more to the "bold, glowing style . . . full of metaphors . . . with all manner of potent words,"[2] which Carlyle's father used with unconscious effort. And finally it owes something

[1]See pp. 106–07.

[2]Carlyle, *Reminiscences* (Everyman's Library), p. 3.

to the example set by Jean Paul. Just as German ideas renewed and strengthened some of Carlyle's beliefs, so the German style, especially as practised by Richter, strengthened and brightened Carlyle's original expression. That the style of *Sartor* is Carlyle's own is beyond doubt. It is not an imitation of Richter; and it is not an artificial style adopted for special occasions. It appears as early as 1814, when his friend Thomas Murray prophetically remarked on Carlyle's "Shandean turn of expression . . . [his] happy flow of language either for pathos, description, or humour . . . [which will make] the name of Carlyle, at least . . . inseparably connected with the literary history of the nineteenth century."[1] It was a style as natural with Carlyle as breathing, and its very audible quality is evidence that his manner of writing was identical with his manner of speaking. That manner, to be sure, was somewhat exaggerated at the time *Sartor* was composed, by frustration and a gloomy outlook on the future. But it was essentially Carlyle.

The "German" quality in the expression of *Sartor* may be seen if we turn to Carlyle's description of Jean Paul's style, an account which, with scarcely a change in wording, describes his own. Jean Paul, says Carlyle, "deals with astonishing liberality in parentheses, dashes, and subsidiary clauses; invents hundreds of new words, alters old ones, or by hyphen chains and pairs and packs them together into most jarring combination . . . Figures without limit; indeed the whole is one tissue of metaphors, and similes, and allusions to all the provinces of Earth, Sea and Air; interlaced with epigrammatic breaks, vehement bursts, or sardonic turns, interjections, quips, puns, and even oaths! . . . Then the style of the whole corresponds, in perplexity and extravagance, with that of the parts . . . embaled in some fantastic wrappage, some mad narrative accounting for its appearance, and connecting it with the author, who generally becomes a person in the drama himself, before all is over." Here we see not only the style but

---

[1]Froude, *Carlyle: First Forty Years*, etc., I, 21.

even something of the pattern of *Sartor*. More of its nature is expressed in another passage: Jean Paul has "an imagination vague, sombre, splendid, or appalling; brooding over the abysses of Being; wandering through Infinitude, and summoning before us, in its dim religious light, shapes of brilliancy, solemnity, or terror . . . He is a humorist from his inmost soul . . . a Titan in his sport as in his earnestness . . . We have Time and Space themselves playing fantastic tricks: it is an infinite masquerade; all Nature is gone forth mumming in the strangest guises."[1] It is small wonder that Thoreau, Lowell, and others assumed that Carlyle's style was an imitation of that of Richter; the two styles are astonishingly similar, and in an *inward* sense it may be said that Richter's style did affect Carlyle's.

The broken, disconnected utterance of *Sartor* was, in some respects, the forerunner of much in our twentieth-century style: the fragmentary, interrupted, implicit manner of the modern novel, the flickering imagery of modern poetry. Carlyle's style should present few difficulties to a generation acquainted with the novel as fashioned by James Joyce, or with the verses of T. S. Eliot. It is a style eminently suited for that characteristically modern type of literary work which Arnold called "the dialogue of the mind with itself."[2] In its shifting broken lights, it symbolizes the universal disintegration which evidences the need for new "social garnitures." Man, stripped of his inherited raiment, alone with his soul, carries on an uneven soliloquy. The poetical, intuitive, and involved style of *Sartor* is an appropriate one for Teufelsdröckh, that "pilgrim of eternity," who belongs in the great line of protesting and searching spirits, in the company of Wilhelm Meister, Faust, Manfred, and Cain.

Sartor Resartus was Carlyle's first and only entirely creative work; and into it he poured the whole force of his genius as it came completely to maturity. He was never again to be so exuberantly enthusiastic, so optimistic, so flexible. *Sartor*

---

[1]Carlyle, "Jean Paul Friedrich Richter," *Ess.*, I, 12, 14–15.

[2]Matthew Arnold, Preface to *Poems*, 1853.

shows him standing on the threshold of a new era, between the age of Romanticism and the age of democracy, science, and the machine. In many ways the style and content of *Sartor* belong to the Romantic period: certainly in its sense of mystery, its "strangeness added to beauty," its inwardness, emotional intensity, and subjective colouring, its Gothic incompleteness, its vindication of imagination over reason, its quest-motif—in all these features, the life and opinions of Teufelsdröckh belong to the age which is commonly thought to end about 1832. On the other hand, the central thought in *Sartor* is *action* rather than yearning, accommodation to prosaic fact in order to actualize the ideal, rather than the *Sehnsucht nach der Unendlichkeit,* the longing for Infinity, which characterized the spirit of the great Romantics. Carlyle in *Sartor* had arrived at all the doctrines which were to make him a mighty prophet in a new and chaotic age: the gospel of work, his canon of reverence for heroes, his faith in the ultimate victory of Right, his mystical sense of the brotherhood of men, his perception of the universe as at once "spectral" and symbolical and instrumental, his keen sense of "fact" in spite of his transcendentalism, his belief in man as spiritually dynamic. *Sartor* set for Carlyle his career of prophecy in an undogmatic ministry to a church as wide as the world. In *Sartor* he mastered his instrument, that program and style which were to appear in his lectures, histories, biographies, and social pamphlets. As a "Satirical Extravaganza on Things in General," it foreshadowed the Carlyle to come, dumbfounded a whole generation, survived to become one of the two or three most influential classics of the Victorian epoch, and remains now an eccentrically beautiful and provocative work of philosophico-literary prose.

SELECTED BIBLIOGRAPHY

[The following is a list of only such works as will assist in an intelligent reading or study of *Sartor Resartus.* For further material, see Dyer's *Carlyle Bibliography,* listed in Sect. IX.]

I. ORIGINAL EDITIONS

"Sartor Resartus." [In Three Books.] *Fraser's Magazine* (London), VIII (Nov., Dec., 1833), 581–92, 669–84; IX (Feb., March, April, June, 1834), 177–95, 301–13, 443–55, 664–74; X (July, Aug., 1834), 77–87, 182–93.

Sartor Resartus. In Three Books. Reprinted for Friends from *Fraser's Magazine.* London: James Fraser. 1834.

This rare privately printed edition was issued in only fifty-eight copies.

Sartor Resartus. In Three Books. Boston: James Munroe and Company. 1836.

This was the first appearance of *Sartor* as a distinct edition. The unsigned Preface is by Emerson. A second American edition, with the same unsigned Preface by Emerson, was issued by James Munroe in 1837. Of each edition there were only 500 copies.

Sartor Resartus; the Life and Opinions of Herr Teufelsdröckh. In Three Books. London: Saunders and Otley. 1838.

The first English edition; and the first to contain "Testimonies of Authors." Issued in five hundred copies, after a requirement of a guarantee subscription for three hundred copies. A second London edition appeared in 1841, a third in 1849, by James Fraser, and Chapman and Hall, respectively.

II. EDITIONS WITH EDITORIAL AIDS

Sartor Resartus. Edited by Archibald MacMechan. Boston and London. 1896.

A monument of research into the allusions of *Sartor,* to which all subsequent editions have been indebted. The Introduction is valuable for its analysis of Carlyle's style, personality, background, and his sources so far as they were then known.

Sartor Resartus: the Life and Opinions of Herr Teufelsdröckh. In Three Books. Edited by H. D. Traill. London. 1896.

Contains the standard text. Traill's Introduction to this and other volumes in the Centenary Edition is marred by irritability and caprice.

———Edited with Introduction and Notes by J. A. S. Barrett. London. 1897.

A scholarly edition produced independently of MacMechan, some of whose findings were incorporated in the Addenda in later reprints and editions (1901, 1905, 1910, 1916, *etc.*). The Introduction was the first to analyze Carlyle's ideas in the light of Hume, Kant, Goethe, and other influences.

———Edited by P. C. Parr. Oxford and London. 1913.

Contains a helpful Introduction. The editor died before the final revision of the Notes; hence a few errors remain to mar this otherwise admirable edition.

[Other noteworthy editions: in the *Collected Works,* London, 1858 ("Testimonies of Authors" omitted); the edition of London, 1869 ("Testimonies" restored; author's Note of 1868 on the date of composition and the original publication, *etc.;* Summary and Index added; making volume I of the Library Edition); in the People's Edition of the *Collected Works,* London, 1872; with Int. by Ernest Rhys, London and New York, 1887 (Camelot Series); with Int. by Edward Dowden, London, 1896; with Int. by Rev. James Wood, London, 1902; with Int. and Notes by Clark S. Northup, New York, 1921; with Int. by Ashley Thorndike, New York, 1921; edited by W. S. Johnson, Boston, 1924; edited by Frederick W. Roe, New York, 1927.]

[Translations: into Dutch, Amsterdam, 1880; into Polish, Warsaw, 1882; into German, ed. by Thomas Fischer, with Notes, Leipzig, 1882; into French, by Edmond Barthélemy, Paris, 1899; into Swedish, by Ellen Ryding, Stockholm, 1903; into Spanish, by Edmundo Gonzalez Blanco, in two volumes, Barcelona, 1905; into Italian, with Int. and Notes, by F. e. G. Chimenti, Bari, Laterza, 1910; into Hungarian, by Tanko Béla, Budapest, 1913; into Danish, by Uffe Birkedal, Copenhagen, 1916].

III. BIOGRAPHY

Nicoll, Henry J. *Thomas Carlyle.* Edinburgh, 1881.

Shepherd, Richard Herne. *Memoirs of the Life and Writings of Thomas Carlyle, with Personal Reminiscences and Selections from his Private Letters to Numerous Correspondents.* 2 volumes. London, 1881.

A mine of bibliographical material.—Dyer.

Froude, James Anthony. *Thomas Carlyle: a History of the First Forty Years of his Life,* 1795–1835. 2 volumes. London, 1882.

———*Thomas Carlyle: a History of his Life in London,* 1834–1881. 2 volumes. London, 1884.

A masterpiece of artistic portraiture, intentionally in the Rembrandt manner; therefore arbitrary in some of its lights and shadows. Champions Mrs. Carlyle; portrays Carlyle as solitary, egoistic, thoughtless of others, "gey ill to deal with." Inaccurate in dates, in the texts of letters, *etc.* Invaluable, however, for its sweep, its illuminating interpretations, its documents. (See Dunn, W. H., *Froude and Carlyle.* New York, 1930.)

Garnett, Richard. *Life of Thomas Carlyle.* London, 1887.

Although superseded in some respects by later biographies, still one of the best short accounts.

Masson, David. *Edinburgh Sketches and Memories.* London, 1892.

Contains invaluable chapters on Carlyle's early Edinburgh years, and a penetrating analysis of his character.

Nichol, John. *Thomas Carlyle.* (English Men of Letters Series.) London and New York, 1892.

Founded on Froude.

Craig, R. S. *The Making of Carlyle: an Experiment in Biographical Explication*. London, 1908.

Attempts to correct Froude. Good on Carlyle's early years.

Archibald, Raymond Clare. *Carlyle's First Love: Margaret Gordon, Lady Bannerman*. An Account of Her Life, Ancestry and Homes, Her Family and Friends. London, 1909.

Valuable as an account of one of the originals of Blumine in *Sartor*.

Wilson, David Alec. *Life of Thomas Carlyle*. London, 1923–34.

Vol. I. Carlyle Till Marriage, 1795–1826. (1923.)
Vol. II. Carlyle to "The French Revolution," 1826–1837. (1924.)
Vol. III. Carlyle on Cromwell and Others, 1837–1848. (1925.)
Vol. IV. Carlyle at his Zenith, 1848–1853. (1927.)
Vol. V. Carlyle to Threescore-and-Ten, 1853–1865. (1929.)
Vol. VI. Carlyle in his Old Age, 1865–1881. (Completed by D. W. MacArthur, 1934.)

The most painstaking and voluminous biography of Carlyle; a mine of information gleaned from every quarter, verbal or printed; but unfortunately marred by the author's indiscriminate championing of Carlyle against Froude, by the absence of any interpretation of Carlyle's work, and by the author's deliberate avoidance of any unified portraiture, either of Carlyle or of his age.

Burdett, Osbert. *The Two Carlyles*. London, 1931.

Neff, Emory. *Carlyle*. New York, 1932.

Excellent on Carlyle's social and economic ideas; very little on his early German interests; interesting passages on early periodicals, "puffing," *etc*.

Lammond, D. *Carlyle* (Great Lives Series). London, 1934.

IV. AUTOBIOGRAPHICAL MATERIAL

Reminiscences by Thomas Carlyle. Edited by James Anthony Froude. 2 volumes. London, 1881.

Inaccurate.

Reminiscences by Thomas Carlyle. Edited by Charles Eliot Norton. 2 volumes. London and New York, 1887.

Corrects errors and supplies omissions in Froude's edition; adds an index, and maps of the Carlyle country.

———Reprinted in Everyman's Library, 1932.

Two Notebooks of Thomas Carlyle. From 23d March 1822 to 16th May 1832. Edited by Charles Eliot Norton. New York: the Grolier Club. 1898.

V. LETTERS

(Containing Material Relevant to *Sartor Resartus*)

Correspondence of Carlyle and Emerson. Edited by Charles Eliot Norton. 2 volumes. London and Boston, 1883.

Early Letters of Carlyle (1814–1826). Edited by Charles Eliot Norton. 2 volumes. London, 1886.

Correspondence between Goethe and Carlyle. Edited by Charles Eliot Norton. London, 1887.

Letters of Thomas Carlyle (1826–1836). Edited by Charles Eliot Norton. 2 volumes. London, 1888.

New Letters of Thomas Carlyle. Edited by Alexander Carlyle. 2 volumes. London, 1904.

Love Letters of Carlyle and Jane Welsh. Edited by Alexander Carlyle. 2 volumes. London, 1909.

"New Letters of Carlyle to Eckermann." Edited by W. A. Speck. *Yale Review,* XV (July, 1926), 736–57.

VI. CRITICAL AND EXPOSITORY WORKS

Wylie, William Howie. *Thomas Carlyle: the Man and his Books.* Illustrated by Personal Reminiscences, Table Talk and Anecdotes of Himself and His Friends. London, 1881.

Abounds in errors, but has considerable anecdotal interest.

Baumgarten, Otto. *Carlyle und Goethe.* Tübingen, 1906.

Excellent general treatment of the subject. English translation, New York, n.d.

Johnson, William Savage. *Thomas Carlyle: a Study of His Literary Apprenticeship, 1814–1831.* New Haven, Conn., 1911.

A useful brief account of the intellectual background of the early Essays, of Carlyle's "spiritual history," of *Sartor Resartus, etc.* An excellent easy introduction to Carlyle.

Cazamian, Louis. *Carlyle* (Les Grands Écrivains Étrangers). Paris, 1913. Translated by E. K. Brown, New York, 1932.

The best one-volume exposition of Carlyle's general point of view; valuable chapters on his "moral formation," the German influence, his early essays, and *Sartor Resartus.*

Perry, Bliss. *Thomas Carlyle.* Indianapolis, 1915.

An easy introduction to Carlyle, with extensive quotations.

Ralli, Augustus. *Guide to Carlyle.* 2 volumes. London, 1920.

Useful analyses of all of Carlyle's works. On *Sartor,* see volume I, Chapters ix and x.

Neff, Emory. *Carlyle and Mill: Mystic and Utilitarian.* New York, 1924. 1926.

A valuable study in contrasts; excellent on Carlyle's economic ideas.

Hagberg, Knut. *Thomas Carlyle: Romantik och Puritanism i Sartor Resartus.* Stockholm, 1925.

A suggestive analysis, deserving an English translation.

Hamilton, Mary Agnes. *Thomas Carlyle.* New York, 1926.

An illuminating and very readable exposition, which brings Carlyle into relationship with twentieth-century thought, especially in Chapters iv and v.

Young, Norwood. *Carlyle: his Rise and Fall.* London, 1927.

A brilliant but vulnerable attack on Carlyle's theory and practice.

Harrold, Charles Frederick. *Carlyle and German Thought: 1819–1834.* New Haven, Conn., 1934.

A study of Carlyle's debt to German literature and philosophy, with reference to the original sources, through the publication of *Sartor Resartus.*

VII. SHORT CRITICAL WORKS: ARTICLES, ESSAYS, CHAPTERS, AND MONOGRAPHS

Sterling, John. "On the Writings of Thomas Carlyle." *London and Westminster Review,* XXXIII (1839), 1–68. Reprinted in *Essays and Tales,* London, 1848.

A penetrating contemporary criticism, of lasting value.

Taine, Hippolyte A. *History of English Literature.* Transl. from the French by H. Van Laun, Edinburgh, 1871. See Book V, Chap. iv.

Thoreau, Henry D. *A Yankee in Canada,* etc. Boston, 1866.

Originates the theory that Carlyle's style comes from Jean Paul; no longer held.

Morley, John. "Carlyle." *Critical Miscellanies* (First Series). London, 1871.

Trenchant criticism, partly adverse.

Conrad, H. "Carlyle und Schiller." *Vierteljahrschriften für Litteraturgeschichte,* II (1889), 195–228.

———"Carlyle und Jean Paul." *Die Gegenwart,* XXXIX (1891), 309–11.

Boyeson, H. H. "Carlyle and Goethe." *Essays on German Literature.* New York, 1892.

Kellner, L. "Goethe und Carlyle." *Die Nation,* XIII (1896), 380–83, 400–03.

Maulsby, D. L. *The Growth of Sartor Resartus.* (Tufts College Studies, Second Series, No. 1) Malden, Mass., 1899.

Derives *Sartor* from Carlyle's previous reading, the *Essays, etc.*

Kraeger, Heinrich. "Carlyles Deutsche Studien und der Wotton Reinfred." *Anglia,* Beibl. IX, Bnd. Nr. VII–VIII (1898), 193–219.

———"Byron und Carlyle." *Der Byronsche Heldentypus.* München, 1898.

———"Carlyles Stellung zur Deutschen Sprache und Literatur." *Anglia,* XXII (1899), 145–343.

———"Zu Carlyles Sartor Resartus." *Anglia,* Beibl., X (1899), 12–13.

Wells, J. T. *Thomas Carlyle: His Religious Experiences as Reflected in Sartor Resartus.* Edinburgh, 1899.

Boeuf, Marie (*Pseud.* Bos, Camille). "Le Kantisme de Carlyle." *Archiv für Geschichte der Philosophie,* XV (1902), 32–41.

Küchler, F. "Carlyle und Schiller." *Anglia,* XXVI (1903), 1–93, 393–446.

Lincke, O. *Über die Wortzusammensetzung in Sartor Resartus.* Berlin, 1904.

Durand, W.Y. "De Quincey and Carlyle in their Relation to the Germans." *Publications of the Modern Language Association of America,* XXII (1907), 521 ff.

Vaughan, C. E. "Carlyle and his German Masters." *Essays and Studies by Members of the English Association.* Oxford, 1910. See pp. 168–96.

Contains some unsound generalizations regarding Carlyle and Fichte; better on Goethe.

Stephen, Leslie. "Carlyle." *Encyclopaedia Britannica,* eleventh edition. (1910). *Cf.* also Leslie Stephen's art. in the *Dictionary of National Biography.* (1887.)

Stawell, F. M. "Goethe's Influence on Carlyle." *International Journal of Ethics,* XXI (1911), 178–89.

Elton, O. "Carlyle." *A Survey of English Literature:* 1780–1880. 4 volumes. London, 1920. See vol. III, pp. 8–40.

Hildebrand, A. *Carlyle und Schiller.* Berlin, 1913.

Fehr, B. "Der deutsche Idealismus in Carlyles Sartor Resartus." *Germanisch-romanische Monatsschrift,* V (1913), 81–101.

Tends to exaggerate the metaphysical in Carlyle, thus to minimize the influence of Goethe; otherwise a very suggestive essay.

Lorenz, A. C. *Diogenes Teufelsdröckh und Thomas Carlyle.* Leipzig, 1913.

Hearn, Lafcadio. "On the Philosophy of Sartor Resartus." *Interpretations of Literature.* Edited by John Erskine. 2 volumes. New York, 1916. See volume I, 208–32.

An excellent popular exposition.

Robertson, J. G. "Carlyle." *Cambridge History of English Literature.* Cambridge, 1916. See vol. XIII, Chap. 1.

Carré, Jean Marie. *Goethe en Angleterre.* Paris, 1920. See pp. 101–187.

Lucid and comprehensive treatment of Carlyle's debt to Goethe, and of his share in the promulgation of Goethe's ideas over England.

Liljegren, S. B. "The Origin of Sartor Resartus." *Palaestra,* No. 148 (1925), 400–33.

Geissendoerfer, Theodore. "Carlyle and Jean Paul Friedrich Richter." *Journal of English and Germanic Philology,* XXV (1926), 540–53.

Harrold, Charles Frederick. "Carlyle's Interpretation of Kant." *Philological Quarterly,* VII (1928), 345–57.

Wellek, René. "Carlyle and German Romanticism." *Xenia Pragensia.* Prague, 1929. See pp. 375–403.

Storrs, Margaret. *The Relation of Carlyle to Kant and Fichte.* Bryn Mawr, Pa., 1929.

A thorough investigation of the metaphysical element in Carlyle's transcendentalism.

Murray, R. H. "Carlyle the Romantic Radical." *Studies in the English Social and Political Thinkers of the Nineteenth Century.* 2 volumes. Cambridge, England, 1929. See volume I, Chap. viii.

Howe, Susanne. "Carlyle and Wilhelm Meister." *Wilhelm Meister and his English Kinsmen.* New York, 1930.

Harrold, Charles Frederick. "Carlyle and Novalis." *Studies in Philology,* XXVII (1930), 47–63.

Muirhead, J. H. "Carlyle's Transcendental Symbolism." *The*

Platonic Tradition in Anglo-Saxon Philosophy. London, 1931. See Part II, Chap. i.

Barrett, J. A. S. "Carlyle's Debt to Goethe." *Hibbert Journal,* XXX (1931), 61–75.

Wellek, René. *Immanuel Kant in England: 1793–1838.* Princeton, N. J., 1931. See pp. 183–202.

Harrold, Charles Frederick. "The Mystical Element in Carlyle (1827–34)." *Modern Philology,* XXIX (1932), 459–75.

Shine, Hill. "Carlyle and the German Philosophy Problem During the Year 1826–1827." *Publications of the Modern Language Association of America,* L (1935), 807–27.

Murphy, Ella M. "Carlyle and the Saint-Simonians." *Studies in Philology,* XXXIII (1936), 93–118.

Shine, Hill. "Carlyle's Views on the Relation between Religion and Poetry up to 1832." *Studies in Philology,* XXXIII (1936), 57–92.

Harrold, Charles Frederick. "The Nature of Carlyle's Calvinism." *Studies in Phililogy,* XXXIII (1936), 475–86.

Shine, Hill. "Carlyle's Views on the Relation between Poetry and History up to Early 1832." *Studies in Philology,* XXXIII (1936), 487–506.

VIII. CARLYLE'S GERMAN SOURCES

(As Cited in the Notes and Introduction to the Present Edition of *Sartor Resartus*)

Fichte, J. G. *Sämmtliche Werke.* Edited by J. H. Fichte. Berlin, 1845–46. 8 volumes.

———*Popular Works.* Translated by William Smith. London, 1873. (Contains *On the Nature of the Scholar, The Vocation of Man,* etc.)

———*Characteristics of the Present Age.* Translated by William Smith. London, 1847.

Goethe, J. W. v. *Sämmtliche Werke.* Jubiläums-Ausgabe. Stuttgart und Berlin, 1902–07. 40 volumes.

———*Wilhelm Meisters Wanderjahre, oder die Entsagenden.* Stuttgart, 1821.

———*Maximen und Reflexionen.* Edited by H. Hecker. Goethe-Gesellschaft, volume 21. Weimar, 1907.

Kant, Immanuel. *Gesammelte Schriften.* Königlich Akademie der Wissenschaft. Berlin, 1902–13. 15 volumes.

———*Critique of Pure Reason.* Translated by Norman Kemp Smith. London, 1929.

Novalis. *Werke.* Edited by H. Friedmann. Berlin, 1908. 2 volumes.

Richter, Jean Paul Friedrich. *Werke.* Berlin, 1879. 60 volumes.

———*Blumen- Frucht- und Dornenstücke: oder Ehestand, Tod, Hochzeit des Armenadvokaten F. St. Siebenkäs.* Berlin, 1818. 4 volumes.

———*Flower, Fruit and Thorn Pieces . . .* Translated by Alexander Ewing. Bohn's Library. London, 1888.

———*Hesperus.* Anonymous translation. Boston, 1865.

———*Levana: oder Erziehlehre.* Stuttgart und Tübingen, 1845.

———*Levana, or the Doctrine of Education.* Anon. transl. London, 1840.

———*Wahrheit aus Jean Pauls Leben.* Breslau, 1826–33. 8 volumes.

Schelling, F. W. J. von. *Sämmtliche Werke.* Stuttgart und Augsburg, 1859–61. 10 volumes.

Schiller, F. von. *Sämmtliche Werke.* Edited by H. Kurz. Hildburghausen, 1868–70. 9 volumes.

Schlegel, A. W. and F. von. *Athenaeum.* Berlin, 1798–1800. 3 volumes.

Schlegel, F. von. *Sämmtliche Werke.* Wien, 1822–23. 10 volumes.

Werner, Zacharias. *Sämmtliche Werke.* Grimma, [1840–44]. 13 volumes.

IX. BIBLIOGRAPHY

Dyer, Isaac Watson. *A Bibliography of Thomas Carlyle's Writings and Ana.* Portland, Maine, 1928.

The standard Carlyle bibliography; comprehensive, and equipped with extensive annotation (see the ten-page note on *Sartor,* pp. 234–43); occasionally inaccurate, but indispensable to the student.

NOTE ON THE TEXT AND FOOTNOTES

The present text of *Sartor Resartus* is that of the Centenary Edition (ed. H. D. Traill, London, 1896–1901). No changes have been made in that text except in the case of obvious misprints, which have been cited in the footnotes. All references to the other works of Carlyle (including his translations) are likewise to the Centenary Edition.

In all cases where there has been more than usual indebtedness to previous editors of *Sartor,* the following initials have been used: B = Barrett; M = MacMechan; N = Northup; P = Parr. Other abbreviations are as follows:

C. E. L. = Froude's *Thomas Carlyle: a History of the First Forty Years of his Life.* 2 volumes. London, 1882.
G.-C. Corr. = *Correspondence between Goethe and Carlyle.* Ed. C. E. Norton. London, 1887.
Ess. = Carlyle's *Critical and Miscellaneous Essays* in the Centenary Edition.

All citations of Carlyle's *Reminiscences* refer to the edition of C. E. Norton, reprinted in the Everyman's Library, 1932, in one volume. Carlyle's unfinished novel, *Wotton Reinfred,* is referred to in the page numbers of the *Last Words of Thomas Carlyle* (London, 1892) where it was first published in a volume, with other uncollected writings.

SARTOR RESARTUS

Die Welt ist ein Universaltropus des Geistes, ein symbolisches Bild desselben. . . .

—NOVALIS

Nicht blosses Wissen, sondern nach deinem Wissen *Thun* ist deine Bestimmung.

—FICHTE

SARTOR RESARTUS

BOOK FIRST

CHAPTER I

PRELIMINARY

No Philosophy of Clothes yet, notwithstanding all our Science. Strangely forgotten that Man is by nature a *naked* animal. The English mind all-too practically absorbed for any such inquiry. Not so, deep-thinking Germany. Advantage of Speculation having free course. Editor receives from Professor Teufelsdröckh his new Work on Clothes.

CONSIDERING our present advanced state of culture, and how the Torch of Science has now been brandished and borne about, with more or less effect, for five thousand years and upwards; how, in these times especially, not only the Torch still burns, and perhaps more fiercely than ever, but innumerable Rush-lights, and Sulphur-matches, kindled thereat, are also glancing in every direction, so that not the smallest cranny or doghole in Nature or Art can remain unilluminated,—it might strike the reflective mind with some surprise that hitherto little or nothing of a fundamental character, whether in the way of Philosophy or History, has been written on the subject of Clothes.

Our Theory of Gravitation[1] is as good as perfect: Lagrange,[2]

[1]Carlyle was at one time (1816) an enthusiastic reader of Sir Isaac Newton, and had written (in 1819–20) an unpublished article on Pictet's *Theory of Gravitation.* (See D. A. Wilson, *Carlyle till Marriage,* pp. 116, 180.)

[2]Joseph Louis, Comte Lagrange (1736–1813): French mathematician and astronomer, author of the *Mécanique analytique* (1788).

it is well known, has proved that the Planetary System, on this scheme, will endure forever; Laplace,[1] still more cunningly, even guesses that it could not have been made on any other scheme. Whereby, at least, our nautical Logbooks can be better kept; and water-transport of all kinds has grown more commodious. Of Geology and Geognosy[2] we know enough: what with the labours of our Werners and Huttons,[3] what with the ardent genius of their disciples, it has come about that now, to many a Royal Society,[4] the Creation of a World is little more mysterious than the cooking of a dumpling; concerning which last, indeed, there have been minds to whom the question, *How the apples were got in,*[5] presented difficulties. Why mention our disquisitions on the Social Contract,[6] on the Standard of Taste,[7] on the Migrations of the Herring?[8] Then, have we not a Doctrine of Rent,[9] a Theory of Value; Philosophies of Language, of History, of Pottery, of Apparitions, of Intoxicating Liquors?[10] Man's whole life and

---

[1]Pierre Simon, Marquis de Laplace (1749–1827): French mathematician and astronomer, author of *Mécanique céleste* (5 vols., 1799–1825).

[2]That part of geology which treats of the materials of the earth.

[3]Abraham Gottlob Werner (1750–1817): founder of German geology, who explained geological formations by the action of water.—James Hutton (1726–97), Scotch geologist, explained such formations by the action of fire.

[4]The Royal Society was founded about 1660, and incorporated in 1662.

[5]In the humorous poem, *The Apple Dumplings and a King,* by John Wolcot (*Pseud.* Peter Pindar), George III, unable to find a seam in the dumplings, asks, "How, how the devil got the apples in?"

[6]Rousseau's *Du Contrat social, ou principes du droit politique* appeared in 1762.

[7]David Hume published an essay, *Of the Standard of Taste,* in 1757. Archibald Alison's *Essays on the Nature and Principles of Taste* appeared in 1790; the second edition (1811) was reviewed by Jeffrey in the *Edinburgh Review* (May, 1811).

[8]Papers on this subject had been published by the American, John Gilpin (*Transactions of the American Philosophical Society,* Philadelphia, 1786), and by Thomas Pennant (1726–98) (*British Zoology,* III, 4th ed., 1776).

[9]See the writings of the early political economists, Adam Smith (1723–90), Thomas R. Malthus (1766–1834), David Ricardo (1772–1823), *etc.*

[10]The philosophy of language and of history was a part of the specula-

environment have been laid open and elucidated; scarcely a fragment or fibre of his Soul, Body, and Possessions, but has been probed, dissected, distilled, desiccated, and scientifically decomposed: our spiritual Faculties, of which it appears there are not a few, have their Stewarts, Cousins, Royer Collards:[1] every cellular, vascular, muscular Tissue glories in its Lawrences, Majendies, Bichâts.[2]

How, then, comes it, may the reflective mind repeat, that the grand Tissue of all Tissues, the only real Tissue, should have been quite overlooked by Science,—the vestural Tissue, namely, of woollen or other cloth; which Man's Soul wears as its outmost wrappage and overall; wherein his whole other Tissues are included and screened, his whole Faculties work, his whole Self lives, moves, and has its being?[3] For if, now and then, some straggling broken-winged thinker has cast an owl's-glance into this obscure region, the most have soared over it altogether heedless; regarding Clothes as a property, not an accident,[4] as quite natural and spontaneous, like the leaves of trees, like the plumage of birds. In all speculations they have tacitly figured man as a *Clothed Animal;* whereas he is by nature a *Naked Animal;* and only in certain circum-

---

tions of F. v. Schlegel (1772–1829), J. G. Fichte (1762–1814), F. W. Schelling (1775–1854), J. G. v. Herder (1744–1803), and of Goethe and Schiller.—Articles on "The Philosophy of Pottery" and "The Philosophy of Apparitions" appeared in *Fraser's Magazine,* April, 1830, pp. 287–91, and August, 1830, pp. 33–41. R. Macnish was the author of *The Anatomy of Drunkenness* (1827) and of *The Philosophy of Sleep* (1830).

[1]Dugald Stewart (1753–1828) was a Scotch philosopher and professor at Edinburgh (1778–1820), much read by the young Carlyle.—Victor Cousin (1792–1867) was a French philosopher, and opponent of materialism.—Pierre Royer-Collard (1763–1845) was an eloquent French teacher of philosophy at the Sorbonne, likewise an opponent of materialism.

[2]Sir William Lawrence (1783–1867), François Magendie (1783–1855), and Maria François Xavier Bichât (1771–1802) were well-known surgeons and physiologists of the day. They are mentioned by Carlyle to parallel their *physical* analysis with the *psychological* or spiritual analysis of Stewart, Cousin, *etc.*

[3]*Cf.* Acts, xvii, 28.

[4]*Property . . . accident:* terms used by logicians and philosophers to distinguish between the essential and the variable features of an object.

stances, by purpose and device, masks himself in Clothes. Shakespeare says, we are creatures that look before and after:[1] the more surprising that we do not look round a little, and see what is passing under our very eyes.

But here, as in so many other cases, Germany, learned, indefatigable, deep-thinking Germany comes to our aid. It is, after all, a blessing that, in these revolutionary times, there should be one country where abstract Thought can still take shelter; that while the din and frenzy of Catholic Emancipations, and Rotten Boroughs, and Revolts of Paris,[2] deafen every French and every English ear, the German can stand peaceful on his scientific watch-tower; and, to the raging, struggling multitude here and elsewhere, solemnly, from hour to hour, with preparatory blast of cowhorn, emit his *Höret ihr Herren und lasset's Euch sagen;*[3] in other words, tell the Universe, which so often forgets that fact, what o'clock it really is. Not unfrequently the Germans have been blamed for an unprofitable diligence; as if they struck into devious courses, where nothing was to be had but the toil of a rough journey; as if, forsaking the gold-mines of finance and that political slaughter of fat oxen whereby a man himself grows fat, they were apt to run goose-hunting into regions of bilberries and crowberries, and be swallowed up at last in remote peat-bogs. Of that unwise science, which, as our Humorist expresses it,

> By geometric scale
> Doth take the size of pots of ale;[4]

---

[1]*Cf. Hamlet,* IV, iv, 37.

[2]*Catholic Emancipations:* civil disabilities were removed from Roman Catholics in 1829.—*Rotten Boroughs:* electoral districts in England which had lost great numbers of voters owing to population shifts caused by the Industrial Revolution, but which still sent their usual number of members to Parliament; largely abolished by the Reform Bill of 1832.—*Revolts of Paris:* an allusion to the Revolution of July 27–29, 1830, which overthrew Charles X.

[3]"Hear ye, gentlemen, and let it be told you." (The first line of a folk-song, supposed to be uttered by the bellman on his nightly rounds. See "Dumb Love," *German Romance,* I, p. 59.)

[4]Butler's *Hudibras,* I, i, 121–22. Slightly inexact; should read: *"could* take."

still more, of that altogether misdirected industry, which is seen vigorously thrashing mere straw, there can nothing defensive be said. In so far as the Germans are chargeable with such, let them take the consequence. Nevertheless be it remarked, that even a Russian steppe has tumuli and gold ornaments; also many a scene that looks desert and rock-bound from the distance, will unfold itself, when visited, into rare valleys. Nay, in any case, would Criticism erect not only finger-posts and turnpikes, but spiked gates and impassable barriers, for the mind of man? It is written, 'Many shall run to and fro, and knowledge shall be increased.'[1] Surely the plain rule is, Let each considerate person have his way, and see what it will lead to. For not this man and that man, but all men make up mankind, and their united tasks the task of mankind.[2] How often have we seen some such adventurous, and perhaps much-censured wanderer light on some out-lying, neglected, yet vitally momentous province; the hidden treasures of which he first discovered, and kept proclaiming till the general eye and effort were directed thither, and the conquest was completed;—thereby, in these his seemingly so aimless rambles, planting new standards, founding new habitable colonies, in the immeasurable circumambient realm of Nothingness and Night![3] Wise man was he who counselled that Speculation should have free course, and look fearlessly towards all the thirty-two points of the compass, whithersoever and howsoever it listed.

Perhaps it is proof of the stunted condition in which pure Science, especially pure moral Science, languishes among us English; and how our mercantile greatness, and invaluable Constitution, impressing a political or other immediately practical tendency on all English culture and endeavour, cramps the free flight of Thought,—that this, not Philosophy

---

[1]Daniel, xii, 4.

[2]From Goethe's *Wilhelm Meister* (Carlyle's transl.), II, p. 131: "It is all men that make up mankind; all powers taken together that make up the world."

[3]*Cf. Paradise Lost,* i, 541–43; ii, 959–63, 970.

of Clothes, but recognition even that we have no such Philosophy, stands here for the first time published in our language. What English intellect could have chosen such a topic, or by chance stumbled on it? But for that same unshackled, and even sequestered condition of the German Learned, which permits and induces them to fish in all manner of waters, with all manner of nets, it seems probable enough, this abstruse Inquiry might, in spite of the results it leads to, have continued dormant for indefinite periods. The Editor of these sheets, though otherwise boasting himself a man of confirmed speculative habits, and perhaps discursive enough, is free to confess, that never, till these last months, did the above very plain considerations, on our total want of a Philosophy of Clothes, occur to him; and then, by quite foreign suggestion. By the arrival, namely, of a new Book from Professor Teufelsdröckh of Weissnichtwo; treating expressly of this subject, and in a style which, whether understood or not, could not even by the blindest be overlooked. In the present Editor's way of thought, this remarkable Treatise, with its Doctrines, whether as judicially acceded to, or judicially denied, has not remained without effect.

'*Die Kleider, ihr Werden und Wirken* (Clothes, their Origin and Influence): *von Diog. Teufelsdröckh, J.U.D. etc. Stillschweigen, und Cognie. Weissnichtwo,* 1831.[1]

'Here,' says the *Weissnichtwo'sche Anzeiger,*[2] 'comes a Volume of that extensive, close-printed, close-meditated sort, which, be it spoken with pride, is seen only in Germany, per-

[1] "*Clothes, their Origin and Influence: by Diogenes Teufelsdröckh, Juris Utriusque Doctor* (Doctor of Civil and of Canon Law, *i.e.,* LL.D.), *etc.* Silence and Co. Know-not-where, 1831." A title undoubtedly suggested to Carlyle by that of a treatise sent to him by Goethe in June, 1830, L. Wachler's *Ueber Werden und Wirken der Literatur,* Breslau, 1829. (*G.-C. Corr.,* pp. 195, 202, etc.) In *Wilhelm Meister* (II, 223), Jarno addresses Wilhelm as "Thou second Diogenes." Jean Paul uses the name in a similar fashion, in describing the typical "Academical burghers" of Germany as "humorists and Diogeneses." ("Quintus Fixlein" *Germ. Romance,* II, 206). These passages may have suggested to Carlyle an appropriate first name for Teufelsdröckh.—*Know-not-where=Kennaquhair,* setting of the opening scene of Scott's *The Monastery.* (M.)

[2] "Weissnichtwo Advertiser."

haps only in Weissnichtwo. Issuing from the hitherto irreproachable Firm of Stillschweigen and Company, with every external furtherance, it is of such internal quality as to set Neglect at defiance.' . . . 'A work,' concludes the well-nigh enthusiastic Reviewer, 'interesting alike to the antiquary, the historian, and the philosophic thinker; a masterpiece of boldness, lynx-eyed acuteness, and rugged independent Germanism and Philanthropy (*derber Kerndeutschheit und Menschenliebe*); which will not, assuredly, pass current without opposition in high places; but must and will exalt the almost new name of Teufelsdröckh to the first ranks of Philosophy, in our German Temple of Honour.'

Mindful of old friendship, the distinguished Professor, in this the first blaze of his fame, which however does not dazzle him, sends hither a Presentation-copy of his Book; with compliments and encomiums which modesty forbids the present Editor to rehearse; yet without indicated wish or hope of any kind, except what may be implied in the concluding phrase: *Möchte es*[1] (this remarkable Treatise) *auch im Brittischen Boden gedeihen!*

CHAPTER II

EDITORIAL DIFFICULTIES

How to make known Teufelsdröckh and his Book to English readers; especially *such* a book? Editor receives from the Hofrath Heuschrecke a letter promising Biographic Documents. Negotiations with Oliver Yorke. *Sartor Resartus* conceived. Editor's assurances and advice to his British reader.

IF FOR a speculative man, 'whose seedfield,' in the sublime words of the Poet, 'is Time,'[2] no conquest is important but that of new ideas, then might the arrival of Professor Teufels-

[1] "May it thrive also on British soil!"

[2] See motto on title page. Carlyle found these verses prefaced to

dröckh's Book be marked with chalk in the Editor's calendar. It is indeed an 'extensive Volume,' of boundless, almost formless contents, a very Sea of Thought; neither calm nor clear, if you will; yet wherein the toughest pearl-diver may dive to his utmost depth, and return not only with sea-wreck but with true orients.[1]

Directly on the first perusal, almost on the first deliberate inspection, it became apparent that here a quite new Branch of Philosophy, leading to as yet undescried ulterior results, was disclosed; farther, what seemed scarcely less interesting, a quite new human Individuality, an almost unexampled personal character, that, namely, of Professor Teufelsdröckh the Discloser. Of both which novelties, as far as might be possible, we resolved to master the significance. But as man is emphatically a proselytising creature, no sooner was such mastery even fairly attempted, than the new question arose: How might this acquired good be imparted to others, perhaps in equal need thereof: how could the philosophy of Clothes, and the Author of such Philosophy, be brought home, in any measure, to the business and bosoms of our own English Nation? For if new-got gold is said to burn the pockets till it be cast forth into circulation, much more may new truth.

Here, however, difficulties occurred. The first thought naturally was to publish Article after Article on this remarkable Volume, in such widely-circulating Critical Journals as the Editor might stand connected with, or by money or love procure access to. But, on the other hand, was it not clear that such matter as must here be revealed, and treated of, might endanger the circulation of any Journal extant? If, indeed, all party-divisions in the State, could have been abolished, Whig, Tory, and Radical, embracing in discrepant union; and all the Journals of the Nation could have been

---

Wilhelm Meisters Wanderjahre (Stuttgart, 1821), and varied his translation of them at different times. See "Characteristics" (*Ess.,* III, 43) for the phrasing as given in the text above:

> My inheritance how wide and fair!
> Time is my fair seed-field, of Time I'm heir.

[1]Pearls. *Cf. Paradise Lost,* v, 1–2.

jumbled into one Journal, and the Philosophy of Clothes poured forth in incessant torrents therefrom, the attempt had seemed possible. But, alas, what vehicle of that sort have we, except *Fraser's Magazine?* A vehicle all strewed (figuratively speaking) with the maddest Waterloo-Crackers,[1] exploding distractively and destructively, wheresoever the mystified passenger stands or sits; nay, in any case, understood to be, of late years, a vehicle full to overflowing, and inexorably shut! Besides, to state the Philosophy of Clothes without the Philosopher, the ideas of Teufelsdröckh without something of his personality, was it not to insure both of entire misapprehension? Now for Biography, had it been otherwise admissible, there were no adequate documents, no hope of obtaining such, but rather, owing to circumstances, a special despair. Thus did the Editor see himself, for the while, shut out from all public utterance of these extraordinary Doctrines, and constrained to revolve them, not without disquietude, in the dark depths of his own mind.

So had it lasted for some months; and now the Volume on Clothes, read and again read, was in several points becoming lucid and lucent; the personality of its Author more and more surprising, but, in spite of all that memory and conjecture could do, more and more enigmatic; whereby the old disquietude seemed fast settling into fixed discontent,—when altogether unexpectedly arrives a Letter from Herr Hofrath Heuschrecke,[2] our Professor's chief friend and associate in Weissnichtwo, with whom we had not previously corresponded. The Hofrath, after much quite extraneous matter, began dilating largely on the 'agitation and attention' which the Philosophy of Clothes was exciting in its own German Republic of Letters; on the deep significance and tendency of his Friend's Volume; and then, at length, with great circumlocution, hinted at the practicability of conveying 'some knowl-

---

[1]Fire-crackers of an unusual size, made to celebrate the victory of the battle of Waterloo.—*Fraser's Magazine* had a reputation for audacity, exuberance, and boisterous humour and satire.

[2]German for "Councillor Grasshopper."

edge of it, and of him, to England, and through England to the distant West': a work on Professor Teufelsdröckh 'were undoubtedly welcome to the *Family,* the *National,*[1] or any other of those patriotic *Libraries,* at present the glory of British Literature'; might work revolutions in Thought; and so forth;—in conclusion, intimating not obscurely, that should the present Editor feel disposed to undertake a Biography of Teufelsdröckh, he, Hofrath Heuschrecke, had it in his power to furnish the requisite Documents.

As in some chemical mixture, that has stood long evaporating, but would not crystallise, instantly when the wire or other fixed substance is introduced, crystallisation commences, and rapidly proceeds till the whole is finished, so was it with the Editor's mind and this offer of Heuschrecke's. Form rose out of void solution and discontinuity; like united itself with like in definite arrangement: and soon either in actual vision and possession, or in fixed reasonable hope, the image of the whole Enterprise had shaped itself, so to speak, into a solid mass. Cautiously yet courageously, through the twopenny post, application to the famed redoubtable Oliver Yorke[2] was now made: an interview, interviews with that singular man have taken place; with more of assurance on our side, with less of satire (at least of open satire) on his, than we anticipated;—for the rest, with such issue as is now visible. As to those same 'patriotic *Libraries,*' the Hofrath's counsel could only be viewed with silent amazement; but with his offer of Documents we joyfully and almost instantaneously closed. Thus, too, in the sure expectation of these, we already see our task begun; and this our *Sartor Resartus,* which is properly a 'Life and Opinions of Herr Teufelsdröckh,'[3] hourly advancing.

Of our fitness for the Enterprise, to which we have such title

---

[1]Reference to actual "libraries," typical of a number, encyclopaedic or periodical in character, which were springing up in the early years of the century. Carlyle's irony is obvious.

[2]Pseudonym of William Maginn (1794–1842), editor of *Fraser's Magazine;* used also to refer to the magazine itself.

[3]A title probably suggested by Sterne's *The Life and Opinions of Tristram Shandy, Gentleman* (1760–67), one of Carlyle's early favourites.

and vocation, it were perhaps uninteresting to say more. Let the British reader study and enjoy, in simplicity of heart, what is here presented him, and with whatever metaphysical acumen and talent for meditation he is possessed of. Let him strive to keep a free, open sense; cleared from the mists of prejudice, above all from the paralysis of cant; and directed rather to the Book itself than to the Editor of the Book. Who or what such Editor may be, must remain conjectural, and even insignificant:[1] it is a voice publishing tidings of the Philosophy of Clothes; undoubtedly a Spirit addressing Spirits: whoso hath ears, let him hear.[2]

On one other point the Editor thinks it needful to give warning: namely, that he is animated with a true though perhaps a feeble attachment to the Institutions of our Ancestors; and minded to defend these, according to ability, at all hazards; nay, it was partly with a view to such defence that he engaged in this undertaking. To stem, or if that be impossible, profitably to divert the current of Innovation, such a Volume as Teufelsdröckh's, if cunningly planted down, were no despicable pile, or floodgate, in the logical wear.[3]

For the rest, be it nowise apprehended, that any personal connection of ours with Teufelsdröckh, Heuschrecke, or this Philosophy of Clothes, can pervert our judgment, or sway us to extenuate or exaggerate. Powerless, we venture to promise, are those private Compliments themselves. Grateful they may well be; as generous illusions of friendship; as fair mementos of bygone unions, of those nights and suppers of the gods,[4] when, lapped in the symphonies and harmonies of Philosophic Eloquence, though with baser accompaniments, the present Editor revelled in that feast of reason,[5] never since

---

[1]With us even he still communicates in some sort of mask, or muffler; and, we have reason to think, under a feigned name!—O. Y. [Carlyle's note.]

[2]*Cf.* Matthew, xiii, 9.

[3]Weir, *i.e.,* a mill dam.

[4]*Cf.* Horace, *Satires,* II, vi, 65.

[5]*Cf.* Pope, *Imitations of Horace,* Satire I, l. 128.

vouchsafed him in so full measure! But what then? *Amicus Plato, magis amica veritas;*[1] Teufelsdröckh is our friend, Truth is our divinity. In our historical and critical capacity, we hope we are strangers to all the world; have feud or favour with no one,—save indeed the Devil, with whom, as with the Prince of Lies[2] and Darkness, we do at all times wage internecine war. This assurance, at an epoch when puffery[3] and quackery have reached a height unexampled in the annals of mankind, and even English Editors, like Chinese Shopkeepers, must write on their door-lintels *No cheating here,*—we thought it good to premise.

CHAPTER III

REMINISCENCES

Teufelsdröckh at Weissnichtwo. Professor of Things in General at the University there: Outward aspect and character; memorable coffee-house utterances; domicile and watch-tower: Sights thence of City-life by day and by night; with reflections thereon. Old 'Liza and her ways. Character of Hofrath Heuschrecke, and his relation to Teufelsdröckh.

To the Author's private circle the appearance of this singular Work on Clothes must have occasioned little less surprise than it has to the rest of the world. For ourselves, at least, few things have been more unexpected. Professor Teufelsdröckh, at the period of our acquaintance with him, seemed to lead a quite still and self-contained life: a man devoted to the higher Philosophies, indeed; yet more likely, if he

---

[1] "Plato is my friend, but Truth is more my friend." Humorously adapted by Sterne, *Tristram Shandy,* Vol. I., Chap. xxi. See Plato, *Phaedo,* 91. (B.)

[2] *Cf. King Lear,* III, iv, 148.

[3] Advertising. (See Bibliography, under Neff, *Carlyle.*)

published at all, to publish a refutation of Hegel and Bardili,[1] both of whom, strangely enough, he included under a common ban; than to descend, as he has here done, into the angry noisy Forum, with an Argument that cannot but exasperate and divide. Not, that we can remember, was the Philosophy of Clothes once touched upon between us. If through the high, silent, meditative Transcendentalism[2] of our Friend we detected any practical tendency whatever, it was at most Political, and towards a certain prospective, and for the present quite speculative, Radicalism; as indeed some correspondence, on his part, with Herr Oken[3] of Jena was now and then suspected; though his special contributions to the *Isis* could never be more than surmised at. But, at all events, nothing Moral, still less anything Didactico-Religious, was looked for from him.

Well do we recollect the last words he spoke in our hearing; which indeed, with the Night they were uttered in, are to be forever remembered. Lifting his huge tumbler of *Gukguk*,[4] and for a moment lowering his tobacco-pipe, he stood up in full coffee-house (it was *Zur Grünen Gans*,[5] the largest in Weissnichtwo, where all the Virtuosity, and nearly all the Intellect of the place assembled of an evening); and there, with low, soul-stirring tone, and the look truly of an angel, though whether of a white or of a black one might be dubious, proposed this toast: *Die Sache der Armen in Gottes und Teufels Namen* (The cause of the Poor, in Heaven's name

---

[1]G. W. F. Hegel (1770–1831): German philosopher.—C. G. Bardili (1761–1808): German philosopher, who attacked Kant.

[2]*Transcendentalism:* a term loosely used here to refer to any philosophy which opposes materialism or empiricism, and which asserts the domination of the intuitive or spiritual over the material. (See Int., Section V, b, for Carlyle's debt to the transcendentalism of the German philosopher, Kant [1724–1804].)

[3]Lorenz Oken (1779–1851): German naturalist and philosopher, founded the *Isis* in 1817 and edited it until 1848.

[4]Gukguk is unhappily only an academical—beer. [Carlyle's note.] *Gukguk* is mentioned in Jean Paul's "Quintus Fixlein" (*German Romance*, II, 205).

[5]"At the Sign of the Green Goose."

and ——'s)! One full shout, breaking the leaden silence; then a gurgle of innumerable emptying bumpers, again followed by universal cheering, returned him loud acclaim. It was the finale of the night: resuming their pipes; in the highest enthusiasm, amid volumes of tobacco-smoke; triumphant, cloud-capt without and within, the assembly broke up, each to his thoughtful pillow. *Bleibt doch ein echter Spass- und Galgen-vogel,*[1] said several; meaning thereby that, one day, he would probably be hanged for his democratic sentiments. *Wo steckt doch der Schalk?*[2] added they, looking round: but Teufelsdröckh had retired by private alleys, and the Compiler of these pages beheld him no more.

In such scenes has it been our lot to live with this Philosopher, such estimate to form of his purposes and powers. And yet, thou brave Teufelsdröckh, who could tell what lurked in thee? Under those thick locks of thine, so long and lank, overlapping roof-wise the gravest face we ever in this world saw, there dwelt a most busy brain. In thy eyes too, deep under their shaggy brows, and looking out so still and dreamy, have we not noticed gleams of an ethereal or else a diabolic fire, and half-fancied that their stillness was but the rest of infinite motion, the *sleep* of a spinning-top? Thy little figure, there as, in loose ill-brushed threadbare habiliments, thou sattest, amid litter and lumber, whole days to 'think and smoke tobacco,'[3] held in it a mighty heart. The secrets of man's Life were laid open to thee; thou sawest into the mystery of the Universe, farther than another; thou hadst *in petto*[4] thy remarkable Volume on Clothes. Nay, was there not in that clear logically-founded Transcendentalism of thine; still more, in thy meek, silent, deep-seated Sansculottism,[5] com-

---

[1] "This merry wag will yet be a gallows-bird."

[2] "Where is the rascal hiding?"

[3] Part of the refrain of a famous drinking song, originally by G. Wither, quoted in D'Urfey's *Pills to Purge Melancholy* (1719–20). (M)

[4] From the Latin *pectus* (breast); in secret, in reserve.

[5] *Sansculottism:* Loosely used here to denote philosophical radicalism, or the spirit of Rousseau and the French Revolution, which attempted to see through the shams and conventions of society. Literal meaning:

bined with a true princely Courtesy of inward nature, the visible rudiments of such speculation? But great men are too often unknown, or what is worse, misknown. Already, when we dreamed not of it, the warp of thy remarkable Volume lay on the loom; and silently, mysterious shuttles were putting-in the woof!

How the Hofrath Heuschrecke is to furnish biographical data, in this case, may be a curious question; the answer of which, however, is happily not our concern, but his. To us it appeared, after repeated trial, that in Weissnichtwo, from the archives or memories of the best-informed classes, no Biography of Teufelsdröckh was to be gathered; not so much as a false one. He was a stranger there, wafted thither by what is called the course of circumstances; concerning whose parentage, birthplace, prospects, or pursuits, curiosity had indeed made inquiries, but satisfied herself with the most indistinct replies. For himself, he was a man so still and altogether unparticipating, that to question him even afar off on such particulars was a thing of more than usual delicacy: besides, in his sly way, he had ever some quaint turn, not without its satirical edge, wherewith to divert such intrusions, and deter you from the like. Wits spoke of him secretly as if he were a kind of Melchizedek,[1] without father or mother of any kind; sometimes, with reference to his great historic and statistic knowledge, and the vivid way he had of expressing himself like an eye-witness of distant transactions and scenes, they called him the *Ewige Jude,* Everlasting, or as we say, Wandering Jew.[2]

"without breeches"; applied to the poorer men of Paris who were active in the Revolution of 1789, and to any Revolutionaries who gave up the knee-breeches of the *ancien régime* and adopted trousers as a symbol of the new era; applied in 1791 to "indigent Patriotism" (Carlyle, *French Revolution,* II, 123 [Bk. III, Ch. iv]).

[1]*Cf.* Hebrews, vii, 1–3: "king of Salem, priest of the most high God . . . without father, without mother, without descent . . . abideth a priest continually." (*Cf.* Genesis, xiv, 17–24; Psalms, cx, 4.)

[2]*Cf.* either the medieval legend of Ahasuerus (Percy's *Reliques*) or the

To the most, indeed, he had become not so much a Man as a Thing; which Thing doubtless they were accustomed to see, and with satisfaction; but no more thought of accounting for than for the fabrication of their daily *Allgemeine Zeitung,*[1] or the domestic habits of the Sun. Both were there and welcome; the world enjoyed what good was in them, and thought no more of the matter. The man Teufelsdröckh passed and repassed, in his little circle, as one of those originals and nondescripts, more frequent in German Universities than elsewhere; of whom, though you see them alive, and feel certain enough that they must have a History, no History seems to be discoverable; or only such as men give of mountain rocks and antediluvian ruins: That they have been created by unknown agencies, are in a state of gradual decay, and for the present reflect light and resist pressure; that is, are visible and tangible objects in this phantasm world, where so much other mystery is.

It was to be remarked that though, by title and diploma, *Professor der Allerley-Wissenschaft,* or as we should say in English, 'Professor of Things in General,' he had never delivered any Course; perhaps never been incited thereto by any public furtherance or requisition. To all appearance, the enlightened Government of Weissnichtwo, in founding their New University, imagined they had done enough, if 'in times like ours,' as the half-official Program expressed it, 'when all things are, rapidly or slowly, resolving themselves into Chaos, a Professorship of this kind had been established; whereby, as occasion called, the task of bodying somewhat forth again from such Chaos might be, even slightly, facilitated.' That actual Lectures should be held, and Public Classes for the 'Science of Things in General,' they doubtless considered premature; on which ground too they had only established the Professorship, nowise endowed it; so that

better known story of the shoemaker who refused Christ permission to rest when he passed his house on the way to the Cross, and was therefore condemned to wander until the Judgement Day.

[1] "Universal Gazette."

Teufelsdröckh, 'recommended by the highest Names,' had been promoted thereby to a Name merely.

Great, among the more enlightened classes, was the admiration of this new Professorship: how an enlightened Government had seen into the Want of the Age (*Zeitbedürfniss*); how at length, instead of Denial and Destruction,[1] we were to have a science of Affirmation and Reconstruction; and Germany and Weissnichtwo were where they should be, in the vanguard of the world. Considerable also was the wonder at the new Professor, dropt opportunely enough into the nascent University; so able to lecture, should occasion call; so ready to hold his peace for indefinite periods, should an enlightened Government consider that occasion did not call. But such admiration and such wonder, being followed by no act to keep them living, could last only nine days; and, long before our visit to that scene, had quite died away. The more cunning heads thought it was all an expiring clutch at popularity, on the part of a Minister, whom domestic embarrassments, court intrigues, old age, and dropsy soon afterwards finally drove from the helm.

As for Teufelsdröckh, except by his nightly appearances at the *Grüne Gans,* Weissnichtwo saw little of him, felt little of him. Here, over his tumbler of Gukguk, he sat reading Journals; sometimes contemplatively looking into the clouds of his tobacco-pipe, without other visible employment: always, from his mild ways, an agreeable phenomenon there; more especially when he opened his lips for speech; on which occasions the whole Coffee-house would hush itself into silence, as if sure to hear something noteworthy. Nay, perhaps to hear a whole series and river of the most memorable

---

[1]*Denial and Destruction:* the principal achievement, as Carlyle believed, of the eighteenth century, of the age of Voltaire and the French Revolution. From Goethe, however, he drew consolation in the doctrine that ages of unbelief and destruction alternate with ages of faith and creativeness. (See the essay on Diderot (*Ess.,* III, p. 248), and Goethe's *West-Oestlicher Divan,* Note on "Israel in der Wüste.")—The vocation of Teufelsdröckh—and of Germany—was (from Carlyle's point of view) to call men to an act of faith and of constructive labour.

utterances; such as, when once thawed, he would for hours indulge in, with fit audience: and the more memorable, as issuing from a head apparently not more interested in them, not more conscious of them, than is the sculptured stone head of some public fountain, which through its brass mouth-tube emits water to the worthy and the unworthy; careless whether it be for cooking victuals or quenching conflagration; indeed, maintains the same earnest assiduous look, whether any water be flowing or not.

To the Editor of these sheets, as to a young enthusiastic Englishman, however unworthy, Teufelsdröckh opened himself perhaps more than to the most. Pity only that we could not then half guess his importance, and scrutinise him with due power of vision! We enjoyed, what not three men in Weissnichtwo could boast of, a certain degree of access to the Professor's private domicile. It was the attic floor of the highest house in the Wahngasse,[1] and might truly be called the pinnacle of Weissnichtwo, for it rose sheer up above the contiguous roofs, themselves rising from elevated ground. Moreover, with its windows it looked towards all the four *Orte,* or as the Scotch say, and we ought to say, *Airts:*[2] the sitting-room itself commanded three; another came to view in the *Schlafgemach* (bed-room) at the opposite end; to say nothing of the kitchen, which offered two, as it were, *duplicates,* and showing nothing new. So that it was in fact the speculum[3] or watch-tower of Teufelsdröckh, wherefrom, sitting at ease, he might see the whole life-circulation of that considerable City; the streets and lanes of which, with all their doing and driving (*Thun und Treiben*), were for the most part visible there.

'I look down into all that wasp-nest or bee-hive,' have we heard him say, 'and witness their wax-laying and honey-

---

[1]*Wahngasse:* Dream-lane, illusion-street, *etc. Grüne Gans* and *Wahngasse* were actual places in Munich which Carlyle's brother John visited and described.

[2]*Airts:* Directions, points of the compass. (*Cf.* Burns, *I Love my Jean.*)

[3]Error for *specula* (watch-tower).

making, and poison-brewing, and choking by sulphur.[1] From the Palace esplanade, where music plays while Serene Highness is pleased to eat his victuals, down to the low lane, where in her door-sill the aged widow, knitting for a thin livelihood, sits to feel the afternoon sun, I see it all; for, except the Schlosskirche[2] weathercock, no biped stands so high. Couriers arrive bestrapped and bebooted, bearing Joy and Sorrow bagged-up in pouches of leather; there, topladen, and with four swift horses, rolls-in the country Baron and his household; here, on timber-leg, the lamed Soldier hops painfully along, begging alms: a thousand carriages, and wains, and cars, come tumbling-in with Food, with young Rusticity, and other Raw Produce, inanimate or animate, and go tumbling out again with Produce manufactured. That living flood, pouring through these streets, of all qualities and ages, knowest thou whence it is coming, whither it is going? *Aus der Ewigkeit, zu der Ewigkeit hin.* From Eternity, onwards to Eternity![3] These are Apparitions: what else?[4] Are they not Souls rendered visible: in Bodies, that took shape and will lose it, melting into air? Their solid Pavement is a Picture of the Sense;[5] they walk on the bosom of Nothing, blank Time is behind them and before them. Or fanciest thou, the red and yellow Clothes-screen yonder, with spurs on its heels and feather in its crown, is but of Today, without a Yesterday or a Tomorrow; and had not rather its Ancestor alive when

---

[1]*Choking by sulphur:* allusion to an old method of obtaining honey by killing a swarm of bees with the fumes of sulphur.

[2]Castle chapel.

[3]*Aus der Ewigkeit, etc:* a favourite thought with Carlyle, as with the German Romanticists. See *C.E.L.*, II, Ch. xiii (letter to John Carlyle); Carlyle, "Quintus Fixlein" (*German Romance*, II, pp. 299–300); Richter, *Flower, Fruit, and Thorn Pieces,* pp. 430–31, *etc.*

[4]*Cf.* Bk. III, Ch. viii, final paragraphs, for Carlyle's most magnificent treatment of this thought.

[5]The pavement can be known only as our sense-experience permits us; the real nature of the pavement is hidden from us. Carlyle had studied the subjective idealism of Bishop Berkeley (1685–1753), who had attacked the old belief in a world of matter independent of mind (*Principles of Human Knowledge,* 1710).

Hengst and Horsa[1] overran thy Island? Friend, thou seest here a living link in that Tissue of History, which inweaves all Being: watch well, or it will be past thee, and seen no more.

'*Ach, mein Lieber!*'[2] said he once, at midnight, when we had returned from the Coffee-house in rather earnest talk, 'it is a true sublimity to dwell here. These fringes of lamplight, struggling up through smoke and thousandfold exhalation, some fathoms into the ancient reign of Night,[3] what thinks Boötes of them, as he leads his Hunting-dogs[4] over the Zenith in their leash of sidereal fire? That stifled hum of Midnight, when Traffic has lain down to rest; and the chariot-wheels of Vanity, still rolling here and there through distant streets, are bearing her to Halls roofed-in, and lighted to the due pitch for her; and only Vice and Misery, to prowl or to moan like nightbirds, are abroad: that hum, I say, like the stertorous, unquiet slumber of sick Life, is heard in Heaven! Oh, under that hideous coverlet of vapours, and putrefactions, and unimaginable gases, what a Fermenting-vat lies simmering and hid! The joyful and the sorrowful are there; men are dying there, men are being born; men are praying,—on the other side of a brick partition, men are cursing; and around them all is the vast, void Night. The proud Grandee still lingers in his perfumed saloons, or reposes within damask curtains; Wretchedness cowers into truckle-beds, or shivers hunger-stricken into its lair of straw: in obscure cellars, *Rouge-et-Noir*[5] languidly emits its voice-of-destiny to haggard hungry Villains; while Councillors of State sit plotting, and playing their high chess-game, whereof the pawns are Men. The Lover whispers his mistress that the coach is ready; and she, full of hope and fear, glides down, to fly with him over the borders: the Thief,

[1]Leaders of Germanic invaders of Britain in the fifth century, founders of the Kingdom of Kent.

[2]"Ah, my dear Sir!"

[3]*Cf. Paradise Lost,* ii, 961 ff.

[4]Northern constellations: *Boötes* (a man with a crook), accompanied by the *Canes Venatici* (Hunting Dogs), driving the Great Bear.

[5]A game, *Trente et quarante,* with diamond-shaped red and black compartments in the gaming-table.

still more silently, sets-to his picklocks and crowbars, or lurks in wait till the watchmen first snore in their boxes. Gay mansions, with supper-rooms, and dancing-rooms, are full of light and music and high-swelling hearts; but, in the Condemned Cells, the pulse of life beats tremulous and faint, and bloodshot eyes look-out through the darkness, which is around and within, for the light of a stern last morning. Six men are to be hanged on the morrow: comes no hammering from the *Rabenstein?*[1]—their gallows must even now be o' building. Upwards of five-hundred-thousand two-legged animals without feathers[2] lie round us, in horizontal positions; their heads all in nightcaps, and full of the foolishest dreams. Riot cries aloud, and staggers and swaggers in his rank dens of shame; and the Mother, with streaming hair, kneels over her pallid dying infant, whose cracked lips only her tears now moisten.—All these heaped and huddled together, with nothing but a little carpentry and masonry between them;—crammed in, like salted fish in their barrel;—or weltering, shall I say, like an Egyptian pitcher of tamed vipers, each struggling to get its *head above* the others: *such* work goes on under that smoke-counterpane!—But I, *mein Werther,*[3] sit above it all; I am alone with the Stars.'

We looked in his face to see whether, in the utterance of such extraordinary Night-thoughts,[4] no feeling might be traced there; but with the light we had, which indeed was only a single tallow-light, and far enough from the window, nothing save that old calmness and fixedness was visible.

These were the Professor's talking seasons: most commonly he spoke in mere monosyllables, or sat altogether silent and smoked; while the visitor had liberty either to say what he listed, receiving for answer an occasional grunt; or to look

---

[1]"Raven-stone," *i.e.,* the gallows.

[2]*Two-legged animals without feathers:* an expression attributed to Plato by Diogenes Laertius.

[3]Literary for "My good friend," *Cf.* Goethe's *Sorrows of Werther* (1774), *etc.;* also *Ess.,* II, 157–58.

[4]Allusion to *The Complaint or Night Thoughts* (1742–45) by Edward Young (1683–1765).

round for a space, and then take himself away. It was a strange apartment; full of books and tattered papers, and miscellaneous shreds of all conceivable substances, 'united in a common element of dust.'[1] Books lay on tables, and below tables; here fluttered a sheet of manuscript, there a torn handkerchief, or nightcap hastily thrown aside; ink-bottles alternated with bread-crusts, coffee-pots, tobacco-boxes, Periodical Literature, and Blücher Boots.[2] Old Lieschen (Lisekin, 'Liza), who was his bed-maker and stove-lighter, his washer and wringer, cook, errand-maid, and general lion's-provider, and for the rest a very orderly creature, had no sovereign authority in this last citadel of Teufelsdröckh; only some once in the month she half-forcibly made her way thither, with broom and duster, and (Teufelsdröckh hastily saving his manuscripts) effected a partial clearance, a jail-delivery[3] of such lumber as was not Literary. These were her *Erdbeben* (earthquakes), which Teufelsdröckh dreaded worse than the pestilence; nevertheless, to such length he had been forced to comply. Glad would he have been to sit here philosophising forever, or till the litter, by accumulation, drove him out of doors: but Lieschen was his right-arm, and spoon, and necessary of life, and would not be flatly gainsayed. We can still remember the ancient woman; so silent that some thought her dumb; deaf also you would often have supposed her; for Teufelsdröckh, and Teufelsdröckh only, would she serve or give heed to; and with him she seemed to communicate chiefly by signs; if it were not rather by some secret divination that she guessed all his wants, and supplied them. Assiduous old dame! she scoured, and sorted, and swept, in her kitchen, with the least possible violence to the ear; yet all was tight and right there: hot and black came the coffee

---

[1]Phrase from *Meister,* I, 88.

[2]Half-boots named after the Prussian general, G. L. von Blücher (1742–1819).

[3]*Jail-delivery:* an expression already used, scathingly, by Carlyle to parody the effect of William Taylor's *Historic Survey of German Poetry* (see *Ess.,* II, 349–50).

ever at the due moment; and the speechless Lieschen herself looked out on you, from under her clean white coif with its lappets,[1] through her clean withered face and wrinkles, with a look of helpful intelligence, almost of benevolence.

Few strangers, as above hinted, had admittance hither: the only one we ever saw there, ourselves excepted, was the Hofrath Heuschrecke, already known, by name and expectation, to the readers of these pages. To us, at that period, Herr Heuschrecke seemed one of those purse-mouthed, crane-necked, clean-brushed, pacific individuals, perhaps sufficiently distinguished in society by this fact, that, in dry weather or in wet, 'they never appear without their umbrella.' Had we not known with what 'little wisdom' the world is governed;[2] and how, in Germany as elsewhere, the ninety-and-nine Public Men can for most part be but mute train-bearers to the hundredth, perhaps but stalking-horses and willing or unwilling dupes,—it might have seemed wonderful how Herr Heuschrecke should be named a *Rath,* or Councillor, and Counsellor, even in Weissnichtwo. What counsel to any man, or to any woman, could this particular Hofrath give; in whose loose, zigzag figure; in whose thin visage, as it went jerking to and fro, in minute incessant fluctuation,—you traced rather confusion worse confounded;[3] at most, Timidity and physical Cold? Some indeed said withal, he was 'the very Spirit of Love embodied': blue earnest eyes, full of sadness and kindness; purse ever open, and so forth; the whole of which, we shall now hope, for many reasons, was not quite groundless. Nevertheless friend Teufelsdröckh's outline, who indeed handled the burin[4] like few in these cases, was probably the best: *Er hat Gemüth und Geist, hat wenigstens gehabt, doch ohne Organ, ohne Schicksals-Gunst; ist gegenwärtig aber halb-zerrüttet, halb-erstarrt,* 'He has heart and

[1]*Coif:* a loose cap, covering the sides of the head; *lappets,* flaps.

[2]A saying attributed to the Swedish statesman, Axel Oxenstiern (1583–1654). (M.)

[3]*Cf. Paradise Lost,* ii, 996.

[4]A pointed, steel cutting-tool, used by an engraver.

talent, at least has had such, yet without fit mode of utterance, or favour of Fortune; and so is now half-cracked, half-congealed.'—What the Hofrath shall think of this when he sees it, readers may wonder: we, safe in the stronghold of Historical Fidelity, are careless.

The main point, doubtless, for us all, is his love of Teufelsdröckh, which indeed was also by far the most decisive feature of Heuschrecke himself. We are enabled to assert that he hung on the Professor with the fondness of a Boswell[1] for his Johnson. And perhaps with the like return; for Teufelsdröckh treated his gaunt admirer with little outward regard, as some half-rational or altogether irrational friend, and at best loved him out of gratitude and by habit. On the other hand, it was curious to observe with what reverent kindness, and a sort of fatherly protection, our Hofrath, being the elder, richer, and as he fondly imagined far more practically influential of the two, looked and tended on his little Sage, whom he seemed to consider as a living oracle. Let but Teufelsdröckh open his mouth, Heuschrecke's also unpuckered itself into a free doorway, besides his being all eye and all ear, so that nothing might be lost: and then, at every pause in the harangue, he gurgled-out his pursy chuckle of a cough-laugh (for the machinery of laughter took some time to get in motion, and seemed crank and slack), or else his twanging nasal, *Bravo! Das glaub' ich;*[2] in either case, by way of heartiest approval. In short, if Teufelsdröckh was Dalai-Lama,[3] of which, except perhaps in his self-seclusion, and godlike indifference, there was no symptom, then might Heuschrecke pass for his chief Talapoin,[4] to whom no dough-pill he could knead and publish was other than medicinal and sacred.

---

[1]James Boswell (1740–95), author of *The Life of Samuel Johnson, LL.D.* (1791).

[2]"I believe that," or "I agree with you."

[3]Grand Lama, or head ("pope") of the Buddhism of Tibet and Mongolia.

[4]*Talapoin:* a Buddhist monk.

In such environment, social, domestic, physical, did Teufelsdröckh, at the time of our acquaintance, and most likely does he still, live and meditate. Here, perched-up in his high Wahngasse watch-tower, and often, in solitude, out-watching the Bear,[1] it was that the indomitable Inquirer fought all his battles with Dulness and Darkness; here, in all probability, that he wrote this surprising Volume on *Clothes.* Additional particulars: of his age, which was of that standing middle sort you could only guess at; of his wide surtout; the colour of his trousers, fashion of his broad-brimmed steeple-hat, and so forth, we might report, but do not. The Wisest truly is, in these times, the Greatest; so that an enlightened curiosity, leaving Kings and suchlike to rest very much on their own basis, turns more and more to the Philosophic Class: nevertheless, what reader expects that, with all our writing and reporting, Teufelsdröckh could be brought home to him, till once the Documents arrive? His Life, Fortunes, and Bodily Presence, are as yet hidden from us, or matter only of faint conjecture. But, on the other hand, does not his Soul lie enclosed in this remarkable Volume, much more truly than Pedro Garcia's did in the buried Bag of Doubloons?[2] To the soul of Diogenes Teufelsdröckh, to his opinions, namely, on the 'Origin and Influence of Clothes,' we for the present gladly return.

[1]See Milton's *Il Penseroso,* l. 87. In northern latitudes, the Great Bear (*Ursa Major*) never sets; hence Teufelsdröckh sat up until daybreak.

[2]See "Preface to the Reader" in *Gil Blas:* "Here lies interred the soul of Pedro Garcia," an inscription on a stone over Garcia's buried gold. *Doubloon:* a Spanish gold coin, no longer used.

CHAPTER IV

CHARACTERISTICS

Teufelsdröckh and his Work on Clothes: Strange freedom of speech; transcendentalism; force of insight and expression; multifarious learning: Style poetic, uncouth: Comprehensiveness of his humour and moral feeling. How the Editor once saw him laugh. Different kinds of Laughter and their significance.

IT WERE a piece of vain flattery to pretend that this Work on Clothes entirely contents us; that it is not, like all works of genius, like the very Sun, which, though the highest published creation, or work of genius, has nevertheless black spots and troubled nebulosities amid its effulgence,—a mixture of insight, inspiration, with dulness, double-vision, and even utter blindness.

Without committing ourselves to those enthusiastic praises and prophesyings of the *Weissnichtwo'sche Anzeiger,*[1] we admitted that the Book had in a high degree excited us to self-activity, which is the best effect of any book; that it had even operated changes in our way of thought; nay, that it promised to prove, as it were, the opening of a new mine-shaft, wherein the whole world of Speculation might henceforth dig to unknown depths. More especially it may now be declared that Professor Teufelsdröckh's acquirements, patience of research, philosophic and even poetic vigour, are here made indisputably manifest; and unhappily no less his prolixity and tortuosity and manifold ineptitude; that, on the whole, as in opening new mine-shafts is not unreasonable, there is much rubbish in his Book, though likewise specimens of almost invaluable ore. A paramount popularity in England we cannot promise him. Apart from the choice of such a topic as Clothes, too often the manner of treating it be-

[1] "*Know-not-where Advertiser.*" (*The Kennaquhair Advertiser.* B.)

tokens in the Author a rusticity and academic seclusion, unblamable, indeed inevitable in a German, but fatal to his success with our public.

Of good society Teufelsdröckh appears to have seen little, or has mostly forgotten what he saw. He speaks-out with a strange plainness; calls many things by their mere dictionary names. To him the Upholsterer is no Pontiff, neither is any Drawing-room a Temple, were it never so begilt and overhung: 'a whole immensity of Brussels carpets, and pier-glasses, and or-molu,' as he himself expresses it, 'cannot hide from me that such Drawing-room is simply a section of Infinite Space, where so many God-created Souls do for the time meet together.' To Teufelsdröckh the highest Duchess is respectable, is venerable; but nowise for her pearl bracelets and Malines[1] laces: in his eyes, the star of a Lord[2] is little less and little more than the broad button of Birmingham spelter[3] in a Clown's smock; 'each is an implement,' he says, 'in its kind; a tag for *hooking-together;* and, for the rest, was dug from the earth, and hammered on a stithy before smith's fingers.' Thus does the Professor look in men's faces with a strange impartiality, a strange scientific freedom; like a man unversed in the higher circles, like a man dropped thither from the Moon. Rightly considered, it is in this peculiarity, running through his whole system of thought, that all these shortcomings, over-shootings, and multiform perversities, take rise: if indeed they have not a second source, also natural enough, in his Transcendental Philosophies, and humour of looking at all Matter and Material things as Spirit;[4] whereby truly his case were but the more hopeless, the more lamentable.

To the Thinkers of this nation, however, of which class it is firmly believed there are individuals yet extant, we can

---

[1]A town between Brussels and Antwerp.

[2]*Star of a Lord:* star-shaped ornament, worn on the breasts of nobles in such orders as the Bath, the Garter, *etc.*

[3]*Spelter:* zinc.

[4]See Int., Section V, b; and Bk. I, Ch. x.

safely recommend the Work: nay, who knows but among the fashionable ranks too, if it be true, as Teufelsdröckh maintains, that 'within the most starched cravat there passes a windpipe and weasand,[1] and under the thickliest embroidered waistcoat beats a heart,'—the force of that rapt earnestness may be felt, and here and there an arrow of the soul pierce through? In our wild Seer, shaggy, unkempt, like a Baptist living on locusts and wild honey,[2] there is an untutored energy, a silent, as it were unconscious, strength, which except in the higher walks of Literature, must be rare. Many a deep glance, and often with unspeakable precision, has he cast into mysterious Nature, and the still more mysterious Life of Man. Wonderful it is with what cutting words, now and then, he severs asunder the confusion; shears down, were it furlongs deep, into the true centre of the matter; and there not only hits the nail on the head, but with crushing force smites it home, and buries it.—On the other hand, let us be free to admit, he is the most unequal writer breathing. Often after some such feat, he will play truant for long pages, and go dawdling and dreaming, and mumbling and maundering the merest commonplaces, as if he were asleep with eyes open, which indeed he is.

Of his boundless Learning, and how all reading and literature in most known tongues, from *Sanchoniathon*[3] to *Dr. Lingard*,[4] from your Oriental *Shasters*, and *Talmuds*, and *Korans*,[5] with Cassini's *Siamese Tables*,[6] and Laplace's

---

[1]*Weasand:* windpipe.

[2]*Cf.* Matthew, iii, 4.

[3]Legendary Phoenician sage, said to have lived "before the Trojan times," author of sacred writings which Philo Herennius Byblius claimed to have translated from the Phoenician original in the second century A.D. Quoted in *Tristram Shandy*, Vol. V, Ch. 28.

[4]Dr. John Lingard (1771–1851), Roman Catholic historian of England, author of *History of England* (1819–1830), *etc.*

[5]*Shasters, and Talmuds, and Korans:* religious and legal books of the Hindus, the Hebrews, and the Mahometans, respectively.

[6]G. D. Cassini (1625–1712), Italian astronomer; became a French subject, and director of the Paris observatory; published "Règles de l'Astronomie Siamoise," *etc.*

Mécanique Céleste,[1] down to *Robinson Crusoe* and the *Belfast Town and Country Almanack,* are familiar to him,—we shall say nothing: for unexampled as it is with us, to the Germans such universality of study passes without wonder, as a thing commendable, indeed, but natural, indispensable, and there of course. A man that devotes his life to learning, shall he not be learned?

In respect of style our Author manifests the same genial capability, marred too often by the same rudeness, inequality, and apparent want of intercourse with the higher classes. Occasionally, as above hinted, we find consummate vigour, a true inspiration; his burning thoughts step forth in fit burning words, like so many full-formed Minervas,[2] issuing amid flame and splendour from Jove's head; a rich, idiomatic diction, picturesque allusions, fiery poetic emphasis, or quaint tricksy turns; all the graces and terrors of a wild Imagination, wedded to the clearest Intellect, alternate in beautiful vicissitude. Were it not that sheer sleeping and soporific passages; circumlocutions, repetitions, touches even of pure doting jargon, so often intervene! On the whole, Professor Teufelsdröckh is not a cultivated writer. Of his sentences perhaps not more than nine-tenths stand straight on their legs; the remainder are in quite angular attitudes, buttressed-up by props (of parentheses and dashes), and ever with this or the other tagrag hanging from them; a few even sprawl-out helplessly on all sides, quite broken-backed and dismembered. Nevertheless, in almost his very worst moods, there lies in him a singular attraction. A wild tone pervades the whole utterance of the man, like its keynote and regulator; now screwing itself aloft as into the Song of Spirits, or else the shrill mockery of Fiends; now sinking in cadences, not without melodious heartiness, though sometimes abrupt enough, into the common pitch, when we hear it only as a monotonous hum; of which hum the true character is extremely difficult to

---

[1]See p. 4, *note* 1.

[2]Minerva, or Athena, Greek goddess of wisdom and war, was supposed to have sprung, fully armed, from the head of Zeus.

fix. Up to this hour we have never fully satisfied ourselves whether it is a tone and hum of real Humour, which we reckon among the very highest qualities of genius, or some echo of mere Insanity and Inanity, which doubtless ranks below the very lowest.

Under a like difficulty, in spite even of our personal intercourse, do we still lie with regard to the Professor's moral feeling. Gleams of an ethereal love burst forth from him, soft wailings of infinite pity; he could clasp the whole Universe into his bosom,[1] and keep it warm; it seems as if under that rude exterior there dwelt a very seraph. Then again he is so sly and still, so imperturbably saturnine; shows such indifference, malign coolness towards all that men strive after; and ever with some half-visible wrinkle of a bitter sardonic humour, if indeed it be not mere stolid callousness,—that you look on him almost with a shudder, as on some incarnate Mephistopheles,[2] to whom this great terrestrial and celestial Round, after all, were but some huge foolish Whirligig, where kings and beggars, and angels and demons, and stars and street-sweepings, were chaotically whirled, in which only children could take interest. His look, as we mentioned, is probably the gravest ever seen: yet it is not of that cast-iron gravity frequent enough among our own Chancery[3] suitors; but rather the gravity as of some silent, high-encircled mountain-pool, perhaps the crater of an extinct volcano; into whose black deeps you fear to gaze: those eyes, those lights that sparkle in it, may indeed be reflexes of the heavenly Stars, but perhaps also glances from the region of Nether Fire!

Certainly a most involved, self-secluded, altogether enigmatic nature, this of Teufelsdröckh! Here, however, we gladly recall to mind that once we saw him *laugh;* once only,

---

[1]See Richter, *Flower, Fruit, and Thorn Pieces,* Bk. III, Ch. ix.

[2]The Devil in *Faust,* the tempter and mocker, "the spirit that denies." See Carlyle's "Goethe's Helena" (*Ess.,* I, 157).

[3]High Court, presided over by the Lord Chancellor, until 1873 the highest court of judicature next to Parliament.

perhaps it was the first and last time in his life; but then such a peal of laughter, enough to have awakened the Seven Sleepers![1] It was of Jean Paul's[2] doing: some single billow in that vast World-Mahlstrom[3] of Humour, with its heaven-kissing coruscations, which is now, alas, all congealed in the frost of death! The large-bodied Poet and the small, both large enough in soul, sat talking miscellaneously together, the present Editor being privileged to listen; and now Paul, in his serious way, was giving one of those inimitable 'Extra-harangues'[4]; and, as it chanced, On the Proposal for a *Cast-metal King:* gradually a light kindled in our Professor's eyes and face, a beaming, mantling, loveliest light; through those murky features, a radiant, ever-young Apollo looked; and he burst forth like the neighing of all Tattersall's,[5]—tears streaming down his cheeks, pipe held aloft, foot clutched into the air,—loud, long-continuing, uncontrollable; a laugh not of the face and diaphragm only, but of the whole man from head to heel. The present Editor, who laughed indeed, yet with measure, began to fear all was not right: however, Teufelsdröckh composed himself, and sank into his old stillness; on his inscrutable countenance there was, if anything, a slight look of shame; and Richter himself could not rouse him again. Readers who have any tincture of Psychology know how much is to be inferred from this; and that no man who has once heartily and wholly laughed can be altogether irreclaimably bad. How much lies in Laughter: the cipher-key, wherewith we decipher the whole man! Some men wear an everlasting barren simper; in the smile of others lies a cold

---

[1]Seven Christian youths of Ephesus, who fled the persecution of Decius (A.D. 250) and concealed themselves in a neighbouring cavern, where they fell asleep, not awakening for nearly two hundred years.

[2]Jean Paul Friedrich Richter (1763–1825), German Romantic humorist, one of Carlyle's favourite authors.

[3]Maelstrom, the famous whirlpool in the Arctic Ocean off the west coast of Norway. (*Cf.* Poe, "A Descent into the Maelstrom.")

[4]Interpolative, digressive discussions, similar to Jean Paul's "Extra-blatt" (Extra-chapter) which he occasionally inserted into his narratives.

[5]A famous horse-market in London.

glitter as of ice: the fewest are able to laugh, what can be called laughing, but only sniff and titter and snigger from the throat outwards; or at best, produce some whiffling husky cachinnation, as if they were laughing through wool: of none such comes good. The man who cannot laugh is not only fit for treasons, stratagems, and spoils;[1] but his whole life is already a treason and a stratagem.

Considered as an Author, Herr Teufelsdröckh has one scarcely pardonable fault, doubtless his worst: an almost total want of arrangement. In this remarkable Volume, it is true, his adherence to the mere course of Time produces, through the Narrative portions, a certain show of outward method; but of true logical method and sequence there is too little. Apart from its multifarious sections and subdivisions, the Work naturally falls into two Parts; a Historical-Descriptive, and a Philosophical-Speculative: but falls, unhappily, by no firm line of demarcation; in that labyrinthic combination, each Part overlaps, and indents, and indeed runs quite through the other. Many sections are of a debatable rubric, or even quite nondescript and unnameable; whereby the Book not only loses in accessibility, but too often distresses us like some mad banquet, wherein all courses had been confounded, and fish and flesh, soup and solid, oyster-sauce, lettuces, Rhine-wine and French mustard, were hurled into one huge tureen or trough, and the hungry Public invited to help itself. To bring what order we can out of this Chaos shall be part of our endeavour.

---

[1] *Cf. Merchant of Venice,* V, i, 85. *Cf.* Carlyle on humour in his two essays on Richter (*Ess.,* I, 16–18; II, 151 ff.)

CHAPTER V

THE WORLD IN CLOTHES

Futile cause-and-effect Philosophies. Teufelsdröckh's Orbis Vestitus. Clothes first invented for the sake of ornament. Picture of our progenitor, the Aboriginal Savage. Wonders of growth and progress in mankind's history. Man defined as a Tool-using Animal.

As Montesquieu wrote a *Spirit of Laws,*' observes our Professor, 'so could I write a *Spirit of Clothes;* thus, with an *Esprit des Lois,* properly an *Esprit de Coutumes,* we should have an *Esprit de Costumes.* For neither in tailoring nor in legislating does man proceed by mere Accident, but the hand is ever guided on by mysterious operations of the mind. In all his Modes, and habilatory endeavours, an Architectural Idea will be found lurking; his Body and the Cloth are the site and materials whereon and whereby his beautified edifice, of a Person, is to be built. Whether he flow gracefully out in folded mantles, based on light sandals; tower-up in high headgear, from amid peaks, spangles and bell-girdles; swell-out in starched ruffs, buckram stuffings, and monstrous tuberosities; or girth himself into separate sections, and front the world an Agglomeration of four limbs,—will depend on the nature of such Architectural Idea: whether Grecian, Gothic, Later-Gothic, or altogether Modern, and Parisian or Anglo-Dandiacal.[1] Again, what meaning lies in Colour! From the soberest drab to the high-flaming scarlet, spiritual idiosyncrasies unfold themselves in choice of Colour: if the Cut betoken Intellect and Talent, so does the Colour betoken Temper and Heart. In all which, among nations as among individuals, there is an incessant, indubitable, though infinitely

[1]Carlyle's allusion to modes in the age of the Dandy, of Beau Brummel (1778–1840) and Count D'Orsay (1801–1852).

complex working of Cause and Effect: every snip of the Scissors has been regulated and prescribed by ever-active Influences, which doubtless to Intelligences of a superior order are neither invisible nor illegible.

'For such superior Intelligences a Cause-and-Effect Philosophy[1] of Clothes, as of Laws, were probably a comfortable winter-evening entertainment: nevertheless, for inferior Intelligences, like men, such Philosophies have always seemed to me uninstructive enough. Nay, what is your Montesquieu[2] himself but a clever infant spelling Letters from a hieroglyphical prophetic Book,[3] the lexicon of which lies in Eternity, in Heaven?—Let any Cause-and-Effect Philosopher explain, not why I wear such and such a Garment, obey such and such a Law; but even why *I* am *here,* to wear and obey anything!—Much, therefore, if not the whole, of that same *Spirit of Clothes* I shall suppress, as hypothetical, ineffectual, and even impertinent: naked Facts, and Deductions drawn therefrom in quite another than that omniscient style, are my humbler and proper province.'

Acting on which prudent restriction, Teufelsdröckh has nevertheless contrived to take-in a well-nigh boundless extent of field; at least, the boundaries too often lie quite beyond our horizon. Selection being indispensable, we shall here glance-over his First Part only in the most cursory manner.

This First Part is, no doubt, distinguished by omnivorous learning, and utmost patience and fairness: at the same time, in its results and delineations, it is much more likely to interest the Compilers of some *Library* of General, Entertain-

---

[1]An allusion to English empirical thinkers, from John Locke (1632–1704) to David Hume (1711–1776). (See Int., II.)

[2]Charles Louis de Secondat, Baron de la Brede et de Montesquieu (1689–1755), French philosophical historian, author of *Esprit des lois* (1748), a comprehensive and monumental work on laws and customs.

[3]Nature as the hieroglyphic expression of the Divine was a favourite theme of Novalis (*Fragmente*), of Schelling (*Methode des Akademischen Studiums*), and of Schiller (*Philosophische Briefe*). "Everything," says Schiller, "within and without me, is the hieroglyphical expression of a power analogous to my own being." (See Schiller's *Werke,* ed. H. Kurtz, Hildburghausen, 1868–70, IX, p. 118.) (See Int., Sect. V, b.)

ing, Useful, or even Useless knowledge[1] than the miscellaneous readers of these pages. Was it this Part of the Book which Heuschrecke had in view, when he recommended us to that joint-stock vehicle of publication, 'at present the glory of British Literature'? If so, the Library Editors are welcome to dig in it for their own behoof.

To the First Chapter, which turns on Paradise and Fig-leaves, and leads us into interminable disquisitions of a mythological, metaphorical, cabalistico-sartorial[2] and quite antediluvian cast, we shall content ourselves with giving an unconcerned approval. Still less have we to do with 'Lilis,[3] Adam's first wife, whom, according to the Talmudists,[4] he had before Eve, and who bore him, in that wedlock, the whole progeny of aerial, aquatic, and terrestrial Devils,'—very needlessly, we think. On this portion of the Work, with its profound glances into the *Adam-Kadmon,*[5] or Primeval Element, here strangely brought into relation with the *Nifl* and *Muspel* (Darkness and Light) of the antique North,[6] it may be enough to say, that its correctness of deduction, and depth of Talmudic and Rabbinical lore have filled perhaps not the worst Hebraist in Britain with something like astonishment.

But, quitting this twilight region, Teufelsdröckh hastens from the Tower of Babel,[7] to follow the dispersion of Mankind

---

[1]A satirical allusion to such cheap methods of popularizing knowledge as the treatises of *The Society for Diffusion of Useful Knowledge,* founded by Lord Brougham in 1825.

[2]Mysteriously relating to clothes, or to tailoring. Cabala, or cabbala: system of occult theosophy or mystical interpretation of the Scriptures among Jewish rabbis and certain medieval Christians.

[3]Or Lilith, Adam's first wife, according to the Talmud. Originally a female Babylonian demon, mentioned in Isaiah, xxxiv, 14, as "screech owl"; introduced as a character in the Walpurgis-Night scenes of Goethe's *Faust.*

[4]See p. 30, *note* 5. The quotation, adapted, is from *The Anatomy of Melancholy* (1621), Part I, Sect. ii, memb. i, subsect. 2; by Robert Burton (1577–1640).

[5]Hebrew for *the first man;* a Cabbalistic term.

[6]In Old Norse mythology, Niflheim, *mist-home,* is the northern region of night; Muspelheim, *bright-home,* the southern region of light.

[7]Genesis, xi, 1–9.

over the whole habitable and habilable globe. Walking by the light of Oriental, Pelasgic,[1] Scandinavian, Egyptian, Otaheitean,[2] Ancient and Modern researches of every conceivable kind, he strives to give us in compressed shape (as the Nürnbergers give an *Orbis Pictus*) an *Orbis Vestitus;*[3] or view of the costumes of all mankind, in all countries, in all times. It is here that to the antiquarian, to the Historian, we can triumphantly say: Fall to! Here is learning: an irregular Treasury, if you will; but inexhaustible as the Hoard of King Nibelung,[4] which twelve wagons in twelve days, at the rate of three journeys a day, could not carry off. Sheep-skin cloaks and wampum[5] belts; phylacteries, stoles, albs; chlamydes, togas, Chinese silks, Afghaun shawls, trunk-hose, leather breeches, Celtic philibegs (though breeches, as the name *Gallia Braccata* indicates, are the more ancient), Hussar cloaks, Vandyke tippets, ruffs, fardingales, are brought vividly before us,—even the Kilmarnock nightcap[6] is not forgotten. For most part, too, we must admit that the Learning, hetero-

---

[1]Prehistoric Mediterranean.

[2]Of Tahiti, an island in the South Pacific.

[3]*Orbis Pictus:* "The World in Pictures." An illustrated school-book (1658) by the Moravian scholar, Amos Comenius (1592–1670); used by Goethe as a youth, and mentioned by Richter in "Quintus Fixlein" (*German Romance,* II, 322.)—*Orbis Vestitus:* The world in clothes, the title of the present chapter.

[4]The hero of a Middle High German epic. See Carlyle's essay on *The Niebelungen Lied.* Correct: four days, rather than twelve.

[5]Beads of shell, used by North American Indians as money, *etc.*

[6]*Phylacteries:* small leather cases containing Scripture texts, the whole worn as an amulet or charm (Matthew, xxiii, 5).—*stoles, albs:* ecclesiastical vestments.—*chlamydes:* short oblong mantles worn by ancient Greek soldiers.—*togas:* loose outer garments worn by Roman citizens when appearing in public.—*trunk-hose:* full breeches reaching just below the thighs, or to the knees, worn chiefly in the 16th and 17th centuries.—*philibegs:* kilts.—*Gallia Braccata:* Gaul wearing breeches (Gaul on the north side of the Alps), in contrast to Romans wearing togas.—*Vandyke tippets:* long hanging garments, or capes, or scarf-like mufflers, as seen in the paintings by Sir Anthony Van Dyck (1599–1641).—*ruff:* a muslin or linen collar, plaited, crimped, or fluted, worn by persons of fashion in the reign of Queen Elizabeth.—*fardingales:* farthingale, a hoop skirt or hoop petticoat.—*Kilmarnock nightcap:* or Kilmarnock cowl, made in Kilmarnock, Ayrshire, Scotland.

geneous as it is, and tumbled-down quite pell-mell, is true concentrated and purified Learning, the drossy parts smelted out and thrown aside.

Philosophical reflections intervene, and sometimes touching pictures of human life. Of this sort the following has surprised us. The first purpose of Clothes, as our Professor imagines, was not warmth or decency, but ornament. 'Miserable indeed,' says he, 'was the condition of the Aboriginal Savage, glaring fiercely from under his fleece of hair, which with the beard reached down to his loins, and hung round him like a matted cloak; the rest of his body sheeted in its thick natural fell. He loitered in the sunny glades of the forest, living on wild-fruits; or, as the ancient Caledonian,[1] squatted himself in morasses, lurking for his bestial or human prey; without implements, without arms, save the ball of heavy Flint, to which, that his sole possession and defence might not be lost, he had attached a long cord of plaited thongs; thereby recovering as well as hurling it with deadly unerring skill. Nevertheless, the pains of Hunger and Revenge once satisfied, his next care was not Comfort but Decoration (*Putz*). Warmth he found in the toils of the chase; or amid dried leaves, in his hollow tree, in his bark shed, or natural grotto: but for Decoration he must have Clothes. Nay, among wild people, we find tattooing and painting even prior to Clothes. The first spiritual want of a barbarous man is Decoration, as indeed we still see among the barbarous classes in civilised countries.

'Reader, the heaven-inspired melodious Singer; loftiest Serene Highness; nay thy own amber-locked, snow-and-rose-bloom Maiden, worthy to glide sylphlike almost on air, whom thou lovest, worshippest as a divine Presence, which, indeed, symbolically taken, she is,—has descended, like thyself, from that same hair-mantled, flint-hurling Aboriginal Anthropophagus![2] Out of the eater cometh forth meat; out

---

[1]Archaic or poetic for "Scotch."

[2]Cannibal. *Cf. Othello,* I, iii, 144.

of the strong cometh forth sweetness.[1] What changes are wrought, not by Time, yet in Time! For not Mankind only, but all that Mankind does or beholds, is in continual growth, re-genesis and self-perfecting vitality. Cast forth thy Act, thy Word, into the ever-living, ever-working Universe: it is a seed-grain that cannot die,[2] unnoticed today (says one), it will be found flourishing as a Banyan-grove (perhaps, alas, as a Hemlock-forest!)[3] after a thousand years.

'He who first shortened the labour of Copyists by device of *Movable Types*[4] was disbanding hired Armies, and cashiering most Kings and Senates, and creating a whole new Democratic world:[5] he had invented the Art of Printing. The first ground handful of Nitre, Sulphur, and Charcoal drove Monk Schwartz's pestle through the ceiling:[6] what will the last do? Achieve the final undisputed prostration of Force under Thought, of Animal courage under Spiritual. A simple invention it was in the old-world Grazier,—sick of lugging his slow Ox about the country till he got it bartered for corn or oil,—to take a piece of Leather, and thereon scratch or stamp the mere Figure of an Ox (or *Pecus*); put it in his pocket, and call it *Pecunia,* Money. Yet hereby did Barter grow Sale, the Leather Money is now Golden and Paper, and all miracles have been out-miracled: for there are Rothschilds and English National Debts; and whoso has sixpence is sovereign (to the length of sixpence) over all men; commands

---

[1]*Cf.* Judges, xiv, 14.

[2]Perhaps suggested by Matthew, xiii, 31–32.

[3]*Banyan-grove:* an East Indian tree; its branches take root and become additional trunks, providing abundant shade.—*Hemlock-forest:* Carlyle evidently unites the hemlock spruce with the poisonous hemlock herb (*Conium maculatum*), with which Socrates was poisoned.

[4]Johann Fust (or Faust) (*c.* 1400–1466), partner of Johann Gutenberg (*c.* 1398–1468), a goldsmith of Mainz, is now generally regarded as the originator of movable types in European printing.

[5]*Cf. On Heroes,* p. 164.

[6]In Europe, gunpowder was produced by Roger Bacon (*c.* 1214–92), through his search for pure nitre. Berthold Schwartz discovered the process of granulating gunpowder early in the fourteenth century.

cooks to feed him, philosophers to teach him, kings to mount guard over him,—to the length of sixpence.—Clothes too, which began in foolishest love of Ornament, what have they not become! Increased Security and pleasurable Heat soon followed: but what of these? Shame, divine Shame, (*Schaam*, Modesty), as yet a stranger to the Anthropophagous bosom, arose there mysteriously under Clothes; a mystic grove-encircled shrine for the Holy in man. Clothes gave us individuality, distinctions, social polity; Clothes have made Men of us; they are threatening to make Clothes-screens of us.

'But, on the whole,' continues our eloquent Professor, 'Man is a Tool-using Animal (*Handthierendes Thier*).[1] Weak in himself, and of small stature, he stands on a basis, at most for the flattest-soled, of some half-square foot, insecurely enough; has to straddle out his legs, lest the very wind supplant him. Feeblest of bipeds! Three quintals[2] are a crushing load for him; the steer of the meadow tosses him aloft, like a waste rag. Nevertheless he can use Tools, can devise Tools: with these the granite mountain melts into light dust before him; he kneads glowing iron, as if it were soft paste; seas are his smooth highway, winds and fire his unwearying steeds. Nowhere do you find him without Tools: without Tools he is nothing, with Tools he is all.'

Here may we not, for a moment, interrupt the stream of Oratory with a remark, that this Definition of the Tool-using Animal appears to us, of all that Animal-sort, considerably the precisest and best? Man is called a Laughing Animal: but do not the apes also laugh, or attempt to do it; and is the manliest man the greatest and oftenest laugher? Teufelsdröckh himself, as we said, laughed only once. Still less do we make of that other French Definition of the Cooking Animal; which, indeed, for rigorous scientific purposes, is as good as useless. Can a Tartar be said to cook, when he only

[1]Man is thus defined in Boswell's *Life of Johnson*, after Benjamin Franklin, (April 7, 1778).

[2]Hundredweights.

readies his steak by riding on it?[1] Again, what Cookery does the Greenlander use, beyond stowing-up his whale-blubber, as a marmot,[2] in the like case, might do? Or how would Monsieur Ude[3] prosper among those Orinocco Indians who, according to Humboldt,[4] lodge in crow-nests, on the branches of trees; and, for half the year, have no victuals but pipe-clay, the whole country being under water? But, on the other hand, show us the human being, of any period or climate, without his Tools: those very Caledonians, as we saw, had their Flint-ball, and Thong to it, such as no brute has or can have.

'Man is a Tool-using Animal,' concludes Teufelsdröckh in his abrupt way; 'of which truth Clothes are but one example: and surely if we consider the interval between the first wooden Dibble[5] fashioned by man, and those Liverpool Steam-carriages,[6] or the British House of Commons, we shall note what progress he has made. He digs up certain black stones from the bosom of the earth, and says to them, *Transport me and this luggage at the rate of five-and-thirty miles an hour;* and they do it: he collects, apparently by lot, six-hundred and fifty-eight miscellaneous individuals, and says to them, *Make this nation toil for us, bleed for us, hunger and sorrow and sin for us;* and they do it.'

---

[1]See *Hudibras,* I, ii, 265–78.

[2]Ground hog.

[3]Louis Eustache Ude, famous French cook of the time.

[4]Alexander von Humboldt (1769–1859), German naturalist and explorer, travelled up the Orinocco in 1800.

[5]A pointed implement used to make holes in the ground, especially for plants or seeds.

[6]The first railroad in England ran between Liverpool and Manchester, and was opened September 15, 1830.

CHAPTER VI

APRONS

Divers Aprons in the world with divers uses. The Military and Police Establishment Society's working Apron. The Episcopal Apron with its corner tucked in. The Laystall. Journalists now our only Kings and Clergy.

ONE of the most unsatisfactory Sections in the whole Volume is that on *Aprons*. What though stout old Gao,[1] the Persian Blacksmith, 'whose Apron, now indeed hidden under jewels, because raised in revolt which proved successful, is still the royal standard of that country'; what though John Knox's Daughter, 'who threatened Sovereign Majesty that she would catch her husband's head in her Apron, rather than he should lie and be a bishop';[2] what though the Landgravine Elizabeth,[3] with many other Apron worthies,—figure here? An idle wire-drawing spirit, sometimes even a tone of levity, approaching to conventional satire, is too clearly discernible. What, for example, are we to make of such sentences as the following?

'Aprons are Defences; against injury to cleanliness, to

---

[1]Or Gaváh, or Kaweh, the Persian blacksmith who led a revolt against the tyrannical Zohák, with his leathern apron on a spear as a standard, which became a royal standard until the reign of Omar.

[2]Elizabeth, youngest daughter of John Knox (1505–72), the Scotch Reformer, married John Welch, minister of Ayr, in 1604. After her husband's banishment, she petitioned the King for his return to Scotland. The King offered to permit it, if Welch would submit to the bishops; whereupon she replied, holding out her apron, that she would rather receive his head in her lap. Mrs. Carlyle (*née* J. B. Welsh) claimed descent from John and Elizabeth Welch.

[3]St. Elizabeth of Hungary (1207–31), who, against her husband's wishes, carried food in a basket to the poor at her gates. When her husband pulled aside her apron where she had hidden the basket, he found the food miraculously changed to roses. See Musaeus's "Melechsala" (*German Romance,* I, 136–40), where Carlyle found the story related at length.

safety, to modesty, sometimes to roguery. From the thin slip of notched silk (as it were, the emblem and beatified ghost of an Apron), which some highest-bred housewife, sitting at Nürnberg Workboxes and Toyboxes,[1] has gracefully fastened on; to the thick-tanned hide, girt round him with thongs, wherein the Builder builds, and at evening sticks his trowel; or to those jingling sheet-iron Aprons, wherein your otherwise half-naked Vulcans hammer and smelt in their smelt-furnace,—is there not range enough in the fashion and uses of this Vestment? How much has been concealed, how much has been defended in Aprons! Nay, rightly considered, what is your whole Military and Police Establishment, charged at uncalculated millions, but a huge scarlet-coloured, iron-fastened Apron, wherein Society works (uneasily enough); guarding itself from some soil and stithy-sparks, in this Devil's-smithy (*Teufelsschmiede*) of a world? But of all Aprons the most puzzling to me hitherto has been the Episcopal or Cassock. Wherein consists the usefulness of this Apron? The Overseer (*Episcopus*) of Souls, I notice, has tucked in the corner of it, as if his day's work were done: what does he shadow forth thereby?'[2] &c. &c.

Or again, has it often been the lot of our readers to read such stuff as we shall now quote?

'I consider those printed Paper Aprons,[3] worn by the Parisian Cooks, as a new vent, though a slight one, for Typography; therefore as an encouragement to modern Literature, and deserving of approval; nor is it without satisfaction that I hear of a celebrated London Firm having in view to introduce the same fashion, with important extensions, in England.'—We who are on the spot hear of no such thing; and indeed have reason to be thankful that hitherto there are other vents for our Literature, exuberant as it is.—

---

[1]Allusion to the toys for which Nürnberg, Germany, was famous.

[2]Note Carlyle's ironic allusion to what he regards as a decline in usefulness of one of the "clothes" of man, namely ecclesiastical authority.

[3]See Carlyle's transl. of Jean Paul's "Quintus Fixlein" (*German Romance*, II), p. 223, for a similar passage.

Teufelsdröckh continues: 'If such supply of printed Paper should rise so far as to choke-up the highways and public thoroughfares, new means must of necessity be had recourse to. In a world existing by Industry, we grudge to employ fire as a destroying element, and not as a creating one. However, Heaven is omnipotent, and will find us an outlet. In the mean while, is it not beautiful to see five-million quintals of Rags picked annually from the Laystall;[1] and annually, after being macerated, hot-pressed, printed-on, and sold,—returned thither; filling so many hungry mouths by the way? Thus is the Laystall, especially with its Rags or Clothes-rubbish, the grand Electric Battery, and Fountain-of-motion, from which and to which the Social Activities (like vitreous and resinous[2] Electricities) circulate, in larger or smaller circles, through the mighty, billowy, stormtost Chaos of Life, which they keep alive!'—Such passages fill us, who love the man, and partly esteem him, with a very mixed feeling.

Farther down we meet with this: 'The Journalists are now the true Kings and Clergy:[3] henceforth Historians, unless they are fools, must write not of Bourbon Dynasties, and Tudors and Hapsburgs;[4] but of Stamped Broad-sheet Dynasties, and quite new successive Names, according as this or the other Able Editor, or Combination of Able Editors, gains the world's ear. Of the British Newspaper Press, perhaps the most important of all, and wonderful enough in its secret constitution and procedure, a valuable descriptive History already exists, in that language, under the title of *Satan's Invisible World Displayed;*[5] which, however, by search in all the Weissnichtwo Libraries, I have not yet succeeded in procuring (*vermöchte nicht aufzutreiben*).'

[1]Rubbish heap. (Archaic).

[2]Positive and negative.

[3]*Cf.* "Quintus Fixlein" (*German Romance,* II, 304–05); *On Heroes,* pp. 162–63; *Ess.,* II, 77.

[4]French, English, and Austrian dynasties or royal families.

[5]Phrase used in the titles of several books on witchcraft in the seventeenth and eighteenth centuries, notably by Cotton Mather in 1692 and George Sinclair in 1685. (M.,B.)

Thus does the good Homer not only nod, but snore.[1] Thus does Teufelsdröckh, wandering in regions where he had little business, confound the old authentic Presbyterian Witchfinder with a new, spurious, imaginary Historian of the *Brittische Journalistik;* and so stumble on perhaps the most egregious blunder in Modern Literature!

CHAPTER VII

MISCELLANEOUS-HISTORICAL

How Men and Fashions come and go. German Costume in the fifteenth century. By what strange chances do we live in History? The costume of Bolivar's Cavalry.

Happier is our Professor, and more purely scientific and historic, when he reaches the Middle Ages in Europe, and down to the end of the Seventeenth Century; the true era of extravagance in Costume. It is here that the Antiquary and Student of Modes comes upon his richest harvest. Fantastic garbs, beggaring all fancy of a Teniers or a Callot,[2] succeeded each other, like monster devouring monster in a Dream. The whole too in brief authentic strokes, and touched not seldom with that breath of genius which makes even old raiment live. Indeed, so learned, precise, graphical, and everyway interesting have we found these Chapters, that it may be thrown-out as a pertinent question for parties concerned, Whether or not a good English translation thereof might henceforth be profitably incorporated with Mr. Merrick's

---

[1]Horace, *Ars Poetica,* l. 359; Pope, *Essay on Criticism,* l. 179 ff.

[2]David Teniers (1582–1649), and his son (1610–90) were famous Flemish painters.—Jacques Callot (1592–1635) was a French painter and engraver. Carlyle probably knew Callot's work from E. T. W. Hoffmann (1776–1822), part of whose *Fantasie-Stücke in Callots Manier* he translated as "The Golden Pot" (*Der Goldne Topf*), a romantic tale. See *German Romance,* II, 23–114.

valuable Work *On Ancient Armour?*[1] Take, by way of example, the following sketch; as authority for which Paulinus's[2] *Zeitkürzende Lust* (ii. 678) is, with seeming confidence, referred to:

'Did we behold the German fashionable dress of the Fifteenth Century, we might smile; as perhaps those bygone Germans, were they to rise again, and see our haberdashery, would cross themselves, and invoke the Virgin. But happily no bygone German, or man, rises again; thus the Present is not needlessly trammelled with the Past; and only grows out of it, like a Tree, whose roots are not intertangled with its branches, but lie peaceably underground. Nay it is very mournful, yet not useless, to see and know, how the Greatest and Dearest, in a short while, would find his place quite filled-up here, and no room for him; the very Napoleon, the very Byron, in some seven years, has become obsolete, and were now a foreigner to his Europe. Thus is the law of Progress secured; and in Clothes, as in all other external things whatsoever, no fashion will continue.

'Of the military classes in those old times, whose buff-belts, complicated chains and gorgets, huge churn-boots,[3] and other riding and fighting gear have been bepainted in modern Romance, till the whole has acquired somewhat of a sign-post character,—I shall here say nothing: the civil and pacific classes, less touched upon, are wonderful enough for us.

'Rich men, I find, have *Teusinke*'[4] (a perhaps untranslateable article); 'also a silver girdle, whereat hang little bells; so that when a man walks, it is with continual jingling. Some few, of musical turn, have a whole chime of bells (*Glocken-*

---

[1]Allusion to Samuel Rush Meyrick's *A Critical Inquiry into Ancient Armour*, London, 1824.

[2]*I.e.*, Paullini, Christian Franz (1643–1712), pedantic German compiler, author of *Zeit-Kürzende erbauliche Lust* (Frankfurt a. M., 1695–1725). Carlyle paraphrases a part of Chapter CXXIII, occasionally interpolating his own remarks.

[3]*Gorgets:* pieces of armour for the throat.—*churn-boots:* boots shaped like a churn.

[4]*Teusincke*, in the original, meaning a bell-shaped girdle. (M.)

spiel) fastened there; which, especially in sudden whirls, and the other accidents of walking, has a grateful effect. Observe too how fond they are of peaks, and Gothic-arch intersections. The male world wears peaked caps, an ell long, which hang bobbing over the side (*schief*): their shoes are peaked in front, also to the length of an ell, and laced on the side with tags; even the wooden shoes have their ell-long noses: some also clap bells on the peak. Further, according to my authority, the men have breeches without seat (*ohne Gesäss*): these they fasten peakwise to their shirts; and the long round doublet must overlap them.

'Rich maidens, again, flit abroad in gowns scolloped out behind and before, so that back and breast are almost bare. Wives of quality, on the other hand, have train-gowns four or five ells in length; which trains there are boys to carry. Brave Cleopatras,[1] sailing in their silk-cloth Galley, with a Cupid for steersman! Consider their welts,[2] a handbreadth thick, which waver round them by way of hem; the long flood of silver buttons, or rather silver shells, from throat to shoe, wherewith these same welt-gowns are buttoned. The maidens have bound silver snoods about their hair, with gold spangles, and pendent flames (*Flammen*), that is, sparkling hair-drops: but of their mothers' headgear who shall speak? Neither in love of grace is comfort forgotten. In winter weather you behold the whole fair creation (that can afford it) in long mantles, with skirts wide below, and, for hem, not one but two sufficient hand-broad welts; all ending atop in a thick well-starched Ruff, some twenty inches broad: these are their Ruff-mantles (*Kragenmäntel*).

'As yet among the womankind hoop-petticoats are not; but the men have doublets of fustian, under which lie multiple ruffs of cloth, pasted together with batter (*mit Teig zusammen-gekleistert*), which create protuberance enough. Thus do the two sexes vie with each other in the art of Decoration; and as usual the stronger carries it.'

---

[1]See *Antony and Cleopatra,* II, ii, 199–226.

[2]Strengthening (and usually ornamental) borders.

Our Professor, whether he have humour himself or not, manifests a certain feeling of the Ludicrous, a sly observance of it, which, could emotion of any kind be confidently predicated of so still a man, we might call a real love. None of those bell-girdles, bushel-breeches, cornuted shoes, or other the like phenomena, of which the History of Dress offers so many, escape him: more especially the mischances, or striking adventures, incident to the wearers of such, are noticed with due fidelity. Sir Walter Raleigh's fine mantle, which he spread in the mud under Queen Elizabeth's feet, appears to provoke little enthusiasm in him; he merely asks, Whether at that period the Maiden Queen 'was red-painted on the nose, and white-painted on the cheeks, as her tire-women, when from spleen and wrinkles she would no longer look in any glass, were wont to serve her?' We can answer that Sir Walter knew well what he was doing, and had the Maiden Queen been stuffed parchment dyed in verdigris,[1] would have done the same.

Thus too, treating of those enormous habiliments, that were not only slashed and galooned,[2] but artificially swollen-out on the broader parts of the body, by introduction of Bran, —our Professor fails not to comment on that luckless Courtier, who having seated himself on a chair with some projecting nail on it, and therefrom rising, to pay his *devoir* on the entrance of Majesty, instantaneously emitted several pecks of dry wheat-dust: and stood there diminished to a spindle, his galoons and slashes dangling sorrowful and flabby round him. Whereupon the Professor publishes this reflection:

'By what strange chances do we live in History? Erostratus by a torch;[3] Milo by a bullock;[4] Henry Darnley, an un-

---

[1]A green dye.

[2]Trimmed with a kind of narrow, close-woven ribbon or braid.

[3]Erostratus, or Eratostratus, or Herostratus, set fire to the temple of Diana at Ephesus in 356 B.C., in order to immortalize himself.

[4]Milo, of Crotona, Magna Graecia, celebrated athlete, was reputed to have carried a heifer four years old through the stadium ot Olympia.

fledged booby and bustard, by his limbs;[1] most Kings and Queens by being born under such and such a bed-tester;[2] Boileau Despréaux (according to Helvetius) by the peck of a turkey;[3] and this ill-starred individual by a rent in his breeches, —for no Memoirist of Kaiser Otto's Court omits him. Vain was the prayer of Themistocles for a talent of Forgetting:[4] my Friends, yield cheerfully to Destiny, and read since it is written.'—Has Teufelsdröckh to be put in mind that, nearly related to the impossible talent of Forgetting, stands that talent of Silence, which even travelling Englishmen manifest?

'The simplest costume,' observes our Professor, 'which I anywhere find alluded to in History, is that used as regimental, by Bolivar's Cavalry,[5] in the late Columbian wars. A square Blanket, twelve feet in diagonal, is provided (some were wont to cut-off the corners, and make it circular): in the centre a slit is effected eighteen inches long; through this the mother-naked Trooper introduces his head and neck; and so rides shielded from all weather, and in battle from many strokes (for he rolls it about his left arm); and not only dressed, but harnessed and draperied.'

With which picture of a State of Nature, affecting by its singularity, and Old-Roman contempt of the superfluous, we shall quit this part of our subject.

---

[1]Henry Stuart, Lord Darnley (1545–1567), second husband of Mary Queen of Scots, was "recommended to kingship for his fine limbs," says Carlyle in his Journal (*C.E.L.*, II, Ch. iv), 1829–30.

[2]Canopy over a bed.

[3]Nicolas Boileau (1636–1711); French poet and critic, author of *L'Art Poétique*. Helvétius (see p. 93, *note* 2) attributed Boileau's coldness and want of feeling as a writer to an injury that he received in his childhood from a frightened turkey-cock. (*De l'Esprit,* Discours III, Ch. i, note [a].)

[4]In Plutarch's *Lives,* the account of Themistocles.

[5]Bolivar, Simon (1783–1830), South American statesman, liberated from Spanish supremacy what are now Venezuela, Colombia, Ecuador, Panama, Peru, and Bolivia. The blanket is the Spanish *poncho*. (B.)

CHAPTER VIII

THE WORLD OUT OF CLOTHES

Teufelsdröckh's Theorem, 'Society founded upon Cloth'; his Method, Intuition quickened by Experience.—The mysterious question, Who am I? Philosophic systems all at fault: A deeper meditation has always taught, here and there an individual, that all visible things are appearances only; but also emblems and revelations of God. Teufelsdröckh first comes upon the question of Clothes: Baseness to which Clothing may bring us.

If in the Descriptive-Historical portion of this Volume, Teufelsdröckh, discussing merely the *Werden* (Origin and successive Improvement) of Clothes, has astonished many a reader, much more will he in the Speculative-Philosophical portion, which treats of their *Wirken,* or Influences. It is here that the present Editor first feels the pressure of his task; for here properly the higher and new Philosophy of Clothes commences: an untried, almost inconceivable region, or chaos; in venturing upon which, how difficult, yet how unspeakably important is it to know what course, of survey and conquest, is the true one; where the footing is firm substance and will bear us, where it is hollow, or mere cloud, and may engulf us! Teufelsdröckh undertakes no less than to expound the moral, political, even religious Influences of Clothes; he undertakes to make manifest, in its thousandfold bearings, this grand Proposition, that Man's earthly interests, 'are all hooked and buttoned together, and held up, by Clothes.' He says in so many words, 'Society is founded upon Cloth'; and again, 'Society sails through the Infinitude on Cloth, as on a Faust's Mantle,[1] or rather like the Sheet of clean and unclean beasts in the Apostle's Dream;[2] and without such Sheet or Mantle,

[1]Goethe's *Faust,* part I, scene iv

[2]Acts, x, 9–18.

would sink to endless depths, or mount to inane limboes,[1] and in either case be no more.'

By what chains, or indeed infinitely complected tissues, of meditation this grand Theorem is here unfolded, and innumerable practical Corollaries are drawn therefrom, it were perhaps a mad ambition to attempt exhibiting. Our Professor's method is not, in any case, that of common school Logic, where the truths all stand in a row, each holding by the skirts of the other; but at best that of practical Reason, proceeding by large Intuition[2] over whole systematic groups and kingdoms; whereby, we might say, a noble complexity, almost like that of Nature, reigns in his Philosophy, or spiritual Picture of Nature: a mighty maze, yet, as faith whispers, not without a plan.[3] Nay we complained above, that a certain ignoble complexity, what we must call mere confusion, was also discernible. Often, also, we have to exclaim: Would to Heaven those same Biographical Documents were come! For it seems as if the demonstration lay much in the Author's individuality; as if it were not Argument that had taught him, but Experience. At present it is only in local glimpses, and by significant fragments, picked often at wide-enough intervals from the original Volume, and carefully collated, that we can hope to impart some outline or foreshadow of this Doctrine. Readers of any intelligence are once more invited to favour us with their most concentrated attention: let these, after intense consideration, and not till then, pronounce, Whether on the utmost verge of our actual horizon there is not a looming as of Land; a promise of new Fortunate Islands,[4] perhaps whole undiscovered Americas, for such as have canvas to sail thither?—As exordium to the whole, stand here the following long citation:

---

[1]*Paradise Lost,* iii, 489–97.

[2]*Practical Reason . . . Intuition:* Kantian terms. (See Int., sect. V, a, b.)

[3]*Mighty maze . . . plan:* Pope, *Essay on Man,* l. 6 ff.

[4]"The Islands of the Blessed" (*Fortunatæ Insulæ*), to which favoured heroes passed without dying, were thought by the ancient Greeks to be located beyond the pillars of Hercules, *i.e.,* off the west coast of Africa. *Cf.* the *Canary* and *Madeira* islands.

'With men of a speculative turn,' writes Teufelsdröckh, 'there come seasons, meditative, sweet, yet awful hours, when in wonder and fear you ask yourself that unanswerable question: Who am *I;* the thing that can say "I" (*das Wesen das sich* Ich *nennt*)?[1] The world, with its loud trafficking, retires into the distance; and, through the paper-hangings, and stone-walls, and thick-plied tissues of Commerce and Polity, and all the living and lifeless integuments (of Society and a Body), wherewith your Existence sits surrounded,—the sight reaches forth into the void Deep, and you are alone with the Universe, and silently commune with it, as one mysterious Presence with another.

'Who am I; what is this Me? A Voice, a Motion, an Appearance;—some embodied, visualised Idea in the Eternal Mind? *Cogito, ergo sum.*[2] Alas, poor Cogitator, this takes us but a little way. Sure enough, I am; and lately was not: but Whence? How? Whereto? The answer lies around, written in all colours and motions, uttered in all tones of jubilee and wail, in thousand-figured, thousand-voiced, harmonious Nature: but where is the cunning eye and ear to whom that God-written Apocalypse will yield articulate meaning? We sit as in a boundless Phantasmagoria and Dream-grotto;[3] boundless, for the faintest star, the remotest century, lies not even nearer the verge thereof: sounds and many-coloured visions flit round our sense; but Him, the Unslumbering, whose work both Dream and Dreamer are, we see not;[4]

---

[1]Jean Paul asks the same question in *Flower, Fruit, and Thorn Pieces* (transl. A. Ewing, London, 1888, p. 429), and deals with it also in his autobiographical work, *Wahrheit aus Jean Pauls Leben* (Breslau, 1826–33, I, 53). Carlyle translates the latter passage in his review of the *Wahrheit* in the *Foreign Review,* Jan., 1830. (See *Ess.,* II, 111.)

[2]"I think, therefore I am." The epoch-making statement of René Descartes (1596–1650), by which, in his *Discours de la méthode* (1637), he indicated that since we can doubt everything but the act of thinking, consciousness must be the ultimate reality. (*Cf.* Richter, *Flower, Fruit, and Thorn Pieces,* p. 471: "I both *think* and *am thought.*")

[3]Apparently an allusion to Plato's *Republic,* Bk. vii.

[4]See Carlyle's *Life of Schiller,* p. 74 (quotation from Schiller's *Don Carlos,* III, x).

except in rare half-waking moments, suspect not. Creation, says one, lies before us, like a glorious Rainbow;[1] but the Sun that made it lies behind us, hidden from us. Then, in that strange Dream, how we clutch at shadows as if they were substances; and sleep deepest while fancying ourselves most awake![2] Which of your Philosophical Systems is other than a dream-theorem; a net quotient, confidently given out, where divisor and dividend are both unknown? What are all your national Wars, with their Moscow Retreats,[3] and sanguinary hate-filled Revolutions, but the Somnambulism of uneasy Sleepers? This Dreaming, this Somnambulism is what we on Earth call Life; wherein the most indeed undoubtedly wander, as if they knew right hand from left;[4] yet they only are wise who know that they know nothing.[5]

'Pity that all Metaphysics had hitherto proved so inexpressibly unproductive! The secret of Man's Being is still like the Sphinx's secret:[6] a riddle that he cannot rede; and for ignorance of which he suffers death, the worst death, a spiritual. What are your Axioms, and Categories, and Systems, and Aphorisms? Words, words. High Air-castles are cunningly built of Words, the Words well bedded also in good Logic-mortar; wherein, however, no Knowledge will come to lodge. *The whole is greater than the part:*[7] how exceedingly true! *Nature abhors a vacuum:* how exceedingly false and calumnious! Again, *Nothing can act but where it*

---

[1]From Richter. See the second essay on Richter, *Ess.,* II, 157.

[2]From Novalis. See essay on Novalis, *Ess.,* II, 39.

[3]*Cf.* Napoleon's disastrous retreat from Moscow in 1812, after having invaded Russia with half a million men, only 25,000 of whom survived the six-months' campaign.

[4]*Cf.* Jonah, iv, 11.

[5]Allusion to Socrates' famous dictum (Plato's *Apology,* ix).

[6]The Sphinx, a fabulous monster near Thebes, put to death all travellers who could not answer the riddle: What creature has four legs in the morning, two in the afternoon, and three in the evening? Oedipus solved the riddle by answering "Man"; and the Sphinx killed herself.

[7]This and the other propositions that follow are from mathematics and science (Euclid, Galileo, Newton, *etc.*), and are set off against the questions prompted by Carlyle's study of Kant and transcendentalism.

is: with all my heart; only, WHERE is it? Be not the slave of Words: is not the Distant, the Dead, while I love it, and long for it, and mourn for it, Here, in the genuine sense, as truly as the floor I stand on? But that same WHERE, with its brother WHEN, are from the first the master-colours of our Dream-grotto; say rather, the Canvas (the warp and woof thereof) whereon all our Dreams and Life-visions are painted. Nevertheless, has not a deeper meditation taught certain of every climate and age, that the WHERE and WHEN, so mysteriously inseparable from all our thoughts, are but superficial terrestrial adhesions to thought; that the Seer may discern them where they mount up out of the celestial EVERYWHERE AND FOREVER: have not all nations conceived their God as Omnipresent and Eternal; as existing in a universal HERE, an everlasting Now? Think well, thou too wilt find that Space is but a mode of our human Sense, so likewise Time; there *is* no Space and no Time:[1] WE are—we know not what;—light-sparkles floating in the æther of Deity!

'So that this so solid-seeming World, after all, were but an air-image, our ME the only reality: and Nature, with its thousandfold production and destruction, but the reflex of our own inward Force,[2] the "phantasy of our Dream";[3] or what the Earth-Spirit in *Faust* names it, *the living visible Garment of God:*

In Being's floods, in Action's storm,
I walk and work, above, beneath,
Work and weave in endless motion!
Birth and Death,
An infinite ocean;
A seizing and giving
The fire of Living:
'Tis thus at the roaring Loom of Time I ply,
And weave for God the Garment thou seest Him by.[4]

---

[1]See Int., Sect. V, b.

[2]*Cf.* Richter, *Flower, Fruit, and Thorn Pieces,* p. 471.

[3]A phrase of Novalis (*Ess.,* II, p. 35).

[4]*Faust,* I, ll. 501–09.

Of twenty millions that have read and spouted this thunder-speech of the *Erdgeist,* are there yet twenty units of us that have learned the meaning thereof?

'It was in some such mood, when wearied and fordone with these high speculations, that I first came upon the question of Clothes. Strange enough, it strikes me, is this same fact of there being Tailors and Tailored. The Horse I ride has his own whole fell: strip him of the girths and flaps and extraneous tags I have fastened round him, and the noble creature is his own sempster and weaver and spinner; nay his own boot-maker, jeweller, and man-milliner; he bounds free through the valleys, with a perennial rainproof court-suit on his body; wherein warmth and easiness of fit have reached perfection; nay, the graces also have been considered, and frills and fringes, with gay variety of colour, featly appended, and ever in the right place, are not wanting. While I—good Heaven!—have thatched myself over with the dead fleeces of sheep, the bark of vegetables, the entrails of worms, the hides of oxen or seals, the felt of furred beasts; and walk abroad a moving Rag-screen, overheaped with shreds and tatters raked from the Charnel-house of Nature, where they would have rotted, to rot on me more slowly! Day after day, I must thatch myself anew; day after day, this despicable thatch must lose some film of its thickness; some film of it, frayed away by tear and wear, must be brushed-off into the Ashpit, into the Laystall; till by degrees the whole has been brushed thither, and I, the dust-making, patent Rag-grinder, get new material to grind down. O subter-brutish! vile! most vile! For have not I too a compact all-enclosing Skin, whiter or dingier? Am I a botched mass of tailors' and cobblers' shreds, then; or a tightly-articulated, homogeneous little Figure, automatic, nay alive?[1]

'Strange enough how creatures of the human-kind shut their eyes to plainest facts; and by the mere inertia of Oblivion and Stupidity, live at ease in the midst of Wonders and Terrors. But indeed man is, and was always, a block-head and dullard;

[1]The whole of this paragraph is a striking expression of the mystic's wonder at the "commonplace."

much readier to feel and digest, than to think and consider. Prejudice, which he pretends to hate, is his absolute lawgiver; mere use-and-wont everywhere leads him by the nose; thus let but a Rising of the Sun, let but a Creation of the World happen *twice,* and it ceases to be marvellous, to be noteworthy, or noticeable. Perhaps not once in a lifetime does it occur to your ordinary biped, of any country or generation, be he gold-mantled Prince, or russet-jerkined Peasant, that his Vestments and his Self are not one and indivisible; that *he* is naked, without vestments, till he buy or steal such, and by forethought sew and button them.

'For my own part, these considerations, of our Clothes-thatch, and how, reaching inwards even to our heart of hearts, it tailorises and demoralises us, fill me with a certain horror at myself and mankind; almost as one feels at those Dutch Cows, which, during the wet season, you see grazing deliberately with jackets and petticoats (of striped sacking), in the meadows of Gouda.[1] Nevertheless there is something great in the moment when a man first strips himself of adventitious wrappages; and sees indeed that he is naked, and, as Swift has it, "a forked straddling animal with bandy legs";[2] yet also a Spirit, and unutterable Mystery of Mysteries.'

CHAPTER IX

ADAMITISM

The universal utility of Clothes, and their higher mystic virtue, illustrated. Conception of Mankind stripped naked; and immediate consequent dissolution of civilized Society.

LET no courteous reader take offence at the opinions broached in the conclusion of the last Chapter. The Editor himself, on first glancing over that singular passage, was inclined

[1]A town in South Holland, famous for its cheese.

[2]*Cf. Lear,* III, iv, 111. (Barrett cites *Martinus Scriblerus,* Ch. xi; Pope, Swift, Arbuthnot.)

to exclaim: What, have we got not only a Sansculottist,[1] but an enemy to Clothes in the abstract? A new Adamite,[2] in this century, which flatters itself that it is the Nineteenth, and destructive both to Superstition and Enthusiasm?

Consider, thou foolish Teufelsdröckh, what benefits unspeakable all ages and sexes derive from Clothes. For example, when thou thyself, a watery, pulpy, slobbery freshman and new-comer in this Planet, sattest muling and puking in thy nurse's arms;[3] sucking thy coral, and looking forth into the world in the blankest manner, what hadst thou been without thy blankets, and bibs, and other nameless hulls?[4] A terror to thyself and mankind! Or hast thou forgotten the day when thou first receivedst breeches, and thy long clothes became short? The village where thou livedst was all apprised of the fact; and neighbour after neighbour kissed thy pudding-cheek, and gave thee, as handsel,[5] silver or copper coins, on that the first gala-day of thy existence. Again, wert not thou, at one period of life, a Buck, or Blood, or Macaroni, or Incroyable, or Dandy,[6] or by whatever name, according to year and place, such phenomenon is distinguished? In that one word lie included mysterious volumes. Nay, now when the reign of folly is over, or altered, and thy clothes are not for triumph but for defence, hast thou always worn them perforce, and as a consequence of Man's Fall; never rejoiced in them as in a warm

---

[1]See p. 16, *note* 5.

[2]Adamites (or Adamians), a sect of heretics which flourished in North Africa in the second and third centuries, hoped to re-establish Adam's state of original innocency. (*Cf.* Genesis, i-iii.)

[3]*Cf. As you Like It,* II, vii, 144.

[4]*Hulls:* any covering; *i.e.,* clothes.

[5]Gift or token to celebrate the beginning of the existence or use of anything.

[6]*Buck:* a dashing young fellow.—*Blood:* a man of fire or spirit, a rake.—*Macaroni:* a travelled young dandy affecting foreign ways.—*Incroyable:* French fop or dandy. (Bloods, Macaronis, and Incroyables were social types of the late-eighteenth century; the Buck appears as early as the sixteenth.)—*Dandy:* a man who gives undue attention to dress, a type appearing between about 1810 and 1830 (*cf.* Byron, Beau Brummel, Count D'Orsay, Bulwer-Lytton, *etc.*).

movable House, a Body round thy Body, wherein that strange Thee of thine sat snug, defying all variations of Climate? Girt with thick double-milled kerseys; half-buried under shawls and broad-brims, and overalls and mud-boots, thy very fingers cased in doeskin and mittens, thou hast bestrode that 'Horse I ride'; and, though it were in wild winter, dashed through the world, glorying in it as if thou wert its lord. In vain did the sleet beat round thy temples; it lighted only on thy impenetrable, felted or woven, case of wool. In vain did the winds howl,—forests sounding and creaking, deep calling unto deep,[1]—and the storms heap themselves together into one huge Arctic whirlpool: thou flewest through the middle thereof, striking fire from the highway; wild music hummed in thy ears, thou too wert as a 'sailor of the air';[2] the wreck of matter and the crash of worlds[3] was thy element and propitiously wafting tide. Without Clothes, without bit or saddle, what hadst thou been; what had thy fleet quadruped been?—Nature is good, but she is not the best: here truly was the victory of Art over Nature. A thunderbolt indeed might have pierced thee; all short of this thou couldst defy.

Or, cries the courteous reader, has your Teufelsdröckh forgotten what he said lately about 'Aboriginal Savages,' and their 'condition miserable indeed'? Would he have all this unsaid; and us betake ourselves again to the 'matted cloak,' and go sheeted in a 'thick natural fell'?

Nowise, courteous reader! The Professor knows full well what he is saying; and both thou and we, in our haste, do him wrong. If Clothes, in these times, 'so tailorise and demoralise us,' have they no redeeming value; can they not be altered to serve better; must they of necessity be thrown to the dogs? The truth is, Teufelsdröckh, though a Sansculottist, is no

---

[1] *Cf.* Psalms xlii, 7.

[2] From Schiller's *Maria Stuart,* III, i, 2098. See Carlyle's *Life of Schiller,* pp. 153–54: "she addresses the clouds, the 'sailors of the air,' who 'are not subjects of Elizabeth,' and bids them carry tidings of her. . . ."

[3] From Addison's *Cato,* V, 1, 31. Properly: "*crush* of worlds."

Adamite; and much perhaps as he might wish to go forth before this degenerate age as 'a Sign,'[1] would nowise wish to do it, as those old Adamites did, in a state of Nakedness. The utility of Clothes is altogether apparent to him: nay perhaps he has an insight into their more recondite, and almost mystic qualities, what we might call the omnipotent virtue of Clothes, such as was never before vouchsafed to any man. For example:

'You see two individuals,' he writes, 'one dressed in fine Red, the other in coarse threadbare Blue: Red says to Blue, "Be hanged and anatomised"; Blue hears with a shudder, and (O wonder of wonders!) marches sorrowfully to the gallows; is there noosed-up, vibrates his hour, and the surgeons dissect him, and fit his bones into a skeleton for medical purposes. How is this; or what make ye of your *Nothing can act but where it is?* Red has no physical hold of Blue, no *clutch* of him, is nowise in *contact* with him: neither are those ministering Sheriffs and Lord-Lieutenants and Hangmen and Tipstaves[2] so related to commanding Red, that he can tug them hither and thither; but each stands distinct within his own skin. Nevertheless, as it is spoken, so is it done: the articulated Word sets all hands in Action; and Rope and Improved-drop perform their work.

'Thinking reader, the reason seems to me twofold: First, that *Man is a Spirit,* and bound by invisible bonds to *All Men;* secondly, that *he wears Clothes,* which are the visible emblems of that fact.[3] Has not your Red hanging-individual a horse-hair wig, squirrel-skins, and a plush-gown; whereby all mortals know that he is a JUDGE?—Society, which the more I think of it astonishes me the more, is founded upon Cloth.[4]

'Often in my atrabiliar moods,[5] when I read of pompous

---

[1]*Cf.* Isaiah, xx, 3.

[2]*Tipstaves:* constables bearing staves tipped with metal.

[3]From Carlyle's Journal, June, 1830 (*C.E.L.,* II, Ch. iv).

[4]See Swift's *Tale of a Tub,* Sect. II.

[5]This whole passage is an expansion of one in Carlyle's Journal for August, 1830 (*C.E.L.,* II, Ch. iv).

ceremonials, Frankfort Coronations, Royal Drawing-rooms, Levees, Couchees;[1] and how the ushers and macers and pursuivants are all in waiting; how Duke this is presented by Archduke that, and Colonel A by General B, and innumerable Bishops, Admirals, and miscellaneous Functionaries, are advancing gallantly to the Anointed Presence; and I strive, in my remote privacy, to form a clear picture of that solemnity,—on a sudden, as by some enchanter's wand, the—shall I speak it? —the Clothes fly-off the whole dramatic corps; and Dukes, Grandees, Bishops, Generals, Anointed Presence itself, every mother's son of them, stand straddling there, not a shirt on them; and I know not whether to laugh or weep. This physical or psychical infirmity, in which perhaps I am not singular, I have, after hesitation, thought right to publish, for the solace of those afflicted with the like.'

Would to Heaven, say we, thou hadst thought right to keep it secret! Who is there now that can read the five columns of Presentations in his Morning Newspaper without a shudder? Hypochondriac men, and all men are to a certain extent hypochondriac, should be more gently treated. With what readiness our fancy, in this shattered state of the nerves, follows out the consequences which Teufelsdröckh, with a devilish coolness, goes on to draw:

'What would Majesty do, could such an accident befall in reality; should the buttons all simultaneously start, and the solid wool evaporate, in very Deed, as here in Dream? *Ach Gott!* How each skulks into the nearest hiding-place; their high State Tragedy (*Haupt- und Staats-Action*)[2] becomes a Pickleherring-Farce[3] to weep at, which is the worst kind of

---

[1]*Frankfort Coronations:* a frequent expression of Richter's. The German emperors were elected at Frankfort and crowned in the cathedral there by the Elector of Mainz.—*Royal Drawing-rooms:* formal receptions at the English court.—*Levees, Couchees:* royal receptions held in the morning and about bedtime, respectively.

[2]Stock-drama of German strolling players of the seventeenth century, similar to the English Heroic Drama of the Restoration.

[3]The stock-name of the fool or merry-andrew in an old English farce became the name of a type of German comedy, *Pickelhäringsspiele,* in the

Farce; *the tables* (according to Horace), and with them, the whole fabric of Government, Legislation, Property, Police, and Civilised Society, *are dissolved,*[1] in wails and howls.'

Lives the man that can figure a naked Duke of Windlestraw[2] addressing a naked House of Lords? Imagination, choked as in mephitic air, recoils on itself, and will not forward with the picture. The Woolsack, the Ministerial, the Opposition Benches—*infandum! infandum!*[3] And yet why is the thing impossible? Was not every soul, or rather every body, of these Guardians of our Liberties, naked, or nearly so, last night; 'a forked Radish[4] with a head fantastically carved'? And why might he not, did our stern fate so order it, walk out to St. Stephen's,[5] as well as into bed, in that no-fashion; and there, with other similar Radishes, hold a Bed of Justice?[6] 'Solace of those afflicted with the like!' Unhappy Teufelsdröckh, had man ever such a 'physical or psychical infirmity' before? And now how many, perhaps, may thy unparalleled confession (which we, even to the sounder British world, and goaded-on by Critical and Biographical duty, grudge to reimpart) incurably infect therewith! Art thou the malignest of Sansculottists, or only the maddest?

'It will remain to be examined,' adds the inexorable Teufelsdröckh, 'in how far the SCARECROW, as a Clothed Person, is not also entitled to benefit of clergy,[7] and English trial by jury:

---

seventeenth century. (See Addison's *Spectator,* No. 47; the German expression *Hanswurst;* and *Wilhelm Meister,* I, 126.)

[1]Horace, *Satires,* II, i, 86: "Solventur risu tabulae." The benches will burst with laughter, or terminate the indictment. Carlyle's meaning: universal collapse.

[2]A grass or grass-straw used for making ropes, *etc.*

[3]"Unheard-of enormities!" From Virgil, *Aeneid,* I, 251.

[4]*Cf. Henry IV, Pt. II,* III, ii, 336–39; *Lear,* III, iv, 109–11.

[5]The Houses of Parliament, Westminster.

[6]The *Lit de justice,* or King's Throne in the French Chamber, in the *ancien régime,* from which the King could compel parliament to do his will. See Carlyle's *French Revolution,* I, 82 (Bk. III, Ch. iv); Richter's "Schmelzle's Journey" (*German Romance,* II, 178); and *Tristram Shandy,* Vol. VI, Chs. xvi and xvii.

[7]*Benefit of clergy:* the privilege claimed by the medieval clergy, later

nay perhaps, considering his high function (for is not he too a Defender of Property, and Sovereign armed with the *terrors* of the Law?), to a certain royal Immunity and Inviolability; which, however, misers and the meaner class of persons are not always voluntarily disposed to grant him.' . . . 'O my friends, we are (in Yorick Sterne's[1] words) but as "turkeys driven,[2] with a stick and red clout, to the market": or if some drivers, as they do in Norfolk, take a dried bladder and put peas in it, the rattle thereof terrifies the boldest!'

CHAPTER X

PURE REASON[3]

A Naked World possible, nay actually exists, under the clothed one. Man, in the eye of Pure Reason, a visible God's Presence. The beginning of all wisdom, to look fixedly on Clothes till they become transparent. Wonder, the basis of Worship: Perennial in man. Modern Sciolists who cannot wonder: Teufelsdröckh's contempt for, and advice to them.

IT MUST now be apparent enough that our Professor, as above hinted, is a speculative Radical, and of the very darkest tinge; acknowledging, for most part, in the solemnities and paraphernalia of civilised Life, which we make so much of, nothing but so many Cloth-rags, turkey-poles, and 'bladders with dried peas.'[4] To linger among such speculations, longer than mere Science requires, a discerning public can have no wish. For our purposes the simple fact that such a *Naked*

---

by any one who could read, of demanding trial and punishment by an ecclesiastical court (which could not inflict the death penalty) when accused of crime before a secular court. Legally repealed in 1827.

[1]Laurence Sterne (1713–68).

[2]See Sterne's *Tristram Shandy,* Vol. V, Ch. vii.

[3]The title of this chapter was undoubtedly suggested by the title of Kant's *Critique of Pure Reason* (*Kritik der reinen Vernunft*) (1781), which Carlyle read, in part, in 1826 and 1827.

[4]See Swift's *Gulliver's Travels* ("Voyage to Laputa," opening paragraph, *etc.*)

World is possible, nay actually exists (under the Clothed one), will be sufficient. Much, therefore, we omit about 'Kings wrestling naked on the green with Carmen,'[1] and the Kings being thrown: 'dissect them with scalpels,' says Teufelsdröckh; 'the same viscera, tissues, livers, lights, and other life-tackle, are there: examine their spiritual mechanism; the same great Need, great Greed, and little Faculty; nay ten to one but the Carman, who understands draught-cattle, the rimming of wheels, something of the laws of unstable and stable equilibrium, with other branches of wagon-science, and has actually put forth his hand and operated on Nature, is the more cunningly gifted of the two. Whence, then, their so unspeakable difference? From Clothes.' Much also we shall omit about confusion of Ranks, and Joan and My Lady,[2] and how it would be everywhere 'Hail fellow well met,' and Chaos were come again:[3] all which to any one that has once fairly pictured-out the grand mother-idea, *Society in a state of Nakedness,* will spontaneously suggest itself. Should some sceptical individual still entertain doubts whether in a world without Clothes, the smallest Politeness, Polity, or even Police, could exist, let him turn to the original Volume, and view there the boundless Serbonian Bog[4] of Sansculottism, stretching sour and pestilential: over which we have lightly flown; where not only whole armies but whole nations might sink! If indeed the following argument, in its brief riveting emphasis, be not of itself incontrovertible and final:

'Are we Opossums; have we natural Pouches, like the Kangaroo? Or how, without Clothes, could we possess the master-organ, soul's seat, and true pineal gland[5] of the Body Social: I mean, a PURSE?'

---

[1]Drivers of carts.

[2]*Cf. Love's Labour's Lost,* III, i, 215; *King John,* I, i, 184.

[3]*Cf. Othello,* III, iii, 92.

[4]Lake Serbonis, in Egypt, near the Suez Canal. Phrasing is from *Paradise Lost,* ii, 592–94.

[5]A small gland at the base of the brain, which Descartes thought to be the seat of the soul. Carlyle may be alluding to a passage in *Tristram Shandy,* Vol. II, ch. xix.

Nevertheless it is impossible to hate Professor Teufelsdröckh; at worst, one knows not whether to hate or to love him. For though, in looking at the fair tapestry of human Life, with its royal and even sacred figures, he dwells not on the obverse alone, but here chiefly on the reverse; and indeed turns out the rough seams, tatters, and manifold thrums[1] of that unsightly wrong side, with an almost diabolic patience and indifference, which must have sunk him in the estimation of most readers,—there is that within which unspeakably distinguishes him from all other past and present Sansculottists. The grand unparalleled peculiarity of Teufelsdröckh is, that with all this Descendentalism,[2] he combines a Transcendentalism, no less superlative; whereby if on the one hand he degrade man below most animals, except those jacketed Gouda Cows,[3] he, on the other, exalts him beyond the visible Heavens, almost to an equality with the Gods.

'To the eye of vulgar Logic,' says he, 'what is man? An omnivorous Biped that wears Breeches. To the eye of Pure Reason[4] what is he? A Soul, a Spirit, and divine Apparition. Round his mysterious Me, there lies, under all those wool-rags, a Garment of Flesh (or of Senses), contextured in the Loom of Heaven; whereby he is revealed to his like, and dwells with them in Union and Division;[5] and sees and fashions for himself a Universe, with azure Starry Spaces, and long Thousands of Years. Deep-hidden is he under that strange Garment; amid Sounds and Colours and Forms, as it were, swathed-in, and inextricably over-shrouded: yet it is sky-woven, and worthy of a God. Stands he not thereby in the

---

[1]The ends of weavers' warp threads.

[2]Carlyle's coinage, to contrast with *trans*cendentalism. Naturalism, empiricism (the philosophy of positive experience.)

[3]See p. 57, *note* 1.

[4]A Kantian term used here in opposition to "vulgar logic" (Kant's "Understanding" [*Verstand*]); for Carlyle, the moral intuition of the world of eternal values.

[5]That is, as a member of society, and as an individual, an impossible relationship except for man's "garment of flesh."

centre of Immensities, in the conflux of Eternities?[1] He feels; power has been given him to know, to believe; nay does not the spirit of Love, free in its celestial primeval brightness, even here, though but for moments, look through? Well said Saint Chrysostom,[2] with his lips of gold, "the true SHEKINAH[3] is Man"; where else is the GOD'S-PRESENCE manifested not to our eyes only, but to our hearts, as in our fellow-man?'

In such passages, unhappily too rare, the high Platonic Mysticism[4] of our Author, which is perhaps the fundamental element of his nature, bursts forth, as it were, in full flood: and, through all the vapour and tarnish of what is often so perverse, so mean in his exterior and environment, we seem to look into a whole inward Sea of Light and Love;—though, alas, the grim coppery clouds soon roll together again, and hide it from view.

Such tendency to Mysticism is everywhere traceable in this man; and indeed, to attentive readers, must have been long ago apparent. Nothing that he sees but has more than a common meaning, but has two meanings: thus, if in the highest Imperial Sceptre and Charlemagne-Mantle,[5] as well as in the poorest Ox-goad and Gipsy-Blanket, he finds Prose, Decay, Contemptibility; there is in each sort Poetry also, and a reverend Worth. For Matter, were it never so despicable,

---

[1]A favourite image of Jean Paul's, in *Flower, Fruit, and Thorn Pieces,* pp. 430–31, *etc.* See also Carlyle's "Signs of the Times" (*Ess.,* II, 59), for a similar passage (1829).

[2]Saint John Chrysostom, the golden-mouthed (Χρυσόστομος) (A.D. c. 345–407), an early Christian Father.

[3]Hebrew Talmud *shekinah,* literally, "the dwelling"; the divine intermediary between God and man, the resting-place or embodiment of the Divine Presence.—The quotation is really from *Tristram Shandy,* Vol. V, ch. i.

[4]*Platonic Mysticism:* used loosely, for neither Carlyle nor Teufelsdröckh was either truly Platonic or mystical. Meaning here: as the sun, though frequently clouded over, sustains all physical life, so the ultimate eternal world of Truth, though imperfectly apprehended by us, sustains our moral life and flashes in upon us during moments of spiritual insight. See Plato's *Republic,* Bks. VI and VII.

[5]The magnificent robe worn by Charlemagne (742[?]–814), said to be preserved in St. Peter's at Rome. (B.)

is Spirit, the manifestation of Spirit: were it never so honourable, can it be more? The thing Visible, nay the thing Imagined, the thing in any way conceived as Visible, what is it but a Garment, a Clothing of the higher, celestial Invisible, 'unimaginable, formless, dark with excess of bright'?[1] Under which point of view the following passage, so strange in purport, so strange in phrase, seems characteristic enough:

'The beginning of all Wisdom is to look fixedly on Clothes, or even with armed eyesight, till they become *transparent*. "The Philosopher," says the wisest of this age,[2] "must station himself in the middle"; how true! The Philosopher is he to whom the Highest has descended, and the Lowest has mounted up; who is the equal and kindly brother of all.

'Shall we tremble before clothwebs and cobwebs, whether woven in Arkwright[3] looms, or by the silent Arachnes[4] that weave unrestingly in our imagination? Or, on the other hand, what is there that we cannot love; since all was created by God?

'Happy he who can look through the Clothes of a Man (the woollen, and fleshly, and official Bank-paper and State-paper Clothes) into the Man himself; and discern, it may be, in this or the other Dread Potentate, a more or less incompetent Digestive-apparatus; yet also an inscrutable venerable Mystery, in the meanest Tinker that sees with eyes!'

For the rest, as is natural to a man of this kind, he deals much in the feeling of Wonder; insists on the necessity and high worth of universal Wonder; which he holds to be the only reasonable temper for the denizen of so singular a Planet as ours. 'Wonder,' says he, 'is the basis of Worship:[5] the reign of wonder is perennial, indestructible in Man; only at

---

[1]*Cf. Paradise Lost,* iii, 380: "Dark with *excessive* bright."

[2]Goethe, in *Wilhelm Meister,* II, 267.

[3]Sir Richard Arkwright (1732–92), inventor of the spinning frame.

[4]Spiders. (Arachne, a Lydian maiden, was turned into a spider by Minerva for competing with her in the arts of weaving and embroidery. —Ovid's *Metamorphoses,* vi.)

[5]From Carlyle's Journal, June 8, 1830, (*C.E.L.,* II, Ch. iv.); a favourite thought with the German Romanticists, *e.g.,* Novalis: "All faith (*Glaube*)

certain stages (as the present), it is, for some short season, a reign *in partibus infidelium*.'[1] That progress of Science, which is to destroy Wonder, and in its stead substitute Mensuration and Numeration, finds small favor with Teufelsdröckh, much as he otherwise venerates these two latter processes.

'Shall your Science,' exclaims he, 'proceed in the small chink-lighted, or even oil-lighted, underground workshop of Logic alone; and man's mind become an Arithmetical Mill, whereof Memory is the Hopper, and mere Tables of Sines and Tangents, Codification, and Treatises of what you call Political Economy, are the Meal? And what is that Science, which the scientific head alone, were it screwed off, and (like the Doctor's in the Arabian Tale)[2] set in a basin to keep it alive, could prosecute without shadow of a heart,—but one other of the mechanical and menial handicrafts, for which the Scientific Head (having a Soul in it) is too noble an organ? I mean that Thought without Reverence is barren, perhaps poisonous; at best, dies like cookery with the day that called it forth; does not live, like sowing, in successive tilths and wider-spreading harvest, bringing food and plenteous increase to all Time.'

In such wise does Teufelsdröckh deal hits, harder or softer, according to ability; yet ever, as we would fain persuade ourselves, with charitable intent. Above all, that class of 'Logic-choppers,[3] and treble-pipe Scoffers, and professed Enemies to Wonder; who, in these days, so numerously patrol as night-constables about the Mechanics' Institute[4] of Science, and

---

is wonderful (*wunderbar*) and wonderworking (*wundertätig*) . . ." (Novalis's *Werke*, ed. H. Friedmann, Berlin, 1908, 4 vols., III, 183.) See Carlyle's essay on Novalis (*Ess.*, II).

[1]"In the country of the unbelievers" (B.). An expression applied in the Roman Catholic Church to a bishop whose titular see is in a country which has ceased to be Roman Catholic.

[2]Allusion to the tale of "The Greek King and Douban the Physician" in *The Arabian Nights.*

[3]*Cf. Romeo and Juliet,* III, v, 150.

[4]A form of working-men's college, with lectures, a library, a museum, *etc.,* which had been developed by George Birkbeck (1776–1841) in Scotland and by Lord Brougham (1778–1868) in London.

cackle like true Old-Roman geese[1] and goslings round their Capitol, on any alarm, or on none; nay who often, as illuminated Sceptics, walk abroad into peaceable society, in full daylight, with rattle and lantern, and insist on guiding you and guarding you therewith, though the Sun is shining, and the street populous with mere justice-loving men': that whole class is inexpressibly wearisome to him. Hear with what uncommon animation he perorates:

'The man who cannot wonder, who does not habitually wonder (and worship), were he President of innumerable Royal Societies, and carried the whole *Mécanique Céleste* and *Hegel's Philosophy,*[2] and the epitome of all Laboratories and Observatories with their results, in his single head,—is but a Pair of Spectacles behind which there is no Eye. Let those who have Eyes look through him, then he may be useful.

'Thou wilt have no Mystery and Mysticism;[3] wilt walk through thy world by the sunshine of what thou callest Truth, or even by the hand-lamp of what I call Attorney-Logic; and "explain" all, "account" for all, or believe nothing of it? Nay, thou wilt attempt laughter; whoso recognises the unfathomable, all-pervading domain of Mystery, which is everywhere under our feet and among our hands; to whom the Universe is an Oracle and Temple, as well as a Kitchen and Cattle-stall, —he shall be a delirious Mystic; to him thou, with sniffing charity, wilt protrusively proffer thy hand-lamp, and shriek, as one injured, when he kicks his foot through it?—*Armer Teufel!*[4] Doth not thy cow calve, doth not thy bull gender?[5]

---

[1]The geese, sacred to Juno, which gave the alarm when the Gauls in B.C. 390 attempted to surprise and take the Capitol.

[2]See pp. 4, 15, *notes.*

[3]This passage is an elaboration upon one in Carlyle's Journal for June 8, 1830 (*C.E.L.,* II, Ch. iv). The derisive charge of "Mystic" was leveled at Carlyle upon the publication of his essays on "Jean Paul," and "The State of German Literature" (June and October, 1827), and also at all of the German transcendentalists and romanticists. From the charge of vague and erratic thinking, Carlyle defended Kant, Fichte, Schelling, Goethe, Schiller, and Novalis in his early essays (*Ess.,* I, 70–86, II, 1–55).

[4]*Armer Teufel:* "Poor devil!"

[5]*Cf.* Job, xxi, 10; xxxix, 1.

Thou thyself, wert thou not born, wilt thou not die? "Explain" me all this, or do one of two things: Retire into private places with thy foolish cackle; or, what were better, give it up, and weep, not that the reign of wonder is done, and God's world all disembellished and prosaic, but that thou hitherto art a Dilettante[1] and sandblind Pedant.'

CHAPTER XI

PROSPECTIVE

Nature not an Aggregate, but a Whole. All visible things are emblems, Clothes; and exist for a time only. The grand scope of the Philosophy of Clothes.—Biographic Documents arrive. Letter from Heuschrecke on the importance of Biography. Heterogeneous character of the documents: Editor sorely perplexed; but desperately grapples with his work.

THE Philosophy of Clothes is now to all readers, as we predicted it would do, unfolding itself into new boundless expansions, of a cloudcapt, almost chimerical aspect, yet not without azure loomings in the far distance, and streaks as of an Elysian brightness;[2] the highly questionable purport and promise of which it is becoming more and more important for us to ascertain. Is that a real Elysian brightness, cries many a timid wayfarer, or the reflex of Pandemonian lava?[3] Is it of a truth leading us into beatific Asphodel meadows,[4] or the yellow-burning marl[5] of a Hell-on-Earth?

---

[1]*Cf.* Carlyle's Journal for September 9, 1830 (*C.E.L.,* Ch. iv). The elegant trifler is dealt with in Bk. III, Ch. X, and more severely in the later, social writings, *Past and Present* (1843) and *Latter-Day Pamphlets* (1850).

[2]Virgil, *Aeneid,* vi, 638–41.

[3]Allusion to the bottom of Pandaemonium, "high Capital of Satan and his Peers" (*Paradise Lost,* i, 227 ff., 296, 756–57).

[4]Fields where the souls of departed heroes dwelt (Homer, *Odyssey,* xi, 539). The asphodel of the Greek poets is supposed to be the narcissus.

[5]*Cf. Paradise Lost,* i, 296.

Our Professor, like other Mystics, whether delirious or inspired, gives an Editor enough to do. Ever higher and dizzier are the heights he leads us to; more piercing, all-comprehending, all-confounding are his views and glances. For example, this of Nature being not an Aggregate but a Whole:

'Well sang the Hebrew Psalmist: "If I take the wings of the morning and dwell in the uttermost parts of the universe, God is there."[1] Thou thyself, O cultivated reader, who too probably art no Psalmist, but a Prosaist, knowing GOD only by tradition, knowest thou any corner of the world where at least FORCE is not? The drop which thou shakest from thy wet hand, rests not where it falls, but tomorrow thou findest it swept away; already on the wings of the Northwind, it is nearing the Tropic of Cancer. How came it to evaporate, and not lie motionless? Thinkest thou there is ought motionless; without Force, and utterly dead?[2]

'As I rode through the Schwarzwald,[3] I said to myself: That little fire which glows star-like across the dark-growing (*nachtende*) moor, where the sooty smith bends over his anvil, and thou hopest to replace thy lost horse-shoe,—is it a detached, separated speck, cut-off from the whole Universe; or indissolubly joined to the whole? Thou fool, that smithy-fire was (primarily) kindled at the Sun; is fed by air that circulates from before Noah's Deluge, from beyond the Dog-star;[4] therein, with Iron Force, and Coal Force, and the far stranger Force of Man, are cunning affinities and battles and victories of Force brought about; it is a little ganglion, or nervous centre, in the great vital system of Immensity. Call it, if thou wilt, an unconscious Altar, kindled on the bosom of the All;[5] whose iron sacrifice, whose iron smoke and influence

[1]Psalms, cxxxix, 9, 10.

[2]*Cf.* Richter's *Flower, Fruit, and Thorn Pieces,* pp. 470–71: "Life and force are at work, with power, everywhere. The grave hillock and the mouldering body are each a *world* of powers at work."

[3]The Black Forest in Germany.

[4]Sirius, the brightest star in the Constellation *Canis Major,* and one of the nearest to earth, 50 million million miles away.

[5]A phrase frequent in Richter. See *Ess.*, II, 155–58.

reach quite through the All; whose dingy Priset, not by word, yet by brain and sinew, preaches forth the mystery of Force; nay preaches forth (exoterically enough) one little textlet from the Gospel of Freedom, the Gospel of Man's Force, commanding, and one day to be all-commanding.

'Detached, separated! I say there is no such separation: nothing hitherto was ever stranded, cast aside; but all, were it only a withered leaf, works together with all;[1] is borne forward on the bottomless, shoreless flood of Action,[2] and lives through perpetual metamorphoses. The withered leaf is not dead and lost, there are Forces in it and around it, though working in inverse order; else how could it *rot?*[3] Despise not the rag from which man makes Paper, or the litter from which the earth makes Corn. Rightly viewed no meanest object is insignificant; all objects are as windows, through which the philosophic eye looks into Infinitude itself.'

Again, leaving that wondrous Schwarzwald Smithy-Altar, what vacant, high-sailing air-ships are these, and whither will they sail with us?

'All visible things are emblems;[4] what thou seest is not there on its own account; strictly taken, is not there at all: Matter exists only spiritually, and to represent some Idea, and *body* it forth.[5] Hence Clothes, as despicable as we think them, are so unspeakably significant. Clothes, from the King's mantle downwards, are emblematic, not of want only,

---

[1]*Cf.* with Bk. III, Ch. vii, "Organic Filaments"; and with Goethe in *Wilhelm Meister,* II, 131: "It is all men that make up mankind," *etc.* This element in Carlyle's philosophy is an often-overlooked complement to his doctrine of "hero-worship."

[2]*Flood of Action: Cf.* Song of the Earth Spirit, from *Faust* on p. 55, and *note* 4.

[3]See p. 55, *note* 2; also *Wilhelm Meister,* I, 106.

[4]*Cf.* with Bk. III, Ch. iii, "Symbols."

[5]*Body it forth: Offenbarung,* or revelation, was the German term for this thought, which Carlyle found in Goethe, Novalis, Fichte, and Schelling; *e.g.,* Goethe: "All the things of which we become cognizant [or perceive, *gewahr werden*] are but manifestations of the Idea" (*Maximen und Reflexionen,* ed. H. Hecker, Weimar, 1907, No. 375). See Int., Sect. V, b.

but of a manifold cunning Victory over Want. On the other hand, all Emblematic things are properly Clothes, thought-woven or hand-woven: must not the Imagination weave Garments, visible Bodies, wherein the else invisible creations and inspirations of our Reason are, like Spirits, revealed, and first become all-powerful;—the rather if, as we often see, the Hand too aid her, and (by wool Clothes or otherwise) reveal such even to the outward eye?

'Men are properly said to be clothed with Authority,[1] clothed with Beauty, with Curses, and the like. Nay, if you consider it, what is Man himself, and his whole terrestrial Life, but an Emblem; a Clothing or visible Garment for that divine ME of his, cast hither, like a light-particle, down from Heaven? Thus is he said also to be clothed with a Body.[2]

'Language is called the Garment of Thought: however, it should rather be, Language is the Flesh-Garment, the Body, of Thought. I said that imagination wove this Flesh-Garment; and does not she? Metaphors are her stuff: examine Language; what, if you except some few primitive elements (of natural sound), what is it all but Metaphors, recognised as such, or no longer recognised; still fluid and florid, or now solid-grown and colourless? If those same primitive elements are the osseous fixtures in the Flesh-Garment, Language,—then are Metaphors its muscles and tissues and living integuments. An unmetaphorical style you shall in vain seek for: is not your very *Attention* a *Stretching-to?*[3] The difference lies here: some styles are lean, adust, wiry, the muscle itself seems osseous; some are even quite pallid, hunger-bitten and dead-looking; while others again glow in the flush of health and vigorous self-growth, sometimes (as in my own case) not without an apoplectic tendency. Moreover, there are sham Metaphors, which overhanging that same Thought's-Body (best naked), and deceptively bedizening, or bolstering it out, may be called its false stuffings,

---

[1] *Cf. Measure for Measure,* II, ii, 117–18.

[2] *Cf.* Job, x, 11.

[3] Latin: *ad* + *tendere,* to *stretch* the neck *towards.*

superfluous show-cloaks (*Putz-Mäntel*), and tawdry woollen rags: whereof he that runs and reads may gather whole hampers,—and burn them.'

Than which paragraph on Metaphors did the reader ever chance to see a more surprisingly metaphorical? However, that is not our chief grievance; the Professor continues:

'Why multiply instances? It is written, the Heavens and the Earth shall fade away like a Vesture;[1] which indeed they are: the Time-vesture of the Eternal. Whatsoever sensibly exists, whatsoever represents Spirit to Spirit, is properly a Clothing, a suit of Raiment, put on for a season, and to be laid off. Thus in this one pregnant subject of CLOTHES, rightly understood, is included all that men have thought, dreamed, done, and been: the whole External Universe and what it holds is but Clothing,[2] and the essence of all Science lies in the PHILOSOPHY OF CLOTHES.'

Towards these dim infinitely-expanded regions, close-bordering on the impalpable Inane, it is not without apprehension, and perpetual difficulties, that the Editor sees himself journeying and struggling. Till lately a cheerful daystar of hope hung before him, in the expected Aid of Hofrath Heuschrecke; which daystar, however, melts now, not into the red of morning, but into a vague, gray half-light, uncertain whether dawn of day or dusk of utter darkness. For the last week, these so-called Biographical Documents are in his hand. By the kindness of a Scottish Hamburg Merchant,[3] whose name, known to the whole mercantile world, he must not mention; but whose honorable courtesy, now and often before spontaneously manifested to him, a mere literary stranger, he cannot soon forget,—the bulky Weissnichtwo Packet, with all its Customhouse seals, foreign hieroglyphs, and miscellaneous tokens of Travel, arrived here in perfect

---

[1]Matthew, iv, 4; see also Psalms, cii, 25, 26.

[2]Swift uses the same phrasing in *A Tale of a Tub,* Section II, also in respect to man's body being but a "micro-coat."

[3]Probably one of the Messrs. Parish & Co., of Hamburg, through whom Goethe and Carlyle exchanged books and packages. (*G.-C. Corr.,* p. 117.)

safety, and free of cost. The reader shall now fancy with what hot haste it was broken up, with what breathless expectation glanced over; and, alas, with what unquiet disappointment it has, since then, been often thrown down, and again taken up.

Hofrath Heuschrecke, in a too long-winded Letter, full of compliments, Weissnichtwo politics, dinners, dining repartees, and other ephemeral trivialities, proceeds to remind us of what we knew well already: that however it may be with Metaphysics, and other abstract Science originating in the Head (*Verstand*) alone, no Life-Philosophy (*Lebensphilosophie*), such as this of Clothes pretends to be, which originates equally in the Character (*Gemüth*), and equally speaks thereto, can attain its significance till the Character itself is known and seen; 'till the Author's View of the World (*Weltansicht*), and how he actively and passively came by such view, are clear: in short till a Biography of him has been philosophico-poetically written,[1] and philosophico-poetically read.' 'Nay,' adds he, 'were the speculative scientific Truth even known, you still, in this inquiring age, ask yourself, Whence came it, and Why, and How?—and rest not, till, if no better may be, Fancy have shaped-out an answer; and either in the authentic lineaments of Fact, or the forged ones of Fiction, a complete picture and Genetical History of the Man and his spiritual Endeavour lies before you. But why,' says the Hofrath, and indeed say we, 'do I dilate on the uses of our Teufelsdröckh's Biography? The great Herr Minister von Goethe[2] has penetratingly remarked that "Man is properly the *only* object that interests man":[3] thus I too have noted, that in Weissnichtwo our whole conversation is little or noth-

---

[1]The method actually employed in Book II of *Sartor.* The *reader's* method is also suggested, in self-defence against the unimaginative responses which Carlyle expected, and received, from many of his earliest readers.

[2]Johann Wolfgang von Goethe (1749–1832), novelist, scientist, critic, dramatist, and greatest of the German poets.

[3]From *Wilhelm Meister,* I, 131: "Man is ever the most interesting object to man, and perhaps should be the only one that interests." The thought in this sentence became one of the two or three master-thoughts of

ing else but Biography or Auto-Biography; ever humano-anecdotical (*menschlich-anekdotisch*). Biography is by nature the most universally profitable, universally pleasant of all things: especially Biography of distinguished individuals.[1]

'By this time, *mein Verehrtester* (my Most Esteemed),' continues he, with an eloquence which, unless the words be purloined from Teufelsdröckh, or some trick of his, as we suspect, is well-nigh unaccountable, 'by this time you are fairly plunged (*vertieft*) in that mighty forest of Clothes-Philosophy; and looking round, as all readers do, with astonishment enough. Such portions and passages as you have already mastered, and brought to paper, could not but awaken a strange curiosity touching the mind they issued from; the perhaps unparalleled psychical mechanism, which manufactured such matter, and emitted it to the light of day. Had Teufelsdröckh also a father and mother; did he, at one time, wear drivel-bibs, and live on spoon-meat? Did he ever, in rapture and tears, clasp a friend's bosom to his; looks he also wistfully into the long burial-aisle of the Past, where only winds, and their low harsh moan, give inarticulate answer? Has he fought duels;—good Heaven! how did he comport himself when in Love? By what singular stair-steps, in short, and subterranean passages, and sloughs of Despair,[2] and steep Pisgah[3] hills, has he reached this wonderful prophetic Hebron[4] (a true Old-Clothes Jewry[5]) where he now dwells?

Carlyle. (See also, Pope, *Essay on Man,* II, 2: "The proper study of mankind is man.")

[1]In this sentence is expressed the germinal idea of *Heroes and Hero-Worship*. *Cf.* the essay, "Biography," *Ess.,* III.

[2]*Cf.* Bunyan's "Slough of Despond," (*Pilgrim's Progress.*)

[3]The mountain from which Moses viewed the Promised Land. (Deuteronomy, xxxiv, 1.)

[4]Residence of King David and burial place of the patriarchs, which Abraham, after his separation from Lot, had received from Jehovah as a place of peace and worship. (Genesis, xiii, 14–18.) Teufelsdröckh, like Moses, sees his own "promised land" (the Clothes philosophy), and, like Abraham, is permitted to live in it, with truth and peace of mind.

[5]A humorous and unexpected allusion to the former Ghetto of London, now a street by that name. (Teufelsdröckh has given up the old

'To all these natural questions the voice of public History is as yet silent. Certain only that he has been, and is, a Pilgrim, and a Traveller from a far Country; more or less footsore and travel-soiled; has parted with road-companions; fallen among thieves,[1] been poisoned by bad cookery, blistered with bugbites; nevertheless, at every stage (for they have let him pass), has had the Bill to discharge. But the whole particulars of his Route, his Weather-observations, the picturesque Sketches he took, though all regularly jotted down (in indelible sympathetic-ink[2] by an invisible interior Penman), are these nowhere forthcoming? Perhaps quite lost: one other leaf of that mighty Volume (of human Memory) left to fly abroad, unprinted, unpublished, unbound up, as waste paper; and to rot, the sport of rainy winds?[3]

'No, *verehrtester Herr Herausgeber,*[4] in no wise! I here, by the unexampled favour you stand in with our Sage, send not a Biography only, but an Autobiography: at least the materials for such; wherefrom, if I misreckon not, your perspicacity will draw fullest insight: and so the whole Philosophy and Philosopher of Clothes will stand clear to the wondering eyes of England, nay thence, through America, through Hindostan, and the antipodal New Holland, finally conquer (*einnehmen*) great part of this terrestrial Planet!'

And now let the sympathising reader judge of our feeling when, in place of this same Autobiography with 'fullest insight,' we find—Six considerable Paper-Bags, carefully sealed, and marked successively, in gilt China-ink, with the symbols

---

and false "clothes"—outworn conceptions of the universe—and has taken up a new Clothes Philosophy; the exchange is a kind of "Jewry," the true kind.)

[1] *Cf.* Luke, x, 30.

[2] A fluid for invisible writing, to be made visible by pressing with a hot iron. Dr. Chalmers had told Carlyle that Christianity is "all written in us already, as in *sympathetic ink;* Bible awakens it, and you can read!" (*Reminiscences,* p. 215.)

[3] Possible allusion to the story of Aeneas's visit to the Cumaean Sibyl (*Aeneid,* Bk. vi), whose answers, committed to leaves, would be blown about on the winds.

[4] "Most esteemed Mr. Editor."

of the Six southern Zodiacal Signs,[1] beginning at Libra; in the inside of which sealed Bags lie miscellaneous masses of Sheets, and oftener Shreds and Snips, written in Professor Teufelsdröckh's scarce legible *cursiv-schrift;*[2] and treating of all imaginable things under the Zodiac and above it, but of his own personal history only at rare intervals, and then in the most enigmatic manner.

Whole fascicles there are, wherein the Professor, or, as he here, speaking in the third person, calls himself, 'the Wanderer,'[3] is not once named. Then again, amidst what seems to be a Metaphysico-theological Disquisition, 'Detached Thoughts on the Steam-engine,' or, 'The continued Possibility of Prophecy,' we shall meet with some quite private, not unimportant Biographical fact. On certain sheets stand Dreams, authentic or not, while the circumjacent waking Actions are omitted. Anecdotes, oftenest without date of place or time, fly loosely on separate slips, like Sibylline leaves.[4] Interspersed also are long purely Autobiographical delineations; yet without connection, without recognisable coherence; so unimportant, so superfluously minute, they almost remind us of 'P.P. Clerk of this Parish.'[5] Thus does famine of intelligence alternate with waste. Selection, order, appears to be unknown to the Professor. In all Bags the same imbroglio; only perhaps in the Bag *Capricorn,* and those near it, the confusion a little worse confounded.[6] Close by a rather eloquent Oration, 'On receiving the Doctor's-Hat,' lie wash-bills, marked *bezahlt*

---

[1]*Six . . . southern Zodiacal Signs:* Libra (Balance) ♎; Scorpio (Scorpion) ♏; Sagittarius (Archer) ♐; Capricornus (Goat) ♑; Aquarius (Water-bearer) ♒; Pisces (Fishes) ♓. The bags seem to cover about five years of the hero's life. (B.)

[2]A small running hand-writing.

[3]Note Bk. II, Ch. vi, "The Sorrows of Teufelsdröckh." The "wanderer" was a stock romantic figure in Carlyle's generation. *Cf.* Goethe's *Wilhelm Meisters Wanderjahre,* Byron's *Childe Harold,* Maturin's *Melmoth the Wanderer,* Coleridge's *The Wanderings of Cain, etc.*

[4]See p. 77, *note* 3.

[5]*Memoirs of P.P., Clerk of this Parish,* variously attributed tc Pope, John Arbuthnot (1667–1735), and Swift. (B.)

[6]*Cf. Paradise Lost,* ii, 996.

(settled). His Travels are indicated by the Street-Advertisements of the various cities he has visited; of which Street-Advertisements, in most living tongues, here is perhaps the completest collection extant.[1]

So that if the Clothes-Volume itself was too like a Chaos, we have now instead of the solar Luminary[2] that should still it, the airy Limbo[3] which by intermixture will farther volatilise and discompose it! As we shall perhaps see it our duty ultimately to deposit these Six Paper-Bags in the British Museum, farther description, and all vituperation of them, may be spared. Biography or Autobiography of Teufelsdröckh there is, clearly enough, none to be gleaned here: at most some sketchy, shadowy fugitive likeness of him may, by unheard-of efforts, partly of intellect, partly of imagination, on the side of Editor and of Reader, rise up between them. Only as a gaseous-chaotic Appendix[4] to that aqueous-chaotic Volume can the contents of the Six Bags hover round us, and portions thereof be incorporated with our delineation of it.

Daily and nightly does the Editor sit (with green spectacles) deciphering these unimaginable Documents from their perplexed *cursiv-schrift;* collating them with the almost equally unimaginable Volume, which stands in legible print. Over such a universal medley of high and low, of hot, cold, moist and dry, is he here struggling (by union of like with like, which is Method) to build a firm Bridge for British travellers. Never perhaps since our first Bridge-builders, Sin and Death, built that stupendous Arch from Hell-gate to the Earth, did any Pontifex,[5] or Pontiff, undertake such a task as the present

---

[1]Allusion to an eccentric hobby of Quintus Fixlein's (*German Romance,* II, 216).

[2]Solar Luminary: *Paradise Lost,* iii, 576; "that great Luminary," *etc.*

[3]*Airy Limbo:* see p. 52, *note* 1.

[4]From these words to the middle of the next paragraph, Carlyle weaves a curious figure from allusions to *Paradise Lost,* ii, 890 to the end; iii, 555–60; and x, 229–397 (Satan's journey from the realm of Chaos to the "empyreal Heaven").—Hot, cold, *etc.*: *Paradise Lost,* ii, 898.—Bridge-builders: *Paradise Lost,* ii, 1024–30.

[5]The reputed etymology is:—Latin: *pons* + *facere,* bridge-builder, origi-

Editor. For in this Arch too, leading, as we humbly presume, far otherwards than that grand primeval one, the materials are to be fished-up from the weltering deep, and down from the simmering air, here one mass, there another, and cunningly cemented, while the elements boil beneath: nor is there any supernatural force to do it with; but simply the Diligence and feeble thinking Faculty of an English Editor, endeavouring to evolve printed Creation out of a German printed and written Chaos, wherein, as he shoots to and fro in it, gathering, clutching, piecing the Why to the far-distant Wherefore, his whole Faculty and Self are like to be swallowed up.

Patiently, under these incessant toils and agitations, does the Editor, dismissing all anger, see his otherwise robust health declining; some fraction of his allotted natural sleep nightly leaving him, and little but an inflamed nervous-system to be looked for.[1] What is the use of health, or of life, if not to do some work therewith? And what work nobler than transplanting foreign Thought into the barren domestic soil;[2] except indeed planting Thought of your own, which the fewest are privileged to do? Wild as it looks, this Philosophy of Clothes, can we ever reach its real meaning, promises to reveal new-coming Eras, the first dim rudiments and already-budding germs of a nobler Era, in Universal History. Is not such a prize worth some striving? Forward with us, courageous reader; be it towards failure, or towards success! The latter thou sharest with us; the former also is not all our own.

---

nally applied to Roman Magistrates whose sacred function it was to superintend the building and demolition of bridges. Later applied to priests at Rome, then to the Pope.

[1]An autobiographical allusion; Carlyle's condition when composing.

[2]*Transplanting foreign Thought:* more autobiography. From contemporary British thought—Utilitarianism, Byronic pessimism, *etc.,*—he turned to "the higher Literature of Germany, [where] there already lies, for him that can read it, the beginning of a new revelation of the Godlike" ("Characteristics," *Ess.,* III, 41).

BOOK SECOND

CHAPTER I

GENESIS

Old Andreas Futteral and Gretchen his wife: their quiet home. Advent of a mysterious stranger, who deposits with them a young infant, the future Herr Diogenes Teufelsdröckh. After-yearnings of the youth for his unknown Father. Sovereign power of Names and Naming. Diogenes a flourishing Infant.

In a psychological point of view, it is perhaps questionable whether from birth and genealogy, how closely scrutinised soever, much insight is to be gained. Nevertheless, as in every phenomenon the Beginning remains always the most notable moment; so, with regard to any great man, we rest not till, for our scientific profit or not, the whole circumstances of his first appearance in this Planet, and what manner of Public Entry he made, are with utmost completeness rendered manifest. To the Genesis of our Clothes-Philosopher, then, be this First Chapter consecrated. Unhappily, indeed, he seems to be of quite obscure extraction; uncertain, we might almost say, whether of any: so that this Genesis of his can properly be nothing but an Exodus (or transit out of Invisibility into Visibility[1]); whereof the preliminary portion is nowhere forthcoming.

'In the village of Entepfuhl,'[2] thus writes he, in the Bag *Libra,* on various Papers, which we arrange with difficulty,

[1]Phrasing similar to Richter's in "Quintus Fixlein" (*German Romance,* II, 299–300: Thiennette's "transition from Nothingness to Existence, from Eternity to Time . . .").

[2]German for *Duckpond:* Ecclefechan, with its large duckpond near the Carlyle cottage.

'dwelt Andreas Futteral and his wife;[1] childless, in still seclusion, and cheerful though now verging towards old age. Andreas had been grenadier Sergeant, and even regimental Schoolmaster under Frederick the Great;[2] but now, quitting the halbert and ferule for the spade and pruning-hook, cultivated a little Orchard, on the produce of which he, Cincinnatus-like,[3] lived not without dignity. Fruits, the peach, the apple, the grape, with other varieties came in their season; all which Andreas knew how to sell: on evenings he smoked largely, or read (as beseemed a regimental Schoolmaster), and talked to neighbours that would listen about the Victory of Rossbach;[4] and how Fritz the Only (*der Einzige*) had once with his own royal lips spoken to him, had been pleased to say, when Andreas as camp-sentinel demanded the pass-word, "*Schweig Hund* (Peace, hound)!" before any of his staff-adjutants could answer. "*Das nenn' ich mir einen König,* There is what I call a King," would Andreas exclaim: "but the smoke of Kunersdorf[5] was still smarting his eyes."

'Gretchen, the housewife, won like Desdemona by the deeds rather than the looks of her now veteran Othello,[6] lived not in altogether military subordination; for, as Andreas said, "the womankind will not drill (*wer kann die Weiberchen dressiren*)": nevertheless she at heart loved him both for valour and wisdom; to her a Prussian grenadier Sergeant and Regiment's Schoolmaster was little other than a Cicero and Cid:[7]

---

[1]*Andreas Futteral and his wife:* slight resemblance to James Carlyle; a little more to Carlyle's mother.

[2]Frederick the Great, of Prussia (1712–86).

[3]Cincinnatus, L. Quintus, hero of the Roman republic, was called from his plough to the dictatorship during a war with the Aequians (B.C. 458). After saving his countrymen, he returned to his farm, having held office but a few days.

[4]*Rossbach:* a town in Saxony, where Frederick won a great victory over the French in 1757.

[5]A village in Brandenburg, where the Austrians and Russians totally defeated Frederick in 1759.

[6]*Othello,* I, iii, 128–68.

[7]Examples of wisdom and courage. Marcus Tullius Cicero (B.C. 106–43): Roman orator and scholar.—Ruy Diaz of Bivar (*c.* 1040–1099):

what you see, yet cannot see over, is as good as infinite. Nay, was not Andreas in very deed a man of order, courage, downrightness (*Geradheit*); that understood Büsching's *Geography*,[1] had been in the victory of Rossbach, and left for dead in the camisade[2] of Hochkirch? The good Gretchen, for all her fretting, watched over him and hovered round him as only a true housemother can: assiduously she cooked and sewed and scoured for him; so that not only his old regimental sword and grenadier-cap, but the whole habitation and environment, where on pegs of honour they hung, looked ever trim and gay: a roomy painted Cottage, embowered in fruit-trees and forest-trees, evergreens and honeysuckles; rising many-coloured from amid shaven grass-plots, flowers struggling-in through the very windows; under its long projecting eaves nothing but garden-tools in methodic piles (to screen them from rain), and seats where, especially on summer nights, a King might have wished to sit and smoke, and call it his. Such a *Bauergut* (Copyhold) had Gretchen given her veteran; whose sinewy arms, and long-disused gardening talent, had made it what you saw.

'Into this umbrageous Man's-nest, one meek yellow evening or dusk, when the Sun, hidden indeed from terrestrial Entepfuhl, did nevertheless journey visible and radiant along the celestial Balance (*Libra*),[3] it was that a Stranger of reverend aspect entered; and, with grave salutation, stood before the two rather astonished housemates. He was close-muffled in a wide mantle; which without farther parley unfolding, he deposited therefrom what seemed some Basket, overhung with green Persian silk; saying only: *Ihr lieben Leute, hier bringe ein unschätzbares Verleihen; nehmt es in aller Acht, sorgfältigst*

---

favourite hero of Spain, and most prominent figure in her literature. Cid=*Seid* (Arabic), Lord Champion.

[1]Büsching, A. F. (1724–93), German geographer, author of *A New Description of the Earth* (8 Vols., 1754–59), which Carlyle frequently consulted.

[2]A night attack.—*Hochkirch* (or Hochkirchen): a town in Saxony, where the Austrians defeated Frederick in 1758.

[3]That is, from September 22 to October 23.

benützt es: mit hohem Lohn, oder wohl mit schweren Zinsen, wird's einst zurückgefordert. "Good Christian people, here lies for you an invaluable Loan; take all heed thereof, in all carefulness employ it: with high recompense, or else with heavy penalty, will it one day be required back." Uttering which singular words, in a clear, bell-like, forever memorable tone, the Stranger gracefully withdrew; and before Andreas or his wife, gazing in expectant wonder, had time to fashion either question or answer, was clean gone. Neither out of doors could aught of him be seen or heard; he had vanished in the thickets, in the dusk; the Orchard-gate stood quietly closed: the Stranger was gone once and always. So sudden had the whole transaction been, in the autumn stillness and twilight, so gentle, noiseless, that the Futterals could have fancied it all a trick of Imagination, or some visit from an authentic Spirit. Only that the green-silk Basket, such as neither Imagination nor authentic Spirits are wont to carry, still stood visible and tangible on their little parlour-table. Towards this the astonished couple, now with lit candle, hastily turned their attention. Lifting the green veil, to see what invaluable it hid, they descried there, amid down and rich white wrappages, no Pitt Diamond[1] or Hapsburg[2] Regalia, but, in the softest sleep, a little red-coloured Infant! Beside it, lay a roll of gold Friedrichs,[3] the exact amount of which was never publicly known; also a *Taufschein* (baptismal certificate), wherein unfortunately nothing but the Name was decipherable; other document or indication none whatever.

'To wonder and conjecture was unavailing, then and always thenceforth. Nowhere in Entepfuhl, on the morrow or next day, did tidings transpire of any such figure as the Stranger; nor could the Traveller, who had passed through the neighbouring Town in coach-and-four, be connected with

---

[1]The Regent Diamond, brought from India in 1702 by Thomas Pitt, Governor of Madras, and grandfather of the first and great Earl of Chatham. It was sold in 1717 to the French Regent for £135,000.

[2]Or Habsburg: name of the former Imperial Family of Austria.

[3]The Friedrichs d'or, an old Prussian gold coin, was worth about $3.98.

this Apparition, except in the way of gratuitous surmise. Meanwhile, for Andreas and his wife, the grand practical problem was: What to do with this little sleeping red-coloured Infant? Amid amazements and curiosities, which had to die away without external satisfying, they resolved, as in such circumstances charitable prudent people needs must, on nursing it, though with spoon-meat, into whiteness, and if possible into manhood. The Heavens smiled on their endeavour: thus has that same mysterious Individual ever since had a status for himself in this visible Universe, some modicum of victual and lodging and parade-ground; and now expanded in bulk, faculty and knowledge of good and evil, he, as HERR DIOGENES TEUFELSDRÖCKH, professes or is ready to profess, perhaps not altogether without effect, in the New University of Weissnichtwo, the new Science of Things in General.'

Our Philosopher declares here, as indeed we should think he well might, that these facts, first communicated, by the good Gretchen Futteral, in his twelfth year, 'produced on the boyish heart and fancy a quite indelible impression. Who this reverend Personage,' he says, 'that glided into the Orchard Cottage when the Sun was in Libra, and then, as on spirit's wings, glided out again, might be? An inexpressible desire, full of love and of sadness, has often since struggled within me to shape an answer. Ever, in my distresses and my loneliness, has Fantasy turned, full of longing (*sehnsuchtsvoll*), to that unknown Father, who perhaps far from me, perhaps near, either way invisible, might have taken me to his paternal bosom, there to lie screened from many a woe. Thou beloved Father, dost thou still, shut out from me only by thin penetrable curtains of earthly Space, wend to and fro among the crowd of the living? Or art thou hidden by those far thicker curtains of the Everlasting Night,[1] or rather of the Everlasting Day, through which my mortal eye and out-

---

[1] *Cf.* Schiller's reference to the "two black impenetrable curtains, which hang down at the two extremities of human life," *etc.* (Quoted by Carlyle in *The Life of Schiller,* p. 50.)

stretched arms need not strive to reach? Alas, I know not, and in vain vex myself to know. More than once, heart-deluded, have I taken for thee this and the other noble-looking Stranger; and approached him wistfully, with infinite regard; but he too had to repel me, he too was not thou.

'And yet, O Man born of Woman,' cries the Autobiographer, with one of his sudden whirls, 'wherein is my case peculiar? Hadst thou, any more than I, a Father whom thou knowest? The Andreas and Gretchen, or the Adam and Eve, who led thee into Life, and for a time suckled and pap-fed thee there, whom thou namest Father and Mother; these were, like mine, but thy nursing-father and nursing-mother: thy true Beginning and Father is in Heaven, whom with the bodily eye thou shalt never behold, but only with the spiritual.'

'The little green veil,' adds he, among much similar moralising, and embroiled discoursing, 'I yet keep; still more inseparably the Name, Diogenes Teufelsdröckh. From the veil can nothing be inferred: a piece of now quite faded Persian silk, like thousands of others. On the Name I have many times meditated and conjectured; but neither in this lay there any clue. That it was my unknown Father's name I must hesitate to believe. To no purpose have I searched through all the Herald's Books, in and without the German Empire, and through all manner of Subscriber-Lists (*Pränumeranten*), Militia-Rolls, and other Name-catalogues; extraordinary names as we have in Germany, the name Teufelsdröckh, except as appended to my own person, nowhere occurs. Again, what may the unchristian rather than Christian "Diogenes" mean?[1] Did that reverend Basket-bearer intend, by such designation, to shadow-forth my future destiny, or his own present malign humour? Perhaps the latter, perhaps both. Thou ill-starred Parent, who like an

---

[1]Diogenes (*God-born*): famous Greek Cynic philosopher of the fifth century B.C., who was said to live in a tub, to go about with a lantern looking for an "honest man," and who was celebrated for extreme self-control and sarcastic wit.

Ostrich[1] hadst to leave thy ill-starred offspring to be hatched into self-support by the mere sky-influences of Chance, can thy pilgrimage have been a smooth one? Beset by Misfortune thou doubtless hast been; or indeed by the worst figure of Misfortune, by Misconduct. Often have I fancied how, in thy hard life-battle, thou wert shot at, and slung at, wounded, hand-fettered, hamstrung, browbeaten and bedevilled by the Time-Spirit (*Zeitgeist*)[2] in thyself and others, till the good soul first given thee was seared into grim rage; and thou hadst nothing for it but to leave in me an indignant appeal to the Future, and living speaking Protest against the Devil, as that same Spirit not of the Time only, but of Time itself, is well named! Which Appeal and Protest, may I now modestly add, was not perhaps quite lost in air.

'For indeed, as Walter Shandy often insisted, there is much, nay almost all, in Names.[3] The Name is the earliest Garment you wrap round the earth-visiting ME; to which it thenceforth cleaves, more tenaciously (for there are Names that have lasted nigh thirty centuries) than the very skin. And now from without, what mystic influences does it not send inwards, even to the centre; especially in those plastic first-times, when the whole soul is yet infantine, soft, and the invisible seedgrain will grow to be an all overshadowing tree! Names? Could I unfold the influence of Names, which are the most important of all Clothings, I were a second greater Trismegistus.[4] Not only all common Speech, but Science,

---

[1]*Cf.* Job, xxxix, 13–18.

[2]Carlyle frequently thinks of Time as the evil or destructive principle in things. *Cf.* Fr. v. Schlegel's conception in Carlyle's "Characteristics" (*Ess.*, III, 34). The enigma of time was a life-long pre-occupation with Carlyle: it was both a "seed-field" (Goethe) and the "element wherein man's soul here below lives imprisoned" (*Ess.*, III, 79). See Int., Sect. V, c.

[3]Allusion to Tristram's father (see *Tristram Shandy,* Vol. I, Ch. xix; also *German Romance,* II, 230, for Quintus Fixlein's concurrence in Walter Shandy's opinion on the importance of names).

[4]Probable allusion to the same chapter in *Tristram Shandy,* as in preceding *note.* Hermes Trismegistus (*Thrice-greatest*): a name given by the Greeks to the Egyptian god Thoth, god of science, letters, speech, *etc.*

Poetry itself is no other, if thou consider it, than a right *Naming*. Adam's first task was giving names to natural Appearances:[1] what is ours still but a continuation of the same; be the Appearances exotic-vegetable, organic, mechanic, stars, or starry movements (as in Science); or (as in Poetry) passions, virtues, calamities, God-attributes, Gods? —In a very plain sense the Proverb says, *Call one a thief, and he will steal;* in an almost similar sense may we not perhaps say, *Call one Diogenes Teufelsdröckh, and he will open the Philosophy of Clothes?*'

'Meanwhile the incipient Diogenes, like others, all ignorant of his Why, his How or Whereabout, was opening his eyes to the kind Light; sprawling-out his ten fingers and toes; listening, tasting, feeling; in a word, by all his Five Senses, still more by his Sixth Sense of Hunger, and a whole infinitude of inward, spiritual, half-awakened Senses, endeavouring daily to acquire for himself some knowledge of this strange Universe where he had arrived, be his task therein what it might. Infinite was his progress; thus in some fifteen months, he could perform the miracle of—Speech! To breed a fresh Soul, is it not like brooding a fresh (celestial) Egg; wherein as yet all is formless, powerless; yet by degrees organic elements and fibres shoot through the watery albumen; and out of vague Sensation grows Thought, grows Fantasy and Force, and we have Philosophies, Dynasties, nay Poetries and Religions!

'Young Diogenes, or rather young Gneschen, for by such diminutive had they in their fondness named him, travelled forward to those high consummations, by quick yet easy stages. The Futterals, to avoid vain talk, and moreover keep the roll of gold Friedrichs safe, gave-out that he was a grandnephew; the orphan of some sister's daughter, suddenly deceased, in Andreas's distant Prussian birthland; of whom, as of her indigent sorrowing widower, little enough was known at Entepfuhl. Heedless of all which, the Nurseling took to

[1]Genesis, ii, 19.

his spoon-meat, and throve. I have heard him noted as a still infant, that kept his mind much to himself; above all, that seldom or never cried. He already felt that time was precious; that he had other work cut-out for him than whimpering.'

Such, after utmost painful search and collation among these miscellaneous Paper-masses, is all the notice we can gather of Herr Teufelsdröckh's genealogy. More imperfect, more enigmatic it can seem to few readers than to us. The Professor, in whom truly we more and more discern a certain satirical turn, and deep under-currents of roguish whim, for the present stands pledged in honour, so we will not doubt him: but seems it not conceivable that, by the 'good Gretchen Futteral,' or some other perhaps interested party, he has himself been deceived? Should these sheets, translated or not, ever reach the Entepfuhl Circulating Library, some cultivated native of that district might feel called to afford explanation. Nay, since Books, like invisible scouts, permeate the whole habitable globe, and Timbuctoo[1] itself is not safe from British Literature, may not some Copy find out even the mysterious basket-bearing Stranger, who in a state of extreme senility perhaps still exists; and gently force even him to disclose himself; to claim openly a son, in whom any father may feel pride?

---

[1](So spelled in Carlyle's youth) A town on the southern edge of the Sahara desert, in the French Sudan. Noteworthy in the second decade of the century because of the murder of Major Gordon Laing there in 1826; René Caillié returned from there and described it in 1828; Tennyson's prize poem *Timbuctoo* was published in 1829.

CHAPTER II

IDYLLIC

Happy Childhood! Entepfuhl: Sights, hearings and experiences of the boy Teufelsdröckh; their manifold teaching. Education; what it can do, what cannot. Obedience our universal duty and destiny. Gneschen sees the good Gretchen pray.

HAPPY season of childhood!' exclaims Teufelsdröckh: 'Kind Nature, that art to all a bountiful mother; that visitest the poor man's hut with auroral radiance; and for thy Nurseling hast provided a soft swathing of Love and infinite Hope, wherein he waxes and slumbers, danced-round (*umgaukelt*) by sweetest Dreams! If the paternal Cottage still shuts us in, its roof still screens us; with a Father we have as yet a prophet, priest and king, and an Obedience that makes us free. The young spirit has awakened out of Eternity, and knows not what we mean by Time; as yet Time is no fast-hurrying stream, but a sportful sunlit ocean,[1] years to the child are as ages: ah! the secret of Vicissitude, of that slower or quicker decay and ceaseless down-rushing of the universal World-fabric, from the granite mountain to the man or day-moth, is yet unknown; and in a motionless Universe, we taste, what afterwards in this quick-whirling Universe, is forever denied us, the balm of Rest. Sleep on, thou fair Child, for thy long rough journey is at hand! A little while, and thou too shalt sleep no more, but thy very dreams shall be mimic battles; thou too, with old Arnauld, wilt have to say in stern patience: "Rest? Rest? Shall I not have all Eternity to rest in?"[2]

---

[1]The idea and the phrasing are similar to Richter's in *Flower, Fruit, etc.*, p. 261 (*Ess.*, II, 156).

[2]Antoine Arnauld (1612–94), French philosopher and Jansenist theologian (the Port Royal School), made the famous reply when his friend Pierre Nicole complained of being tired of his life of controversy with Jesuits, Calvinists, and other opponents.

Celestial Nepenthe![1] though a Pyrrhus[2] conquer empires, and an Alexander[3] sack the world, he finds thee not; and thou hast once fallen gently, of thy own accord, on the eyelids, on the heart of every mother's child. For as yet, sleep and waking are one: the fair Life-garden rustles infinite around, and everywhere is dewy fragrance, and the budding of Hope; which budding, if in youth, too frostnipt, it grow to flowers, will in manhood yield no fruit, but a prickly, bitter-rinded stone-fruit, of which the fewest can find the kernel.'

In such rose-coloured light does our Professor, as Poets are wont, look back on his childhood; the historical details of which (to say nothing of much other vague oratorical matter) he accordingly dwells on with an almost wearisome minuteness. We hear of Entepfuhl standing 'in trustful derangement' among the woody slopes; the paternal Orchard flanking it as extreme outpost from below; the little Kuhbach[4] gushing kindly by, among beech-rows, through river after river, into the Donau,[5] into the Black Sea, into the Atmosphere and Universe; and how 'the brave old Linden,' stretching like a parasol of twenty ells in radius, overtopping all other rows and clumps, towered-up from the central *Agora* and *Campus Martius*[6] of the Village, like its Sacred Tree; and how the old men sat talking under its shadow (Gneschen often greedily listening), and the wearied labourers reclined, and the unwearied children sported, and the young men and maidens often danced to flute-music. 'Glorious summer twilights,' cries Teufelsdröckh, 'when the Sun, like a proud Conqueror

---

[1]*Nepenthe:* a potion or drug used by the ancients to give relief or forgetfulness. *Cf.* Milton, *Comus,* 675; Homer, *Odyssey,* iv, 221.

[2]Pyrrhus (B.C. 318–272), King of Epirus, twice defeated the Romans, but was conquered in the battle of Beneventum in 275.

[3]Alexander the Great (B.C. 356–323), King of Macedon, conquered the Persians and most of the known (ancient) world.

[4]*Kuhbach* (*Cowbrook*): a burn, or brook, flowed down the centre of the single street of Ecclefechan.

[5]Danube.

[6]*Agora:* Market-place in Greek cities.—*Campus Martius:* Field of Mars, place of assembly in Rome.

and Imperial Taskmaster, turned his back, with his gold-purple emblazonry, and all his fireclad body-guard (of Prismatic Colours); and the tired brickmakers of this clay Earth might steal a little frolic, and those few meek Stars would not tell of them!'

Then we have long details of the *Weinlesen* (Vintage), the Harvest-Home, Christmas, and so forth; with a whole cycle of the Entepfuhl Children's-games, differing apparently by mere superficial shades from those of other countries. Concerning all which, we shall here, for obvious reasons, say nothing. What cares the world for our as yet miniature Philosopher's achievements under that 'brave old Linden'? Or even where is the use of such practical reflections as the following? 'In all the sports of Children, were it only in their wanton breakages and defacements, you shall discern a creative instinct (*schaffenden Trieb*): the Mankin feels that he is a born Man, that his vocation is to work. The choicest present you can make him is a Tool; be it knife or pen-gun,[1] for construction or for destruction; either way it is for Work, for Change. In gregarious sports of skill or strength, the boy trains himself to Coöperation, for war or peace, as governor or governed:[2] the little Maid again, provident of her domestic destiny, takes with preference to Dolls.'

Perhaps, however, we may give this anecdote, considering who it is that relates it: 'My first short-clothes were of yellow serge; or rather, I should say, my first short-cloth, for the vesture was one and indivisible, reaching from neck to ankle, a mere body with four limbs: of which fashion how little could I then divine the architectural, how much less the moral significance!'

More graceful is the following little picture: 'On fine evenings I was wont to carry-forth my supper (bread-crumb boiled in milk), and eat it out-of-doors. On the coping of the

---

[1]Pop-gun.

[2]Once more the reference to unity and multiplicity, the oneness of *society*, and the division of society into leaders ("heroes") and the followers. See p. 65, *note* 5.

Orchard-wall, which I could reach by climbing, or still more easily if Father Andreas would set-up the pruning-ladder, my porringer was placed: there, many a sunset, have I, looking at the distant western Mountains, consumed, not without relish, my evening meal. Those hues of gold and azure, that hush of World's expectation as Day died, were still a Hebrew Speech for me; nevertheless I was looking at the fair illuminated Letters, and had an eye for their gilding.'

With 'the little one's friendship for cattle and poultry' we shall not much intermeddle. It may be that hereby he acquired a 'certain deeper sympathy with animated Nature': but when, we would ask, saw any man, in a collection of Biographical Documents, such a piece as this: 'Impressive enough (*bedeutungsvoll*) was it to hear, in early morning, the Swineherd's horn; and know that so many hungry happy quadrupeds were, on all sides, starting in hot haste to join him, for breakfast on the Heath. Or to see them at eventide, all marching-in again, with short squeak, almost in military order; and each, topographically correct, trotting-off in succession to the right or left, through its own lane, to its own dwelling; till old Kunz, at the Village-head, now left alone, blew his last blast, and retired for the night. We are wont to love the Hog chiefly in the form of Ham; yet did not these bristly thick-skinned beings here manifest intelligence, perhaps humour of character; at any rate, a touching, trustful submissiveness to Man,—who, were he but a Swineherd, in darned gabardine,[1] and leather breeches more resembling slate or discoloured-tin breeches, is still the Hierarch of this lower world?'

It is maintained, by Helvetius[2] and his set, that an infant of genius is quite the same as any other infant, only that certain surprisingly favourable influences accompany him through life, especially through childhood, and expand him, while

[1] A coarse loose frock or coat, or smock frock.

[2] Claude Adrien Helvétius (1715–71), French philosopher and *littérateur,* was one of the Encyclopaedists, and author of *De l'Homme, de ses facultés intellectuelles, et de son education* (1772), and of the more famous work, *De l'Esprit* (1758).

others lie closefolded and continue dunces. Herein, say they, consists the whole difference between an inspired Prophet and a double-barrelled Game-preserver:[1] the inner man of the one has been fostered into generous development; that of the other, crushed-down perhaps by vigour of animal digestion, and the like, has exuded and evaporated, or at best sleeps now irresuscitably stagnant at the bottom of his stomach. 'With which opinion,' cries Teufelsdröckh, 'I should as soon agree as with this other, that an acorn might, by favourable or unfavourable influences of soil and climate, be nursed into a cabbage, or the cabbage-seed into an oak.

'Nevertheless,' continues he, 'I too acknowledge the all-but omnipotence of early culture and nurture: hereby we have either a doddered dwarf bush, or a high-towering, wide-shadowing tree; either a sick yellow cabbage, or an edible luxuriant green one. Of a truth, it is the duty of all men, especially of all philosophers, to note-down with accuracy the characteristic circumstances of their Education,[2] what furthered, what hindered, what in any way modified it: to which duty, nowadays so pressing for many a German Autobiographer, I also zealously address myself.'—Thou rogue! Is it by short-clothes of yellow serge, and swineherd horns, that an infant of genius is educated? And yet, as usual, it ever remains doubtful whether he is laughing in his sleeve at these Autobiographical times of ours, or writing from the abundance of his own fond ineptitude. For he continues: 'If among the ever-streaming currents of Sights, Hearings, Feelings for Pain or Pleasure, whereby, as in a Magic Hall, young Gneschen went about environed, I might venture to select and specify, perhaps these following were also of the number:

'Doubtless, as childish sports call forth Intellect, Activity,

---

[1]See the end of Ch. iv of B. III; and Carlyle's frequent satirical references to champions of the Corn-laws, the game-laws, and the idle ("do-nothing") Aristocracy, in *Past and Present,* III, viii, ix, *etc.* (*Cf.* also Carlyle's Journal for June 30, 1830, in *C.E.L.,* II, Ch. iv.)

[2]Goethe had written of his own education in *Dichtung und Wahrheit,* and of an *ideal* method of education in *Wilhelm Meisters Wanderjahre,* Chapters x–xi (on the "Pedagogical Province").

so the young creature's Imagination was stirred up, and a Historical tendency given him by the narrative habits of Father Andreas; who, with his battle-reminiscences, and gray austere yet hearty patriarchal aspect, could not but appear another Ulysses and "much-enduring Man."[1] Eagerly I hung upon his tales, when listening neighbours enlivened the hearth; from these perils and these travels, wild and far almost as Hades[2] itself, a dim world of Adventure expanded itself within me. Incalculable also was the knowledge I acquired in standing by the Old Men under the Linden-tree: the whole of Immensity was yet new to me; and had not these reverend seniors, talkative enough, been employed in partial surveys thereof for nigh fourscore years? With amazement I began to discover that Entepfuhl stood in the middle of a Country, of a World; that there was such a thing as History, as Biography; to which I also, one day, by hand and tongue, might contribute.

'In a like sense worked the *Postwagen* (Stage-coach),[3] which, slow-rolling under its mountains of men and luggage, wended through our Village: northwards, truly, in the dead of night; yet southwards visibly at eventide. Not till my eighth year did I reflect that this Postwagen could be other than some terrestrial Moon, rising and setting by mere Law of Nature, like the heavenly one; that it came on made highways, from far cities towards far cities; weaving them like a monstrous shuttle into closer and closer union. It was then that, independently of Schiller's *Wilhelm Tell,* I made this not quite insignificant reflection (so true also in spiritual things): *Any road, this simple Entepfuhl road, will lead you to the end of the World!*[4]

---

[1]*Cf.* "Long-tried" (πολύτλας), *etc.,* an epithet constantly applied by Homer to Ulysses.

[2]The gloomy subterranean abode of the dead, or departed spirits, in Greek mythology.

[3]In Carlyle's youth, Ecclefechan was a stopping-place for the London, Carlisle, and Glasgow coaches.

[4]From Schiller's *Wilhelm Tell,* IV, iii, 2619: "Denn jede Strasse führt ans End' der Welt."

'Why mention our Swallows, which, out of far Africa, as I learned, threading their way over seas and mountains, corporate cities and belligerent nations, yearly found themselves, with the month of May, snug-lodged in our Cottage Lobby? The hospitable Father (for cleanliness' sake) had fixed a little bracket plumb under their nest: there they built, and caught flies, and twittered, and bred; and all, I chiefly, from the heart loved them. Bright, nimble creatures, who taught *you* the mason-craft; nay, stranger still, gave you a masonic incorporation, almost social police? For if, by ill chance, and when time pressed, your House fell, have I not seen five neighbourly Helpers appear next day; and swashing to and fro, with animated, loud, long-drawn chirpings, and activity almost super-hirundine, complete it again before nightfall?

'But undoubtedly the grand summary of Entepfuhl child's-culture, where as in a funnel its manifold influences were concentrated and simultaneously poured-down on us, was the annual Cattle-fair.[1] Here, assembling from all the four winds, came the elements of an unspeakable hurlyburly.[2] Nutbrown maids[3] and nutbrown men, all clear-washed, loud-laughing, bedizened and beribanded; who came for dancing, for treating, and if possible, for happiness. Topbooted Graziers from the North; Swiss Brokers, Italian Drovers, also topbooted, from the South; these with their subalterns in leather jerkins, leather skull-caps, and long oxgoads; shouting in half-articulate speech, amid the inarticulate barking and bellowing. Apart stood Potters from far Saxony, with their crockery in fair rows; Nürnberg Pedlars,[4] in booths that to me seemed richer than Ormuz bazaars;[5] Showmen from the Lago Maggiore;[6]

---

[1]A cattle-fair was held annually, in Carlyle's early years, in Ecclefechan.

[2]*Hurlyburly: cf. Macbeth,* I, i, 3.

[3]*Cf.* the fifteenth-century poem of that name, included in Percy's *Reliques* (1765).

[4]See p. 44, *note* 1.

[5]Ormuz, or Hormuz, an island in the Strait of Ormuz, off the coast of Persia, was formerly celebrated for its wealthy market in the trade with India. "Wealth of Ormus and of Ind" (*Paradise Lost*, ii, 2).

[6]A large lake in northern Italy.

detachments of the *Wiener Schub* (Offscourings of Vienna) vociferously superintending games of chance. Ballad-singers brayed, Auctioneers grew hoarse; cheap New Wine (*heuriger*) flowed like water, still worse confounding the confusion; and high over all, vaulted, in ground-and-lofty tumbling, a parti-coloured Merry-Andrew,[1] like the genius of the place and of Life itself.

'Thus encircled by the mystery of Existence; under the deep heavenly Firmament; waited-on by the four golden Seasons, with their vicissitudes of contribution, for even grim Winter brought its skating-matches and shooting-matches, its snow-storms and Christmas-carols,—did the Child sit and learn. These things were the Alphabet, whereby in aftertime he was to syllable and partly read the grand Volume of the World:[2] what matters it whether such Alphabet be in large gilt letters or in small ungilt ones, so you have an eye to read it? For Gneschen, eager to learn, the very act of looking thereon was a blessedness that gilded all: his existence was a bright, soft element of Joy; out of which, as in Prospero's Island,[3] wonder after wonder bodied itself forth, to teach by charming.

'Nevertheless, I were but a vain dreamer to say, that even then my felicity was perfect. I had, once for all, come down from Heaven into the Earth. Among the rainbow colours that glowed on my horizon, lay even in childhood a dark ring of Care, as yet no thicker than a thread, and often quite over-shone; yet always it reappeared, nay ever waxing broader and broader; till in after-years it almost over-shadowed my whole canopy, and threatened to engulf me in final night. It was the ring of Necessity[4] whereby we are all begirt; happy he for

---

[1]A clown or buffoon. One of the chief characters in the Prelude to Goethe's *Faust*.

[2]*Cf*. p. 36, *note* 3, on "hieroglyphics," and Bk. III, Ch. viii, "Natural Supernaturalism"; also Sir Thomas Browne, *Religio Medici* (Everyman ed.), pp. 17–18, for similar passage.

[3]*Cf*. Shakespeare's *The Tempest, passim*. ("Charming" = enchantment. B.)

[4]A foreshadowing of the gospel of Work in "The Everlasting Yea"

whom a kind heavenly Sun brightens it into a ring of Duty, and plays round it with beautiful prismatic diffractions; yet ever, as basis and as bourne for our whole being, it is there.

'For the first few years of our terrestrial Apprenticeship, we have not much work to do; but, boarded and lodged gratis, are set down mostly to look about us over the workshop, and see others work, till we have understood the tools a little, and can handle this and that. If good Passivity alone, and not good Passivity and good Activity together,[1] were the thing wanted, then was my early position favourable beyond the most. In all that respects openness of Sense, affectionate Temper, ingenuous Curiosity, and the fostering of these, what more could I have wished? On the other side, however, things went not so well. My Active Power (*Thatkraft*) was unfavourably hemmed-in; of which misfortune how many traces yet abide with me! In an orderly house, where the litter of children's sports is hateful enough, your training is too stoical; rather to bear and forbear than to make and do. I was forbid much:[2] wishes in any measure bold I had to renounce; everywhere a strait bond of Obedience inflexibly held me down. Thus already Freewill often came in painful collision with Necessity; so that my tears flowed, and at seasons the Child itself might taste that root of bitterness,[3] wherewith the whole fruitage of our life is mingled and tempered.

'In which habituation to Obedience, truly, it was beyond measure safer to err by excess than by defect. Obedience is our universal duty and destiny; wherein whoso will not bend must break: too early and too thoroughly we cannot be

---

(Bk. II, Ch. ix), of turning one's limitations into creative directions (see p. 119, *note* 2); *cf. Wilhelm Meister,* II, 54, and the essay on Burns (*Ess.,* I, 295): "Manhood begins when we have in any way made truce with Necessity . . . felt that in Necessity we are free."

[1]A foreshadowing of the doctrines of Renunciation and Work, respectively (see chapter, "Everlasting Yea," *etc.*).

[2]Possible allusion to the sternness of Carlyle's father. (See R. S. Craig, *The Making of Carlyle,* pp. 27–29.)

[3]*Cf.* Hebrews, xii, 15.

trained to know that Would, in this world of ours, is as mere zero to Should, and for most part as the smallest of fractions even to Shall. Hereby was laid for me the basis of worldly Discretion, nay of Morality itself. Let me not quarrel with my upbringing.[1] It was rigorous, too frugal, compressively secluded, everyway unscientific: yet in that very strictness and domestic solitude might there not lie the root of deeper earnestness, of the stem from which all noble fruit must grow? Above all, how unskilful soever, it was loving, it was well-meant, honest; whereby every deficiency was helped. My kind Mother, for as such I must ever love the good Gretchen, did me one altogether invaluable service: she taught me, less indeed by word than by act and daily reverent look and habitude, her own simple version of the Christian Faith. Andreas too attended Church; yet more like a parade-duty, for which he in the other world expected pay with arrears,—as, I trust, he has received; but my Mother, with a true woman's heart, and fine though uncultivated sense, was in the strictest acceptation Religious. How indestructibly the Good grows, and propagates itself, even among the weedy entanglements of Evil! The highest whom I knew on Earth I here saw bowed down, with awe unspeakable, before a Higher in Heaven: such things, especially in infancy, reach inwards to the very core of your being; mysteriously does a Holy of Holies[2] build itself into visibility in the mysterious deeps; and Reverence, the divinest in man, springs forth undying from its mean envelopment of Fear.[3] Wouldst thou rather be a peasant's son that knew, were it never so rudely, there was a God in Heaven and in Man; or a duke's son that only knew there were two-and-thirty quarters[4] on the family-coach?'

---

[1]The last paragraph in the present chapter is strikingly autobiographical, and should be read in the light of Chapter I ("James Carlyle") of the *Reminiscences;* Wilson, *Carlyle till Marriage;* Froude's *Life, etc.*

[2]*Cf.* Exodus, xxvi, 33, 34.

[3]See the famous chapter on the "three Reverences," *Wilhelm Meister,* II, Ch. x (reverence is to be developed in children out of the inborn primitive instinct of Fear [p. 266]).

[4]The divisions of the shield in heraldry.

To which last question we must answer: Beware, O Teufelsdröckh, of spiritual pride!

CHAPTER III

PEDAGOGY

Teufelsdröckh's School. His Education. How the ever-flowing Kuhbach speaks of Time and Eternity. The Hinterschlag Gymnasium: rude Boys; and pedant Professors. The need of true Teachers, and their due recognition. Father Andreas dies; and Teufelsdröckh learns the secret of his birth: His reflections thereon. The Nameless University. Statistics of Imposture much wanted. Bitter fruits of Rationalism: Teufelsdröckh's religious difficulties. The young Englishman Herr Towgood. Modern Friendship.

Hitherto we see young Gneschen, in his indivisible case of yellow serge, borne forward mostly on the arms of kind Nature alone; seated, indeed, and much to his mind, in the terrestrial workshop, but (except his soft hazel eyes, which we doubt not already gleamed with a still intelligence) called upon for little voluntary movement there. Hitherto, accordingly, his aspect is rather generic, that of an incipient Philosopher and Poet in the abstract; perhaps it would puzzle Herr Heuschrecke himself to say wherein the special Doctrine of Clothes is as yet foreshadowed or betokened. For with Gneschen, as with others, the Man may indeed stand pictured in the Boy (at least all the pigments are there); yet only some half of the Man stands in the Child, or young Boy, namely, his Passive endowment, not his Active. The more impatient are we to discover what figure he cuts in this latter capacity; how, when, to use his own words, 'he understands the tools a little, and can handle this or that,' he will proceed to handle it.

Here, however, may be the place to state that, in much of our Philosopher's history, there is something of an almost

Hindoo character:[1] nay perhaps in that so well-fostered and every-way excellent 'Passivity' of his, which, with no free development of the antagonist Activity, distinguished his childhood, we may detect the rudiments of much that, in after days, and still in these present days, astonishes the world. For the shallow-sighted, Teufelsdröckh is oftenest a man without Activity of any kind, a No-man; for the deep-sighted, again, a man with Activity almost superabundant, yet so spiritual, close-hidden, enigmatic, that no mortal can foresee its explosions, or even when it has exploded, so much as ascertain its significance. A dangerous, difficult temper for the modern European; above all, disadvantageous in the hero of a Biography! Now as heretofore it will behove the Editor of these pages, were it never so unsuccessfully, to do his endeavour.

Among the earliest tools of any complicacy which a man, especially a man of letters, gets to handle, are his Class-books. On this portion of his History, Teufelsdröckh looks down professedly as indifferent. Reading he 'cannot remember ever to have learned';[2] so perhaps had it by nature.[3] He says generally: 'Of the insignificant portion of my Education, which depended on Schools, there need almost no notice be taken. I learned what others learn; and kept it stored-by in a corner of my head, seeing as yet no manner of use in it. My Schoolmaster,[4] a downbent, brokenhearted, underfoot martyr, as others of that guild are, did little for me, except discover that he could do little: he, good soul, pronounced me a genius, fit for the learned professions; and that I must be sent to the Gymnasium,[5] and one day to the University. Meanwhile, what printed thing soever I could meet with I read. My very

---

[1]A possible allusion to Hindu habits of patience, spiritual contemplation, receptivity, *etc.*

[2]An autobiographical fact (see *C.E.L.*, I, Ch. ii.)

[3]*Cf. Much Ado about Nothing,* III, iii, 14–16.

[4]Carlyle's early teacher was William Gullen. (Wilson, *Carlyle till Marriage,* p. 24.)

[5]Grammar school (so named in Germany); in Scotland, the Academy.

copper pocket-money I laid-out on stall-literature;[1] which, as it accumulated, I with my own hands sewed into volumes. By this means was the young head furnished with a considerable miscellany of things and shadows of things: History in authentic fragments lay mingled with Fabulous chimeras,[2] wherein also was reality; and the whole not as dead stuff, but as living pabulum, tolerably nutritive for a mind as yet so peptic.'

That the Entepfuhl Schoolmaster judged well, we now know. Indeed, already in the youthful Gneschen, with all his outward stillness, there may have been manifest an inward vivacity that promised much; symptoms of a spirit singularly open, thoughtful, almost poetical. Thus, to say nothing of his Suppers on the Orchard-wall, and other phenomena of that earlier period, have many readers of these pages stumbled, in their twelfth year, on such reflections as the following? 'It struck me much, as I sat by the Kuhbach, one silent noontide, and watched it flowing, gurgling, to think how this same streamlet had flowed and gurgled, through all changes of weather and of fortune, from beyond the earliest date of History. Yes, probably on the morning when Joshua forded Jordan;[3] even as at the mid-day when Cæsar, doubtless with difficulty, swam the Nile, yet kept his *Commentaries* dry,[4]—this little Kuhbach, assiduous as Tiber,[5] Eurotas[6] or Siloa,[7] was murmuring on across the wilderness, as yet unnamed, unseen: here, too, as in the Euphrates and the Ganges, is a vein or veinlet of the grand World-circulation of Waters, which, with its atmospheric arteries, has lasted and lasts simply with the World. Thou fool! Nature alone is antique, and

---

[1]Periodicals and pamphlets sold at a bookseller's "stall" or bench.

[2]Such as that described in the *Iliad*, Bk. vi.

[3]Joshua, iii, 14–17.

[4]Related in Plutarch's *Lives*.

[5]A river in Italy, on the banks of which stood Rome.

[6]The chief river in Laconia (in ancient Greece), on which Sparta stood.

[7]Or Siloam. A river and pool near Jerusalem. (*Cf.* Isaiah, viii, 6; John, ix, 7; *Paradise Lost*, i, 11.)

the oldest art a mushroom; that idle crag thou sittest on is six-thousand years of age.'[1] In which little thought, as in a little fountain, may there not lie the beginning of those well-nigh unutterable meditations on the grandeur and mystery of TIME, and its relation to ETERNITY, which play such a part in this Philosophy of Clothes?

Over his Gymnasic and Academic years the Professor by no means lingers so lyrical and joyful as over his childhood. Green sunny tracts there are still; but intersected by bitter rivulets of tears, here and there stagnating into sour marshes of discontent. 'With my first view of the Hinterschlag[2] Gymnasium,' writes he, 'my evil days began. Well do I still remember the red sunny Whitsuntide morning, when, trotting full of hope by the side of Father Andreas, I entered the main street of the place, and saw its steeple-clock (then striking Eight) and *Schuldthurm* (Jail), and the aproned or disaproned Burghers moving-in to breakfast: a little dog, in mad terror, was rushing past; for some human imps had tied a tin-kettle to its tail; thus did the agonised creature, loud-jingling, career through the whole length of the Borough, and become notable enough. Fit emblem of many a Conquering Hero, to whom Fate (wedding Fantasy to Sense, as it often elsewhere does) has malignantly appended a tin-kettle of Ambition, to chase him on; which the faster he runs, urges him the faster, the more loudly and more foolishly! Fit emblem also of much that awaited myself, in that mischievous Den; as in the World, whereof it was a portion and epitome!

'Alas, the kind beech-rows of Entepfuhl were hidden in the distance: I was among strangers, harshly, at best indifferently, disposed towards me; the young heart felt, for the first time, quite orphaned and alone.' His schoolfellows, as is usual, persecuted him: 'They were Boys,' he says, 'mostly rude Boys, and obeyed the impulse of rude Nature, which bids the deer-herd fall upon any stricken hart, the duck-flock put to death

---

[1]Biblical chronology dated the creation at 4004 B.C.

[2]"Smite-behind." (*Cf. Reminiscences,* pp. 29–30).

any broken-winged brother or sister, and on all hands the strong tyrannise over the weak.' He admits that though 'perhaps in an unusual degree morally courageous,' he succeeded ill in battle, and would fain have avoided it; a result, as would appear, owing less to his small personal stature (for in passionate seasons he was 'incredibly nimble'), than to his 'virtuous principles': 'if it was disgraceful to be beaten,' says he, 'it was only a shade less disgraceful to have so much as fought; thus was I drawn two ways at once, and in this important element of school-history, the war-element, had little but sorrow.' On the whole, that same excellent 'Passivity,' so notable in Teufelsdröckh's childhood, is here visibly enough again getting nourishment. 'He wept often; indeed to such a degree that he was nicknamed *Der Weinende* (the Tearful),[1] which epithet, till towards his thirteenth year, was indeed not quite unmerited. Only at rare intervals did the young soul burst-forth into fire-eyed rage, and, with a stormfulness (*Ungestüm*) under which the boldest quailed, assert that he too had Rights of Man, or at least of Mankin.' In all which, who does not discern a fine flower-tree and cinnamon-tree (of genius) nigh choked among pumpkins, reed-grass and ignoble shrubs; and forced if it would live, to struggle upwards only, and not outwards; into a *height* quite sickly, and disproportioned to its *breadth?*

We find, moreover, that his Greek and Latin were 'mechanically' taught; Hebrew scarce even mechanically; much else which they called History, Cosmography, Philosophy, and so forth, no better than not at all. So that, except inasmuch as Nature was still busy; and he himself 'went about, as was of old his wont, among the Craftsmen's workshops, there learning many things';[2] and farther lighted on some small store of curious reading, in Hans Wachtel the Cooper's house, where he lodged,—his time, it would appear, was utterly wasted. Which facts the Professor has not yet learned to look upon

---

[1]Autobiographical fact. (*C.E.L.*, I, Ch. ii; Nichol, *Life*, p. 18; Craig, p. 50; *Wotton Reinfred*, p. 22 ff., *etc.*).

[2]From Goethe's *Autobiography*, Bk. iv, quoted in the essay on "Goethe's Works" (*Ess.*, II, 415).

with any contentment. Indeed, throughout the whole of this Bag *Scorpio,* where we now are, and often in the following Bag, he shows himself unusually animated on the matter of Education, and not without some touch of what we might presume to be anger.

'My Teachers,' says he, 'were hide-bound Pedants, without knowledge of man's nature, or of boy's; or of aught save their lexicons and quarterly account-books. Innumerable dead Vocables (no dead Language, for they themselves knew no Language) they crammed into us, and called it fostering the growth of mind. How can an inanimate, mechanical Gerund grinder,[1] the like of whom will, in a subsequent century, be manufactured at Nürnberg[2] out of wood and leather, foster the growth of anything; much more of Mind, which grows, not like a vegetable (by having its roots littered with etymological compost), but like a spirit, by mysterious contact of Spirit; Thought kindling itself at the fire of living Thought? How shall *he* give kindling, in whose own inward man there is no live coal, but all is burnt-out to a dead grammatical cinder? The Hinterschlag Professors knew syntax enough; and of the human soul thus much: that it had a faculty called Memory, and could be acted-on through the muscular integument by appliance of birch-rods.

'Alas, so is it everywhere, so will it ever be; till the Hodman[3] is discharged, or reduced to hodbearing; and an Architect is hired, and on all hands fitly encouraged: till communities and individuals discover, not without surprise, that fashioning the souls of a generation by Knowledge can rank on a level with blowing their bodies to pieces by Gunpowder; that with Generals and Fieldmarshals for killing, there should be world-

---

[1]Satirical Carlylese for pedantic grammarian. From *Tristram Shandy,* Vol. V, Ch. xxxii.

[2]Allusion to Pope, *Martinus Scriblerus,* Ch. xii, paraphrased in essay on Richter, prefaced to "Quintus Fixlein" (*German Romance,* II, 124) in describing Richter's failure to delineate exalted heroes. (B.)

[3]*Hodman:* an expression from Fichte ("State of German Literature," *Ess.,* I, 58–61); Fichte's *On the Nature of the Scholar,* transl. William Smith, London, 1873, p. 141.

honoured Dignitaries, and were it possible, true God-ordained Priests, for teaching. But as yet, though the Soldier wears openly, and even parades, his butchering-tool, nowhere, far as I have travelled, did the Schoolmaster make show of his instructing-tool: nay, were he to walk abroad with birch girt on thigh, as if he therefrom expected honour, would there not, among the idler class, perhaps a certain levity be excited?'

In the third year of this Gymnasic period, Father Andreas seems to have died: the young Scholar, otherwise so maltreated, saw himself for the first time clad outwardly in sables, and inwardly in quite inexpressible melancholy. 'The dark bottomless Aybss,[1] that lies under our feet, had yawned open; the pale kingdoms of Death,[2] with all their innumerable silent nations and generations, stood before him; the inexorable word, NEVER! now first showed its meaning. My Mother wept, and her sorrow got vent; but in my heart there lay a whole lake of tears, pent-up in silent desolation. Nevertheless the unworn Spirit is strong; Life is so healthful that it even finds nourishment in Death: these stern experiences, planted down by Memory in my Imagination, rose there to a whole cypress-forest, sad but beautiful; waving, with not unmelodious sighs, in dark luxuriance, in the hottest sunshine, through long years of youth:—as in manhood also it does, and will do; for I have now pitched my tent under a Cypress-tree; the Tomb is now my inexpugnable Fortress, ever close by the gate of which I look upon the hostile armaments, and pains and penalties of tyrannous Life placidly enough, and listen to its loudest threatenings with a still smile. O ye loved ones, that already sleep in the noiseless Bed of Rest, whom in life I could only weep for and never help; and ye, who wide-scattered still toil lonely in the monster-bearing Desert, dyeing the flinty ground with your blood,—yet a little while, and we shall all meet THERE, and our Mother's bosom will screen us all; and Oppression's harness, and Sorrow's fire-whip, and all

---

[1] *Cf. Paradise Lost,* ii, 405.

[2] *Cf.* Virgil, *Aeneid,* vi, 269 ff.

the Gehenna[1] Bailiffs that patrol and inhabit ever-vexed Time, cannot thenceforth harm us any more!'

Close by which rather beautiful apostrophe, lies a laboured Character[2] of the deceased Andreas Futteral; of his natural ability, his deserts in life (as Prussian Sergeant); with long historical inquiries into the genealogy of the Futteral Family, here traced back as far as Henry the Fowler:[3] the whole of which we pass over, not without astonishment. It only concerns us to add, that now was the time when Mother Gretchen revealed to her foster-son that he was not at all of this kindred; or indeed of any kindred, having come into historical existence in the way already known to us. 'Thus was I doubly orphaned,' says he; 'bereft not only of Possession, but even of Remembrance. Sorrow and Wonder, here suddenly united, could not but produce abundant fruit. Such a disclosure, in such a season, struck its roots through my whole nature: ever till the years of mature manhood, it mingled with my whole thoughts, was as the stem whereon all my day-dreams and night-dreams grew. A certain poetic elevation, yet also a corresponding civic depression, it naturally imparted: *I was like no other;*[4] in which fixed-idea, leading sometimes to highest, and oftener to frightfullest results, may there not lie the first spring of tendencies, which in my Life have become remarkable enough? As in birth, so in action, speculation, and social position, my fellows are perhaps not numerous.'

In the Bag *Sagittarius,* as we at length discover, Teufelsdröckh has become a University man; though how, when, or of what quality, will nowhere disclose itself with the smallest

---

[1]The valley of Hinnom, near Jerusalem, where some of the Israelites sacrificed their children to Moloch (Jeremiah, vii, 31); afterwards a place of abomination and refuse, where perpetual fires were kept burning to prevent pestilence; hence, later, Hell (*cf. Paradise Lost,* i, 405). Here, with *Bailiffs:* hell-sorrows or torments. (B.)

[2]A character-sketch.

[3]Henry I (876?–936), Emperor of Germany (919–36).

[4]One of the marks of the contemporary romantic hero. *Cf.* Karl von Moor in Schiller's *The Robbers* (Carlyle's *Life of Schiller,* pp. 14–16.)

certainty. Few things, in the way of confusion and capricious indistinctness, can now surprise our readers; not even the total want of dates, almost without parallel in a Biographical work. So enigmatic, so chaotic we have always found, and must always look to find, these scattered Leaves. In *Sagittarius,* however, Teufelsdröckh begins to show himself even more than usually Sibylline:[1] fragments of all sorts; scraps of regular Memoir, College-Exercises, Programs, Professional Testimoniums, Milkscores, torn Billets, sometimes to appearance of an amatory cast; all blown together as if by merest chance, henceforth bewilder the sane Historian. To combine any picture of these University, and the subsequent, years; much more, to decipher therein any illustrative primordial elements of the Clothes-Philosophy, becomes such a problem as the reader may imagine.

So much we can see; darkly, as through the foliage of some wavering thicket: a youth of no common endowment, who has passed happily through Childhood, less happily yet still vigorously through Boyhood, now at length perfect in 'dead vocables,' and set down, as he hopes, by the living Fountain, there to superadd Ideas and Capabilities. From such Fountain he draws, diligently, thirstily, yet never or seldom with his whole heart, for the water nowise suits his palate; discouragements, entanglements, aberrations are discoverable or supposable. Nor perhaps are even pecuniary distresses wanting; for 'the good Gretchen, who in spite of advices from not disinterested relatives has sent him hither, must after a time withdraw her willing but too feeble hand.' Nevertheless in an atmosphere of Poverty and manifold Chagrin, the Humour of that young Soul, what character is in him, first decisively reveals itself; and, like strong sunshine in weeping skies, gives out variety of colours, some of which are prismatic. Thus, with the aid of Time and of what Time brings, has the stripling Diogenes Teufelsdröckh waxed into manly stature; and into so questionable an aspect,[2] that we ask with new

[1]See p. 77, *note* 3.

[2]*Hamlet,* I, iv, 43: "Thou com'st in such a questionable shape."

eagerness, How he specially came by it, and regret anew that there is no more explicit answer. Certain of the intelligible and partially significant fragments, which are few in number, shall be extracted from that Limbo[1] of a Paper-bag, and presented with the usual preparation.

As if, in the Bag *Scorpio,* Teufelsdröckh had not already expectorated his antipedagogic spleen; as if, from the name *Sagittarius,* he had thought himself called upon to shoot arrows, we here again fall-in with such matter as this: 'The University where I was educated still stands vivid enough in my remembrance,[2] and I know its name well; which name, however, I, from tenderness to existing interests and persons, shall in nowise divulge. It is my painful duty to say that, out of England and Spain, ours was the worst of all hitherto discovered Universities. This is indeed a time when right Education is, as nearly as may be, impossible: however, in degrees of wrongness there is no limit: nay, I can conceive a worse system than that of the Nameless itself; as poisoned victual may be worse than absolute hunger.

'It is written, When the blind lead the blind, both shall fall into the ditch:[3] wherefore, in such circumstances, may it not sometimes be safer, if both leader and led simply—sit still? Had you, anywhere in Crim Tartary,[4] walled-in a square enclosure; furnished it with a small, ill-chosen Library; and then turned loose into it eleven-hundred Christian striplings, to tumble about as they listed, from three to seven years: certain persons, under the title of Professors, being stationed at the gates, to declare aloud that it was a University, and exact considerable admission-fees,—you had, not indeed in mechanical structure, yet in spirit and result, some

---

[1]See p. 52, *note* 1.

[2]Carlyle attended Edinburgh University, 1809–13, and had much the same experience as Teufelsdröckh's. (See Masson's *Edinburgh Sketches,* pp. 226–44). See, however, Carlyle's Rectorial Address (*Ess.,* IV, 449 ff.), and *Reminiscences,* p. 84, *n,* for his later love of his *alma mater.*

[3]Matthew, xv, 14.

[4]That part of the Crimea which, in the Middle Ages, was inhabited by the Tartars.

imperfect resemblance of our High Seminary. I say, imperfect; for if our mechanical structure was quite other, so neither was our result altogether the same: unhappily, we were not in Crim Tartary, but in a corrupt European city, full of smoke and sin; moreover, in the middle of a Public, which, without far costlier apparatus than that of the Square Enclosure, and Declaration aloud, you could not be sure of gulling.

'Gullible, however, by fit apparatus, all Publics are; and gulled, with the most surprising profit. Towards anything like a *Statistics of Imposture,* indeed, little as yet has been done: with a strange indifference, our Economists, nigh buried under Tables for minor Branches of Industry, have altogether overlooked the grand all-overtopping Hypocrisy Branch; as if our whole arts of Puffery,[1] of Quackery, Priestcraft, Kingcraft, and the innumerable other crafts and mysteries of that genus, had not ranked in Productive Industry at all! Can any one, for example, so much as say, What moneys, in Literature and Shoeblacking, are realised by actual instruction and actual jet Polish; what by fictitious-persuasive Proclamation of such; specifying, in distinct items, the distributions, circulations, disbursements, incomings of said moneys, with the smallest approach to accuracy? But to ask, How far, in all the several infinitely-complected departments of social business, in government, education, in manual, commercial, intellectual fabrication of every sort, man's Want is supplied by true Ware; how far by the mere Appearance of true Ware:—in other words, To what extent, by what methods, with what effects, in various times and countries, Deception takes the place and wages of Performance: here truly is an Inquiry big with results for the future time, but to which hitherto only the vaguest answer can be given. If for the present, in our Europe, we estimate the ratio of Ware to Appearance of Ware so high even as at One to a Hundred (which, considering the Wages of a Pope, Russian Autocrat, or English Game-Preserver,[2] is

[1]See p. 14, *note* 3.

[2]See p. 94, *note* 1.

probably not far from the mark),—what almost prodigious saving may there not be anticipated, as the *Statistics of Imposture* advances, and so the manufacturing of Shams (that of Realities rising into clearer and clearer distinction therefrom) gradually declines, and at length becomes all but wholly unnecessary!

'This for the coming golden ages. What I had to remark, for the present brazen one, is, that in several provinces, as in Education, Polity, Religion, where so much is wanted and indispensable, and so little can as yet be furnished, probably Imposture is of sanative, anodyne nature, and man's Gullibility not his worst blessing. Suppose your sinews of war quite broken; I mean your military chest insolvent, forage all but exhausted; and that the whole army is about to mutiny, disband, and cut your and each other's throat,—then were it not well could you, as if by miracle, pay them in any sort of fairy-money, feed them on coagulated water, or mere imagination of meat; whereby, till the real supply came up, they might be kept together and quiet? Such perhaps was the aim of Nature, who does nothing without aim, in furnishing her favourite, Man, with this his so omnipotent or rather omnipatient Talent of being Gulled.[1]

'How beautifully it works, with a little mechanism; nay, almost makes mechanism for itself! These Professors in the Nameless lived with ease, with safety, by a mere Reputation, constructed in past times, and then too with no great effort, by quite another class of persons. Which Reputation, like a strong, brisk-going undershot wheel,[2] sunk into the general current, bade fair, with only a little annual repainting on their part, to hold long together, and of its own accord assiduously grind for them. Happy that it was so, for the Millers! They themselves needed not to work; their attempts at working, at what they called Educating, now when I look back on it, fill me with a certain mute admiration.

[1]This whole passage is in the spirit of *A Tale of a Tub* (Sect. IX) and *Hudibras* (II, iii, 1 ff.).

[2]A mill-wheel moved by water passing beneath.

'Besides all this, we boasted ourselves a Rational University; in the highest degree hostile to Mysticism; thus was the young vacant mind furnished with much talk about Progress of the Species, Dark Ages, Prejudice,[1] and the like; so that all were quickly enough blown out into a state of windy argumentativeness; whereby the better sort had soon to end in sick, impotent Scepticism; the worser sort explode (*crepiren*) in finished Self-conceit, and to all spiritual intents become dead.—But this too is portion of mankind's lot. If our era is the Era of Unbelief, why murmur under it; is there not a better coming, nay come? As in long-drawn systole and long-drawn diastole,[2] must the period of Faith alternate with the period of Denial;[3] must the vernal growth, the summer luxuriance of all Opinions, Spiritual Representations and Creations, be followed by, and again follow, the autumnal decay, the winter dissolution. For man lives in Time, has his whole earthly being, endeavour and destiny shaped for him by Time: only in the transitory Time-Symbol is the ever-motionless Eternity we stand on made manifest.[4] And yet, in such winter-seasons of Denial, it is for the nobler-minded perhaps a comparative misery to have been born, and to be awake and work; and for the duller a felicity, if, like hibernating animals, safe-lodged in some Salamanca University,[5] or Sybaris City,[6] or other superstitious or voluptuous Castle

[1]Popular watchwords of the day.

[2]*Systole . . . diastole:* contraction and dilation, as of the heart.

[3]The alternation of ages of faith and of doubt was a theory proposed by Goethe (see p. 19, *note* 1), which, with Carlyle, became a part of the "Phoenix doctrine" (see Book III, Chapter v.)

[4]Compare with p. 87, *note* 2. Here, time is considered as the revelation of Eternity, a Fichtean conception (*Characteristics of the Present Age,* pp. 4, 11) which Carlyle united with Goethe's "time is my seed-field" to express the idea that we embody, or "clothe," eternal values or truths when we labour creatively in our space-time world.

[5]A school of theology and law, founded about 1230, famous throughout Europe during the fifteenth and sixteenth centuries. Salamanca was known as the "little Rome" of Spain.

[6]A celebrated Greek town in Lucania (southern Italy), founded B.C. 720, and mentioned in Herodotus and Aristotle as famed for its wealth and luxury.

of Indolence,[1] they can slumber-through in stupid dreams, and only awaken when the loud-roaring hailstorms have all done their work, and to our prayers and martyrdoms the new Spring has been vouchsafed.'

That in the environment, here mysteriously enough shadowed forth, Teufelsdröckh must have felt ill at ease, cannot be doubtful. 'The hungry young,' he says, 'looked up to their spiritual Nurses; and, for food, were bidden eat the east-wind.[2] What vain jargon of controversial Metaphysic, Etymology, and mechanical Manipulation falsely named Science, was current there, I indeed learned, better perhaps than the most. Among eleven-hundred Christian youths, there will not be wanting some eleven eager to learn. By collision with such, a certain warmth, a certain polish was communicated; by instinct and happy accident, I took less to rioting (*renommiren*), than to thinking and reading, which latter also I was free to do. Nay from the chaos of that Library, I succeeded in fishing-up more books perhaps than had been known to the very keepers thereof. The foundation of a Literary Life was hereby laid. I learned, on my own strength, to read fluently in almost all cultivated languages, on almost all subjects and sciences; farther, as man is ever the prime object to man, already it was my favourite employment to read character in speculation, and from the Writing to construe the Writer. A certain groundplan of Human Nature and Life began to fashion itself in me; wondrous enough, now when I look back on it; for my whole Universe, physical and spiritual, was as yet a Machine! However, such a conscious, recognised groundplan, the truest I had, *was* beginning to be there, and by additional experiments might be corrected and indefinitely extended.'

Thus from poverty does the strong educe nobler wealth; thus in the destitution of the wild desert does our young

---

[1]*Castle of Indolence:* the title of a poem by James Thomson (1700–1748).

[2]*Cf.* Milton, *Lycidas,* 125 ff.; Job, xv, 2.

Ishmael[1] acquire for himself the highest of all possessions, that of Self-help. Nevertheless a desert this was, waste, and howling with savage monsters. Teufelsdröckh gives us long details of his 'fever-paroxysms of Doubt';[2] his Inquiries concerning Miracles, and the Evidences of religious Faith; and how 'in the silent night-watches, still darker in his heart than over sky and earth, he has cast himself before the All-seeing, and with audible prayers cried vehemently for Light, for deliverance from Death and the Grave. Not till after long years, and unspeakable agonies, did the believing heart surrender; sink into spell-bound sleep, under the nightmare Unbelief;[3] and, in this hag-ridden dream, mistake God's fair living world for a pallid, vacant Hades and extinct Pandemonium.[4] But through such Purgatory pain,' continues he, 'it is appointed us to pass; first must the dead Letter of Religion own itself dead, and drop piecemeal into dust, if the living Spirit of Religion, freed from this its charnel-house,[5] is to arise on us, newborn of Heaven, and with new healing under its wings.'[6]

To which Purgatory pains, seemingly severe enough, if we add a liberal measure of Earthly distresses, want of practical guidance, want of sympathy, want of money, want of hope; and all this in the fervid season of youth, so exaggerated in imagining, so boundless in desires, yet here so poor in means, —do we not see a strong incipient spirit oppressed and overloaded from without and from within; the fire of genius struggling-up among fuel-wood of the greenest, and as yet with more of bitter vapour than of clear flame?

From various fragments of Letters and other documentary

---

[1]*Cf.* Genesis, xvi, 1–16; xxi, 12–21.

[2]After Schiller, in the "Philosophical Letters" (*Werke,* IX, 112): "Skepticism and Free-thinking are but the fever-paroxysms of the human spirit. . . ."

[3]See Int., Sect. V, c.

[4]See p. 70, *note* 3.

[5]A house or vault, where dead bodies, or the bones of the dead, are deposited. An expression frequent in Richter.

[6]*Cf.* Malachi, iv, 2.

scraps, it is to be inferred that Teufelsdröckh, isolated, shy, retiring as he was, had not altogether escaped notice: certain established men are aware of his existence;[1] and, if stretching-out no helpful hand, have at least their eyes on him. He appears, though in dreary enough humour, to be addressing himself to the Profession of Law;[2]—whereof, indeed, the world has since seen him, a public graduate. But omitting these broken, unsatisfactory thrums of Economical relation, let us present rather the following small thread of Moral relation; and therewith, the reader for himself weaving it in at the right place, conclude our dim arras-picture of these University years.

'Here also it was that I formed acquaintance with Herr Towgood,[3] or, as it is perhaps better written, Herr Toughgut; a young person of quality (*von Adel*), from the interior parts of England. He stood connected, by blood and hospitality, with the Counts von Zähdarm,[4] in this quarter of Germany; to which noble Family I likewise was, by his means, with all friendliness, brought near. Towgood had a fair talent, unspeakably ill-cultivated; with considerable humour of character: and, bating his total ignorance, for he knew nothing except Boxing and a little Grammar, showed less of that aristocratic impassivity, and silent fury, than for most part belongs to Travellers of his nation. To him I owe my first practical knowledge of the English and their ways; perhaps also something of the partiality with which I have ever since regarded that singular people. Towgood was not without an eye, could he have come at any light. Invited doubtless by the presence of the Zähdarm Family, he had travelled hither, in the almost

[1]In the dark years of Carlyle's apprenticeship (1816–21), he gradually won the attention of Professor John Leslie of Edinburgh University, Dr. (afterwards Sir) David Brewster, and Edward Irving, rising young schoolmaster at Kirkaldy. (Wilson, *Carlyle till Marriage.*)

[2]On Carlyle and the law, see Wilson, *Carlyle till Marriage,* p. 179.

[3]The original of Herr Towgood is supposed to be Charles Buller (1806–48), whose tutor was Carlyle, and who became a member of Parliament (1830).

[4]*Zähdarm:* German for "Tough-gut."

frantic hope of perfecting his studies; he, whose studies had as yet been those of infancy, hither to a University where so much as the notion of perfection, not to say the effort after it, no longer existed! Often we would condole over the hard destiny of the Young in this era: how, after all our toil, we were to be turned-out into the world, with beards on our chins indeed, but with few other attributes of manhood; no existing thing that we were trained to Act on, nothing that we could so much as Believe. "How has our head on the outside a polished Hat," would Towgood exclaim, "and in the inside Vacancy, or a froth of Vocables and Attorney-Logic! At a small cost men are educated to make leather into shoes; but at a great cost, what am I educated to make? By Heaven, Brother! what I have already eaten and worn, as I came thus far, would endow a considerable Hospital of Incurables."—"Man, indeed," I would answer, "has a Digestive Faculty, which must be kept working, were it even partly by stealth. But as for our Miseducation, make not bad worse; waste not the time yet ours, in trampling on thistles because they have yielded us no figs.[1] *Frisch zu, Bruder!*[2] Here are Books, and we have brains to read them; here is a whole Earth and a whole Heaven, and we have eyes to look on them: *Frisch zu!*"

'Often also our talk was gay; not without brilliancy, and even fire. We looked-out on Life, with its strange scaffolding, where all at once harlequins dance, and men are beheaded and quartered: motley, not unterrific was the aspect; but we looked on it like brave youths. For myself, these were perhaps my most genial hours. Towards this young warmhearted, strongheaded and wrongheaded Herr Towgood I was even near experiencing the now obsolete sentiment of Friendship. Yes, foolish Heathen that I was, I felt that, under certain conditions, I could have loved this man, and taken him to my bosom, and been his brother once and always. By degrees, however, I understood the new time, and its wants. If man's

---

[1] *Cf.* Matthew, vii, 16.

[2] "Quickly to work, Brother!"

Soul is indeed, as in the Finnish Language,[1] and Utilitarian Philosophy,[2] a kind of *Stomach,* what else is the true meaning of Spiritual Union but an Eating together? Thus we, instead of Friends, are Dinner-guests; and here as elsewhere have cast away chimeras.'

So ends, abruptly as is usual, and enigmatically, this little incipient romance. What henceforth becomes of the brave Herr Towgood, or Toughgut? He has dived-under, in the Autobiographical Chaos, and swims we see not where. Does any reader 'in the interior parts of England' know of such a man?

CHAPTER IV

GETTING UNDER WAY

The grand thaumaturgic Art of Thought. Difficulty in fitting Capability to Opportunity, or of getting under way. The advantage of Hunger and Bread-Studies. Teufelsdröckh has to enact the stern monodrama of *No object and no rest.* Sufferings as Auscultator. Given up as a man of genius. Zähdarm House. Intolerable presumption of young men. Irony and its consequences. Teufelsdröckh's Epitaph on Count Zähdarm.

'THUS nevertheless,' writes our Autobiographer, apparently as quitting College, 'was there realised Somewhat; namely, I, Diogenes Teufelsdröckh: a visible Temporary Figure (*Zeitbild*), occupying some cubic feet of Space, and

[1]Barrett: "A Finnish scholar informs me that there is nothing in the Finnish language to support Carlyle's allusion."

[2]Identified especially with the names of Jeremy Bentham (1748–1832), James Mill (1773–1836), and John Stuart Mill (1806–73). "The creed which accepts as the foundation of morals, Utility, or the Greatest Happiness Principle . . . By happiness is intended pleasure and the absence of pain . . ." for the greatest number. (J. S. Mill, *Utilitarianism,* 1863, Ch. ii.) The word "Utilitarian" was adopted by J. S. Mill in 1823 from Galt's *Annals of the Parish* (1821), after being first suggested by Bentham. (See Mill's *Autobiography,* London, 1873, Ch. iii. pp. 79–80.)

containing within it Forces both physical and spiritual; hopes, passions, thoughts; the whole wondrous furniture, in more or less perfection, belonging to that mystery, a Man. Capabilities there were in me to give battle, in some small degree, against the great Empire of Darkness: does not the very Ditcher and Delver, with his spade, extinguish many a thistle and puddle; and so leave a little Order, where he found the opposite? Nay your very Daymoth has capabilities in this kind; and ever organises something (into its own Body, if no otherwise), which was before Inorganic; and of mute dead air makes living music, though only of the faintest, by humming.

'How much more, one whose capabilities are spiritual; who has learned, or begun learning, the grand thaumaturgic art of Thought! Thaumaturgic[1] I name it; for hitherto all Miracles have been wrought thereby, and henceforth innumerable will be wrought; whereof we, even in these days, witness some. Of the Poet's and Prophet's inspired Message, and how it makes and unmakes whole worlds, I shall forbear mention: but cannot the dullest hear Steam-Engines clanking around him? Has he not seen the Scottish Brassmith's[2] IDEA (and this but a mechanical one) travelling on fire-wings round the Cape, and across two Oceans; and stronger than any other Enchanter's Familiar, on all hands unweariedly fetching and carrying: at home, not only weaving Cloth; but rapidly enough overturning the whole old system of Society; and, for Feudalism and Preservation of the Game, preparing us, by indirect but sure methods, Industrialism and the Government of the Wisest? Truly a Thinking Man is the worst enemy the Prince of Darkness can have; every time such a one announces himself, I doubt not, there runs a shudder through the Nether Empire; and new Emissaries are trained, with new tactics, to, if possible, entrap him, and hoodwink and handcuff him.

---

[1]Wonder-working.

[2]An allusion to James Watt (1736–1819), inventor of the "Watt steam-engine" (1769), and for some years a mathematical instrument-maker in Glasgow.

'With such high vocation had I too, as denizen of the Universe, been called. Unhappy it is, however, that though born to the amplest Sovereignty, in this way, with no less than sovereign right of Peace and War against the Time-Prince (*Zeitfürst*), or Devil,[1] and all his Dominions, your coronation-ceremony costs such trouble, your sceptre is so difficult to get at, or even to get eye on!'

By which last wiredrawn similitude does Teufelsdröckh mean no more than that young men find obstacles in what we call 'getting under way'? 'Not what I Have,' continues he, 'but what I Do is my Kingdom. To each is given a certain inward Talent, a certain outward Environment of Fortune; to each, by wisest combination of these two, a certain maximum of Capability.[2] But the hardest problem were ever this first: To find by study of yourself, and of the ground you stand on, what your combined inward and outward Capability specially is. For, alas, our young soul is all budding with Capabilities, and we see not yet which is the main and true one. Always too the new man is in a new time, under new conditions; his course can be the *fac-simile* of no prior one, but is by its nature original. And then how seldom will the outward Capability fit the inward: though talented wonderfully enough, we are poor, unfriended, dyspeptical, bashful; nay what is worse than all, we are foolish. Thus, in a whole imbroglio of Capabilities, we go stupidly groping about, to grope which is ours, and often clutch the wrong one: in this mad work must several years of our small term be spent, till the purblind Youth, by practice, acquire notions of distance, and become a seeing Man. Nay, many so spend their whole term, and in ever-new expectation, ever-new disappointment, shift from enterprise to enterprise, and from side to side: till

---

[1]See p. 87, *note* 2.

[2]The Goethean doctrine of *Bildung* as found in *Wilhelm Meister, passim* (esp. I, 100, 300–01, 328–29, 386–87, *etc.*). *Bildung:* Harmonious self-development by cultivating the special, not the vague or general, capabilities which are innate in us, and by properly utilizing our immediate surroundings. The key to Carlyle's doctrine of Work. (See Susanne Howe, *Wilhelm Meister and his English Kinsmen,* N. Y., 1930.)

at length, as exasperated striplings of threescore-and-ten, they shift into their last enterprise, that of getting buried.

'Such, since the most of us are too ophthalmic, would be the general fate; were it not that one thing saves us: our Hunger. For on this ground, as the prompt nature of Hunger is well known, must a prompt choice be made: hence have we, with wise foresight, Indentures and Apprenticeships for our irrational young; whereby, in due season, the vague universality of a Man shall find himself ready-moulded into a specific Craftsman; and so thenceforth work, with much or with little waste of Capability as it may be; yet not with the worst waste, that of time. Nay even in matters spiritual, since the spiritual artist too is born blind, and does not, like certain other creatures, receive sight in nine days, but far later, sometimes never,—is it not well that there should be what we call Professions, or Bread-studies[1] (*Brodzwecke*), pre-appointed us? Here, circling like the gin-horse, for whom partial or total blindness is no evil, the Bread-artist can travel contentedly round and round, still fancying that it is forward and forward; and realise much: for himself victual; for the world an additional horse's power in the grand corn-mill or hemp-mill of Economic Society. For me too had such a leading-string been provided;[2] only that it proved a neck-halter, and had nigh throttled me, till I broke it off. Then, in the words of Ancient Pistol,[3] did the world generally become mine oyster, which I, by strength or cunning, was to open, as I would and could. Almost had I deceased (*fast wär ich umgekommen*), so obstinately did it continue shut.'

We see here, significantly foreshadowed, the spirit of much that was to befall our Autobiographer; the historical embodiment of which, as it painfully takes shape in his Life, lies

---

[1]*Bread-studies:* a term adapted from Carlyle's German sources (*Ess.*, I, 57).

[2]For Teufelsdröckh, it was Law; for Carlyle, the ministry, which he gave up in 1818, in order to study Law.

[3]*Cf. Merry Wives of Windsor.* II. ii. 2.

scattered, in dim disastrous details, through this Bag *Pisces,* and those that follow. A young man of high talent, and high though still temper, like a young mettled colt, 'breaks-off his neck-halter,' and bounds forth, from his peculiar manger, into the wide world; which, alas, he finds all rigorously fenced-in. Richest clover-fields tempt his eye; but to him they are forbidden pasture: either pining in progressive starvation, he must stand; or, in mad exasperation, must rush to and fro, leaping against sheer stone-walls, which he cannot leap over, which only lacerate and lame him; till at last, after thousand attempts and endurances, he, as if by miracle, clears his way; not indeed into luxuriant and luxurious clover, yet into a certain bosky wilderness where existence is still possible, and Freedom, though waited on by Scarcity, is not without sweetness. In a word, Teufelsdröckh having thrown-up his legal Profession, finds himself without landmark of outward guidance; whereby his previous want of decided Belief, or inward guidance, is frightfully aggravated. Necessity urges him on; Time will not stop, neither can he, a Son of Time;[1] wild passions without solacement, wild faculties without employment, ever vex and agitate him. He too must enact that stern Monodrama, *No Object and no Rest;*[2] must front its successive destinies, work through to its catastrophe, and deduce therefrom what moral he can.

Yet let us be just to him, let us admit that his 'neck-halter' sat nowise easy on him; that he was in some degree forced to break it off. If we look at the young man's civic position, in this Nameless capital, as he emerges from its Nameless University, we can discern well that it was far from enviable. His first Law-Examination he has come through triumphantly; and can even boast that the *Examen Rigorosum* need not have frightened him: but though he is hereby 'an *Auscultator*[3]

---

[1]*Son of Time:* a phrase from Goethe ("Ihr Söhne der Zeit"), *Gott, Gemüth und Welt.*

[2]*No Object and no Rest:* from Goethe's *Faust,* I, 3349: "Der Unmensch ohne Zweck und Ruh'."

[3]*Examen Rigorosum:* the third and final Law Examination in a German

of respectability,' what avails it? There is next to no employment to be had. Neither, for a youth without connexions, is the process of Expectation very hopeful in itself; nor for one of his disposition much cheered from without. 'My fellow Auscultators,' he says, 'were Auscultators: they dressed, and digested, and talked articulate words; other vitality showed they almost none. Small speculation in those eyes, that they did glare withal![1] Sense neither for the high nor for the deep, nor for aught human or divine, save only for the faintest scent of coming Preferment.' In which words, indicating a total estrangement on the part of Teufelsdröckh, may there not also lurk traces of a bitterness as from wounded vanity? Doubtless these prosaic Auscultators may have sniffed at him, with his strange ways; and tried to hate, and what was much more impossible, to despise him. Friendly communion, in any case, there could not be: already has the young Teufelsdröckh left the other young geese; and swims apart, though as yet uncertain whether he himself is cygnet[2] or gosling.

Perhaps, too, what little employment he had was performed ill, at best unpleasantly. 'Great practical method and expertness' he may brag of; but is there not also great practical pride, though deep-hidden, only the deeper-seated? So shy a man can never have been popular. We figure to ourselves, how in those days he may have played strange freaks with his independence, and so forth: do not his own words betoken as much? 'Like a very young person, I imagined it was with Work alone, and not also with Folly and Sin, in myself and others, that I had been appointed to struggle.' Be this as it may, his progress from the passive Auscultatorship, towards any active Assessorship,[3] is evi-

---

University.—*Auscultator:* a young lawyer who has passed his first examination and practices in the lower courts; a lawyer's assistant. (Both terms are used in *German Romance,* II, 6, 7, 229, *etc.; Ess.,* II, 419.)

[1] *Cf. Macbeth,* III, iv, 95.

[2] Young swan.

[3] Assistant judgeship.

dently of the slowest. By degrees, those same established men, once partially inclined to patronise him, seem to withdraw their countenance, and give him up as 'a man of genius': against which procedure he, in these Papers, loudly protests. 'As if,' says he, 'the higher did not presuppose the lower; as if he who can fly into heaven, could not also walk post if he resolved on it! But the world is an old woman, and mistakes any gilt farthing for a gold coin; whereby being often cheated, she will thenceforth trust nothing but the common copper.'

How our winged sky-messenger, unaccepted as a terrestrial runner, contrived, in the mean while, to keep himself from flying skyward without return, is not too clear from these Documents. Good old Gretchen seems to have vanished from the scene, perhaps from the Earth; other Horn of Plenty, or even of Parsimony, nowhere flows for him; so that 'the prompt nature of Hunger being well known,' we are not without our anxiety. From private Tuition,[1] in never so many languages and sciences, the aid derivable is small; neither, to use his own words, 'does the young Adventurer hitherto suspect in himself any literary gift; but at best earns bread-and-water wages, by his wide faculty of Translation.[2] Nevertheless,' continues he, 'that I subsisted is clear, for you find me even now alive.' Which fact, however, except upon the principle of our true-hearted, kind old Proverb, that 'there is always life for a living one,'[3] we must profess ourselves unable to explain.

Certain Landlords' Bills, and other economic Documents, bearing the mark of Settlement, indicate that he was not without money; but, like an independent Hearth-holder, if not House-holder, paid his way. Here also occur, among

[1]Carlyle was a private tutor at various times from 1818 to 1824.

[2]Carlyle's translations: Berzelius's *Chemistry* (1819); Moh's *Crystallography and Mineralogy* (1820); Legendre's *Geometry* (1824); *Wilhelm Meisters Lehrjahre* (1824); *German Romance* (stories from Musaeus, de la Motte Fouque, Tieck, Hoffmann, Richter; and Goethe's *Wilhelm Meisters Wanderjahre*) (1827).

[3]*Cf. Wilhelm Meister,* II, 215: "Life belongs to the living."

many others, two little mutilated Notes, which perhaps throw light on his condition. The first has now no date, or writer's name, but a huge Blot; and runs to this effect: 'The (*Inkblot*),[1] tied-down by previous promise, cannot, except by best wishes, forward the Herr Teufelsdröckh's views on the Assessorship in question; and sees himself under the cruel necessity of forbearing, for the present, what were otherwise his duty and joy, to assist in opening the career for a man of genius, on whom far higher triumphs are yet waiting.' The other is on gilt paper; and interests us like a sort of epistolary mummy now dead, yet which once lived and beneficently worked. We give it in the original: *'Herr Teufelsdröckh wird von der Frau Gräfinn, auf Donnerstag, zum* AESTHETISCHEN THEE *schönstens eingeladen.'*[2]

Thus, in answer to a cry for solid pudding,[3] whereof there is the most urgent need, comes, epigrammatically enough, the invitation to a wash of quite fluid *Æsthetic Tea!* How Teufelsdröckh, now at actual handgrips with Destiny herself, may have comported himself among these Musical and Literary Dilettanti of both sexes, like a hungry lion invited to a feast of chickenweed, we can only conjecture. Perhaps in expressive silence, and abstinence: otherwise if the lion, in such case, is to feast at all, it cannot be on the chickenweed, but only on the chickens. For the rest, as this Frau Gräfinn dates from the *Zähdarm House,* she can be no other than the Countess and mistress of the same; whose intellectual tendencies, and good-will to Teufelsdröckh, whether on the footing of Herr Towgood, or on his own footing, are hereby manifest. That some sort of relation, indeed, continued, for a time, to connect our Autobiographer, though perhaps feebly enough, with this noble House, we have elsewhere express evidence. Doubtless, if he expected patronage, it

---

[1]This may refer vaguely to Carlyle's non-appointment to the chair of Moral Philosophy in St. Andrews University, 1828 (B.).

[2]"The Countess cordially invites Herr Teufelsdröckh to aesthetic tea on Thursday." (Dilettante tea-party.)

[3]*Cf.* Pope, *Dunciad,* I, 54.

was in vain; enough for him if he here obtained occasional glimpses of the great world, from which we at one time fancied him to have been always excluded. 'The Zähdarms,'[1] says he, 'lived in the soft, sumptuous garniture of Aristocracy; whereto Literature and Art, attracted and attached from without, were to serve as the handsomest fringing. It was to the *Gnädigen Frau* (her Ladyship) that this latter improvement was due: assiduously she gathered, dextrously she fitted-on, what fringing was to be had; lace or cobweb, as the place yielded.' Was Teufelsdröckh also a fringe, of lace or cobweb; or promising to be such? 'With his *Excellenz* (the Count),' continues he, 'I have more than once had the honour to converse; chiefly on general affairs, and the aspect of the world, which he, though now past middle life, viewed in no unfavourable light; finding indeed, except the Outrooting of Journalism[2] (*die auszurottende Journalistik*), little to desiderate therein. On some points, as his *Excellenz* was not uncholeric, I found it more pleasant to keep silence. Besides, his occupation being that of Owning Land, there might be faculties enough, which, as superfluous for such use, were little developed in him.'

That to Teufelsdröckh the aspect of the world was nowise so faultless, and many things besides 'the Outrooting of Journalism' might have seemed improvements, we can readily conjecture. With nothing but a barren Auscultatorship from without, and so many mutinous thoughts and wishes from within, his position was no easy one. 'The Universe,' he says, 'was as a mighty Sphinx-riddle,[3] which I knew so little of, yet must rede, or be devoured. In red streaks of

[1]The originals: Judge and Mrs. Buller, parents of Charles Buller to whom Carlyle had been a tutor. Zähdarm House: the home of the Bullers, Kinnaird House, in Perthshire. The Bullers were very wealthy people, the first with whom Carlyle had come in contact (M.).

[2]A deep conviction of Fichte's (*Characteristics of the Present Age*, pp. 86–90). Carlyle shared Fichte's repugnance for popular journalism, reviewing, *etc.*

[3]See p. 54, *note* 6.

unspeakable grandeur, yet also in the blackness of darkness,[1] was Life, to my too-unfurnished Thought, unfolding itself. A strange contradiction lay in me; and I as yet knew not the solution of it; knew not that spiritual music can spring only from discords set in harmony; that but for Evil there were no Good,[2] as victory is only possible by battle.'

'I have heard affirmed (surely in jest),' observes he elsewhere, 'by not unphilanthropic persons, that it were a real increase of human happiness, could all young men from the age of nineteen be covered under barrels, or rendered otherwise invisible; and there left to follow their lawful studies and callings, till they emerged, sadder and wiser,[3] at the age of twenty-five. With which suggestion, at least as considered in the light of a practical scheme, I need scarcely say that I nowise coincide. Nevertheless it is plausibly urged that, as young ladies (*Mädchen*) are, to mankind, precisely the most delightful in those years; so young gentlemen (*Bübchen*)[4] do then attain their maximum of detestability. Such gawks (*Gecken*) are they, and foolish peacocks, and yet with such a vulturous hunger for self-indulgence; so obstinate, obstreperous, vain-glorious; in all senses, so froward and so forward. No mortal's endeavour or attainment will, in the smallest, content the as yet unendeavouring, unattaining young gentleman; but he could make it all infinitely better, were it worthy of him. Life everywhere is the most manageable matter, simple as a question in the Rule-of-Three:[5] multiply

---

[1]Jude, 13.

[2]One of the chief doctrines set forth in "Characteristics" (1831), derived largely from Goethe, as part of the doctrine of *Bildung* (development of character out of the warring opposites of choice and necessity). (See *Ess.* III, 28.) Evil as a necessary factor in attaining good is, of course, a cardinal principle in the philosophy of Browning, who in his formative years was an admirer of Carlyle.

[3]*Cf. Ancient Mariner*, 624.

[4]*Bübchen* = *"Baby-boys,"* not "young gentlemen." (Fischer) *Cf.* Goethe, *Gott, Gemüth und Welt.*

[5]Paraphrase of a passage in *Wotton Reinfred*, p. 64 ff.; *cf.* Book II, Ch. ix, "Everlasting Yea." *Cf.* similar passage in *Wilhelm Meister*, I, 306.

your second and third term together, divide the product by the first, and your quotient will be the answer,—which you are but an ass if you cannot come at. The booby has not yet found-out, by any trial, that, do what one will, there is ever a cursed fraction, oftenest a decimal repeater, and no net integer quotient so much as to be thought of.'

In which passage does not there lie an implied confession that Teufelsdröckh himself, besides his outward obstructions, had an inward, still greater, to contend with; namely, a certain temporary, youthful, yet still afflictive derangement of head? Alas, on the former side alone, his case was hard enough. 'It continues ever true,' says he, 'that Saturn, or Chronos, or what we call TIME, devours all his Children:[1] only by incessant Running, by incessant Working, may you (for some threescore-and-ten years) escape him; and you too he devours at last. Can any Sovereign, or Holy Alliance of Sovereigns,[2] bid Time stand still; even in thought, shake themselves free of Time? Our whole terrestrial being is based on Time, and built of Time; it is wholly a Movement, a Time-impulse; Time is the author of it, the material of it. Hence also our Whole Duty, which is to move, to work,—in the right direction. Are not our Bodies and our Souls in continual movement, whether we will or not; in a continual Waste, requiring a continual Repair? Utmost satisfaction of our whole outward and inward Wants were but satisfaction for a space of Time; thus, whatso we have done, is done, and for us annihilated, and ever must we go and do anew. O Time-Spirit, how hast thou environed and imprisoned us, and sunk us so deep in thy troublous dim Time-Element, that only in lucid moments can so much as glimpses of our upper Azure Home be revealed to us! Me, however, as a Son of Time, unhappier than some others, was Time threatening to

---

[1]Kronos, an early Greek divinity, dethroned his father Uranos, and then devoured his own children to escape a like fate; later identified with Saturn, Latin god of agriculture. By a confusion of his name with Chronos ("Time"), he came to be erroneously regarded as a god of Time.

[2]An allusion to the agreement among Prussia, Austria, and Russia to preserve the existing dynasties, made at Paris in September, 1815.

eat quite prematurely;[1] for, strive as I might, there was no good Running, so obstructed was the path, so gyved[2] were the feet.' That is to say, we presume, speaking in the dialect of this lower world, that Teufelsdröckh's whole duty and necessity was, like other men's, 'to work,—in the right direction,' and that no work was to be had; whereby he became wretched enough. As was natural: with haggard Scarcity threatening him in the distance; and so vehement a soul languishing in restless inaction, and forced thereby, like Sir Hudibras's sword[3] by rust,

> To eat into itself, for lack
> Of something else to hew and hack!

But on the whole, that same 'excellent Passivity,'[4] as it has all along done, is here again vigorously flourishing; in which circumstance may we not trace the beginnings of much that now characterises our Professor; and perhaps, in faint rudiments, the origin of the Clothes-Philosophy itself? Already the attitude he has assumed towards the World is too defensive; not, as would have been desirable, a bold attitude of attack. 'So far hitherto,' he says, 'as I had mingled with mankind, I was notable, if for anything, for a certain stillness of manner, which, as my friends often rebukingly declared, did but ill express the keen ardour of my feelings. I, in truth, regarded men with an excess both of love and of fear. The mystery of a Person, indeed, is ever divine to him that has a sense for the Godlike. Often, notwithstanding, was I blamed, and by half-strangers hated, for my so-called Hardness (*Härte*), my Indifferentism towards men; and the seemingly ironic tone I had adopted, as my favourite dialect in

---

[1]Note that Carlyle has now used Time in four different senses: (1) as the symbol of evil and destruction (Schlegel), (2) as the symbol, garment, or revelation of eternity (Goethe, Fichte), (3), as man's "seed-field" (opportunity), and (4) as the prison which shuts us out from the truth of Eternity. (See p. 87, *note* 2; p. 112, *note* 4; p. 119, *note* 2; p. 127, *note* 1.)

[2]*Gyved:* shackled, or fettered (archaic).

[3]*Hudibras,* I, i, 359–62.

[4]See p. 101, *note* 1.

conversation.[1] Alas, the panoply of Sarcasm was but as a buckram case, wherein I had striven to envelope myself; that so my own poor Person might live safe there, and in all friendliness, being no longer exasperated by wounds. Sarcasm I now see to be, in general, the language of the Devil; for which reason I have long since as good as renounced it. But how many individuals did I, in those days, provoke into some degree of hostility thereby! An ironic man, with his sly stillness, and ambuscading ways, more especially an ironic young man, from whom it is least expected, may be viewed as a pest to society. Have we not seen persons of weight and name coming forward, with gentlest indifference, to tread such a one out of sight, as an insignificancy and worm, start ceiling-high (*balkenhoch*), and thence fall shattered and supine, to be borne home on shutters, not without indignation, when he proved electric and a torpedo!'

Alas, how can a man with this devilishness of temper make way for himself in Life; where the first problem, as Teufelsdröckh too admits, is 'to unite yourself with some one and with somewhat (*sich anzuschliessen*)'?[2] Division, not union, is written on most part of his procedure. Let us add too that, in no great length of time, the only important connexion he had ever succeeded in forming, his connexion with the Zähdarm Family, seems to have been paralysed, for all practical uses, by the death of the 'not uncholeric' old Count. This fact stands recorded, quite incidentally, in a certain *Discourse on Epitaphs,* huddled into the present Bag, among so much else; of which Essay the learning and curious penetration are more to be approved of than the spirit. His grand principle is, that lapidary inscriptions, of what sort soever, should be Historical rather than Lyrical. 'By request of that worthy Nobleman's survivors,' says he, 'I undertook to compose his Epitaph; and not unmindful of my own rules, produced the following; which however, for an alleged defect

---

[1]The rest of the paragraph is closely autobiographical. See Masson, *Edinburgh Sketches;* Carlyle, *Reminiscences; C.E.L.* I, Ch. v, *etc.*

[2]Adapted from *Wilhelm Meister,* II, 277.

of Latinity, a defect never yet fully visible to myself, still remains unengraven';—wherein, we may predict, there is more than the Latinity that will surprise an English reader:

HIC JACET

PHILIPPUS ZAEHDARM, COGNOMINE MAGNUS,

ZAEHDARMI COMES,

EX IMPERII CONCILIO,

VELLERIS AUREI, PERISCELIDIS, NECNON VULTURIS NIGRI

EQUES.

QUI DUM SUB LUNA AGEBAT,

QUINQUIES MILLE PERDICES

PLUMBO CONFECIT:

VARII CIBI

CENTUMPONDIA MILLIES CENTENA MILLIA,

PER SE, PERQUE SERVOS QUADRUPEDES BIPEDESVE,

HAUD SINE TUMULTU DEVOLVENS,

IN STERCUS

PALAM CONVERTIT.

NUNC A LABORE REQUIESCENTEM

OPERA SEQUUNTUR.

SI MONUMENTUM QUÆRIS,

FIMETUM ADSPICE.

PRIMUM IN ORBE DEJECIT [*sub dato*]; POSTREMUM [*sub dato*].[1]

[1]"Here lies Philip Zaehdarm, surnamed the Great, Count of Zaehdarm, of the Council of the Empire, Knight of the Golden Fleece, of the Garter [*lit.* Anklet], and of the Black Vulture. Who during his sublunary existence, shot five thousand partridges: A hundred million hundredweights of foods of various kinds, through himself, and through his servants, quadrupeds or bipeds, not by any means without racket in its course, he openly converted into manure. Now resting from labour, his works follow him [Revelation, xiv, 13]. If you seek his monument, look at this heap [*cf.* the inscription to Sir Christopher Wren, the architect, in St. Paul's, (*Si monumentum requiris, circumspice*)]. Begun (*as given*); finished (*as given*)."—The epitaph is a satire on the "Corn-law, game-preserving Aristocracy." See p. 94, *note* 1.

CHAPTER V

ROMANCE

Teufelsdröckh gives up his Profession. The heavenly mystery of Love. Teufelsdröckh's feeling of worship towards women. First and only love. Blumine. Happy hearts and free tongues. The infinite nature of Fantasy. Love's joyful progress; sudden dissolution; and final catastrophe.

For long years,' writes Teufelsdröckh, 'had the poor Hebrew, in this Egypt of an Auscultatorship, painfully toiled, baking bricks without stubble,[1] before ever the question once struck him with entire force: For what?—*Beym Himmel!* For Food and Warmth! And are Food and Warmth nowhere else, in the whole wide Universe, discoverable?—Come of it what might, I resolved to try.'

Thus then are we to see him in a new independent capacity, though perhaps far from an improved one. Teufelsdröckh is now a man without Profession. Quitting the common Fleet of herring-busses and whalers,[2] where indeed his leeward, laggard condition was painful enough, he desperately steers off, on a course of his own, by sextant and compass of his own. Unhappy Teufelsdröckh! Though neither Fleet, nor Traffic nor Commodores pleased thee, still was it not *a Fleet,* sailing in prescribed track, for fixed objects; above all, in combination, wherein, by mutual guidance, by all manner of loans and borrowings, each could manifoldly aid the other? How wilt thou sail in unknown seas; and for thyself find that shorter North-west Passage[3] to thy fair Spice-country of a

[1] *Cf.* Exodus, v, 6–19.

[2] That is, taking his career in his own hands. Herring-busses were small boats used by the Dutch in the herring-fishery.

[3] To the Indies. In 1818 and in 1829, Capt. John Ross had attempted such a passage. The idea is borrowed from *Tristram Shandy,* Bk. V, Ch. xlii: "a north-west passage to the intellectual world."

Nowhere?—A solitary rover, on such a voyage, with such nautical tactics, will meet with adventures. Nay, as we forthwith discover, a certain Calypso-Island[1] detains him at the very outset; and as it were falsifies and oversets his whole reckoning.

'If in youth,' writes he once, 'the Universe is majestically unveiling, and everywhere Heaven revealing itself on Earth, nowhere to the Young Man does this Heaven on Earth so immediately reveal itself as in the Young Maiden. Strangely enough, in this strange life of ours, it has been so appointed. On the whole, as I have often said, a Person (*Persönlichkeit*) is ever holy to us; a certain orthodox Anthropomorphism connects my *Me* with all *Thees* in bonds of Love: but it is in this approximation of the Like and Unlike, that such heavenly attraction, as between Negative and Positive,[2] first burns-out into a flame. Is the pitifullest mortal Person, think you, indifferent to us? Is it not rather our heartfelt wish to be made one with him; to unite him to us, by gratitude, by admiration, even by fear; or failing all these, unite ourselves to him? But how much more, in this case of the Like-Unlike! Here is conceded us the higher mystic possibility of such a union, the highest in our Earth; thus, in the conducting medium of Fantasy, flames-forth that *fire*-development of the universal Spiritual Electricity, which, as unfolded between man and woman, we first emphatically denominate LOVE.

'In every well-conditioned stripling, as I conjecture, there already blooms a certain prospective Paradise, cheered by some fairest Eve; nor, in the stately vistas, and flowerage and foliage of that Garden, is a Tree of Knowledge,[3] beautiful and awful in the midst thereof, wanting. Perhaps too the whole is but the lovelier, if Cherubim and a Flaming Sword divide it from all footsteps of men; and grant him, the imaginative

---

[1]The Island of Ogygia, where the nymph Calypso detained Ulysses for seven years. *Odyssey*, ii.

[2]An idea treated by Goethe in *Gott, Gemüth und Welt*.

[3]Adapted from a passage in "Quintus Fixlein" (*German Romance*, II, 221–22) and Genesis, ii, 8–25, *etc*.

stripling, only the view, not the entrance. Happy season of virtuous youth, when shame is still an impassable celestial barrier; and the sacred air-cities of Hope have not shrunk into the mean clay-hamlets of Reality; and man, by his nature, is yet infinite and free!

'As for our young Forlorn,' continues Teufelsdröckh, evidently meaning himself, 'in his secluded way of life, and with his glowing Fantasy, the more fiery that it burnt under cover, as in a reverberating furnace, his feeling towards the Queens of this Earth was, and indeed is, altogether unspeakable. A visible Divinity dwelt in them; to our young Friend all women were holy, were heavenly. As yet he but saw them flitting past, in their many-coloured angel-plumage; or hovering mute and inaccessible on the outskirts of *Æsthetic Tea:* all of air they were, all Soul and Form; so lovely, like mysterious priestesses, in whose hand was the invisible Jacob's-ladder,[1] whereby man might mount into very Heaven. That he, our poor Friend, should ever win for himself one of these Gracefuls (*Holden*)—*Ach Gott!* how could he hope it; should he not have died under it? There was a certain delirious vertigo in the thought.

'Thus was the young man, if all-sceptical of Demons and Angels such as the vulgar had once believed in, nevertheless not unvisited by hosts of true Sky-born, who visibly and audibly hovered round him wheresoever he went; and they had that religious worship in his thought, though as yet it was by their mere earthly and trivial name that he named them. But now, if on a soul so circumstanced, some actual Air-maiden, incorporated into tangibility and reality, should cast any electric glance of kind eyes, saying thereby, "Thou too mayst love and be loved"; and so kindle him,—good Heaven, what a volcanic, earthquake-bringing, all consuming fire were probably kindled!'

Such a fire, it afterwards appears, did actually burst-forth, with explosions more or less Vesuvian, in the inner man of

---

[1]Genesis, xxviii, 10–15.

Herr Diogenes; as indeed how could it fail? A nature, which, in his own figurative style, we might say, had now not a little carbonised tinder, of Irritability; with so much nitre of latent Passion, and sulphurous Humour enough; the whole lying in such hot neighbourhood, close by 'a reverberating furnace of Fantasy':[1] have we not here the components of driest Gunpowder, ready, on occasion of the smallest spark, to blaze-up? Neither, in this our Life-element, are sparks anywhere wanting. Without doubt, some Angel, whereof so many hovered round, would one day, leaving 'the outskirts of *Æsthetic Tea,*' flit nigher; and, by electric Promethean[2] glance, kindle no despicable firework. Happy, if it indeed proved a Firework,[3] and flamed-off rocket-wise, in successive beautiful bursts of splendour, each growing naturally from the other, through the several stages of a happy Youthful Love; till the whole were safely burnt-out; and the young soul relieved with little damage! Happy, if it did not rather prove a Conflagration and mad Explosion; painfully lacerating the heart itself; nay perhaps bursting the heart in pieces (which were Death); or at best, bursting the thin walls of your 'reverberating furnace,' so that it rage thenceforth all unchecked among the contiguous combustibles (which were Madness): till of the so fair and manifold internal world of our Diogenes, there remained Nothing, or only the 'crater of an extinct volcano'!

From multifarious Documents in this Bag *Capricornus,* and in the adjacent ones on both sides thereof, it becomes manifest that our philosopher, as stoical and cynical as he now looks, was heartily and even frantically in Love: here therefore may our old doubts whether his heart were of stone or of flesh give way. He loved once; not wisely but too well.[4] And

---

[1]A furnace or kiln in which the flame is reflected from the roof on the material treated. The expression, "reverberating furnace of a noble anger," is used by Richter, in *Flower, Fruit, etc.,* p. 54.

[2]Fire-bearing. *Cf. Love's Labour's Lost,* IV, iii, 304.

[3]The rest of the paragraph is an elaboration upon a similar passage in *Wilhelm Meister,* I, 105–07 (Bk. II, Ch. i).

[4]*Othello,* V, ii, 343.

once only: for as your Congreve[1] needs a new case or wrappage for every new rocket, so each human heart can properly exhibit but one Love, if even one; the 'First Love which is infinite'[2] can be followed by no second like unto it. In more recent years, accordingly, the Editor of these Sheets was led to regard Teufelsdröckh as a man not only who would never wed, but who would never even flirt; whom the grand-climacteric[3] itself, and *St. Martin's Summer*[4] of incipient Dotage, would crown with no new myrtle-garland.[5] To the Professor, women are henceforth Pieces of Art; of Celestial Art, indeed; which celestial pieces he glories to survey in galleries, but has lost thought of purchasing.

Psychological readers are not without curiosity to see how Teufelsdröckh, in this for him unexampled predicament, demeans himself; with what specialties of successive configuration, splendour and colour, his Firework blazes-off. Small, as usual, is the satisfaction that such can meet with here. From amid these confused masses of Eulogy and Elegy, with their mad Petrarchan[6] and Werterean[7] ware lying madly scattered among all sorts of quite extraneous matter, not so much as the fair one's name can be deciphered. For, without doubt, the title *Blumine,* whereby she is here designated, and which means simply Goddess of Flowers, must be fictitious. Was her real name Flora, then? But what was her surname, or had she none? Of what station in Life was she; of what parentage, fortune, aspect? Specially,

---

[1]A powerful form of rocket, formerly used in war, inclosed in a metallic case; named after Sir William Congreve (1772–1828), the inventor.

[2]From Goethe (*Autobiography and Travels,* transl. J. Oxenford, London, 1874 [Bohn Stand. Libr.], I, 503).

[3]*climacteric:* turning-point. Formerly thought to be any year produced by multiplying seven by the odd numbers, 3, 5, 7, *etc.* A man's grand climacteric is his sixty-third year.

[4]Warm or mild weather in November (St. Martin's Day is November 11); in America, Indian Summer.

[5]The myrtle was sacred to Venus.

[6]Petrarch (1304–74), Italian poet, wrote a series of sonnets to Laura.

[7]Allusion to Goethe's *Die Leiden des Jungen Werthers* (1774), a novel of unhappy love. See Bk. II, Ch. vi.

by what Preëstablished Harmony[1] of occurrences did the Lover and the Loved meet one another in so wide a world; how did they behave in such a meeting? To all which questions, not unessential in a Biographic work, mere Conjecture must for most part return answer. 'It was appointed,' says our Philosopher, 'that the high celestial orbit of Blumine should intersect the low sublunary one of our Forlorn; that he, looking in her empyrean eyes, should fancy the upper Sphere of Light was come down into this nether sphere of Shadows; and finding himself mistaken, make noise enough.'

We seem to gather that she was young, hazel-eyed, beautiful, and some one's Cousin; highborn, and of high spirit; but unhappily dependent and insolvent; living, perhaps, on the not too gracious bounty of moneyed relatives. But how came 'the Wanderer' into her circle? Was it by the humid vehicle of *Æsthetic Tea,* or by the arid one of mere Business? Was it on the hand of Herr Towgood; or of the Gnädige Frau, who, as an ornamental Artist, might sometimes like to promote flirtation, especially for young cynical Nondescripts? To all appearance, it was chiefly by Accident, and the grace of Nature.

'Thou fair Waldschloss,'[2] writes our Autobiographer, 'what stranger ever saw thee, were it even an absolved[3] Auscultator, officially bearing in his pocket the last *Relatio ex Actis*[4] he would ever write, but must have paused to wonder! Noble Mansion! There stoodest thou, in deep Mountain Amphitheatre, on umbrageous lawns, in thy serene solitude; stately, massive, all of granite; glittering in the western sunbeams, like a palace of El Dorado,[5] overlaid with precious metal. Beautiful rose up, in wavy curvature, the slope of thy guardian Hills; of the greenest was their sward, embossed with its

[1]The theory propounded by Leibnitz (1646–1716) that changes in matter and mind are not mutually causal but merely concomitant, from a preëstablished pattern.

[2]Forest-castle.

[3]*Absolved:* from the German "absolviren," to finish one's studies.

[4]Law reports; MS. (*Cf. German Romance,* II, 12).

[5]Land of Gold (Spanish).

dark-brown frets of crag, or spotted by some spreading solitary Tree and its shadow. To the unconscious Wayfarer thou wert also as an Ammon's Temple[1] in the Libyan Waste; where, for joy and woe, the tablet of his Destiny lay written. Well might he pause and gaze; in that glance of his were prophecy and nameless forebodings.'

But now let us conjecture that the so presentient Auscultator has handed-in his *Relatio ex Actis;* been invited to a glass of Rhine-wine; and so, instead of returning dispirited and athirst to his dusty Town-home, is ushered into the Gardenhouse, where sit the choicest party of dames and cavaliers: if not engaged in Æsthetic Tea, yet in trustful evening conversation, and perhaps Musical Coffee, for we hear of 'harps and pure voices making the stillness live.' Scarcely, it would seem, is the Gardenhouse inferior in respectability to the noble mansion itself. 'Embowered amid rich foliage, rose-clusters, and the hues and odours of thousand flowers, here sat that brave company; in front, from the wide-opened doors, fair outlook over blossom and bush, over grove and velvet green, stretching, undulating onwards to the remote Mountain peaks: so bright, so mild, and everywhere the melody of birds and happy creatures: it was all as if man had stolen a shelter from the Sun in the bosom-vesture of Summer herself. How came it that the Wanderer advanced thither with such forecasting heart (*ahndungsvoll*),[2] by the side of his gay host? Did he feel that to these soft influences his hard bosom ought to be shut; that here, once more, Fate had it in view to try him; to mock him, and see whether there were Humour in him?

'Next moment he finds himself presented to the party; and especially by name to—Blumine![3] Peculiar among all

---

[1]Ammon, or Amûn, an Egyptian divinity, had a celebrated temple and oracle in the oasis of Ammonium in the Libyan desert, which was visited by Alexander the Great.

[2]Parr notes that Carlyle probably meant to write *ahnungsvoll* ("full of foreboding") rather than *ahndungsvoll* ("full of revenge").

[3]*Cf.* Quintus Fixlein's "lily of Heaven" (*German Romance,* II, 287). Blumine is a combination of three women in Carlyle's life: (i) Margaret

dames and damosels glanced Blumine, there in her modesty, like a star among earthly lights. Noblest maiden! whom he bent to, in body and in soul; yet scarcely dared look at, for the presence filled him with painful yet sweetest embarrassment.

'Blumine's was a name well known to him; far and wide was the fair one heard of, for her gifts, her graces, her caprices: from all which vague colourings of Rumour, from the censures no less than from the praises, had our friend painted for himself a certain imperious Queen of Hearts,[1] and blooming warm Earth-angel, much more enchanting than your mere white Heaven-angels of women, in whose placid veins circulates too little naphtha-fire. Herself also he had seen in public places; that light yet so stately form; those dark tresses, shading a face where smiles and sunlight played over earnest deeps: but all this he had seen only as a magic vision, for him inaccessible, almost without reality. Her sphere was too far from his; how should she ever think of him; O Heaven! how should they so much as once meet together? And now that Rose-goddess sits in the same circle with him; the light of *her* eyes has smiled on him; if he speak, she will hear it! Nay, who knows, since the heavenly Sun looks into lowest valleys, but Blumine herself might have aforetime noted the so unnotable; perhaps, from his very gainsayers, as

---

Gordon, of Prince Edward Island, whom Carlyle met, through Irving, her former tutor, at Kirkaldy, in 1816–17, and who recognized Carlyle's genius beneath his harsh exterior; (ii) Catherine Aurora Kirkpatrick, daughter of an Irish soldier and an Indian princess, whom Mrs. Strachey identifies with Blumine, and who evidently is "Jane Montagu" in *Wotton Reinfred;* (iii) Jane Welsh Carlyle, who also appears to be the original of "Jane Montagu" in *Wotton Reinfred,* owing to her sharp wit and vivacity. The fictitious figure of Jane Montagu herself may also contribute to the creation of Blumine, who, after all, is patterned to some extent on a contemporary romantic character, the fragile, flowerlike young woman who nevertheless has strength of will when occasions demand. *Cf.* Thiennette in "Quintus Fixlein," the "fair Amazon" in *Wilhelm Meister's Apprenticeship,* Bk. IV, Ch. vi; the romantic heroines in Scott, *etc., etc.* (See Dyer's *Bibliography of Carlyle,* 239–40).

[1]*Queen of Hearts:* Elizabeth (1596–1662), daughter of James I, of England, the unfortunate queen of Bohemia;—so called because of her engaging manner.

he had from hers, gathered wonder, gathered favour for him? Was the attraction, the agitation mutual, then; pole and pole trembling towards contact, when once brought into neighbourhood? Say rather, heart swelling in presence of the Queen of Hearts; like the Sea swelling when once near its Moon![1] With the Wanderer it was even so: as in heavenward gravitation, suddenly as at the touch of a Seraph's wand, his whole soul is roused from its deepest recesses; and all that was painful and that was blissful there, dim images, vague feelings of a whole Past and a whole Future, are heaving in unquiet eddies within him.

'Often, in far less agitating scenes, had our still Friend shrunk forcibly together; and shrouded-up his tremors and flutterings, of what sort soever, in a safe cover of Silence, and perhaps of seeming Stolidity. How was it, then, that here, when trembling to the core of his heart, he did not sink into swoons, but rose into strength, into fearlessness and clearness? It was his guiding genius (*Dämon*)[2] that inspired him; he must go forth and meet his Destiny. Show thyself now, whispered it, or be forever hid. Thus sometimes it is even when your anxiety becomes transcendental, that the soul first feels herself able to transcend it; that she rises above it, in fiery victory; and borne on new-found wings of victory, moves so calmly, even because so rapidly, so irresistibly. Always must the Wanderer remember, with a certain satisfaction and surprise, how in this case he sat not silent, but struck adroitly into the stream of conversation; which thenceforth, to speak with an apparent not a real vanity, he may say that he continued to lead. Surely, in those hours, a certain inspiration was imparted him, such inspiration as is still possible in our late era. The self-secluded unfolds himself in noble thoughts, in free, glowing words; his soul is as one sea of light, the

---

[1]So in "Quintus Fixlein" (*German Romance,* II, 331).

[2]Not the δαίμων of Plato's Socrates, but the German-Romantic term meaning mental endowment peculiar to an individual, determining his vocation and destiny. *Cf.* Josiah Royce, *The Spirit of Modern Philosophy,* Boston, 1892, pp. 171, 173.

peculiar home of Truth and Intellect; wherein also Fantasy bodies-forth form after form, radiant with all prismatic hues.'

It appears, in this otherwise so happy meeting, there talked one 'Philistine';[1] who even now, to the general weariness, was dominantly pouring-forth Philistinism (*Philistriositäten*);[2] little witting what hero was here entering to demolish him! We omit the series of Socratic,[3] or rather Diogenic utterances, not unhappy in their way, whereby the monster, 'persuaded into silence,' seems soon after to have withdrawn for the night. 'Of which dialectic marauder,' writes our hero, 'the discomfiture was visibly felt as a benefit by most: but what were all applauses to the glad smile, threatening every moment to become a laugh, wherewith Blumine herself repaid the victor? He ventured to address her, she answered with attention: nay what if there were a slight tremor in that silver voice; what if the red glow of evening were hiding a transient blush!

'The conversation took a higher tone, one fine thought called forth another: it was one of those rare seasons, when the soul expands with full freedom, and man feels himself brought near to man. Gaily in light, graceful abandonment, the friendly talk played round that circle; for the burden was rolled from every heart; the barriers of Ceremony, which are indeed the laws of polite living, had melted as into vapour; and the poor claims of *Me* and *Thee,* no longer parted by rigid fences, now flowed softly into one another; and Life lay all harmonious, many-tinted, like some fair royal champaign, the sovereign and owner of which were Love only. Such

---

[1]From the German *Philister,* University slang term applied to every non-student, also in the period of Goethe's and Schiller's *Xenien* (1796) to narrow-minded, uncultivated, utilitarian opponents to the spirit of art and enlightenment. Carlyle used the term in "The State of German Literature" (*Ess.,* I, 68); but later preferred the term *gigmanity* ("respectability with its thousand gigs," *etc.;* see *Ess.,* II, 130, *n*). Matthew Arnold in *Essays in Criticism* (1865) did most to spread the use of the term.

[2]*Philistriositäten:* Fischer (p. 276) corrects to *Philistrositäten.*

[3]Allusion to Socrates' method of eliciting contradictory responses to his questions by assuming an appearance of ignorance.

music springs from kind hearts, in a kind environment of place and time. And yet as the light grew more aërial on the mountain-tops, and the shadows fell longer over the valley, some faint tone of sadness may have breathed through the heart; and, in whispers more or less audible, reminded every one that as this bright day was drawing towards its close, so likewise must the Day of Man's Existence decline into dust and darkness; and with all its sick toilings, and joyful and mournful noises, sink in the still Eternity.

'To our Friend the hours seemed moments; holy was he and happy: the words from those sweetest lips came over him like dew on thirsty grass; all better feelings in his soul seemed to whisper, It is good for us to be here.[1] At parting, the Blumine's hand was in his: in the balmy twilight, with the kind stars above them, he spoke something of meeting again, which was not contradicted; he pressed gently those small soft fingers, and it seemed as if they were not hastily, not angrily withdrawn.'

Poor Teufelsdröckh! it is clear to demonstration thou art smit: the Queen of Hearts would see a 'man of genius' also sigh for her; and there, by art-magic, in that preternatural hour, has she bound and spell-bound thee. 'Love is not altogether a Delirium,' says he elsewhere; 'yet has it many points in common therewith. I call it rather a discerning of the Infinite in the Finite, of the Idea made Real; which discerning again may be either true or false, either seraphic or demoniac, Inspiration or Insanity. But in the former case too, as in common Madness, it is Fantasy that superadds itself to sight; on the so petty domain of the Actual plants its Archimedes-lever,[2] whereby to move at will the infinite Spiritual. Fantasy I might call the true Heaven-gate and Hell-gate of man:[3] his sensuous life is but the small temporary

---

[1] *Cf.* Matthew, xvii, 4.

[2] Archimedes (B.C. 287–212), philosopher and mathematician of Syracuse, discovered the principle of the lever, and is reputed to have said, "Give me a place to stand on, and I will move the world."

[3] Carlyle relates fantasy and love in much the same manner as do Richter and Novalis, to denote the imaginative power which transcends

stage (*Zeitbühne*), whereon thick-streaming influences from both these far yet near regions meet visibly, and act tragedy and melodrama. Sense can support herself handsomely, in most countries, for some eighteen-pence a day; but for Fantasy planets and solar-systems will not suffice. Witness your Pyrrhus conquering the world, yet drinking no better red wine than he had before.'[1] Alas! witness also your Diogenes, flame-clad, scaling the upper Heaven, and verging towards Insanity, for prize of a 'high-souled Brunette,' as if the earth held but one and not several of these!

He says that, in Town, they met again: 'day after day, like his heart's sun, the blooming Blumine shone on him. Ah! a little while ago, and he was yet in all darkness: him what Graceful (*Holde*) would ever love? Disbelieving all things, the poor youth had never learned to believe in himself.[2] Withdrawn, in proud timidity, within his own fastnesses; solitary from men, yet baited by night-spectres enough, he saw himself, with a sad indignation, constrained to renounce the fairest hopes of existence. And now, O now! "She looks on thee," cried he: "she the fairest, noblest; do not her dark eyes tell thee, thou art not despised? The Heaven's-Messenger! All Heaven's blessings be hers!" Thus did soft melodies flow through his heart; tones of an infinite gratitude; sweetest intimations that he also was a man, that for him also unutterable joys had been provided.

'In free speech, earnest or gay, amid lambent glances, laughter, tears, and often with the inarticulate mystic speech

---

the real. "Reason plus Phantasy," said Novalis, "gives Religion; Reason plus Understanding gives Science . . . The Content of Phantasy (*Phantasiebegriff*) is an Intuition (*Anschauung*)" (*Werke,* III, 75, 114). (*Cf.* first paragraph of Ch. iii of Bk. III.) Barrett notes the Miltonic use of "Heaven-gate" and "Hell-gate" (*Paradise Lost,* iii, 541; ii, 725) to indicate the "bridge from the sensuous life to the unseen Beyond."

[1]From Plutarch's *Lives;* related therefrom in the *Spectator,* No. 180.

[2]A foreshadowing, in psychological terms, of the philosophical and religious dilemma, "The Everlasting No," of Bk. II, Ch. vii. This predicament, together with the "proud timidity," the solitariness, and the "sad indignation" of Teufelsdröckh, is of course definitely autobiographical.

of Music: such was the element they now lived in; in such a many-tinted, radiant Aurora,[1] and by this fairest of Orient Light-bringers must our Friend be blandished, and the new Apocalypse of Nature unrolled to him.[2] Fairest Blumine! And, even as a Star, all Fire and humid Softness, a very Light-ray incarnate! Was there so much as a fault, a "caprice," he could have dispensed with? Was she not to him in very deed a Morning-Star; did not her presence bring with it airs from Heaven?[3] As from Æolian Harps in the breath of dawn, as from the Memnon's Statue[4] struck by the rosy finger of Aurora, unearthly music was around him, and lapped[5] him into untried balmy Rest. Pale Doubt fled away to the distance; Life bloomed-up with happiness and hope. The past, then, was all a haggard dream; he had been in the Garden of Eden, then, and could not discern it! But lo now, the black walls of his prison melt away; the captive is alive, is free. If he loved his Disenchantress? *Ach Gott!* His whole heart and soul and life were hers, but never had he named it Love: existence was all a Feeling, not yet shaped into a Thought.'

Nevertheless, into a Thought, nay into an Action, it must be shaped; for neither Disenchanter nor Disenchantress, mere 'Children of Time,' can abide by Feeling alone. The Professor knows not, to this day, 'how in her soft, fervid bosom the Lovely found determination, even on hest of Necessity, to cut

---

[1]Words which point to the half-*Oriental* Catherine *Aurora* Kirkpatrick as one of the originals of Blumine.

[2]A revelation or disclosure of the divine by means of Nature. *Cf.* Bk. I, Ch. viii.

[3]*Cf. Hamlet,* I, iv, 41.

[4]*Æolian harps:* Aeolus was god of winds, whose currents of air produced music when they passed through the harp.—*Memnon's Statue:* Memnon was the son of Tithonus and Eos (or Aurora, the dawn), a king of Aethiopia, and a hero in the Trojan war. A statue erected by, or in honour of, Memnon, in the Theban plain, was supposed to emit a sound like the snapping asunder of a chord, when struck by the first rays of "rosy-fingered" Aurora; see Tacitus' *Annals,* ii, 61; Homer's *Odyssey, etc.* Richter is fond of using "Aeolian harp" in his romances.

[5]*Cf. Comus,* 257; *L'Allegro,* 136: "Lap me in soft Lydian Aires."

asunder these so blissful bonds.' He even appears surprised at the 'Duenna Cousin,'[1] whoever she may have been, 'in whose meagre, hunger-bitten[2] philosophy, the religion of young hearts was, from the first, faintly approved of.' We, even at such distance, can explain it without necromancy. Let the Philosopher answer this one question. What figure, at that period, was a Mrs. Teufelsdröckh likely to make in polished society? Could she have driven so much as a brass-bound Gig,[3] or even a simple iron-spring one? Thou foolish 'absolved Auscultator,' before whom lies no prospect of capital, will any yet known 'religion of young hearts' keep the human kitchen warm? Pshaw! thy divine Blumine, when she 'resigned herself to wed some richer,' shows more philosophy, though but 'a woman of genius,' than thou, a pretended man.

Our readers have witnessed the origin of this Love-mania, and with what royal splendour it waxes, and rises. Let no one ask us to unfold the glories of its dominant state; much less the horrors of its almost instantaneous dissolution. How from such inorganic masses, henceforth madder than ever, as lie in these Bags, can even fragments of a living delineation be organised? Besides, of what profit were it? We view, with a lively pleasure, the gay silk Montgolfier[4] start from the ground, and shoot upwards, cleaving the liquid deeps, till it dwindle to a luminous star: but what is there to look longer on, when once, by natural elasticity, or accident of fire, it has

---

[1]The "Aunt" of Margaret Gordon, one of the originals of Blumine; the aunt in *Wotton Reinfred*.

[2]*Meagre, hunger-bitten:* an expression from "Quintus Fixlein" (*German Romance*, II, 238–39).

[3]*Gig:* a term later used by Carlyle as a symbol of "respectability," from the ingenuous use of the expression, "keeping a gig," as a definition of "respectability," in the trial of Thurtell, the murderer. (See *Ess.,* II, 130; III, 71, *n.*)

[4]A balloon, inflated with hot air, so called from the inventors, Stephen and Joseph Montgolfier, who in 1782–83, succeeded in sending up a small balloon at Annonay, France. (See Carlyle's *French Revolution,* I, 51 [Bk. II, Ch. vi].)

exploded? A hapless air-navigator, plunging, amid torn parachutes, sand-bags, and confused wreck, fast enough into the jaws of the Devil! Suffice it to know that Teufelsdröckh rose into the highest regions of the Empyrean,[1] by a natural parabolic track, and returned thence in a quick perpendicular one. For the rest, let any feeling reader, who has been unhappy enough to do the like, paint it out for himself: considering only that if he, for his perhaps comparatively insignificant mistress, underwent such agonies and frenzies, what must Teufelsdröckh's have been, with a fire-heart, and for a nonpareil Blumine! We glance merely at the final scene:

'One morning,[2] he found his Morning-star all dimmed and dusky-red; the fair creature was silent, absent, she seemed to have been weeping. Alas, no longer a Morning-star, but a troublous skyey Portent, announcing that the Doomsday had dawned! She said, in a tremulous voice, They were to meet no more.' The thunderstruck Air-sailor is not wanting to himself in this dread hour: but what avails it? We omit the passionate expostulations, entreaties, indignations, since all was vain, and not even an explanation was conceded him; and hasten to the catastrophe. '"Farewell, then, Madam!" said he, not without sternness, for his stung pride helped him. She put her hand in his, she looked in his face, tears started to her eyes; in wild audacity he clasped her to his bosom; their lips were joined, their two souls, like two dew-drops,[3] rushed into one,—for the first time, and for the last!' Thus was Teufelsdröckh made immortal by a kiss.[4] And then? Why, then—'thick curtains of Night rushed over his soul, as rose

---

[1]In ancient and medieval cosmology, the highest heaven or heavenly sphere, composed of a kind of sublimated fire. *Cf. Paradise Lost,* ii, 927–38.

[2]This final paragraph follows closely a somewhat longer passage in *Wotton Reinfred,* pp. 36, 129 ff.

[3]"Like two tears, melted into one," "Quintus Fixlein" (*German Romance,* II, 253).

[4]*Cf.* Marlowe, *Dr. Faustus,* sc. xiii.

the immeasurable Crash of Doom; and through the ruins as of a shivered Universe was he falling, falling, towards the Abyss.'[1]

CHAPTER VI

SORROWS OF TEUFELSDRÖCKH

Teufelsdröckh's demeanour thereupon. Turns pilgrim. A last wistful look on native Entepfuhl: Sunset amongst primitive Mountains. Basilisk-glance of the Barouche-and-four. Thoughts on View-hunting. Wanderings and Sorrowings.

WE HAVE long felt that, with a man like our Professor, matters must often be expected to take a course of their own; that in so multiplex, intricate a nature, there might be channels, both for admitting and emitting, such as the Psychologist had seldom noted; in short, that on no grand occasion and convulsion, neither in the joy-storm nor in the woe-storm, could you predict his demeanour.

To our less philosophical readers, for example, it is now clear that the so passionate Teufelsdröckh, precipitated through 'a shivered Universe' in this extraordinary way, has only one of three things which he can next do: Establish himself in Bedlam;[2] begin writing Satanic Poetry;[3] or blow-out his brains. In the progress towards any of which consummations, do not such readers anticipate extravagance enough; breast-beating, brow-beating (against walls), lion-bellowings of

[1]This last, rhetorical sentence follows the pattern of Jean Paul's characteristic passages. *Cf.* the Vision of the Dead Christ, quoted in the second essay on Richter (*Ess.*, II, 156–58).

[2]A corruption of *Bethlehem,* famous asylum for lunatics, St. Mary of Bethlehem in London.

[3]The Satanic School of poetry included Byron and Shelley and their followers:—so called first by Southey in the preface to his "Vision of Judgment" (1821), as being in his opinion "especially characterized by a Satanic spirit of pride and audacious impiety." (For Carlyle's opinion of the Byronic solution, see references in Froude's *Life,* but especially the essay on Goethe [*Ess.*, I, 217 ff.]).

blasphemy and the like, stampings, smitings, breakages of furniture, if not arson itself?

Nowise so does Teufelsdröckh deport him. He quietly lifts his *Pilgerstab* (Pilgrim-staff),[1] 'old business being soon wound-up'; and begins a perambulation and circumambulation of the terraqueous Globe! Curious it is, indeed, how with such vivacity of conception, such intensity of feeling, above all, with these unconscionable habits of Exaggeration in speech, he combines that wonderful stillness of his, that stoicism in external procedure. Thus, if his sudden bereavement, in this matter of the Flower-goddess, is talked of as a real Doomsday and Dissolution of Nature, in which light doubtless it partly appeared to himself, his own nature is nowise dissolved thereby; but rather is compressed closer. For once, as we might say, a Blumine by magic appliances has unlocked that shut heart of his, and its hidden things rush-out tumultuous, boundless, like genii[2] enfranchised from their glass phial: but no sooner are your magic appliances withdrawn, than the strange casket of a heart springs-to again; and perhaps there is now no key extant that will open it; for a Teufelsdröckh, as we remarked, will not love a second time. Singular Diogenes! No sooner has that heart-rending occurrence fairly taken place, than he affects to regard it as a thing natural, of which there is nothing more to be said. 'One highest hope, seemingly legible in the eyes of an Angel, had recalled him as out of Death-shadows into celestial Life: but a gleam of Tophet[3] passed over the face of his Angel; he was rapt away in whirlwinds, and heard the laughter of Demons. It was a Calenture,'[4] adds he, 'whereby the Youth saw green Paradise-groves

---

[1]Pilgrim's (wanderer's) staff. A regular literary "property" in German poems and tales (M.).

[2]As in the Tale of the Fisherman, *Arabian Nights*.

[3]Hebrew: *Tōpheth*. An Old Testament term of uncertain meaning and etymology. In Milton, another name for Hinnom, Gehenna, *etc*. See p. 107, *note* 1. Carlyle was very fond of the metaphorical use of the word.

[4]Spanish for *fever*, with delirium, in which sailors may imagine they see green fields, *etc*.

in the waste Ocean-waters: a lying vision, yet not wholly a lie, for *he* saw it.' But what things soever passed in him, when he ceased to see it; what ragings and despairings soever Teufelsdröckh's soul was the scene of, he has the goodness to conceal under a quite opaque cover of Silence. We know it well; the first mad paroxysm past, our brave Gneschen collected his dismembered philosophies, and buttoned himself together; he was meek, silent, or spoke of the weather and the Journals: only by a transient knitting of those shaggy brows, by some deep flash of those eyes, glancing one knew not whether with tear-dew or with fierce fire,—might you have guessed what a Gehenna was within; that a whole Satanic School were spouting, though inaudibly, there. To consume your own choler, as some chimneys consume their own smoke; to keep a whole Satanic School spouting, if it must spout, inaudibly, is a negative yet no slight virtue, nor one of the commonest in these times.

Nevertheless, we will not take upon us to say, that in the strange measure he fell upon, there was not a touch of latent Insanity; whereof indeed the actual condition of these Documents in *Capricornus* and *Aquarius* is no bad emblem. His so unlimited Wanderings, toilsome enough, are without assigned or perhaps assignable aim; internal Unrest seems his sole guidance; he wanders, wanders, as if that curse of the Prophet had fallen on him, and he were 'made like unto a wheel.'[1] Doubtless, too, the chaotic nature of these Paper-bags aggravates our obscurity. Quite without note of preparation, for example, we come upon the following slip: 'A peculiar feeling it is that will rise in the Traveller, when turning some hill-range in his desert road, he descries lying far below, embosomed among its groves and green natural bulwarks, and all diminished to a toybox,[2] the fair Town, where so many souls, as it were seen and yet unseen, are driving their multifarious traffic. Its white steeple is then truly a starward-

[1] *Cf.* Psalms, lxxxiii, 13; *Tristram Shandy,* Vol. VII, Ch. xiii. (Aimless, restless wandering.)

[2] *Cf.* "Quintus Fixlein" (*German Romance,* II, 193).

pointing finger; the canopy of blue smoke seems like a sort of Life-breath: for always, of its own unity, the soul gives unity to whatsoever it looks on with love; thus does the little Dwellingplace of men, in itself a congeries of houses and huts, become for us an individual, almost a person. But what thousand other thoughts unite thereto, if the place has to ourselves been the arena of joyous or mournful experiences; if perhaps the cradle we were rocked in still stands there, if our Loving ones still dwell there, if our Buried ones there slumber!' Does Teufelsdröckh, as the wounded eagle is said to make for its own eyrie, and indeed military deserters, and all hunted outcast creatures, turn as if by instinct in the direction of their birthland,—fly first, in this extremity, towards his native Entepfuhl; but reflecting that there no help awaits him, take only one wistful look from the distance, and then wend elsewhither?

Little happier seems to be his next flight: into the wilds of Nature; as if in her mother-bosom he would seek healing. So at least we incline to interpret the following Notice, separated from the former by some considerable space, wherein, however, is nothing noteworthy:

'Mountains were not new to him,[1] but rarely are Mountains seen in such combined majesty and grace as here. The rocks are of that sort called Primitive by the mineralogists, which always arrange themselves in masses of a rugged, gigantic character; which ruggedness, however, is here tempered by a singular airiness of form, and softness of environment: in a climate favourable to vegetation, the gray cliff, itself covered with lichens, shoots-up through a garment of foliage or verdure; and white, bright cottages, tree-shaded, cluster round the everlasting granite. In fine vicissitude, Beauty alternates with Grandeur: you ride through stony hollows, along strait passes, traversed by torrents, overhung by high walls of rock; now winding amid broken shaggy chasms, and huge frag-

---

[1]This paragraph follows closely a passage in *Wotton Reinfred,* p. 49 ff. (*Cf.* Wilhelm Meister's wanderings among mountains, in his period of sorrow and "renunciation," in the *Wanderjahre, passim.*)

ments; now suddenly emerging into some emerald valley, where the streamlet collects itself into a Lake, and man has again found a fair dwelling, and it seems as if Peace had established herself in the bosom of Strength.

'To Peace, however, in this vortex of existence, can the Son of Time not pretend: still less if some Spectre haunt him from the Past; and the Future is wholly a Stygian Darkness, spectre-bearing.[1] Reasonably might the Wanderer exclaim to himself: Are not the gates of this world's Happiness inexorably shut against thee; hast thou a hope that is not mad? Nevertheless, one may still murmur audibly, or in the original Greek if that suit thee better: "Whoso can look on Death will start at no shadows."[2]

'From such meditations is the Wanderer's attention called outwards; for now the Valley closes-in abruptly, intersected by a huge mountain mass, the stony water-worn ascent of which is not to be accomplished on horseback. Arrived aloft, he finds himself again lifted into the evening sunset light; and cannot but pause, and gaze round him, some moments there. An upland irregular expanse of wold, where valleys in complex branchings are suddenly or slowly arranging their descent towards every quarter of the sky. The mountain-ranges are beneath your feet, and folded together: only the loftier summits look down here and there as on a second plain; lakes also lie clear and earnest in their solitude. No trace of man now visible; unless indeed it were he who fashioned that little visible link of Highway, here, as would seem, scaling the inaccessible, to unite Province with Province. But sun-wards, lo you! how it towers sheer up, a world of Mountains, the diadem and centre of the mountain region! A hundred and a hundred savage peaks, in the last light of Day; all glowing, of gold and amethyst, like giant spirits of the wilderness; there in their silence, in their solitude, even as on the night when

---

[1] *Cf.* Virgil, *Aeneid,* vi, 290–94. (Pertaining to the darkness of the river Styx, in Hades.)

[2] A proverb of many versions and of uncertain origin. Carlyle attributes it to Euripides, in *Wotton Reinfred,* p. 119. Quoted also in *Ess.,* II, 121

Noah's Deluge first dried! Beautiful, nay solemn, was the sudden aspect to our Wanderer. He gazed over those stupendous masses with wonder, almost with longing desire; never till this hour had he known Nature, that she was One, that she was his Mother and divine. And as the ruddy glow was fading into clearness in the sky, and the Sun had now departed, a murmur of Eternity and Immensity, of Death and of Life, stole through his soul; and he felt as if Death and Life were one, as if the Earth were not dead, as if the Spirit of the Earth had its throne in that splendour, and his own spirit were therewith holding communion.

'The spell was broken by a sound of carriage-wheels. Emerging from the hidden Northward, to sink soon into the hidden Southward, came a gay Barouche[1]-and-four: it was open; servants and postillions wore wedding-favours: that happy pair, then, had found each other, it was their marriage evening! Few moments brought them near: *Du Himmel!*[2] It was Herr Towgood and——Blumine! With slight unrecognising salutation they passed me; plunged down amid the neighbouring thickets, onwards, to Heaven, and to England; and I, in my friend Richter's words, *I remained alone, behind them, with the Night.*'[3]

Were it not cruel in these circumstances, here might be the place to insert an observation, gleaned long ago from the great *Clothes-Volume,* where it stands with quite other intent: 'Some time before Small-pox was extirpated,' says the Professor, 'there came a new malady of the spiritual sort on Europe: I mean the epidemic, now endemical, of View-hunting.[4] Poets

---

[1]A four-wheeled carriage, with a seat in front for the driver, two double seats inside, one facing back and the other front, and a folding top over the back seat.

[2]"Good Heavens!"

[3]"Quintus Fixlein" (*German Romance,* II, 331).

[4]Carlyle's repugnance for the romantic's luxuriating in natural scenery, as in Wordsworth, De Quincey, Byron. Although Teufelsdröckh is made un-romantic in many respects—in his vindication of self-control, of realistic and constructive work, *etc.*—nevertheless Carlyle, as a child of his own time, inevitably gives him a deeply romantic character, as a dreamy, love-lorn, defiant wanderer, consuming his heart over the enigmas

of old date, being privileged with Senses, had also enjoyed external Nature; but chiefly as we enjoy the crystal cup which holds good or bad liquor for us; that is to say, in silence, or with slight incidental commentary: never, as I compute, till after the *Sorrows of Werter*,[1] was there man found who would say: Come let us make a Description! Having drunk the liquor, come let us eat the glass! Of which endemic the Jenner[2] is unhappily still to seek.' Too true!

We reckon it more important to remark that the Professor's Wanderings, so far as his stoical and cynical envelopment admits us to clear insight, here first take their permanent character, fatuous or not. That Basilisk-glance[3] of the Barouche-and-four seems to have withered-up what little remnant of a purpose may have still lurked in him: Life has become wholly a dark labyrinth; wherein, through long years, our Friend, flying from spectres, has to stumble about at random, and naturally with more haste than progress.

Foolish were it in us to attempt following him, even from afar, in this extraordinary world-pilgrimage of his; the simplest record of which, were clear record possible, would fill volumes. Hopeless is the obscurity, unspeakable the confusion. He glides from country to country, from condition to condition; vanishing and re-appearing, no man can calculate how or where. Through all quarters of the world he wanders, and apparently through all circles of society. If in any scene, perhaps difficult to fix geographically, he settles for a time, and forms connexions, be sure he will snap them abruptly asunder. Let him sink out of sight as Private Scholar

---

of the universe and of human experience, among romantic mountain scenery which he enjoys for itself as well as for its symbolism of the divine "Immensity."

[1]See p. 23, *note* 3. Other passages on "view-hunting" as a mark of "Werterism" may be found in "Characteristics" (*Ess.*, III, 24) and in "Goethe" (*Ess.*, I, 211).

[2]Jenner, Edward (1749–1823), an English physician, first vaccinated from cow pox in 1796.

[3]*Basilisk:* a fabulous serpent, lizard, or dragon whose glance was supposed to be fatal.

(*Privatisirender*), living by the grace of God in some European capital, you may next find him as Hadjee[1] in the neighbourhood of Mecca. It is an inexplicable Phantasmagoria, capricious, quick-changing; as if our Traveller, instead of limbs and highways, had transported himself by some wishing-carpet,[2] or Fortunatus' Hat.[3] The whole, too, imparted emblematically, in dim multifarious tokens (as that collection of Street-Advertisements);[4] with only some touch of direct historical notice sparingly interspersed: little light-islets in the world of haze! So that, from this point, the Professor is more of an enigma than ever. In figurative language, we might say he becomes, not indeed a spirit, yet spiritualised, vaporised. Fact unparalleled in Biography: The river of his History, which we have traced from its tiniest fountains, and hoped to see flow onward, with increasing current, into the ocean, here dashes itself over that terrific Lover's Leap;[5] and, as a mad-foaming cataract, flies wholly into tumultuous clouds of spray! Low down it indeed collects again into pools and plashes; yet only at a great distance, and with difficulty, if at all, into a general stream. To cast a glance into certain of those pools and plashes, and trace whither they run, must, for a chapter or two, form the limit of our endeavour.

For which end doubtless those direct historical Notices, where they can be met with, are the best. Nevertheless, of this sort too there occurs much, which, with our present light, it were questionable to emit. Teufelsdröckh, vibrating everywhere between the highest and the lowest levels, comes into contact with public History itself. For example, those con-

---

[1]*Hadjee* (or hadji): a Moslem who has made his *hadj*, or pilgrimage to Mecca.

[2]As in the story of Ahmed and Peribanou, *Arabian Nights*.

[3]The hero of a popular European tale, Fortunatus received from Fortune an inexhaustible purse and from the Sultan a wishing cap which transported him to any place where he wished to be. The story appeared in German and in French in the sixteenth century, and was dramatized by Hans Sachs in German and by Thomas Dekker in English.

[4]See p. 79, *note* 1.

[5]Cape Ducato, in the Ionian Sea, the promontory from which Sappho is fabled to have thrown herself into the sea for love of Phaon.

versations and relations with illustrious Persons, as Sultan Mahmoud,[1] the Emperor Napoleon, and others, are they not as yet rather of a diplomatic character than of a biographic? The Editor, appreciating the sacredness of crowned heads, nay perhaps suspecting the possible trickeries of a Clothes-Philosopher, will eschew this province for the present; a new time may bring new insight and a different duty.

If we ask now, not indeed with what ulterior Purpose, for there was none, yet with what immediate outlooks; at all events, in what mood of mind, the Professor undertook and prosecuted this world-pilgrimage,—the answer is more distinct than favourable. 'A nameless Unrest,' says he, 'urged me forward; to which the outward motion was some momentary lying solace. Whither should I go? My Loadstars[2] were blotted out; in that canopy of grim fire shone no star. Yet forward must I; the ground burnt under me; there was no rest for the sole of my foot. I was alone, alone! Ever too the strong inward longing shaped Fantasms for itself: towards these, one after the other, must I fruitlessly wander. A feeling I had, that for my fever-thirst there was and must be somewhere a healing Fountain. To many fondly imagined Fountains, the Saints' Wells[3] of these days, did I pilgrim; to great Men, to great Cities, to great Events: but found there no healing. In strange countries, as in the well-known; in savage deserts, as in the press of corrupt civilisation, it was ever the same: how could your Wanderer escape from—*his own Shadow*?[4] Nevertheless still Forward! I felt as if in great

[1]Mahmud II (1785–1839), Sultan of Turkey 1808–39.

[2]Stars that guide. The lodestar: *Cynosure*, or the northern constellation Ursa Minor (Little Bear), containing the North Star, hence used by mariners as a guide.

[3]Allusion to belief in the curative properties of wells and fountains dedicated to saints, who replaced the earlier pagan presiding spirits. (N.)

[4]*Cf.* Goethe's epigram:

Was lehr' ich dich vor allen Dingen?—
Könntest mich lehren von meiner Schatte zu springen!

What shall I teach thee, the foremost thing?
Couldst teach me off my own shadow to spring!

(See Carlyle's *Life of John Sterling*, p. 130.)

haste; to do I saw not what. From the depths of my own heart, it called to me, Forwards! The winds and the streams, and all Nature sounded to me, Forwards! *Ach Gott,* I was even, once for all, a Son of Time.'

From which is it not clear that the internal Satanic School was still active enough? He says elsewhere: 'The *Enchiridion of Epictetus*[1] I had ever with me, often as my sole rational companion; and regret to mention that the nourishment it yielded was trifling.' Thou foolish Teufelsdröckh! How could it else? Hadst thou not Greek enough to understand thus much: *The end of Man is an Action, and not a Thought,*[2] though it were the noblest?

'How I lived?' writes he once: 'Friend, hast thou considered the "rugged all-nourishing Earth," as Sophocles well names her;[3] how she feeds the sparrow on the house-top,[4] much more her darling, man?[5] While thou stirrest and livest, thou hast a probability of victual. My breakfast of tea has been cooked by a Tartar woman, with water of the Amur,[6] who wiped her earthen kettle with a horse-tail. I have roasted wild-eggs in the sand of Sahara; I have awakened in Paris *Estrapades*[7] and Vienna *Malzleins,*[8] with no prospect of breakfast beyond ele-

[1]The manual or handbook (Εγχειρίδιου) of the Stoic philosopher, Epictetus, once a slave, afterwards a freedman, of the first century at Rome, was a compilation of his discourses by his pupil, Arrian. Carlyle knew the book well, and admired its counsel to desire nothing but freedom and peace, to regard evil as appearance, and to find happiness in the exercise of will.

[2]A free adaptation from Aristotle, *Ethics,* I, iii; X, ix, *etc.* One of Carlyle's favourite quotations, as supporting Goethe's dictum, "Doubt of any kind can be removed by nothing but activity" (*Wilhelm Meister,* I, 386). *Cf.* p. 196.

[3]In *Philoctetes,* 391 (δρεστέρα παμβῶτι Γᾶ). *Cf. Wotton Reinfred,* p. 169.

[4]Psalms, cii, 7.

[5]*Her darling, man:* so in *Wilhelm Meister,* I, 106.

[6]Chief river in Eastern Asia.

[7]A street near the Pantheon, so named from the torturing of Protestants by the "strappado," *i.e.,* by hoisting the victim by a rope and letting him fall so as to dislocate the arms.

[8]A suburb of Vienna, mentioned in Jean Paul's "Journey to Flaetz" (*German Romance,* II, 142).

mental liquid. That I had my Living to seek saved me from Dying,—by suicide. In our busy Europe, is there not an everlasting demand for Intellect, in the chemical, mechanical, political, religious, educational, commercial departments? In Pagan countries, cannot one write Fetishes?[1] Living! Little knowest thou what alchemy[2] is in an inventive Soul; how, as with its little finger, it can create provision enough for the body (of a Philosopher); and then, as with both hands, create quite other than provision; namely, spectres to torment itself withal.'

Poor Teufelsdröckh! Flying with Hunger always parallel to him; and a whole Infernal Chase in his rear; so that the countenance of Hunger is comparatively a friend's! Thus must he, in the temper of ancient Cain, or of the modern Wandering Jew,[3]—save only that he feels himself not guilty and but suffering the pains of guilt,—wend to and fro with aimless speed. Thus must he, over the whole surface of the Earth (by footprints), write his *Sorrows of Teufelsdröckh;* even as the great Goethe, in passionate words, had to write his *Sorrows of Werter,*[4] before the spirit freed herself, and he could become a Man. Vain truly is the hope of your swiftest Runner to escape 'from his own Shadow'! Nevertheless, in these sick days, when the Born of Heaven first descries himself (about the age of twenty) in a world such as ours, richer than usual in two things, in Truths grown obsolete, and Trades grown obsolete,—what can the fool think but that it is all a Den of Lies, wherein whoso will not speak Lies and act Lies, must stand idle and despair? Whereby it happens that, for your nobler minds, the publishing of some such Work of Art, in one or the other dialect, becomes almost a necessity. For what is it properly but an Altercation with the Devil, before you begin honestly Fighting him? Your Byron publishes his

---

[1]Material objects to which magical powers are ascribed.

[2]The medieval chemical science, which aimed at transmuting baser metals into gold.

[3]See p. 17, *note* 2.

[4]See p. 23, *note* 3.

Sorrows of Lord George, in verse and in prose, and copiously otherwise:[1] your Bonaparte represents his *Sorrows of Napoleon* Opera, in an all-too stupendous style; with music of cannon-volleys, and murder-shrieks of a world; his stage-lights are the fires of Conflagration; his rhyme and recitative are the tramp of embattled Hosts and the sound of falling Cities.—Happier is he who, like our Clothes-Philosopher, can write such matter, since it must be written, on the insensible Earth, with his shoe-soles only; and also survive the writing thereof!

CHAPTER VII

THE EVERLASTING NO[2]

Loss of Hope, and of Belief. Profit-and-Loss Philosophy. Teufelsdröckh in his darkness and despair still clings to Truth and follows Duty. Inexpressible pains and fears of Unbelief. Fever-crisis: Protest against the Everlasting No: Baphometic Fire-Baptism.

UNDER the strange nebulous envelopment, wherein our Professor has now shrouded himself, no doubt but his spiritual nature is nevertheless progressive, and growing: for how can the 'Son of Time,' in any case, stand still? We be-

---

[1] "Byron we call 'a dandy of sorrows and acquainted with grief' " (*C.E.L.,* II, Ch. iv, Carlyle's Journal for Oct. 28, 1830); *cf.* "Goethe's Works" (*Ess.,* II, 436).

[2] "Carlyle often said [that] it was his reflections on the death of this uncle [Thomas, born 1776, died 1816] that suggested to him the subject of his chapter on 'The Everlasting No' in *Sartor Resartus.*"—C. E. Norton, in *Carlyle's Reminiscences,* p. 22, *n. Cf. C.E.L.* I, xx: "It was God that said Yes. It is the Devil that forever says No."—Goethe's Mephistopheles, in *Faust,* "is a *philosophe,* and doubts most things. . . . He is the Devil, not of Superstition, but of Knowledge. . . . He despises all things, human and divine. . . . He calls himself the Denier . . . detecting the false, but without force to bring forth, or even to discern, any glimpse of the true. . . . A combination of perfect Understanding with perfect Selfishness . . ." ("Goethe's Helena" [*Ess.,* I, 157–58]). In

hold him, through those dim years, in a state of crisis, of transition: his mad Pilgrimings, and general solution into aimless Discontinuity, what is all this but a mad Fermentation; wherefrom, the fiercer it is, the clearer product will one day evolve itself?

Such transitions are ever full of pain: thus the Eagle when he moults is sickly;[1] and, to attain his new beak, must harshly dash-off the old one upon rocks. What Stoicism soever[2] our Wanderer, in his individual acts and motions, may affect, it is clear that there is a hot fever of anarchy and misery raging within; coruscations of which flash out: as, indeed, how could there be other? Have we not seen him disappointed, bemocked of Destiny, through long years? All that the young heart might desire and pray for has been denied; nay, as in the last worst instance, offered and then snatched away. Ever an 'excellent Passivity';[3] but of useful, reasonable Activity, essential to the former as Food to Hunger, nothing granted: till at length, in this wild Pilgrimage, he must forcibly seize for himself an Activity, though useless, unreasonable. Alas, his cup of bitterness, which had been filling drop by drop, ever since that first 'ruddy morning' in the Hinterschlag Gymnasium, was at the very lip; and then with that poisondrop, of the Towgood-and-Blumine business, it runs over, and even hisses over in a deluge of foam.

He himself says once, with more justice than originality: 'Man is, properly speaking, based upon Hope, he has no other possession but Hope; this world of his is emphatically the

---

short, the "Everlasting No" is that attitude which accepts evil, necessity, limitation, and suffering as alone real, and therefore *denies a moral order* in the universe, and regards all faith, goodness, apparent freedom, and happiness as a contemptible illusion.

[1]*Cf.* Psalms, ciii, 5; St. Augustine comments on the passage (Migne, *Patrologiae Latinae Cursus Completus,* xxxvii, 1323 ff. [N.]), but refers to the eagle in *old age*.

[2]That is, whatever moral stamina was exalted by Epictetus. See p. 155, *note* 1.

[3]Renunciation, denial of self-satisfaction, as yet forced upon Teufelsdröckh *from without;* later to be adopted by him, by a free choice, as the way to moral insight and wholesomeness. See "The Everlasting Yea."

"Place of Hope."'[1] What, then, was our Professor's possession? We see him, for the present, quite shut-out from Hope; looking not into the golden orient, but vaguely all round into a dim copper firmament, pregnant with earthquake and tornado.

Alas, shut-out from Hope, in a deeper sense than we yet dream of! For, as he wanders wearisomely through this world, he has now lost all tidings of another and higher. Full of religion, or at least of religiosity, as our Friend has since exhibited himself, he hides not that, in those days, he was wholly irreligious: 'Doubt had darkened into Unbelief,' says he; 'shade after shade goes grimly over your soul, till you have the fixed, starless, Tartarean black.'[2] To such readers as have reflected, what can be called reflecting, on man's life, and happily discovered, in contradiction to much Profit-and-Loss Philosophy,[3] speculative and practical, that Soul is *not* synonymous with Stomach; who understand, therefore, in our Friend's words, 'that, for man's well-being, Faith is properly the one thing needful; how, with it, Martyrs, otherwise weak, can cheerfully endure the shame and the cross; and without it, Worldlings puke-up their sick existence, by suicide, in the midst of luxury': to such it will be clear that, for a pure moral nature, the loss of his religious Belief was the loss of everything. Unhappy young man! All wounds, the crush of long-continued Destitution, the stab of false Friendship and of false Love, all wounds in thy so genial heart, would have healed again, had not its life-warmth been withdrawn. Well might he exclaim, in his wild way: 'Is there no God, then; but at best an absentee God, sitting idle, ever since the first Sabbath, at the outside of his Universe, and *see*ing it go?[4] Has

---

[1]These words are a constant refrain throughout Carlyle's writings and correspondence. Hope in the sense here intended means dynamic, creative faith, a *religious* attitude rather than a merely practical one.

[2]Gloomy and dark as Tartarus, the inner region of Hell in the *Iliad,* where the rebel Titans were confined. *Cf. Paradise Lost,* ii, 858: "This gloom of Tartarus profound."

[3]Utilitarianism, materialism. See p. 117, *note* 2.

[4]Allusion to the eighteenth-century deistic conception of God as an

the word Duty no meaning; is what we call Duty no divine Messenger and Guide, but a false earthly Fantasm, made-up of Desire and Fear, of emanations from the Gallows and from Doctor Graham's Celestial-Bed?[1] Happiness of an approving Conscience! Did not Paul of Tarsus, whom admiring men have since named Saint, feel that *he* was "the chief of sinners";[2] and Nero of Rome, jocund in spirit (*wohlgemuth*), spend much of his time in fiddling?[3] Foolish Wordmonger and Motive-grinder, who in thy Logic-mill hast an earthly mechanism for the Godlike itself, and wouldst fain grind me out Virtue from the husks of Pleasure,[4]—I tell thee, Nay! To the unregenerate Prometheus Vinctus[5] of a man, it is ever the bitterest aggravation of his wretchedness that he is conscious of Virtue, that he feels himself the victim not of suffering only, but of injustice. What then? Is the heroic inspiration we name Virtue but some Passion; some bubble of the blood, bubbling in the direction others *profit* by? I know not: only this I know, If what thou namest Happiness be our true aim, then are we all astray. With Stupidity and sound Digestion man may front much. But what, in these dull unimaginative days, are the terrors of Conscience to the diseases of the Liver!

Artificer who, having created the universe according to a design visible to man, now lets it run without his presence (see Paley's *Natural Theology,* 1802). Goethe satirized this view of the universe in a celebrated epigram which Carlyle quotes in "Diderot" (*Ess.,* III, 233): "Think ye that God made the Universe, and then let it run round his finger (*am Finger laufen liesse*)?"

[1]An elaborate bed supposed to cure sterility in married people, invented by the notorious quack doctor, James Graham (1745–94). Mentioned in Musaeus's "Melechsala" (*German Romance,* I, 200).

[2]I Timothy, i, 15.

[3]Related in Tacitus's *Annals,* xiv, 14.

[4]Jeremy Bentham, the Utilitarian, had formulated a "calculus" of pleasure and pain, whereby ethical action (virtue) would be rewarded by pleasure, vice by pain (*Principles of Morals and Legislation,* 1780).

[5]Prometheus Bound, the title of Aeschylus's drama, representing the conflict of audacious genius with Fate. Prometheus (Forethought) stole fire from heaven, and was therefore condemned by Zeus to be chained to a rock on Mount Caucasus while a vulture gnawed his liver. *Cf.* Goethe's poem, "Prometheus," and Shelley's *Prometheus Unbound.*

Not on Morality, but on Cookery, let us build our stronghold: there brandishing our frying-pan, as censer, let us offer sweet incense to the Devil, and live at ease on the fat things *he* has provided for his Elect!'

Thus has the bewildered Wanderer to stand, as so many have done, shouting question after question into the Sibyl-cave of Destiny,[1] and receive no Answer but an Echo. It is all a grim Desert, this once-fair world of his; wherein is heard only the howling of wild-beasts, or the shrieks of despairing, hate-filled men; and no Pillar of Cloud by day, and no Pillar of Fire by night,[2] any longer guides the Pilgrim. To such length has the spirit of Inquiry carried him. 'But what boots it (*was thut's*)?' cries he: 'it is but the common lot in this era. Not having come to spiritual majority prior to the *Siècle de Louis Quinze,*[3] and not being born purely a Loghead (*Dummkopf*), thou hadst no other outlook. The whole world is, like thee, sold to Unbelief; their old Temples of the Godhead, which for long have not been rainproof, crumble down; and men ask now: where is the Godhead; our eyes never saw him?'

Pitiful enough were it, for all these wild utterances, to call our Diogenes wicked. Unprofitable servants as we all are,[4] perhaps at no era of his life was he more decisively the Servant of Goodness, the Servant of God, than even now when doubting God's existence. 'One circumstance I note,' says he: 'after all the nameless woe that Inquiry, which for me, what it is not always, was genuine Love of Truth, had wrought me, I nevertheless still loved Truth, and would bate no jot[5] of my allegiance to her. "Truth!" I cried, "though the Heavens crush me for following her: no Falsehood! though a whole

[1]See p. 77, *note* 3.

[2]*Cf.* Exodus, xiii, 21. A frequent metaphor of Jean Paul's (B.).

[3]The title of a history by Voltaire, and the name of the age of the Encyclopaedists, of Reason, scepticism, and *persiflage*. See Carlyle's essays on Diderot and Voltaire, *etc.*

[4]Luke, xvii, 10.

[5]*Bate no jot:* phrasing from Milton's sonnet, "To Mr. Cyriack Skinner upon his Blindness."

celestial Lubberland[1] were the price of Apostasy." In conduct it was the same. Had a divine Messenger from the clouds, or miraculous Handwriting on the wall,[2] convincingly proclaimed to me *This thou shalt do,* with what passionate readiness, as I often thought, would I have done it, had it been leaping into the infernal Fire. Thus, in spite of all Motive-grinders, and Mechanical Profit-and-Loss Philosophies, with the sick ophthalmia and hallucination they had brought on, was the Infinite nature of Duty[3] still dimly present to me: living without God in the world,[4] of God's light I was not utterly bereft; if my as yet sealed eyes, with their unspeakable longing, could nowhere see Him, nevertheless in my heart He was present,[5] and His heaven-written Law still stood legible and sacred there.'

Meanwhile, under all these tribulations, and temporal and spiritual destitutions, what must the Wanderer, in his silent soul, have endured! 'The painfullest feeling,' writes he, 'is that of your own Feebleness (*Unkraft*); ever, as the English Milton says, to be weak is the true misery.[6] And yet of your Strength there is and can be no clear feeling, save by what you have prospered in, by what you have done. Between vague wavering Capability and fixed indubitable Performance, what a difference![7] A certain inarticulate Self-consciousness dwells dimly in us; which only our Works can render articulate and decisively discernible. Our Works are the mirror wherein the spirit first sees its natural lineaments. Hence,

---

[1]Land of Cockaigne, or of plenty. *Cf.* Hans Sachs's *Das Schlaraffenland* (land of sluggards) (M.).

[2]*Cf.* Daniel, v, 5–28.

[3]That is, that duty is to be performed, not from considerations of reward and punishment—from space-time considerations—but from a conviction of the non-temporal, non-spatial (or absolute) good in performing it; also that the results of duty performed or neglected go on through endless time and infinite space. (*Cf.* the chapter on "Organic Filaments"; also *Ess.,* I, 397.)

[4]Ephesians, ii, 12.

[5]*Cf.* Proverbs, vii, 3.

[6]*Paradise Lost,* i, 157: "Fallen Cherub, to be weak is miserable."

[7]See p. 119, *note* 2.

too, the folly of that impossible Precept, *Know thyself;*[1] till it be translated into this partially possible one, *Know what thou canst work at.*

'But for me, so strangely unprosperous had I been, the net-result of my Workings amounted as yet simply to—Nothing. How then could I believe in my Strength, when there was as yet no mirror to see it in? Ever did this agitating, yet, as I now perceive, quite frivolous question, remain to me insoluble: Hast thou a certain Faculty, a certain Worth, such even as the most have not; or art thou the completest Dullard of these modern times? Alas, the fearful Unbelief is unbelief in yourself;[2] and how could I believe? Had not my first, last Faith in myself, when even to me the Heavens seemed laid open, and I dared to love, been all-too cruelly belied? The speculative Mystery of Life grew ever more mysterious to me: neither in the practical Mystery had I made the slightest progress, but been everywhere buffeted, foiled, and contemptuously cast out. A feeble unit in the middle of a threatening Infinitude, I seemed to have nothing given me but eyes, whereby to discern my own wretchedness. Invisible yet impenetrable walls, as of Enchantment, divided me from all living: was there, in the wide world, any true bosom I could press trustfully to mine? O Heaven, No, there was none! I kept a lock upon my lips: why should I speak much with that shifting variety of so-called Friends, in whose withered, vain and too-hungry souls Friendship was but an incredible tradition? In such cases, your resource is to talk little, and that little mostly from the Newspapers. Now when I look back, it was a strange isolation I then lived in.[3] The men and women

---

[1]A maxim attributed to Solon, Socrates, Thales, *etc.;* inscribed over the portico of the temple at Delphi. Carlyle objected to this maxim as leading to morbid self-analysis, Byronic despair, and the "disease of metaphysics" ("Characteristics," *Ess.,* III, 40–43).

[2]See p. 159.

[3]Autobiographical. The unhappiest period in Carlyle's life came between the years 1816 and 1822, when he suffered from ill health, frustrated designs, and religious doubt. See *C.E.L.,* I, iv–ix; Wilson, *Carlyle till Marriage, passim; Reminiscences,* pp. 182–210.

around me, even speaking with me, were but Figures; I had, practically, forgotten that they were alive, that they were not merely automatic. In the midst of their crowded streets and assemblages, I walked solitary; and (except as it was my own heart, not another's, that I kept devouring) savage also, as the tiger in his jungle. Some comfort it would have been, could I, like a Faust, have fancied myself tempted and tormented of the Devil; for a Hell, as I imagine, without Life, though only diabolic Life, were more frightful: but in our age of Down-pulling and Disbelief, the very Devil has been pulled down, you cannot so much as believe in a Devil. To me the Universe was all void of Life, of Purpose, of Volition, even of Hostility: it was one huge, dead, immeasurable Steam-engine, rolling on, in its dead indifference, to grind me limb from limb. O, the vast, gloomy, solitary Golgotha,[1] and Mill of Death![2] Why was the Living banished thither companionless, conscious? Why, if there is no Devil; nay, unless the Devil is your God?'

A prey incessantly to such corrosions, might not, moreover, as the worst aggravation to them, the iron constitution even of a Teufelsdröckh threaten to fail? We conjecture that he has known sickness; and, in spite of his locomotive habits, perhaps sickness of the chronic sort. Hear this, for example: 'How beautiful to die of broken-heart, on Paper! Quite another thing in practice; every window of your Feeling, even of your Intellect, as it were, begrimed and mud-bespattered, so that no pure ray can enter; a whole Drugshop in your inwards; the fordone soul drowning slowly in quagmires of Disgust!'

Putting all which external and internal miseries together,

---

[1]Hebrew: *gulgōleth,* skull; place of skulls; Calvary. *Cf.* Matthew, xxvii, 33.

[2]From Novalis's *Die Lehrlinge zu Sais* (The Pupils at Sais) and *Die Christenheit oder Europa* (Christianity, or Europe), in *Werke,* II, 33–35; IV, 138–39, passages from which Carlyle quotes in the essay on Novalis (*Ess.,* II, 30–35, 42–43, *etc.*). Novalis attempts to show that knowledge without religious imagination places man in a mechanical universe, a vast mill (*einer ungeheuren Mühle*), without architect (*Baumeister*) or miller (*Müller*). "Mill of Death" is Carlyle's literal translation of Novalis's *eine furchtbare Mühle des Todes.*

may we not find in the following sentences, quite in our Professor's still vein, significance enough? 'From Suicide a certain aftershine (*Nachschein*) of Christianity withheld me:[1] perhaps also a certain indolence of character; for, was not that a remedy I had at any time within reach? Often, however, was there a question present to me: Should some one now, at the turning of that corner, blow thee suddenly out of Space, into the other World, or other No-world, by pistol-shot,—how were it? On which ground, too, I often, in sea-storms and sieged cities and other death-scenes, exhibited an imperturbability, which passed, falsely enough, for courage.'

'So had it lasted,' concludes the Wanderer, 'so had it lasted, as in bitter protracted Death-agony, through long years. The heart within me, unvisited by any heavenly dew-drop was smouldering in sulphurous, slow-consuming fire. Almost since earliest memory I had shed no tear; or once only when I, murmuring half-audibly, recited Faust's Death-song, that wild *Selig der den er im Siegesglanze findet* (Happy whom *he* finds in Battle's splendour),[2] and thought that of this last Friend even I was not forsaken, that Destiny itself could not

---

[1]As late as 1823, it is evident, in spite of Carlyle's words, that he had contemplated suicide. (See his Journal for December 31, 1823, in *C.E.L.*, I, Ch. xii.) Like Teufelsdröckh, he was suffering from ill health, from failure to find congenial occupation, and from an unhappy—or at least unsuccessful—courtship. On the other hand, suicide was, in Teufelsdröckh's day, a romantic subject; Goethe's Werther was a suicide, and Goethe himself dallied with the thought in his earlier, *Sturm-und-Drang* period (see his *Autobiography,* Bk. XIII). Karl Moor, in Schiller's *The Robbers,* considers blowing himself "companionless to some burnt and blasted circle of the Universe" by pistol-shot. (See *Ess.,* II, 206).

[2]Not quoted literally, but adapted. Mephistopheles asks Faust if Death is never an entirely welcome guest; Faust replies that happy is the man for whom Death weaves a laurel in "victory's hour," and who, after the mad dance, is found in his lover's arms, *etc. Faust,* I, sc. iv, ll. 1573–76. In Carlyle's own "Everlasting No," it was not Faust's Deathsong but his *Curse* which expressed his state of mind (see *Faust,* I, ll. 1583–1606): Faust curses all frivolous pleasures, all reputation, delusions, dreams, all pride, worldly gain, wine and love—then adds, "Cursed be Hope's vision, Faith's delusion, and cursed, thrice cursed, be Patience meek! (*Und Fluch vor allen der Geduld!*)." See *Love Letters of T.C.,* II, 351; *G.-Carlyle Corr.,* p. 34.

doom me not to die.[1] Having no hope, neither had I any definite fear, were it of Man or of Devil: nay, I often felt as if it might be solacing, could the Arch-Devil himself, though in Tartarean terrors,[2] but rise to me, that I might tell him a little of my mind. And yet, strangely enough, I lived in a continual, indefinite, pining fear; tremulous, pusillanimous, apprehensive of I knew not what; it seemed as if all things in the Heavens above and the Earth beneath would hurt me; as if the Heavens and the Earth were but boundless jaws of a devouring monster, wherein I, palpitating, waited to be devoured.

'Full of such humour, and perhaps the miserablest man in the whole French Capital or Suburbs, was I, one sultry Dog-day, after much perambulation, toiling along the dirty little *Rue Saint-Thomas de l'Enfer,*[3] among civic rubbish enough, in

---

[1]Barrett: "Carlyle connected this with Dante (Cary's), *Hell,* iii, 45; but *cf.* especially Milton, *Paradise Lost,* x, 770–844."

[2]See p. 159, *note* 2.

[3]The experience of Teufelsdröckh, says Carlyle, "is symbolical myth all, except that of the incident in the Rue St. Thomas de l'Enfer, which occurred quite literally to myself in Leith Walk [Edinburgh], during three weeks of total sleeplessness, in which almost my one solace was that of a daily bathe on the sands between Leith and Portobello. Incident was as I went down; coming up I generally felt refreshed for the hour. I remember it well, and could go straight to about the place." (*C.E.L.,* I, Ch. vii. See also Masson's *Edinburgh Sketches,* pp. 295–300.) *Rue de l'Enfer:* Hell Street. St. Thomas, the doubting disciple, gives further appropriateness to the title.—The exact date of Carlyle's "conversion," according to Froude (*op. cit.*), was some time in June, 1821. Alexander Carlyle, however, after a careful examination of all the facts, places the event "in July or early in August, 1822" (*Love Letters of T.C.,* ed. Alexander Carlyle, London, 1909 [2 vols], II, 381). It is important to note that neither Teufelsdröckh nor Carlyle experienced a "conversion" to any particular religious belief; there was nothing Pauline or apocalyptic in it. Contrary to the interpretation by Garnett (*Life of T.C.,* London, 1887, p. 25), the "conversion" cannot "be paralleled from the experiences of St. Paul, Mahomet, Luther." It was merely the regaining of a sense of inner resources, of the mystery of consciousness and freedom, with which to front an apparently mechanical and hostile world. The religious implications, constructively considered, were to come later. The whole subject of Teufelsdröckh's and Carlyle's "conversion" is dealt with in the present editor's *Carlyle and German Thought: 1819–1834,* pp. 41–44.

a close atmosphere, and over pavements hot as Nebuchadnezzar's Furnace;[1] whereby doubtless my spirits were little cheered; when, all at once, there rose a Thought in me, and I asked myself: "What *art* thou afraid of? Wherefore, like a coward, dost thou forever pip and whimper, and go cowering and trembling? Despicable biped! what is the sum-total of the worst that lies before thee? Death? Well, Death; and say the pangs of Tophet[2] too, and all that the Devil and Man may, will or can do against thee! Hast thou not a heart; canst thou not suffer whasoever it be; and, as a Child of Freedom, though outcast, trample Tophet itself under thy feet, while it consumes thee? Let it come, then; I will meet it and defy it!"[3] And as I so thought, there rushed like a stream of fire over my whole soul; and I shook base Fear away from me forever. I was strong, of unknown strength; a spirit, almost a god. Ever from that time, the temper of my misery was changed: not Fear or whining Sorrow was it, but Indignation and grim fire-eyed Defiance.

'Thus had the EVERLASTING NO (*das ewige Nein*) pealed authoritatively through all the recesses of my Being, of my ME; and then was it that my whole ME stood up, in native God-created majesty, and with emphasis recorded its Protest. Such a Protest,[4] the most important transaction in Life, may that same Indignation and Defiance, in a psychological point of view, be fitly called. The Everlasting No had said: "Be-

---

[1]Daniel, iii, 19.

[2]See p. 147, *note* 3.

[3]As Barrett notes, Carlyle's account of his own case is coloured by his subsequent reading. Teufelsdröckh's decision is precisely that of Karl Moor in Schiller's *The Robbers,* IV, vi, as quoted in *Ess.,* II, 206: "Shall I give wretchedness the victory over me?—No, I will endure it . . . . Let misery blunt itself on my pride! I will go through with it." Both the phrasing and the motive resemble Teufelsdröckh's.

[4]Teufelsdröckh's "protest" is *against* the "Everlasting No"; the "NO" (a denial of the validity and dignity of faith in the goodness of things) had "pealed authoritatively" throughout his being (held him in complete bondage). His *ability* to protest demonstrates to Teufelsdröckh that he is somehow not wholly a part of the natural order (of death, necessity, limitation, *etc.*).

hold, thou art fatherless, outcast, and the Universe is mine (the Devil's)"; to which my whole Me now made answer: "*I* am not thine, but Free, and forever hate thee!"

'It is from this hour that I incline to date my Spiritual New-birth, or Baphometic[1] Fire-baptism; perhaps I directly thereupon began to be a Man.'[2]

---

[1]A word of very uncertain derivation; meaning here merely a sudden culmination of suffering leading to a blinding (flame-like) spiritual illumination or understanding.—Originally, Baphomet was the imaginary symbol or double-headed idol which the Knights Templars were accused of worshipping in their secret rites, supposedly reviving the impurities of early Gnostic heresies. Etymologically, the word is apparently a corruption of *Mahomet* or *Mohammed* (*Webst. Int. Dict.*), though some writers derive it from the Greek (βαφή, baptism, +μῆτις, wisdom [symbolized by fire]).—Carlyle adopted the phrase from Zacharias Werner's *Die Söhne des Thals* (The Sons of the Valley), Act V, Sc. ii, the "Story of the Fallen Master," Baffometus, who having refused to build the Lord a temple, is made an outcast, in the shape of a monster, and languishes for four thousand years, until "a Saviour from his own seed, redeem his trespass and deliver him." (See Carlyle's translation of the passage in *Ess.* I, 100 ff.) Teufelsdröckh's spirit of denial, his life as a spiritual outcast, and his sufferings, all make him a kind of Baffometus; but he has now had his "fire-baptism," an experience still to come to Werner's character.

[2]Began, that is, to realize his true humanity, as a "son of freedom" as well as a "Son of Time" (or limitation), in so far as struggle and aspiration, triumphant over the shallow illusions of youth, define true manhood.

CHAPTER VIII

CENTRE OF INDIFFERENCE[1]

Teufelsdröckh turns now outwardly to the *Not-me;* and finds wholesomer food. Ancient Cities: Mystery of their origin and growth: Invisible inheritances and possessions. Power and virtue of a true Book. Wagram Battlefield: War. Great Scenes beheld by the Pilgrim: Great Events, and Great Men. Napoleon, a divine missionary, preaching *La carrière ouverte aux talens.* Teufelsdröckh at the North Cape: Modern means of self-defence. Gunpowder and duelling. The Pilgrim, despising his miseries, reaches the Centre of Indifference.

THOUGH, after this 'Baphometic Fire-baptism' of his, our Wanderer signifies that his Unrest was but increased; as, indeed, 'Indignation and Defiance,' especially against things in general, are not the most peaceable inmates; yet can the Psychologist surmise that it was no longer a quite hopeless Unrest; that henceforth it had at least a fixed centre to revolve round. For the fire-baptised soul, long so scathed and thunder-riven, here feels its own Freedom, which feeling is its Baphometic Baptism: the citadel of its whole kingdom it has thus gained by assault, and will keep inexpugnable; outwards from which the remaining dominions, not indeed without hard battling, will doubtless by degrees be conquered and pacificated. Under another figure, we might say, if in that great moment, in the *Rue Saint-Thomas de l'Enfer,* the old inward Satanic School[2] was not yet thrown out of doors, it received peremptory judicial notice to quit;—whereby, for

[1]Teufelsdröckh's indifference arises from his having discovered his ego, or self, without as yet having seized upon any creative channels for the development of his personality and for the intellectual construction of his new universe (or his new religious outlook). The phrase is from Musaeus (*German Romance,* I, 80).

[2]See p. 146, *note* 3.

the rest, its howl-chantings, Ernulphus-cursings,[1] and rebellious gnashings of teeth, might, in the meanwhile, become only the more tumultuous, and difficult to keep secret.

Accordingly, if we scrutinise these Pilgrimings well, there is perhaps discernible henceforth a certain incipient method in their madness.[2] Not wholly as a Spectre does Teufelsdröckh now storm through the world; at worst as a spectre-fighting Man, nay who will one day be a Spectre-queller. If pilgriming restlessly to so many 'Saints' Wells,'[3] and ever without quenching of his thirst, he nevertheless finds little secular wells, whereby from time to time some alleviation is ministered. In a word, he is now, if not ceasing, yet intermitting to 'eat his own heart'; and clutches round him outwardly on the NOT-ME[4] for wholesomer food. Does not the following glimpse exhibit him in a much more natural state?

'Towns also and Cities, especially the ancient, I failed not to look upon with interest. How beautiful to see thereby, as through a long vista, into the remote Time; to have as it were, an actual section of almost the earliest Past brought safe into the Present, and set before your eyes! There, in that old City, was a live ember of Culinary Fire put down, say only two-thousand years ago; and there, burning more or less triumphantly, with such fuel as the region yielded, it has burnt,

[1]Ernulf (1040–1124) was Bishop of Rochester. The text of the Bishop's curse is in *Tristram Shandy,* Vol. III, Ch. xi. *Cf.* Faust's Curse (p. 165, *note* 2).

[2]*Cf. Hamlet,* II, ii, 211–12.

[3]See p. 154, *note* 3.

[4]In German, *das Nicht-Ich,* an expression from Fichte, and from Novalis who interpreted Fichte, meaning the external world, all that is not mind or consciousness. In Teufelsdröckh's "conversion," his first discovery (or re-discovery) was his Me or ego (Fichte's *Ich*); his second discovery was the fundamental character of the outer world, as being *not-conscious,* as material for the conscious self to work upon. This seemed to Carlyle to solve the riddle of matter: it made matter the raw material of spirit, no longer an independent and autonomous realm, but a derivative of mind. Novalis had said: "The *Nicht-Ich* is the symbol of the *Ich,* and serves only for the ego's knowledge of itself . . . One understands the *Ich* only in so far as it is represented by the *Nicht-Ich.*" (*Werke,* III, 90; also Fichte, *Die Bestimmung des Menschen* [The Vocation of Man], Zweites Buch: Wissen [Book II: Knowledge].) *Cf. Ess.,* II, 25.

and still burns, and thou thyself seest the very smoke thereof. Ah! and the far more mysterious live ember of Vital Fire was then also put down there; and still miraculously burns and spreads; and the smoke and ashes thereof (in these Judgment-Halls and Churchyards), and its bellows-engines (in these Churches), thou still seest; and its flame, looking out from every kind countenance, and every hateful one, still warms thee or scorches thee.

'Of Man's Activity and Attainment the chief results are aeriform, mystic, and preserved in Tradition only:[1] such are his Forms of Government, with the Authority they rest on; his Customs, or Fashions both of Cloth-habits and of Soul-habits; much more his collective stock of Handicrafts, the whole Faculty he has acquired of manipulating Nature: all these things, as indispensable and priceless as they are, cannot in any way be fixed under lock and key, but must flit, spirit-like, on impalpable vehicles, from Father to Son; if you demand sight of them, they are nowhere to be met with. Visible Plowmen and Hammermen there have been, ever from Cain and Tubalcain downwards:[2] but where does your accumulated Agricultural, Metallurgic, and other Manufacturing SKILL lie warehoused? It transmits itself on the atmospheric air, on the sun's rays (by Hearing and by Vision); it is a thing aeriform, impalpable, of quite spiritual sort. In like manner, ask me not, Where are the LAWS; where is the GOVERNMENT? In vain wilt thou go to Schönbrunn,[3] to Downing Street,[4] to the Palais Bourbon:[5] thou findest nothing

[1]The rest of the chapter shows Teufelsdröckh looking on the world with new eyes: all forms of human activity—governments, occupations, books, wars, heroisms, inventions—are but evidences of mind at work with matter, "manipulating Nature," the ego (*Ich*) expressing itself by means of the non-ego (*Nicht-Ich*), the whole process "mystically" carried on by tradition (itself a form of the ego's activity).

[2]See Genesis, iv, 1–22.

[3]An imperial palace on the outskirts of Vienna, where important treaties were signed during the Napoleonic wars.

[4]A street in London, containing the Government Offices and the official residence of the Prime Minister.

[5]The Chamber of Deputies in Paris, seat of the French parliament.

there but brick or stone houses, and some bundles of Papers tied with tape. Where, then, is that same cunningly-devised almighty GOVERNMENT of theirs to be laid hands on? Everywhere, yet nowhere: seen only in its works, this too is a thing aeriform, invisible; or if you will, mystic and miraculous. So spiritual (*geistig*) is our whole daily Life: all that we do springs out of Mystery, Spirit, invisible Force; only like a little Cloud-image, or Armida's Palace,[1] air-built, does the Actual body itself forth from the great mystic Deep.

'Visible and tangible products of the Past, again, I reckon-up to the extent of three. Cities, with their Cabinets and Arsenals; then tilled Fields, to either or to both of which divisions Roads with their Bridges, may belong; and thirdly ——Books. In which third truly, the last invented, lies a worth far surpassing that of the two others. Wondrous indeed is the virtue of a true Book. Not like a dead city of stones, yearly crumbling, yearly needing repair; more like a tilled field, but then a spiritual field: like a spiritual tree, let me rather say, it stands from year to year, and from age to age (we have Books that already number some hundred-and-fifty human ages); and yearly comes its new produce of leaves (Commentaries, Deductions, Philosophical, Political Systems; or were it only Sermons, Pamphlets, Journalistic Essays), every one of which is talismanic and thaumaturgic,[2] for it can persuade men. O thou who art able to write a Book, which once in the two centuries or oftener there is a man gifted to do, envy not him whom they name City-builder, and inexpressibly pity him whom they name Conqueror or City-burner! Thou too art a Conqueror and Victor; but of the true sort, namely over the Devil: thou too hast built what will outlast all marble and metal, and be a wonder-bringing City of the Mind, a Temple

---

[1]The castle of the enchantress in Tasso's *Jerusalem Delivered*.

[2]Wonder-working. Apparently Carlyle, in his reading of Novalis, had caught some of that mystic's belief in the "magical" nature of the spiritual life. Novalis's *magischer Idealismus* is expressed in a section of his *Fragmente,* labelled as "Magische Fragmente." From these Carlyle quotes in his essay on Novalis (*Ess.,* II, 39–43).

and Seminary and Prophetic Mount, whereto all kindreds of the Earth will pilgrim.—Fool! why journeyest thou wearisomely, in thy antiquarian fervour, to gaze on the stone pyramids of Geeza, or the clay ones of Sacchara?[1] These stand there, as I can tell thee, idle and inert, looking over the Desert, foolishly enough, for the last three-thousand years: but canst thou not open thy Hebrew BIBLE, then, or even Luther's Version[2] thereof?'

No less satisfactory is his sudden appearance not in Battle, yet on some Battle-field; which, we soon gather, must be that of Wagram;[3] so that here, for once, is a certain approximation to distinctiveness of date. Omitting much, let us impart what follows:

'Horrible enough! A whole Marchfeld[4] strewed with shell-splinters, cannon-shot, ruined tumbrils, and dead men and horses; stragglers still remaining not so much as buried. And those red mould heaps: ay, there lie the Shells of Men, out of which all the Life and Virtue has been blown; and now are they swept together, and crammed-down out of sight, like blown Egg-shells!—Did Nature, when she bade the Donau bring down his mould-cargoes from the Carinthian and Carpathian Heights, and spread them out here into the softest, richest level,—intend thee, O Marchfeld, for a corn-bearing Nursery, whereon her children might be nursed; or for a Cockpit, wherein they might the more commodiously be throttled and tattered? Were thy three broad Highways, meeting here from the ends of Europe, made for Ammunition-wagons, then? Were thy Wagrams and Still-

[1]*Geeza . . . Sacchara* (or Ghizeh, and Sakkara): the sites of the most notable pyramids in Egypt, near Cairo.

[2]Appeared in 1534–35.

[3]A village near Vienna where Napoleon defeated the Austrians, July 5, 6, 1809.

[4]A plain near Vienna, north of the Danube (Donau), where Ottokar, King of Bohemia, was slain by Rudolph of Hapsburg, in the battle of Stillfried (or Stielfried) in 1278. More than five centuries later, at Wagram, in the same plain, Napoleon conquered the Hapsburgs. See "Early German Literature," *Ess.*, II, 277, note.

frieds but so many ready-built Casemates, wherein the house of Hapsburg might batter with artillery, and with artillery be battered? König Ottokar, amid yonder hillocks, dies under Rodolf's truncheon; here Kaiser Franz falls a-swoon under Napoleon's: within which five centuries, to omit the others, how has thy breast, fair Plain, been defaced and defiled! The greensward is torn-up and trampled-down; man's fond care of it, his fruit-trees, hedge-rows, and pleasant dwellings, blown away with gunpowder; and the kind seedfield lies a desolate, hideous Place of Sculls.[1]—Nevertheless, Nature is at work; neither shall these Powder-Devilkins with their utmost devilry gainsay her: but all that gore and carnage will be shrouded-in, absorbed into manure; and next year the Marchfeld will be green, nay greener. Thrifty unwearied Nature, ever out of our great waste educing some little profit of thy own,—how dost thou, from the very carcass of the Killer, bring Life for the Living![2]

'What, speaking in quite unofficial language, is the net-purport and upshot of war? To my own knowledge, for example, there dwell and toil, in the British village of Dumdrudge,[3] usually some five-hundred souls. From these, by certain "Natural Enemies"[4] of the French, there are successively selected, during the French war, say thirty able-bodied men: Dumdrudge, at her own expense, has suckled and nursed them: she has, not without difficulty and sorrow, fed them up to manhood, and even trained them to crafts, so that one can weave, another build, another hammer, and the weakest can stand under thirty stone avoirdupois. Nevertheless, amid much weeping and swearing, they are selected; all dressed in red; and shipped away, at the public charges, some two-

---

[1]Golgotha. (See p. 164, *note* 1.)

[2]*Cf.* Judges, xiv, 9.

[3]Carlyle's coinage for many of the British villages he knew in the 1830's.

[4]An expression used at the time in respect to the English and the French. Barrett notes Hobbes's "homo homini lupus" (applied to the Orangemen by the Catholics in 1824), as a possible source.

thousand miles, or say only to the south of Spain;[1] and fed there till wanted. And now to that same spot, in the south of Spain, are thirty similar French artisans, from a French Dumdrudge, in like manner wending: till at length, after infinite effort, the two parties come into actual juxtaposition; and Thirty stands fronting Thirty, each with a gun in his hand. Straightway the word "Fire!" is given: and they blow the souls out of one another; and in place of sixty brisk useful craftsmen, the world has sixty dead carcasses, which it must bury, and anew shed tears for. Had these men any quarrel? Busy as the Devil is, not the smallest! They lived far enough apart; were the entirest strangers; nay, in so wide a Universe, there was even, unconsciously, by Commerce, some mutual helpfulness between them. How then? Simpleton! their Governors had fallen-out; and, instead of shooting one another, had the cunning to make these poor blockheads shoot.—Alas, so is it in Deutschland, and hitherto in all other lands; still as of old, "what devilry soever Kings do, the Greeks must pay the piper!"[2]—In that fiction of the English Smollet,[3] it is true, the final Cessation of War is perhaps prophetically shadowed forth; where the two Natural Enemies, in person, take each a Tobacco-pipe, filled with Brimstone; light the same, and smoke in one another's faces, till the weaker gives in: but from such predicted Peace-Era, what blood-filled trenches, and contentious centuries, may still divide us!'

Thus can the Professor, at least in lucid intervals, look away from his own sorrows, over the many-coloured world, and pertinently enough note what is passing there. We may remark, indeed, that for the matter of spiritual culture, if for nothing else, perhaps few periods of his life were richer than this. Internally, there is the most momentous instructive Course of Practical Philosophy, with Experiments, going on;

---

[1]To fight in the Peninsular War, 1808–14, in which the British were engaged against Napoleon.

[2]A free adaptation of Horace, *Epistles*, I, ii, 14.

[3]Smollett (1721–71), *The Adventures of Ferdinand Count Fathom*, Ch. xli.

towards the right comprehension of which his Peripatetic[1] habits, favourable to Meditation, might help him rather than hinder. Externally, again, as he wanders to and fro, there are, if for the longing heart little substance, yet for the seeing eye sights enough: in these so boundless Travels of his, granting that the Satanic School was even partially kept down, what an incredible knowledge of our Planet, and its Inhabitants and their Works, that is to say, of all knowable things, might not Teufelsdröckh acquire!

'I have read in most Public Libraries,' says he, 'including those of Constantinople[2] and Samarcand:[3] in most Colleges, except the Chinese Mandarin ones, I have studied, or seen that there was no studying. Unknown Languages have I oftenest gathered from their natural repertory, the Air, by my organ of Hearing; Statistics, Geographics, Topographics came, through the Eye, almost of their own accord. The ways of Man, how he seeks food, and warmth, and protection for himself, in most regions, are ocularly known to me. Like the great Hadrian,[4] I meted-out much of the terraqueous Globe with a pair of Compasses that belonged to myself only.

'Of great Scenes why speak? Three summer days, I lingered reflecting, and even composing (*dichtete*), by the Pine-chasms of Vaucluse;[5] and in that clear Lakelet moistened my bread. I have sat under the Palm-trees of Tadmor;[6] smoked a pipe

[1]Walking about; itinerant. Humorously adapted from the name given to the followers of Aristotle, who walked about as he lectured in the Lyceum at Athens.

[2]The library in the Mosque of St. Sophia.

[3]In Turkestan, an important seat of learning in the fifteenth century.

[4]Hadrian (76–138) spent the greater part of his reign in travelling through the provinces of the empire, in order that he might personally inspect their condition; holding that the emperor should be like the sun and visit every part of his dominions. So *Wilhelm Meister,* II, 414.

[5]A village near Avignon, in South-East France, famous as the home of Petrarch.

[6]*I. e.,* Palmyra (called "Tadmor in the wilderness" in II Chronicles, viii, 4; and "Tamar" in Ezekiel, xlvii, 19, *etc.*), a celebrated city in the Syrian Desert, built by Solomon, and called the "City of Palms." It was independent of Rome under Zenobia, but was captured by Aurelian and destroyed in 273. It has splendid ruins.

among the ruins of Babylon. The great Wall of China I have seen; and can testify that it is of gray brick, coped and covered with granite, and shows only second-rate masonry.—Great Events, also, have not I witnessed? Kings sweated-down (*ausgemergelt*) into Berlin-and-Milan Customhouse-Officers;[1] the World well won, and the World well lost;[2] oftener than once a hundred-thousand individuals shot (by each other) in one day. All kindreds and peoples and nations dashed together, and shifted and shovelled into heaps, that they might ferment there, and in time unite. The birth-pangs of Democracy,[3] wherewith convulsed Europe was groaning in cries that reached Heaven, could not escape me.

'For great Men I have ever had the warmest predilection; and can perhaps boast that few such in this era have wholly escaped me. Great Men are the inspired (speaking and acting) Texts of that divine Book of Revelation, whereof a Chapter is completed from epoch to epoch, and by some named History; to which inspired Texts your numerous talented men, and your innumerable untalented men, are the better or worse exegetic Commentaries,[4] and wagonload of too-stupid, heretical or orthodox, weekly Sermons. For my study, the inspired Texts themselves! Thus did not I, in very early days, having disguised me as tavern-waiter, stand

---

[1]Allusion to the low estate to which Kings under Napoleon fell after the British-exports decree of 1806.

[2]*Cf. All for Love, or the World Well Lost,* a play by Dryden, 1678.

[3]Probable allusion to the famous Three Days Revolution in Paris, July 27–29, 1830, in which Charles X was overthrown. During 1830 and 1831 riots took place in many towns in Great Britain, as a part of the Reform agitation, which eventuated in the Reform Bill of 1832.

[4]The germ of Carlyle's doctrine of heroes and hero-worship. He had been reading Fichte's *Über das Wesen des Gelehrten* (On the Nature of the Scholar): the hero (or leader) "is the most direct revelation (*Erscheinung*) of God in the world" (*Werke,* VI, 427). Both Fichte and Novalis held that "the whole of history is an Evangel (*Evangelium*)," of which great men are the most important features (Novalis, *Werke,* III, 192). See *Heroes and Hero-Worship.*—It must not be forgotten, however, that Carlyle's whole hero-theory lay implicit in the Calvinist doctrine of "the Elect." See Int., V, a.

behind the field-chairs, under that shady Tree at Treisnitz[1] by the Jena Highway; waiting upon the great Schiller and greater Goethe; and hearing what I have not forgotten. For——'

——But at this point the Editor recalls his principle of caution, some time ago laid down, and must suppress much. Let not the sacredness of Laurelled, still more, of Crowned Heads, be tampered with. Should we, at a future day, find circumstances altered, and the time come for Publication, then may these glimpses into the privacy of the Illustrious be conceded; which for the present were little better than treacherous, perhaps traitorous Eavesdroppings. Of Lord Byron, therefore, of Pope Pius,[2] Emperor Tarakwang,[3] and the 'White Water-roses' (Chinese Carbonari)[4] with their mysteries, no notice here! Of Napoleon himself we shall only, glancing from afar, remark that Teufelsdröckh's relation to him seems to have been of very varied character. At first we find our poor Professor on the point of being shot as a spy; then taken into private conversation, even pinched on the ear, yet presented with no money; at last indignantly dismissed, almost thrown out of doors, as an 'Ideologist.' 'He himself,' says the Professor, 'was among the completest Ideologists, at least Ideopraxists:[5] in the Idea (*in der Idee*)[6] he lived, moved and fought. The man was a Divine Missionary, though unconscious of it; and preached, through the cannon's throat, that great doctrine, *La carrière ouverte aux talens* (The Tools to

[1]*I.e.,* Triesnitz. Near Jena in Germany. Where Goethe and Schiller sometimes met in the period of the *Musen-Almanach,* on which they collaborated, in 1796–97, *etc.* See Carlyle's *Life of Schiller,* p. 124.

[2]Probably Pius VII, who was Pope from 1800 to 1823.

[3]The Chinese Emperor Tao Kuang (1781–1850) ascended the throne in 1821.

[4]Carbonari: *Charcoal-burners:* secret revolutionary society in Italy, in the early nineteenth century.

[5]*Ideologist:* a theorist, dreamer, visionary. The term was applied by Napoleon to those who remained faithful to the doctrines of the French Revolution of 1789.—*Ideopraxists:* those who put ideas into practice.

[6]A probable adaptation of Goethe's *Spruch:* "Napoleon . . . lived altogether in the Idea . . ." (*Maximen und Reflexionen,* Nos. 262–64).

him that can handle them),[1] which is our ultimate Political Evangel, wherein alone can liberty lie. Madly enough he preached, it is true, as Enthusiasts[2] and first Missionaries are wont, with imperfect utterance, amid much frothy rant; yet as articulately perhaps as the case admitted. Or call him, if you will, an American Backwoodsman, who had to fell unpenetrated forests, and battle with innumerable wolves, and did not entirely forbear strong liquor, rioting, and even theft; whom, notwithstanding, the peaceful Sower will follow, and, as he cuts the boundless harvest, bless.'

More legitimate and decisively authentic is Teufelsdröckh's appearance and emergence (we know not well whence) in the solitude of the North Cape, on that June Midnight. He has a 'light-blue Spanish cloak' hanging round him, as his 'most commodious, principal, indeed sole upper-garment'; and stands there, on the World-promontory, looking over the infinite Brine, like a little blue Belfry (as we figure), now motionless indeed, yet ready, if stirred, to ring quaintest changes.

'Silence as of death,' writes he; 'for Midnight, even in the Arctic latitudes, has its character: nothing but the granite cliffs ruddy-tinged, the peaceable gurgle of that slow-heaving Polar Ocean, over which in the utmost North the great Sun hangs low and lazy, as if he too were slumbering. Yet is his cloud-couch wrought of crimson and cloth-of-gold; yet does his light stream over the mirror of waters, like a tremulous fire-pillar, shooting downwards to the abyss, and hide itself under my feet. In such moments, Solitude also is invaluable; for who would speak, or be looked on, when behind him lies all Europe and Africa, fast asleep, except the watchmen; and before him the silent Immensity, and Palace of the Eternal, whereof our Sun is but a porch-lamp?

'Nevertheless, in this solemn moment comes a man, or

---

[1]Expanded a little in *Heroes and Hero-Worship,* p. 276. During the Napoleonic wars, the English Whig statesmen, Fox and Grenville, effected a coalition known as the "Ministry of All-the-Talents," 1806–1807.

[2]Used in its older sense, to mean *religious madmen.*

monster, scrambling from among the rock-hollows; and, shaggy, huge as the Hyperborean[1] Bear, hails me in Russian speech: most probably, therefore, a Russian Smuggler. With courteous brevity, I signify my indifference to contraband trade, my humane intentions, yet strong wish to be private. In vain: the monster, counting doubtless on his superior stature, and minded to make sport for himself, or perhaps profit, were it with murder, continues to advance; ever assailing me with his importunate train-oil[2] breath; and now has advanced, till we stand both on the verge of the rock, the deep Sea rippling greedily down below. What argument will avail? On the thick Hyperborean, cherubic reasoning, seraphic eloquence were lost. Prepared for such extremity, I, deftly enough, whisk aside one step; draw out, from my interior reservoirs, a sufficient Birmingham Horse-pistol, and say, "Be so obliging as retire, Friend (*Er ziehe sich zurück, Freund*), and with promptitude!" This logic even the Hyperborean understands: fast enough, with apologetic, petitionary growl, he sidles off; and, except for suicidal as well as homicidal purposes, need not return.

'Such I hold to be the genuine use of Gunpowder: that it makes all men alike tall. Nay, if thou be cooler, cleverer than I, if thou have more *Mind,* though all but no *Body* whatever, then canst thou kill me first, and art the taller. Hereby, at last, is the Goliath powerless, and the David resistless; savage Animalism is nothing, inventive Spiritualism is all.[3]

'With respect to Duels, indeed, I have my own ideas. Few things, in this so surprising world, strike me with more surprise. Two little visual Spectra of men, hovering with insecure enough cohesion in the midst of the UNFATHOMABLE,

---

[1]Probably from the Greek, meaning beyond Boreas (the North Wind); hence most northern.

[2]Whale oil.

[3]The sum and substance of the present chapter. Mind, or Spirit is the true power; material things and organization are but the evidence and means of that power; and the more subtle the means the nearer they are to the spiritual. Barrett notes Carlyle's ranking of Christian humility over Norse valour (in *On Heroes*) as an example.

and to dissolve therein, at any rate, very soon,—make pause at the distance of twelve paces asunder; whirl round; and, simultaneously by the cunningest mechanism, explode one another into Dissolution; and off-hand become Air, and Non-extant! Deuce on it (*verdammt*), the little spitfires!—Nay, I think with old Hugo von Trimberg:[1] "God must needs laugh outright, could such a thing be, to see his wondrous Manikins here below." '

But amid these specialties, let us not forget the great generality, which is our chief quest here: How prospered the inner man of Teufelsdröckh under so much outward shifting? Does Legion[2] still lurk in him, though repressed; or has he exorcised that Devil's Brood? We can answer that the symptoms continue promising. Experience is the grand spiritual Doctor; and with him Teufelsdröckh has been long a patient, swallowing many a bitter bolus.[3] Unless our poor Friend belong to the numerous class of Incurables, which seems not likely, some cure will doubtless be effected. We should rather say that Legion, or the Satanic School, was now pretty well extirpated and cast out, but next to nothing introduced in its room; whereby the heart remains, for the while, in a quiet but no comfortable state.

'At length, after so much roasting,' thus writes our Autobiographer, 'I was what you might name calcined. Pray only that it be not rather, as is the more frequent issue, reduced to a *caput-mortuum!*[4] But in any case, by mere dint of practice, I had grown familiar with many things. Wretchedness was still wretched; but I could now partly see through it, and despise it. Which highest mortal, in this inane Existence, had I not found a Shadow-hunter, or Shadow-hunted; and,

---

[1]Medieval moralist, schoolmaster, and Meistersinger (1260–1309). See Carlyle's "Early German Literature" (*Ess.,* II, 287–94).

[2]*Cf.* Mark, v, 9; Luke, viii, 30.

[3]Large mass of material, or pill, such as is used in veterinary practice. (Carlylean humour.)

[4]Literally a death's head. In old chemistry, the residuum after distillation or sublimation; hence any worthless residue.

when I looked through his brave garnitures, miserable enough? Thy wishes have all been sniffed aside, thought I: but what, had they even been all granted! Did not the Boy Alexander weep because he had not two Planets to conquer; or a whole Solar System; or after that, a whole Universe?[1] *Ach Gott,* when I gazed into these Stars, have they not looked-down on me as if with pity, from their serene spaces; like Eyes glistening with heavenly tears over the little lot of man! Thousands of human generations, all as noisy as our own, have been swallowed-up of Time, and there remains no wreck[2] of them any more; and Arcturus and Orion and Sirius and the Pleiades are still shining in their courses, clear and young, as when the Shepherd first noted them in the plain of Shinar.[3] Pshaw! what is this paltry little Dog-cage[4] of an Earth; what art thou that sittest whining there? Thou art still Nothing, Nobody: true; but who, then, is Something, Somebody? For thee the Family of Man has no use; it rejects thee; thou art wholly as a dissevered limb:[5] so be it; perhaps it is better so!'

Too-heavy-laden Teufelsdröckh! Yet surely his bands are loosening; one day he will hurl the burden far from him, and bound forth free and with a second youth.

'This,' says our Professor, 'was the CENTRE OF INDIFFERENCE[6] I had now reached; through which whoso travels from the Negative Pole to the Positive must necessarily pass.'

---

[1]So *Hudibras,* I, iii, 1022 (B.). *Cf.* Juvenal, *Satires,* x, 168.

[2]*Wreck:* in the older meaning of *wrack,* ruin or remains.

[3]The tower of Babel was built on "a plain in the land of Shinar" (Genesis, xi, 1–9; *Paradise Lost,* iii, 466–67).

[4]A wheel-like cage in which a dog was placed to turn the jack of a turnspit, and so roast the meat. The term here suggests the aimless and mechanical nature of the world when seen without the eyes of faith. "Dog-hutch" is another term of which Carlyle was fond.

[5]Adapted from the Journal Sept. 21, 1825 (*C.E.L.,* I, Ch. xvii), *etc.*

[6]The expression is here used as in physics, to denote that point midway between two extremes of a magnet, where the attractive force of the two poles is stable; the equator of the magnet.

CHAPTER IX

THE EVERLASTING YEA

Temptations in the Wilderness: Victory over the Tempter. Annihilation of self. Belief in God, and love to Man. The Origin of Evil, a problem ever requiring to be solved anew: Teufelsdröckh's solution. Love of Happiness a vain whim: A Higher in man than Love of Happiness. The Everlasting Yea. Worship of Sorrow. Voltaire: his task now finished. Conviction worthless, impossible, without Conduct. The true Ideal, the Actual: Up and work!

TEMPTATIONS in the Wilderness!'[1] exclaims Teufelsdröckh: 'Have we not all to be tried with such? Not so easily can the old Adam,[2] lodged in us by birth, be dispossessed. Our Life is compassed round with Necessity; yet is the meaning of Life itself no other than Freedom, than Voluntary Force:[3] thus have we a warfare; in the beginning, especially, a hard-fought battle. For the God-given mandate, *Work thou in Welldoing,*[4] lies mysteriously written, in Promethean[5] Prophetic Characters, in our hearts; and leaves us no rest,[6] night

[1]See Matthew, iv, 1; *Paradise Regained,* i, 193 ff.

[2]*Cf.* I Corinthians, xv, 21–22; Colossians, iii, 9: "put off the old man," *etc.*

[3]The discovery made in Teufelsdröckh's "conversion"—that life is consciousness, will, inner force, though "compassed round with Necessity [natural law]." The "old Adam" in man perpetually tempts him to make his home comfortably with nature and her laws, accepting life on an animal plane (the perpetual "temptation in the Wilderness") and to regard his sense of freedom and moral superiority over blind force as a delusion.

[4]Probably adapted from II Thessalonians, iii, 13.

[5]Fire-bearing, *etc.* See p. 134, *note* 2.

[6]Carlyle is following Goethe here, *Wilhelm Meister,* I, 444: "Deep within us lies the creative force, which out of these [the elements of Nature, the Not-Me] can produce what they were meant to be; and which *leaves us neither sleep nor rest* till . . . that same have been produced." (Italics added.)

or day, till it be deciphered and obeyed; till it burn forth, in our conduct, a visible, acted Gospel of Freedom. And as the clay-given mandate, *Eat thou and be filled*, at the same time persuasively proclaims itself through every nerve,—must not there be a confusion, a contest, before the better Influence can become the upper?

'To me nothing seems more natural than that the Son of Man, when such God-given mandate first prophetically stirs within him, and the Clay must now be vanquished or vanquish,—should be carried of the spirit into grim Solitudes, and there fronting the Tempter do grimmest battle with him; defiantly setting him at naught, till he yield and fly. Name it as we choose: with or without visible Devil, whether in the natural Desert of rocks and sands, or in the populous moral Desert of selfishness and baseness,—to such Temptation are we all called. Unhappy if we are not! Unhappy if we are but Half-men, in whom that divine handwriting has never blazed forth, all-subduing, in true sun-splendour; but quivers dubiously amid meaner lights: or smoulders, in dull pain, in darkness, under earthly vapours!—Our Wilderness is the wide World in an Atheistic Century; our Forty Days are long years of suffering and fasting: nevertheless, to these also comes an end. Yes, to me also was given, if not Victory, yet the consciousness of Battle, and the resolve to persevere therein while life or faculty is left. To me also, entangled in the enchanted forests, demon-peopled, doleful of sight and of sound, it was given, after weariest wanderings, to work out my way into the higher sunlight slopes—of that Mountain[1] which has no summit, or whose summit is in Heaven only!'

He says elsewhere, under a less ambitious figure; as figures are, once for all, natural to him: 'Has not thy Life been that of most sufficient men (*tüchtigen Männer*) thou hast known in this generation? An outflush of foolish young Enthusiasm,

[1]Symbol of spiritual insight, revelation of a mighty truth, *etc.* Barrett cites Dante's "Mountain of Purification" and *On Heroes* ("Hero as Poet"), *etc.*

like the first fallow-crop, wherein are as many weeds as valuable herbs: this all parched away, under the Droughts of practical and spiritual Unbelief, as Disappointment, in thought and act, often-repeated gave rise to Doubt, and Doubt gradually settled into Denial! If I have had a second-crop, and now see the perennial greensward, and sit under umbrageous cedars, which defy all Drought (and Doubt); herein too, be the Heavens praised, I am not without examples, and even examplars.'

So that, for Teufelsdröckh also, there has been a 'glorious revolution': these mad shadow-hunting and shadow-hunted Pilgrimings of his were but some purifying 'Temptation in the Wilderness,' before his apostolic work (such as it was) could begin; which Temptation is now happily over, and the Devil once more worsted! Was 'that high moment in the *Rue de l'Enfer,*' then, properly the turning-point of the battle; when the Fiend said, *Worship me, or be torn in shreds;* and was answered valiantly with an *Apage Satana?*[1]—Singular Teufelsdröckh, would thou hadst told thy singular story in plain words! But it is fruitless to look there, in those Paper-bags, for such. Nothing but innuendoes, figurative crotchets: a typical Shadow, fitfully wavering, prophetico-satiric; no clear logical Picture. 'How paint to the sensual eye,' asks he once, 'what passes in the Holy-of-Holies[2] of Man's Soul; in what words, known to these profane times, speak even afar-off of the unspeakable?' We ask in turn: Why perplex these times, profane as they are, with needless obscurity, by omission and by commission? Not mystical only is our Professor, but whimsical; and involves himself, now more than ever, in eye-bewildering *chiaroscuro.*[3] Successive glimpses, here faithfully imparted, our more gifted readers must endeavour to combine for their own behoof.

---

[1]"Get thee hence, Satan!" Matthew, iv, 8–10.

[2]See p. 99, *note* 2. An early expression of Carlyle's doctrine of silence. See Bk. III, Ch. iii, "Symbols"; also *Wilhelm Meister,* II, 76: "The best is not to be explained by words."

[3]Italian: *chiaro-oscuro:* clear-obscure; hence light and shade.

He says: 'The hot Harmattan wind[1] had raged itself out; its howl went silent within me; and the long-deafened soul could now hear. I paused in my wild wanderings; and sat me down to wait, and consider; for it was as if the hour of change drew nigh. I seemed to surrender, to renounce utterly, and say: Fly, then, false shadows of Hope; I will chase you no more, I will believe you no more. And ye too, haggard spectres of Fear, I care not for you; ye too are all shadows and a lie. Let me rest here: for I am way-weary and life-weary; I will rest here, were it but to die: to die or to live is alike to me;[2] alike insignificant.'—And again: 'Here, then, as I lay in that Centre of Indifference; cast, doubtless by benignant upper Influence, into a healing sleep, the heavy dreams rolled gradually away, and I awoke to a new Heaven and a new Earth.[3] The first preliminary moral Act, Annihilation of Self (*Selbst-tödtung*),[4] had been happily accomplished; and my mind's eyes were now unsealed, and its hands ungyved.'[5]

Might we not also conjecture that the following passage refers to his Locality, during this same 'healing sleep'; that his Pilgrim-staff lies cast aside here, on 'the high table-land'; and indeed that the repose is already taking wholesome effect on him? If it were not that the tone, in some parts, has more of riancy, even of levity, than we could have expected! However, in Teufelsdröckh, there is always the strangest Dualism:

---

[1]A dry dust-laden wind blowing from the interior on the Atlantic coast of Africa in certain seasons, withering vegetation and drying the skin. *Cf.* "the Harmattan breath of Doubt . . . where the Tree of Life once bloomed", *etc.* ("Goethe," *Ess.*, I, 216).

[2]Barrett notes this as attributed to Thales (Seventh Century B.C.) by Diogenes Laertius.

[3]*Cf.* Revelation, xxi, 1.

[4]Though the idea is essentially Christian (Matthew, xvi, 24–25, *etc.*), the phrasing is, roughly, that of Novalis, for whom, however, *Selbsttödtung* was the first preliminary act of *philosophic thinking,* not of moral action. See the essay on Novalis (*Ess.*, II, 39) and Novalis's *Werke,* III, 32. Carlyle's idea is closer to Goethe's *Entsagen* (Renunciation), though closer still to the Christian ideal of "losing one's life to save it." For a complete analysis, see *Carlyle and German Thought,* Ch. viii, Sect. 4.

[5]Unfettered. See p. 128, *note* 2.

light dancing, with guitar-music, will be going on in the fore-court, while by fits from within comes the faint whimpering of woe and wail. We transcribe the piece entire.

'Beautiful it was to sit there, as in my skyey Tent, musing and meditating; on the high table-land, in front of the Mountains; over me, as roof, the azure Dome, and around me, for walls, four azure-flowing curtains,—namely, of the Four azure Winds, on whose bottom-fringes also I have seen gilding. And then to fancy the fair Castles that stood sheltered in these Mountain hollows; with their green flower-lawns, and white dames and damosels, lovely enough: or better still, the straw-roofed Cottages, wherein stood many a Mother baking bread, with her children round her:—all hidden and protectingly folded-up in the valley-folds; yet there and alive, as sure as if I beheld them. Or to see, as well as fancy, the nine Towns and Villages, that lay round my mountain-seat, which, in still weather, were wont to speak to me (by their steeple-bells) with metal tongue; and, in almost all weather, proclaimed their vitality by repeated Smoke-clouds; whereon, as on a culinary horologe, I might read the hour of the day. For it was the smoke of cookery, as kind housewives at morning, midday, eventide, were boiling their husbands' kettles; and ever a blue pillar rose up into the air, successively or simultaneously, from each of the nine, saying, as plainly as smoke could say: Such and such a meal is getting ready here. Not uninteresting! For you have the whole Borough, with all its love-makings and scandal-mongeries, contentions and contentments, as in miniature, and could cover it all with your hat.—If, in my wide Wayfarings, I had learned to look into the business of the World in its details, here perhaps was the place for combining it into general propositions, and deducing inferences therefrom.

'Often also could I see the black Tempest marching in anger through the Distance: round some Schreckhorn,[1] as yet grim-blue, would the eddying vapour gather, and there tumul-

[1]"Peak of Terror." One of the principal summits of the Bernese Alps, in Switzerland.

tuously eddy, and flow down like a mad witch's hair; till, after a space, it vanished, and, in the clear sunbeam, your Schreckhorn stood smiling grim-white, for the vapour had held snow. How thou fermentest and elaboratest, in thy great fermenting-vat and laboratory of an Atmosphere, of a World, O Nature! —Or what is Nature? Ha! why do I not name thee GOD? Art not thou the "Living Garment of God"?[1] O Heavens, is it, in very deed, HE, then, that ever speaks through thee; that lives and loves in thee, that lives and loves in me?

'Fore-shadows, call them rather fore-splendours, of that Truth, and Beginning of Truths, fell mysteriously over my soul. Sweeter than Dayspring to the Ship-wrecked in Nova Zembla;[2] ah, like the mother's voice to her little child that strays bewildered, weeping, in unknown tumults; like soft streamings of celestial music to my too-exasperated heart, came that Evangel. The Universe is not dead and demoniacal, a charnel-house[3] with spectres; but godlike, and my Father's!

'With other eyes, too, could I now look upon my fellow man: with an infinite Love, an infinite Pity. Poor, wandering, wayward man! Art thou not tried, and beaten with stripes, even as I am? Ever, whether thou bear the royal mantle or the beggar's gabardine, art thou not so weary, so heavy-laden; and thy Bed of Rest is but a Grave. O my Brother, my Brother, why cannot I shelter thee in my bosom, and wipe away all tears from thy eyes![4]—Truly, the din of

---

[1]See p. 55, *note* 4. Carlyle is tempted to name Nature, God (possibly after Goethe and Schelling); but note p. 59: "Nature is good, but she is not the best," in which statement Carlyle's Calvinism breaks through his preoccupation with German ideas.

[2]Possibly an allusion to the expedition of Willem Barents, Dutch navigator, who left Amsterdam in 1594 with two ships to search for a north-west passage to eastern Asia. On a third voyage in 1596 his ship was frozen off the north coast of Novaya Zemlya during the winter. Barents died on the way home the following summer (1597). Jean Paul refers to "the winter history of the four Russian sailors on Nova Zembla" ("Quintus Fixlein," *German Romance,* II, 295).

[3]*Cf.* similar passage in Jean Paul's *Flower, Fruit, etc.,* in *Ess.,* II, 156.

[4]*Cf.* Revelation, xxi, 4.

many-voiced Life, which, in this solitude, with the mind's organ, I could hear, was no longer a maddening discord, but a melting one; like inarticulate cries, and sobbings of a dumb creature, which in the ear of Heaven are prayers. The poor Earth, with her poor joys, was now my needy Mother, not my cruel Stepdame; Man, with his so mad Wants and so mean Endeavours, had become the dearer to me; and even for his sufferings and his sins, I now first named him Brother. Thus was I standing in the porch of that *"Sanctuary of Sorrow"*;[1] by strange, steep ways had I too been guided thither; and ere long its sacred gates would open, and the *"Divine Depth of Sorrow"*[2] lie disclosed to me.'

The Professor says, he here first got eye on the Knot that had been strangling him, and straightway could unfasten it, and was free. 'A vain interminable controversy,' writes he, 'touching what is at present called Origin of Evil, or some such thing, arises in every soul, since the beginning of the world; and in every soul, that would pass from idle Suffering into actual Endeavouring, must first be put an end to. The most, in our time, have to go content with a simple, incomplete enough Suppression of this controversy; to a few some Solution of it is indispensable. In every new era, too, such Solution comes-out in different terms; and ever the Solution of the last era has become obsolete, and is found unserviceable. For it is man's nature to change his Dialect from century to century; he cannot help it though he would. The authentic *Church-Catechism* of our present century has not yet fallen into my hands: meanwhile, for my own private

---

[1]The name of the hall into which Wilhelm Meister is to be taken to view the remaining murals representing the life of Christ; used here to denote a state of soul, later the state of the whole world.

[2]Christ's sorrow; applied here to Teufelsdröckh's new knowledge-through-sorrow; also to the sacredness of suffering everywhere. (See *Wilhelm Meister,* II, 274–75; *Carlyle and German Thought,* pp. 222–30.) These expressions occur frequently throughout Carlyle's works and correspondence, and show how far Carlyle remained faithful to the essence of Christianity, under the intellectual terms of his German authors; *i.e.,* to the acceptance of pain, humility, suffering, *etc.,* as "the furtherances of what is holy." (See Int., Sect. V, c.)

behoof, I attempt to elucidate the matter so. Man's Unhappiness, as I construe, comes of his Greatness;[1] it is because there is an Infinite in him, which with all his cunning he cannot quite bury under the Finite. Will the whole Finance Ministers and Upholsterers and Confectioners of modern Europe undertake, in joint-stock company, to make one Shoeblack HAPPY? They cannot accomplish it, above an hour or two: for the Shoeblack also has a Soul quite other than his Stomach; and would require, if you consider it, for his permanent satisfaction and saturation, simply this allotment, no more, and no less: *God's infinite Universe altogether to himself,* therein to enjoy infinitely, and fill every wish as fast as it rose. Oceans of Hochheimer,[2] a Throat like that of Ophiuchus:[3] speak not of them; to the infinite Shoeblack they are as nothing. No sooner is your ocean filled, than he grumbles that it might have been of better vintage. Try him with half of a Universe, of an Omnipotence, he sets to quarrelling with the proprietor of the other half, and declares himself the most maltreated of men.—Always there is a black spot in our sunshine: it is even, as I said, the *Shadow of Ourselves.*[4]

'But the whim we have of Happiness is somewhat thus. By certain valuations, and averages, of our own striking, we come upon some sort of average terrestrial lot; this we fancy belongs to us by nature, and of indefeasible right. It is simple payment of our wages, of our deserts; requires neither thanks nor complaint; only such *overplus* as there may be do we account Happiness; any *deficit* again is Misery. Now consider that we have the valuation of our own deserts ourselves,

---

[1]Teufelsdröckh has simply reversed his point of view: hitherto his unhappiness came of his overestimating his insignificance in the physical universe; now his own physical insignificance is forgotten in a realization of his spiritual infinitude, which makes him unhappy in a *newer* dynamically creative way, rather than in a static acquisitive fashion.

[2]A Rhine wine from Hochheim near Mainz.

[3]Evidently the throat of the serpent in the Constellation south of Hercules, known as *Serpentarius,* a man holding a serpent in his hands.

[4]See p. 154, *note* 4.

and what a fund of Self-conceit there is in each of us,—do you wonder that the balance should so often dip the wrong way, and many a Blockhead cry: See there, what a payment; was ever worthy gentleman so used!—I tell thee, Blockhead, it all comes of thy Vanity; of what thou *fanciest* those same deserts of thine to be. Fancy that thou deservest to be hanged (as is most likely), thou wilt feel it happiness to be only shot: fancy that thou deservest to be hanged in a hair-halter, it will be a luxury to die in hemp.

'So true is it, what I then said, that *the Fraction of Life can be increased in value not so much by increasing your Numerator as by lessening your Denominator.*[1] Nay, unless my Algebra deceive me, *Unity* itself divided by *Zero* will give *Infinity.* Make thy claim of wages a zero, then; thou hast the world under thy feet. Well did the Wisest of our time write: "It is only with Renunciation (*Entsagen*) that Life, properly speaking, can be said to begin."[2]

'I asked myself: What is this that, ever since earliest years, thou hast been fretting and fuming, and lamenting and self-tormenting, on account of? Say it in a word: is it not because thou art not HAPPY? Because the THOU (sweet gentleman) is not sufficiently honoured, nourished, soft-bedded, and lovingly cared-for? Foolish soul! What Act of Legislature was there that *thou* shouldst be Happy? A little while ago thou hadst no right to *be* at all. What if thou wert born and predestined not to be Happy, but to be Unhappy! Art thou nothing other than a Vulture, then, that fliest through the Universe seeking after somewhat to *eat;* and shrieking dole-

[1]Adapted from the Journal for March 1827 (M.). See p. 126, *note* 5.

[2]Goethe, in *Wilhelm Meister,* II, 334: ". . . the high meaning of Renunciation, by which alone the first real entrance into life is conceivable." For Goethe, Renunciation (*Entsagen*) was a part of *Bildung* (harmonious self-development), a subordination of the parts to the whole, or of one part until a later and more propitious time for activity; for Carlyle, however, it has a Christian, a Calvinistic significance, a "dying to the flesh." Yet it is true that Goethe developed his conception of *Entsagen* in his later, neo-Christian period, and, in view of the latter chapters of the *Wanderjahre,* perhaps Carlyle is not very far from what Goethe at times intended to mean. (See Int., Sect. V. c.)

fully because carrion enough is not given thee? Close thy *Byron;* open thy *Goethe.*'[1]

'*Es leuchtet mir ein,*[2] I see a glimpse of it!' cries he elsewhere: 'there is in man a HIGHER than Love of Happiness: he can do without Happiness, and instead thereof find Blessedness![3] Was it not to preach-forth this same HIGHER that sages and martyrs, the Poet and the Priest, in all times, have spoken and suffered; bearing testimony, through life and through death, of the Godlike that is in Man, and how in the Godlike only has he Strength and Freedom? Which God-inspired Doctrine art thou also honoured to be taught; O Heavens! and broken with manifold merciful Afflictions, even till thou become contrite, and learn it! O, thank thy Destiny for these; thankfully bear what yet remain: thou hadst need of them; the Self in thee needed to be annihilated. By benignant fever-paroxysms is Life rooting out the deep-seated chronic Disease, and triumphs over Death. On the roaring billows of Time, thou art not engulfed, but borne aloft into the azure of Eternity. Love not Pleasure; love God.[4] This is the EVERLASTING YEA, wherein all contradiction is solved: wherein whoso walks and works, it is well with him.'

And again: 'Small is it that thou canst trample the Earth with its injuries under thy feet, as old Greek Zeno[5] trained

---

[1]This is Carlyle's announcement that the age of *Kraftmänner* (Powermen) like Byron, which had followed on the age of Voltaire, has given place to a new era of practical idealism, the age of Goethe in his *Wilhelm Meister.* See "Goethe," *Ess.*, I, 216–24, for Carlyle's comparison of the Goethe of *Werther* with the Byron of *Manfred.*

[2]Meister's exclamation when he catches a glimpse of the significance of the "three reverences" in Chapter x of the *Wanderjahre.*

[3]In obeying the dictates of duty (the key to the Everlasting Yea). Happiness had been sought in satisfying natural impulses, infinite in number, therefore leading to despair and denial of the reality of moral values above the material (the Everlasting No). Duty for the sake of duty is a Kantian principle, developed also by Fichte.

[4]*Cf.* II Timothy, iii, 4.

[5]A Greek Stoic philosopher of the third century B.C. (not to be confused with Zeno the Eleatic, of the fifth century B.C.); whose primary doctrines confirmed Carlyle's Calvinism: the world as an organic harmony; man the microcosm, epitome of the Whole; moral duty as action in

thee: thou canst love the Earth while it injures thee, and even because it injures thee; for this a Greater than Zeno was needed, and he too was sent. Knowest thou that "*Worship of Sorrow*"?[1] The Temple thereof, founded some eighteen centuries ago, now lies in ruins, overgrown with jungle, the habitation of doleful creatures:[2] nevertheless, venture forward; in a low crypt, arched out of falling fragments, thou findest the Altar still there, and its sacred Lamp perennially burning.'

Without pretending to comment on which strange utterances, the Editor will only remark, that there lies beside them much of a still more questionable character; unsuited to the general apprehension; nay wherein he himself does not see his way. Nebulous disquisitions on Religion, yet not without bursts of splendour; on the 'perennial continuance of Inspiration'; on Prophecy; that there are 'true Priests, as well as Baal-Priests,[3] in our own day': with more of the like sort. We select some fractions, by way of finish to this farrago.

'Cease, my much respected Herr von Voltaire,'[4] thus apostrophises the Professor: 'shut thy sweet voice; for the task appointed thee seems finished. Sufficiently hast thou

---

harmony with the divine law of the world, absolute submission to that law, rather than pleasure or happiness; evil to be turned to good through right action; determinism (fate) in metaphysics, but free will in ethics (moral responsibility); acceptance of adversity as a discipline and moulder of personality.

[1]Carlyle's Christian expansion upon Goethe's *sanctuary* and *divine depths of sorrow;* to Stoic fortitude we are to add Christian patience, and *love* of sorrow. "Religion," said Novalis, "contains infinite sadness (*Wehmut*). . . . Man can become holy only through sorrow (*Unglück*)" (*Ess.,* II, 42; Novalis, *Werke,* III, 180, 183).

[2]*Cf.* Isaiah, xiii, 21.—Christian theology, dogmas, and creeds (the clothes of religion) are worn out; the soul is still alive.

[3]I Kings, xviii, 17–40.—False priests.

[4]Voltaire (1694–1778), to Carlyle, was "emphatically the man of his century," summing all the mockery, wit, cold understanding, and lack of religious imagination of the eighteenth century; the antithesis of Goethe, who saw more deeply, passed through his sceptical period, and said in *Wilhelm Meister* (II, 267) that "the Christian religion having once appeared, cannot again vanish" but will take progressively newer forms. See Carlyle's essay on Voltaire, *Ess.,* I, 396 ff.

demonstrated this proposition, considerable or otherwise: That the Mythus of the Christian Religion looks not in the eighteenth century as it did in the eighth. Alas, were thy six-and-thirty quartos, and the six-and-thirty thousand other quartos and folios, and flying sheets or reams, printed before and since on the same subject, all needed to convince us of so little! But what next? Wilt thou help us to embody the divine Spirit of that Religion in a new Mythus, in a new vehicle and vesture, that our Souls, otherwise too like perishing, may live? What! thou hast no faculty in that kind? Only a torch for burning, no hammer for building? Take our thanks, then, and ——— thyself away.

'Meanwhile what are antiquated Mythuses to me? Or is the God present, felt in my own heart, a thing which Herr von Voltaire will dispute out of me; or dispute into me? To the *"Worship of Sorrow"* ascribe what origin and genesis thou pleasest, *has* not that Worship originated, and been generated; is it not *here?* Feel it in thy heart, and then say whether it is of God! This is Belief; all else is Opinion,—for which latter whoso will, let him worry and be worried.'

'Neither,' observes he elsewhere, 'shall ye tear-out one another's eyes, struggling over "Plenary Inspiration,"[1] and such-like: try rather to get a little even Partial Inspiration, each of you for himself. One Bible I know, of whose Plenary Inspiration doubt is not so much as possible; nay with my own eyes I saw the God's-Hand writing it: thereof all other Bibles are but Leaves,—say, in Picture-Writing to assist the weaker faculty.'

Or, to give the wearied reader relief, and bring it to an end, let him take the following perhaps more intelligible passage:

'To me, in this our life,' says the Professor, 'which is an

---

[1]The theological doctrine of plenary inspiration, against which Voltaire was particularly violent, regards supernatural inspiration as extending to all subjects dealt with in the Bible, and therefore to be accepted as true and authoritative. Carlyle regarded Voltaire's attack as beside the point, since "Christianity, the worship of Sorrow," does not rest upon "miracles" and other "evidences," but has its verification "in mysterious, ineffaceable characters . . . written in the purest nature of man" (*Ess.,* I, 457).

internecine warfare with the Time-spirit,[1] other warfare seems questionable. Hast thou in any way a Contention with thy brother, I advise thee, think well what the meaning thereof is. If thou gauge it to the bottom, it is simply this: "Fellow, see! thou art taking more than thy share of Happiness in the world, something from *my* share: which, by the Heavens, thou shalt not; nay I will fight thee rather."—Alas, and the whole lot to be divided is such a beggarly matter, truly a "feast of shells,"[2] for the substance has been spilled out: not enough to quench one Appetite; and the collective human species clutching at them!—Can we not, in all such cases, rather say: "Take it, thou too-ravenous individual; take that pitiful additional fraction of a share, which I reckoned mine, but which thou so wantest; take it with a blessing: would to Heaven I had enough for thee!"—If Fichte's *Wissenschaftslehre* be, "to a certain extent, Applied Christianity,"[3] surely to a still greater extent, so is this. We have here not a Whole Duty of Man,[4] yet a Half Duty, namely the Passive half:[5] could we but do it, as we can demonstrate it!

'But indeed Conviction, were it never so excellent, is worthless till it convert itself into Conduct. Nay properly Conviction is not possible till then; inasmuch as all Speculation is by nature endless, formless, a vortex amid vortices:[6] only by a

[1]One of several somewhat puzzling references to Time; here probably meaning our struggle to express the eternal within the limits of time. See p. 87, *note* 2.

[2]That is, of shells from which the yolks have been blown; adapted from the Journal, Jan. 14, 1830 (*C.E.L.*, II, Ch. iv.).

[3]From Novalis's *Fragmente,* quoted in *Ess.,* II, 43. The significance of Novalis's statement no doubt escaped Carlyle, for there is no evidence that he ever read the *Wissenschaftslehre* (Doctrine of Knowledge) (1794). It is true, however, that some of the doctrines not only of Fichte but of Novalis, the Schlegels, Goethe, and Schiller were "applied Christianity" (an interpretation in modern terms); otherwise Carlyle would never have composed *Sartor Resartus.*

[4]*Whole Duty of Man:* the title of an anonymous devotional work published in 1659. *Cf.* Ecclesiastes, xii, 13.

[5]That is, acceptance of suffering, humility, pain, *etc.* Work is the active half of duty.

[6]Evidence of the mystical element in Carlyle. The deepest knowledge

felt indubitable certainty of Experience does it find any centre to revolve round, and so fashion itself into a system. Most true is it, as a wise man teaches us, that "Doubt of any sort cannot be removed except by Action."[1] On which ground, too, let him who gropes painfully in darkness or uncertain light, and prays vehemently that the dawn may ripen into day, lay this other precept well to heart, which to me was of invaluable service: *"Do the Duty which lies nearest thee,"*[2] which thou knowest to be a Duty! Thy second Duty will already have become clearer.

'May we not say, however, that the hour of Spiritual Enfranchisement is even this: When your Ideal World, wherein the whole man has been dimly struggling and inexpressibly languishing to work, becomes revealed, and thrown open; and you discover, with amazement enough, like the Lothario in *Wilhelm Meister,* that your "America is here or nowhere"?[3] The Situation that has not its Duty, its Ideal, was never yet occupied by man. Yes here, in this poor, miserable, hampered, despicable Actual,[4] wherein thou even now standest, here or nowhere is thy Ideal: work it out therefrom; and working, believe, live, be free. Fool! the Ideal is in thyself, the impediment too is in thyself:[5] thy Condition is but the

---

comes through other channels than logic. *Cf.* Carlyle's rejection of metaphysics as a "disease," in "Characteristics," *Ess.,* III, 25.

[1]From *Wilhelm Meister,* I, 386.

[2]From *Wilhelm Meister,* II, 2 (Bk. VII, Ch. i).

[3]*Wilhelm Meister,* II, 11: "In America, [says Lothario] I fancied I might accomplish something; . . . if any task was not begirt with a thousand dangers, I considered it trivial, unworthy of me. How differently do matters now appear! How precious, how important seems the duty which is nearest me, whatever it may be!"—"I recollect the letter which you sent me from the Western world," said Jarno: "it contained the words: 'I will return, and in my house, amid my fields, among my people, I will say: *Here or nowhere is America!*' "

[4]Another term for the "Time-Spirit" which has "environed and imprisoned us . . ."; the "troublous dim Time-Element," which is yet "the author, the material" of "our whole terrestrial being . . ." (See Bk. II, Ch. iv).

[5]*Wilhelm Meister,* I, 83: "Not in thy condition, but in thyself lies the mean impediment over which thou canst not gain the mastery."

stuff thou art to shape that same Ideal out of: what matters whether such stuff be of this sort or that, so the Form thou give it be heroic, be poetic? O thou that pinest in the imprisonment of the Actual, and criest bitterly to the gods for a kingdom wherein to rule and create, know this of a truth: the thing thou seekest is already with thee, "here or nowhere," couldst thou only see!

'But it is with man's Soul as it was with Nature: the beginning of Creation is—Light.[1] Till the eye have vision, the whole members are in bonds.[2] Divine moment, when over the tempest-tossed Soul, as once over the wild-weltering Chaos, it is spoken: Let there be Light! Ever to the greatest that has felt such moment, is it not miraculous and God-announcing;[3] even as, under simpler figures, to the simplest and least. The mad primeval Discord is hushed; the rudely-jumbled conflicting elements bind themselves into separate Firmaments: deep silent rock-foundations are built beneath; and the skyey vault with its everlasting Luminaries above: instead of a dark wasteful Chaos, we have a blooming, fertile, heaven-encompassed World.

'I too could now say to myself: Be no longer a Chaos, but a World, or even Worldkin. Produce! Produce! Were it but the pitifullest infinitesimal fraction of a Product, produce it, in God's name! 'Tis the utmost thou hast in thee: out with it, then. Up, up! Whatsoever thy hand findeth to do, do it with thy whole might. Work while it is called Today; for the Night cometh, wherein no man can work.'[4]

---

[1]*Cf.* Genesis, i, 3.

[2]Adapted from Matthew, vi, 22, 23.

[3]"Is not real Conviction (*Überzeugung*)," asks Novalis, "the only true God-announcing Miracle (*Gott verkündende Wunder*)?" See *Ess.*, II, 42; Novalis, *Werke*, III, 183.

[4]*Cf.* Ecclesiastes, ix, 10; John, ix, 4.—This is the first great climax in *Sartor*, for which the whole preceding development was a preparation. The next climax comes at the end of Book III, Chapter viii.

CHAPTER X

PAUSE

Conversion; a spiritual attainment peculiar to the modern Era. Teufelsdröckh accepts Authorship as his divine calling. The scope of the command *Thou shalt not steal.*—Editor begins to suspect the authenticity of the Biographical documents; and abandons them for the great Clothes volume. Result of the preceding ten Chapters: Insight into the character of Teufelsdröckh: His fundamental beliefs, and how he was forced to seek and find them.

THUS have we, as closely and perhaps satisfactorily as, in such circumstances, might be, followed Teufelsdröckh through the various successive states and stages of Growth, Entanglement, Unbelief, and almost Reprobation, into a certain clearer state of what he himself seems to consider as Conversion. 'Blame not the word,' says he; 'rejoice rather that such a word, signifying such a thing, has come to light in our modern Era, though hidden from the wisest Ancients. The Old World knew nothing of Conversion;[1] instead of an *Ecce Homo,*[2] they had only some *Choice of Hercules.*[3] It was a new-attained progress in the Moral Development of man: hereby has the Highest come home to the bosoms of the most Limited; what to Plato was but a hallucination, and to Socrates a Chimera, is now clear and certain to your Zinzendorfs,[4] your Wesleys,[5] and the poorest of their Pietists and Methodists.'

---

[1]Carlyle's real conversion came at Hoddam Hill in 1826, when he had found his "nearest duty"—the translating of *German Romance*—and had conquered all his "scepticisms, agonising doubtings," *etc.,* winning at last "a constant inward happiness." *Reminiscences,* pp. 281–82.

[2]"Behold the man!" (John, xix, 5 [Vulgate]); Christ.

[3]Between two women, Virtue and Vice, abstractions, rather than a way of life as suggested in *Ecce Homo.* (See Cicero, *De Officiis,* I, xxxii. Barrett cites Xenophon, *Mem.,* II, i, 21 ff.)

[4]Followers of Nicolaus Ludwig, Count of Zinzendorf and Pottendorf (1700–60), German religious and social reformer, who revived and led the sect of Moravians or United Brethren; mentioned in *Wilhelm Meister.*

[5]Wesley, John (1703–91), founder of the sect called Methodists.

It is here, then, that the spiritual majority of Teufelsdröckh commences: we are henceforth to see him 'work in well-doing,' with the spirit and clear aims of a Man. He has discovered that the Ideal Workshop he so panted for is even this same Actual ill-furnished Workshop he has so long been stumbling in. He can say to himself: 'Tools? Thou hast no Tools? Why, there is not a Man, or a Thing, now alive but has tools. The basest of created animalcules, the Spider itself, has a spinning-jenny,[1] and warping-mill, and power-loom within its head: the stupidest of Oysters has a Papin's-Digester,[2] with stone-and-lime house to hold it in: every being that can live can do something: this let him *do*.—Tools? Hast thou not a Brain, furnished, furnishable with some glimmerings of Light; and three fingers to hold a Pen withal? Never since Aaron's rod[3] went out of practice, or even before it, was there such a wonder-working Tool: greater than all recorded miracles have been performed by Pens. For strangely in this so solid-seeming World, which nevertheless is in continual restless flux, it is appointed that *Sound,* to appearance the most fleeting, should be the most continuing of all things. The WORD[4] is well said to be omnipotent in this world; man, thereby divine, can create as by a *Fiat.* Awake, arise! Speak forth what is in thee; what God has given thee, what the Devil shall not take away. Higher task than that of Priesthood was allotted to no man: wert thou but the meanest in that sacred Hierarchy, is it not honour enough therein to spend and be spent?[5]

'By this Art, which whoso will may sacrilegiously degrade into a handicraft,' adds Teufelsdröckh, 'have I thenceforth abidden. Writings of mine, not indeed known as mine (for

---

[1]*Cf. Hudibras,* III, i, 1461 (B.).

[2]Famous "steam-digester," a closed vessel in which the boiling point of water was considerably raised; invented by Denis Papin (1647–c.1712), French physicist, and one of the inventors of the steam-engine.

[3]*Aaron's rod:* Exodus, vii, viii.

[4]John, i, 1–3.

[5]*Cf.* II Corinthians, xii, 15.

what am *I?*), have fallen, perhaps not altogether void, into the mighty seed-field of Opinion;[1] fruits of my unseen sowing gratifyingly meet me here and there. I thank the Heavens that I have now found my Calling; wherein, with or without perceptible result, I am minded diligently to persevere.

'Nay how knowest thou,' cries he, 'but this and the other pregnant Device, now grown to be a world-renowned far-working Institution; like a grain of right mustard-seed[2] once cast into the right soil, and now stretching-out strong boughs to the four winds, for the birds of the air to lodge in,—may have been properly my doing? Some one's doing, it without doubt was; from some Idea, in some single Head, it did first of all take beginning: why not from some Idea in mine?' Does Teufelsdröckh here glance at that 'SOCIETY FOR THE CONSERVATION OF PROPERTY (*Eigenthums-conservirende Gesellschaft*),'[3] of which so many ambiguous notices glide spectre-like through these inexpressible Paper-bags? 'An Institution,' hints he, 'not unsuitable to the wants of the time; as indeed such sudden extension proves: for already can the Society number, among its office-bearers or corresponding members, the highest Names, if not the highest Persons, in Germany, England, France; and contributions, both of money and of meditation, pour in from all quarters; to, if possible, enlist the remaining Integrity of the world, and, defensively and with forethought, marshal it round this Palladium.'[4] Does Teufelsdröckh mean, then, to give himself out as the originator of that so notable *Eigenthums-conservirende* ('Owndom-conserving') *Gesellschaft;* and if so, what, in the Devil's name,

---

[1]Adapted from Goethe's "Time is my seed-field," *etc.*

[2]*Cf.* Matthew, xiii, 31, 32.

[3]The passage which follows, dealing whimsically with the idea of property, material and mental, rests upon a passage in Locke's *Two Treatises of Government* (1690); see the second treatise, ch. 9, in which men are said to quit the state of nature and to form a society "for the mutual preservation of their lives, liberties and estates, which I call by the general name—property." *Cf. Ess.*, II, 66–67; IV, 163.

[4]An image of the goddess Pallas Athena on which the safety of Troy was thought to depend; hence any especially valued safeguard.

is it? He again hints: 'At a time when the divine Commandment, *Thou shalt not steal,* wherein truly, if well understood, is comprised the whole Hebrew Decalogue, with Solon's and Lycurgus's[1] Constitutions, Justinian's[2] Pandects, the Code Napoléon,[3] and all Codes, Catechisms, Divinities, Moralities whatsoever, that man has hitherto devised (and enforced with Altar-fire and Gallows-ropes) for his social guidance: at a time, I say, when this divine Commandment has all-but faded away from the general remembrance; and, with little disguise, a new opposite Commandment, *Thou shalt steal,* is everywhere promulgated,—it perhaps behoved, in this universal dotage and deliration, the sound portion of mankind to bestir themselves and rally. When the widest and wildest violations of that divine right of Property, the only divine right now extant or conceivable, are sanctioned and recommended by a vicious Press, and the world has lived to hear it asserted that *we have no Property in our very Bodies, but only an accidental Possession and Life-rent,*[4] what is the issue to be looked for? Hangmen and Catchpoles may, by their noose-gins and baited fall-traps, keep down the smaller sort of vermin; but what, except perhaps some such Universal Association, can protect us against whole meat-devouring and man-devouring hosts of Boa-constrictors? If, therefore, the more sequestered Thinker have wondered, in his privacy, from what hand that perhaps not ill-written *Program* in the Public Journals, with its high *Prize-Questions* and so liberal *Prizes,* could have proceeded,—let him now cease such wonder; and, with un-

---

[1]*Solon:* Athenian lawgiver of the seventh century B.C.—*Lycurgus:* Spartan lawgiver of the ninth century B.C.

[2]Justinian (A.D. 483–565), Emperor of Constantinople, is famous for his appointment of a commission of jurists who compiled a *Digesta* or *Pandectae,* in fifty books, containing all that was valuable in the work of previous jurists.

[3]The code or compilation of the laws of France, drawn up at the instigation of Napoleon, in 1802–08, forming the basis of the French system to the present day.

[4]Adapted from a longer passage in Carlyle's Journal, Oct. 28, 1830 (*C.E.L.*, II, Ch. iv).

divided faculty, betake himself to the *Concurrenz* (Competition).'

We ask: Has this same 'perhaps not ill-written *Program,*' or any other authentic Transaction of that Property-conserving Society, fallen under the eye of the British Reader, in any Journal foreign or domestic? If so, what are those *Prize-Questions;* what are the terms of Competition, and when and where? No printed Newspaper-leaf, no farther light of any sort, to be met with in these Paper-bags! Or is the whole business one other of those whimsicalities and perverse inexplicabilities, whereby Herr Teufelsdröckh, meaning much or nothing, is pleased so often to play fast-and-loose with us?

Here, indeed, at length, must the Editor give utterance to a painful suspicion, which, through late Chapters, has begun to haunt him; paralysing any little enthusiasm that might still have rendered his thorny Biographical task a labor of love. It is a suspicion grounded perhaps on trifles, yet confirmed almost into certainty by the more and more discernible humouristico-satirical tendency of Teufelsdröckh, in whom under-ground humours, and intricate sardonic rogueries, wheel within wheel, defy all reckoning: a suspicion, in one word, that these Autobiographical Documents are partly a mystification! What if many a so-called Fact were little better than a Fiction; if here we had no direct Camera-obscura Picture of the Professor's History; but only some more or less fantastic Adumbration, symbolically, perhaps significantly enough, shadowing-forth the same! Our theory begins to be that, in receiving as literally authentic what was but hieroglyphically so, Hofrath Heuschrecke, whom in that case we scruple not to name Hofrath Nose-of-Wax,[1] was made a fool of, and set adrift to make fools of others. Could it be expected, indeed, that a man so known for impenetrable reticence as Teufelsdröckh, would all at once frankly unlock his private citadel to an English Editor and a German Hofrath; and not rather deceptively

[1]From Burton's *Anatomy of Melancholy* (Preface); Massinger's *The Unnatural Combat,* V, ii; meaning a pliable person.

*in*lock both Editor and Hofrath in the labyrinthic tortuosities and covered-ways of said citadel (having enticed them thither), to see, in his half-devilish way, how the fools would look?

Of one fool, however, the Herr Professor will perhaps find himself short. On a small slip, formerly thrown aside as blank, the ink being all-but invisible, we lately notice, and with effort decipher, the following: 'What are your historical Facts; still more your biographical? Wilt thou know a Man, above all a Mankind, by stringing-together beadrolls of what thou namest Facts? The Man is the spirit he worked in;[1] not what he did, but what he became. Facts are engraved Hierograms,[2] for which the fewest have the key. And then how your Block-head (*Dummkopf*) studies not their Meaning; but simply whether they are well or ill cut, what he calls Moral or Immoral! Still worse is it with your Bungler (*Pfuscher*):[3] such I have seen reading some Rousseau,[4] with pretenses of interpretation; and mistaking the ill-cut Serpent-of-Eternity for a common poisonous reptile.' Was the Professor apprehensive lest an Editor, selected as the present boasts himself, might mistake the Teufelsdröckh Serpent-of-Eternity in like manner? For which reason it was to be altered, not without underhand satire, into a plainer Symbol? Or is this merely one of his half-sophisms, half-truisms, which if he can but set

[1]This thought became one of the dominating ideas in the nineteenth century, especially in Browning. Carlyle is here adapting *Wilhelm Meister,* II, 76: "The spirit in which we act is the highest matter."

[2]See p. 36, *note* 3. Schelling in *Die Methode des akademischen Studiums* (The Method of Academical Studies) says: "Nature is for us a primeval author, who has written in hieroglyphs, and whose pages are colossal" (*Werke,* V, 246; also Carlyle's *Ess.,* I, 83, *n*). Novalis laments that "the significance of the hieroglyph [of Nature] is wanting (*fehlt*)" (*Werke,* III, 116).

[3]A term borrowed from Fichte (*On the Nature of the Scholar*), to denote the unimaginative interpreter. (*Ess.,* I, 58–61).

[4]Rousseau, Jean Jacques (1712–78) regarded duty (Carlyle's "serpent of eternity"—infinite nature of duty) as less a guide of life than sensibility, desire, and a return to "the noble savage."—The Serpent-with-tail-in-mouth is an emblem of Eternity, and was adopted by Carlyle for his Seal.

on the back of a Figure, he cares not whither it gallop? We say not with certainty; and indeed, so strange is the Professor, can never say. If our suspicion be wholly unfounded, let his own questionable ways, not our necessary circumspectness, bear the blame.

But be this as it will, the somewhat exasperated and indeed exhausted Editor determines here to shut these Paper-bags for the present. Let it suffice that we know of Teufelsdröckh, so far, if 'not what he did, yet what he became': the rather, as his character has now taken its ultimate bent, and no new revolution, of importance, is to be looked for. The imprisoned Chrysalis is now a winged Psyche:[1] and such, wheresoever be its flight, it will continue. To trace by what complex gyrations (flights or involuntary waftings) through the mere external Life-element, Teufelsdröckh reaches his University Professorship, and the Psyche clothes herself in civic Titles, without altering her now fixed nature,—would be comparatively an unproductive task, were we even unsuspicious of its being, for us at least, a false and impossible one. His outward Biography, therefore, which, at the Blumine Lover's-Leap,[2] we saw churned utterly into spray-vapour, may hover in that condition, for aught that concerns us here. Enough that by survey of certain 'pools and plashes,' we have ascertained its general direction; do we not already know that, by one way and other, it *has* long since rained-down again into a stream; and even now, at Weissnichtwo, flows deep and still, fraught with the *Philosophy of Clothes,* and visible to whoso will cast eye thereon? Over much invaluable matter, that lies scattered, like jewels among quarry-rubbish, in those Paper-catacombs, we may have occasion to glance back, and somewhat will demand insertion at the right place: meanwhile be our tiresome diggings therein suspended.

If now, before reopening the great *Clothes-Volume,* we ask what our degree of progress, during these Ten Chapters, has

---

[1]Psyche was the Greek personification of the human soul; her emblem is the butterfly. See Apuleius, *The Golden Ass.*

[2]See p. 153, *note* 5.

been, towards right understanding of the *Clothes-Philosophy,* let not our discouragement become total. To speak in that old figure of the Hell-gate Bridge over Chaos,[1] a few flying pontoons have perhaps been added, though as yet they drift straggling on the Flood; how far they will reach, when once the chains are straightened and fastened, can, at present, only be matter of conjecture.

So much we already calculate: Through many a little loophole, we have had glimpses into the internal world of Teufelsdröckh; his strange mystic, almost magic Diagram of the Universe, and how it was gradually drawn, is not henceforth altogether dark to us. Those mysterious ideas on TIME, which merit consideration, and are not wholly unintelligible with such, may by and by prove significant. Still more may his somewhat peculiar view of Nature, the decisive Oneness he ascribes to Nature.[2] How all Nature and Life are but one *Garment,* a 'Living Garment,' woven and ever aweaving in the 'Loom of Time'[3] is not here, indeed, the outline of a whole *Clothes-Philosophy;* at least the arena it is to work in? Remark, too, that the Character of the Man, nowise without meaning in such a matter, becomes less enigmatic: amid so much tumultuous obscurity, almost like diluted madness, do not a certain indomitable Defiance and yet a boundless Reverence seem to loom forth, as the two mountain-summits, on whose rock-strata all the rest were based and built?

Nay further, may we not say that Teufelsdröckh's Biography, allowing it even, as suspected, only a hieroglyphical truth, exhibits a man, as it were preappointed for Clothes-Philosophy? To look through the Shows of things into Things themselves[4] he is led and compelled. The 'Passivity'[5]

---

[1]See p. 79, *note* 4.

[2]See pp. 150–151.

[3]See p. 55, *note* 4.

[4]This ability Carlyle later ascribes to the Hero: "He is . . . a *seer;* seeing through the shows of things" (*Heroes and Hero-Worship,* p. 116). Carlyle's context relates to the hero as priest, but the ability is also ascribed to the hero as a type.

[5]See p. 98, *note* 1.

given him by birth is fostered by all turns of his fortune. Everywhere cast out, like oil out of water, from mingling in any Employment, in any public Communion, he has no portion but Solitude, and a life of Meditation. The whole energy of his existence is directed, through long years, on one task: that of enduring pain, if he cannot cure it. Thus everywhere do the Shows of things oppress him, withstand him, threaten him with fearfullest destruction: only by victoriously penetrating into Things themselves can he find peace and a stronghold. But is not this same looking-through the Shows, or Vestures, into the Things, even the first preliminary to a *Philosophy of Clothes?* Do we not, in all this, discern some beckonings towards the true higher purport of such a Philosophy; and what shape it must assume with such a man, in such an era?

Perhaps in entering on Book Third, the courteous Reader is not utterly without guess whither he is bound: nor, let us hope, for all the fantastic Dream-Grottoes[1] through which, as is our lot with Teufelsdröckh, he must wander, will there be wanting between whiles some twinkling of a steady Polar Star.

---

[1]See p. 53, *note* 3.

BOOK THIRD

CHAPTER I

INCIDENT IN MODERN HISTORY

Story of George Fox the Quaker; and his perennial suit of Leather. A man God-possessed, witnessing for spiritual freedom and manhood.

As a wonder-loving and wonder-seeking man, Teufelsdröckh, from an early part of this Clothes-Volume, has more and more exhibited himself. Striking it was, amid all his perverse cloudiness, with what force of vision and of heart he pierced into the mystery of the World; recognising in the highest sensible phenomena, so far as Sense went, only fresh or faded Raiment; yet ever, under this, a celestial Essence thereby rendered visible: and while, on the one hand, he trod the old rags of Matter, with their tinsels, into the mire, he on the other everywhere exalted Spirit above all earthly principalities and powers, and worshipped it, though under the meanest shapes, with a true Platonic mysticism.[1] What the man ultimately purposed by thus casting his Greek-fire[2] into the general Wardrobe of the Universe; what such, more or less complete, rending and burning of Garments throughout the whole compass of Civilised Life and Speculation, should lead to; the rather as he was no Adamite,[3] in any sense, and could not, like

---

[1]See p. 66, *note* 4.

[2]A combustible composition which burns under water, the constituents of which are supposed to be asphalt, nitre, and sulphur; known previously in India and China, and used by Eastern Greeks and Mohammedans.

[3]See p. 58, *note* 2.

Rousseau, recommend either bodily or intellectual Nudity, and a return to the savage state: all this our readers are now bent to discover; this is, in fact, properly the gist and purport of Professor Teufelsdröckh's Philosophy of Clothes.[1]

Be it remembered, however, that such purport is here not so much evolved, as detected to lie ready for evolving. We are to guide our British Friends into the new Gold-country, and show them the mines; nowise to dig-out and exhaust its wealth, which indeed remains for all time inexhaustible. Once there, let each dig for his own behoof, and enrich himself.

Neither, in so capricious inexpressible a Work as this of the Professor's, can our course now more than formerly be straightforward, step by step, but at best leap by leap. Significant Indications stand-out here and there; which for the critical eye, that looks both widely and narrowly, shape themselves into some ground-scheme of a Whole: to select these with judgment, so that a leap from one to the other be possible, and (in our old figure) by chaining them together, a passable Bridge be effected: this, as heretofore, continues our only method. Among such light-spots, the following, floating in much wild matter about *Perfectibility,*[2] has seemed worth clutching at:

'Perhaps the most remarkable incident in Modern History,' says Teufelsdröckh, 'is not the Diet of Worms,[3] still less the Battle of Austerlitz, Waterloo, Peterloo,[4] or any other Battle;

---

[1]True. This opening paragraph is indeed, as MacMechan says, "the key to the whole mystery of Clothes Philosophy."

[2]*Perfectibility:* a term frequent in the literature of the Enlightenment (Voltaire, Rousseau, Tom Paine, *etc.*), for the doctrine that man, naturally good, can be redeemed entirely from his present low and enslaved state.

[3]Celebrated Imperial assembly of councillors, held in 1521, to check the Reformation and to condemn Luther.

[4]*Austerlitz:* a town in Moravia, where Napoleon defeated the Austrians and Russians, December 2, 1805.—*Waterloo:* June 18, 1815.—*Peterloo,* a name, after "Waterloo," for the attack by the military upon a crowd of Lancashire workers assembled in St. Peter's Field, Manchester, August 16, 1819; a few were killed, hundreds injured.

but an incident passed carelessly over by most Historians, and treated with some degree of ridicule by others: namely, George Fox's making to himself a suit of Leather.[1] This man, the first of the Quakers, and by trade a Shoemaker, was one of those, to whom, under ruder or purer form, the Divine Idea of the Universe[2] is pleased to manifest itself; and, across all the hulls of Ignorance and earthly Degradation, shine through, in unspeakable Awfulness, unspeakable Beauty, on their souls: who therefore are rightly accounted Prophets, God-possessed; or even Gods, as in some periods it has chanced. Sitting in his stall; working on tanned hides, amid pincers, paste-horns, rosin, swine-bristles, and a nameless flood of rubbish, this youth had, nevertheless, a Living Spirit belonging to him; also an antique Inspired Volume, through which, as through a window, it could look upwards, and discern its celestial Home. The task of a daily pair of shoes, coupled even with some prospect of victuals, and an honourable Mastership in Cordwainery,[3] and perhaps the post of Third-borough in his hundred,[4] as the crown of long faithful sewing, —was nowise satisfaction enough to such a mind: but ever amid the boring and hammering came tones from that far country, came Splendours and Terrors; for this poor Cordwainer, as we said, was a Man; and the Temple of Immensity, wherein as Man he had been sent to minister, was full of holy mystery to him.

'The Clergy of the neighbourhood, the ordained Watchers and Interpreters of that same holy mystery, listened with un-

---

[1]George Fox (1624–91), founder of the Society of Friends (Quakers), agent to a grazier and wool-dealer, left home at 21 and turned itinerant preacher, organizing the Friends in 1669. In his travels Fox was called the "man in leather breeches." For his having worn a *suit* of leather there is no evidence.

[2]The ultimate and divine principle "pervading the visible Universe; which visible Universe is indeed but its symbol and sensible manifestation, having in itself no meaning, or even true existence independent of it." *Ess.*, I, 58. Derived from Fichte's *On the Nature of the Scholar*, Novalis's *Fragments, etc.*

[3]Shoemaking in cordovan (Spanish) leather.

[4]Constable in his district.

affected tedium to his consultations, and advised him, as the solution of such doubts, to "drink beer and dance with the girls." Blind leaders of the blind![1] For what end were their tithes levied and eaten; for what were their shovel-hats[2] scooped-out, and their surplices and cassock-aprons girt-on; and such a church-repairing, and chaffering, and organing, and other racketing, held over that spot of God's Earth,—if Man were but a Patent Digester,[3] and the Belly with its adjuncts the grand Reality? Fox turned from them, with tears and a sacred scorn, back to his Leather-parings and his Bible. Mountains of encumbrance, higher than Ætna, had been heaped over that Spirit: but it was a Spirit, and would not lie buried there. Through long days and nights of silent agony, it struggled and wrestled, with a man's force, to be free; how its prison-mountains heaved and swayed tumultuously, as the giant spirit shook them to this hand and that, and emerged into the light of Heaven! That Leicester shoe-shop, had men known it, was a holier place than any Vatican or Loretto-shrine.[4]—"So bandaged, and hampered, and hemmed in," groaned he, "with thousand requisitions, obligations, straps, tatters, and tagrags, I can neither see nor move: not my own am I, but the World's; and Time flies fast, and Heaven is high, and Hell is deep: Man! bethink thee, if thou hast power of Thought! Why not; what binds me here? Want, want!—Ha, of what? Will all the shoe-wages under the Moon ferry me across into that far Land of Light? Only Meditation can, and devout Prayer to God. I will to the woods: the hollow of a tree will lodge me, wild-berries feed me; and for Clothes, cannot I stitch myself one perennial suit of Leather!"

---

[1]*Cf.* Matthew, xv, 14.

[2]Broad-brimmed hats, turned up at the sides, and projecting in front, like a shovel, worn by some clergy of the English Church. "Shovel-hattery" became Carlyle's satirical term for religious hypocrisy.

[3]*I.e.,* Papin's-Digester. See p. 199, *note* 2.

[4]The house in Ancona which is said to be the one in which Jesus lived, and to have been transported by angels from Nazareth.

'Historical Oil-painting,' continues Teufelsdröckh, 'is one of the Arts I never practised; therefore shall I not decide whether this subject were easy of execution on the canvas. Yet often has it seemed to me as if such first outflashing of man's Freewill, to lighten, more and more into Day, the Chaotic Night that threatened to engulf him in its hindrances and its horrors, were properly the only grandeur there is in History. Let some living Angelo[1] or Rosa,[2] with seeing eye and understanding heart, picture George Fox on that morning, when he spreads-out his cutting-board for the last time, and cuts cowhides by unwonted patterns, and stitches them together into one continuous all-including Case, the farewell service of his awl! Stitch away, thou noble Fox: every prick of that little instrument is pricking into the heart of Slavery, and World-worship, and the Mammon-god. Thy elbows jerk, as in strong swimmer-strokes, and every stroke is bearing thee across the Prison-ditch, within which Vanity holds her Workhouse and Ragfair, into lands of true Liberty; were the work done, there is in broad Europe one Free Man, and thou art he!

'Thus from the lowest depth there is a path to the loftiest height; and for the Poor also a Gospel has been published. Surely if, as D'Alembert[3] asserts, my illustrious namesake, Diogenes,[4] was the greatest man of Antiquity, only that he wanted Decency, then by stronger reason is George Fox the greatest of the Moderns, and greater than Diogenes himself: for he too stands on the adamantine basis of his Manhood, casting aside all props and shoars; yet not, in half-savage Pride, undervaluing the Earth; valuing it rather, as a place to yield him warmth and food, he looks Heavenward from his

[1]Michelangelo (1475–1564), the famous Italian painter and sculptor.

[2]Salvator Rosa (1615–73), Italian painter of romantic landscapes and battle-pieces.—Carlyle professed both an ignorance of, and a lack of interest in art. Neither Michelangelo nor Salvator Rosa would probably have chosen Fox and his stitching as an inspiring subject.

[3]D'Alembert, Jean (1717–83), French mathematician and encyclopaedist.

[4]See p. 86, *note* 1.

Earth, and dwells in an element of Mercy and Worship, with a still Strength, such as the Cynic's Tub[1] did nowise witness. Great, truly, was that Tub; a temple from which man's dignity and divinity was scornfully preached abroad: but greater is the Leather Hull, for the same sermon was preached there, and not in Scorn but in Love.'

George Fox's 'perennial suit,' with all that it held, has been worn quite into ashes for nigh two centuries: why, in a discussion on the *Perfectibility of Society,* reproduce it now? Not out of blind sectarian partisanship: Teufelsdröckh himself is no Quaker; with all his pacific tendencies, did not we see him, in that scene at the North Cape, with the Archangel Smuggler, exhibit fire-arms?

For us, aware of his deep Sansculottism,[2] there is more meant in this passage than meets the ear.[3] At the same time, who can avoid smiling at the earnestness and Bœotian[4] simplicity (if indeed there be not an underhand satire in it) with which that 'Incident' is here brought forward; and, in the Professor's ambiguous way, as clearly perhaps as he durst in Weissnichtwo, recommended to imitation! Does Teufelsdröckh anticipate that, in this age of refinement, any considerable class of the community, by way of testifying against the 'Mammon-god,' and escaping from what he calls 'Vanity's Workhouse and Ragfair,' where doubtless some of them are toiled and whipped and hood-winked sufficiently,—will sheathe themselves in close-fitting cases of Leather? The idea is ridiculous in the extreme. Will Majesty lay aside its robes of state, and Beauty its frills and train-gowns, for a second-skin of tanned hide? By which change Huddersfield and

---

[1]The tub in which Diogenes is reputed to have lived. See p. 86, *note* 1.

[2]See p. 16, *note* 5.

[3]*Cf. Il Penseroso,* 120.—The Centenary Edition misprints "that" for "than."

[4]The inhabitants of Boeotia were famed for their dull wit, which passed into a proverb, *Boeoticum ingenium.* Horace, *Epistles,* II, i, 244; Pope, *Dunciad,* iii, 50.

Manchester, and Coventry and Paisley,[1] and the Fancy-Bazaar,[2] were reduced to hungry solitudes; and only Day and Martin[3] could profit. For neither would Teufelsdröckh's mad day-dream, here as we presume covertly intended, of levelling Society (*levelling* it indeed with a vengeance, into one huge drowned marsh!), and so attaining the political effects of Nudity without its frigorific or other consequences,—be thereby realised. Would not the rich man purchase a water-proof suit of Russia Leather; and the high-born Belle step-forth in red or azure morocco, lined with shamoy: the black cowhide being left to the Drudges and Gibeonites[4] of the world; and so all the old Distinctions be reëstablished?

Or has the Professor his own deeper intention; and laughs in his sleeve at our strictures and glosses, which indeed are but a part thereof?

CHAPTER II

CHURCH–CLOTHES

Church-Clothes defined; the Forms under which the Religious Principle is temporarily embodied. Outward Religion originates by Society: Society becomes possible by Religion. The condition of Church-Clothes in our time.

NOT less questionable is his Chapter on *Church-Clothes,* which has the farther distinction of being the shortest in the Volume. We here translate it entire:

'By Church-Clothes, it need not be premised that I mean infinitely more than Cassocks and Surplices; and do not at all mean the mere haberdasher Sunday Clothes that men go to

[1]Cities famous, respectively, for the production of woolen goods, cotton goods, ribbons and watches, and shawls.

[2]The bazaar in Soho, London.

[3]Manufacturers of blacking, in London.

[4]Condemned by Joshua to be hewers of wood and drawers of water, for having deceived him. Joshua, ix, 3–27.

Church in. Far from it! Church-Clothes, are, in our vocabulary, the Forms, the *Vestures,* under which men have at various periods embodied and represented for themselves the Religious Principle; that is to say, invested the Divine Idea of the World[1] with a sensible and practically active Body, so that it might dwell among them as a living and life-giving WORD.[2]

'These are unspeakably the most important of all the vestures and garnitures of Human Existence. They are first spun and woven, I may say, by that wonder of wonders, SOCIETY;[3] for it is still only when "two or three are gathered together,"[4] that Religion, spiritually existent, and indeed indestructible, however latent, in each, first outwardly manifests itself (as with "cloven tongues of fire"),[5] and seeks to be embodied in a visible Communion and Church Militant. Mystical, more than magical, is that Communing of Soul with Soul, both looking heavenward: here properly Soul first speaks with Soul; for only in looking heavenward, take it in what sense you may, not in looking earthward, does what we can call Union, mutual Love, Society, begin to be possible. How true is that of Novalis: "It is certain, my Belief gains quite *infinitely* the moment I can convince another mind thereof"![6] Gaze thou in the face of thy Brother, in those eyes

---

[1]See p. 209, *note* 2.

[2]See p. 72, *note* 5.—The present chapter is of fundamental importance; it expresses the very purpose for which *Sartor Resartus* was composed: to rehabilitate religion for modern man by vindicating its essential truth and showing the need of new forms for expressing it.

[3]*Cf.* "Characteristics" (*Ess.,* III, 12): "Society is the standing wonder of our existence."—By maintaining the mysterious and spiritual nature of society, Carlyle is preparing us for his anti-democratic standpoint, *i.e.,* his conviction that society cannot be saved by debate, discussion, rationalization, but only through silent leadership and unquestioning obedience. For this emphasis on the mystical influence of spiritual communion among men of like purpose, Carlyle is indebted to Fichte and Novalis as well as to Goethe.

[4]Matthew, xviii, 20.

[5]Acts, ii, 3.

[6]Novalis: pseudonym of Friedrich v. Hardenberg (1772–1801), German poet and mystic, one of the pioneers of the Romantic movement. He attempted to blend his philosophical and his mystical conceptions into

where plays the lambent fire of Kindness, or in those where rages the lurid conflagration of Anger; feel how thy own so quiet Soul is straightway involuntarily kindled with the like, and ye blaze and reverberate on each other, till it is all one limitless confluent flame (of embracing Love, or of deadly-grappling Hate); and then say what miraculous virtue goes out of man into man. But if so, through all the thick-plied hulls of our Earthly Life; how much more when it is of the Divine Life we speak, and inmost ME is, as it were, brought into contact with inmost ME!

'Thus was it that I said, the Church-Clothes are first spun and woven by Society; outward Religion originates by Society, Society becomes possible by Religion. Nay, perhaps, every conceivable Society, past and present, may well be figured as properly and wholly a Church, in one or other of these three predicaments: an audibly preaching and prophesying Church, which is the best; second, a Church that struggles to preach and prophesy, but cannot as yet, till its Pentecost come; and third and worst, a Church gone dumb with old age, or which only mumbles delirium prior to dissolution. Whoso fancies that by Church is here meant Chapterhouses and Cathedrals, or by preaching and prophesying, mere speech and chanting, let him,' says the oracular Professor, 'read on, light of heart (*getrosten Muthes*).

'But with regard to your Church proper, and the Church-Clothes specially recognised as Church-Clothes, I remark, fearlessly enough, that without such Vestures and sacred Tissues Society has not existed, and will not exist.[1] For if

---

a harmonious whole, uniting life and poetry, science and religion; but was cut off by an early death, his lovable personality leaving, however, a strong mark on the Romantic school in Germany. Carlyle (see *Ess.*, II, 1 ff.) admitted his despair of ever understanding Novalis's character, but regarded his works as "an unfathomed mine of philosophical ideas." The passage quoted is from Novalis's *Werke,* III, 74–75; and appears in *Ess.*, III, 11.

[1]That religion is the basis of society is a doctrine of many times and places; but it was especially developed by the German Romantics in a form which attracted Carlyle. It was from them that Coleridge adopted

Government is, so to speak, the outward Skin of the Body Politic, holding the whole together and protecting it; and all your Craft-Guilds, and Associations for Industry, of hand or of head, are the Fleshly Clothes, the muscular and osseous Tissues (Lying *under* such Skin), whereby Society stands and works;—then is Religion the inmost Pericardial and Nervous Tissue, which ministers Life and warm Circulation to the whole. Without which Pericardial Tissue the Bones and Muscles (of Industry) were inert, or animated only by a Galvanic vitality; the Skin would become a shrivelled pelt, or fast-rotting raw-hide; and Society itself a dead carcass, —deserving to be buried. Men were no longer Social, but Gregarious; which latter state also could not continue, but must gradually issue in universal selfish discord, hatred, savage isolation, and dispersion;—whereby, as we might continue to say, the very dust and dead body of Society would have evaporated and become abolished. Such, and so all-important, all-sustaining, are the Church-Clothes to civilised or even to rational men.

'Meanwhile, in our era of the World, those same Church-Clothes have gone sorrowfully out-at-elbows: nay, far worse, many of them have become mere hollow Shapes, or Masks, under which no living Figure or Spirit any longer dwells; but only spiders and unclean beetles, in horrid accumulation, drive their trade; and the mask still glares on you with its glass-eyes, in ghastly affectation of Life,—some generation-and-half after Religion has quite withdrawn from it, and in unnoticed nooks is weaving for herself new Vestures, wherewith to reappear, and bless us, or our sons or grandsons. As a Priest, or Interpreter of the Holy, is the noblest and highest of all men, so is a Sham-priest (*Schein-priester*) the falsest and basest; neither is it doubtful that his Canonicals, were they Popes' Tiaras, will one day be torn from him, to make

---

his idea of *Schwärmerei,* which Carlyle muses upon in his Journal, in connection with Novalis's equating religion and social unity. (*C.E.L.,* II, Ch. iv: *Schwärmerei* = swarming, "to crowd together and excite one another.") Barrett cites Bacon's essay on Religion.

bandages for the wounds of mankind; or even to burn into tinder, for general scientific or culinary purposes.

'All which, as out of place here, falls to be handled in my Second Volume, *On the Palingenesia, or Newbirth of Society;*[1] which volume, as treating practically of the Wear, Destruction, and Retexture of Spiritual Tissues, or Garments, forms, properly speaking, the Transcendental or ultimate Portion of this my work *on Clothes,* and is already in a state of forwardness.'

And herewith, no farther exposition, note, or commentary being added, does Teufelsdröckh, and must his Editor now, terminate the singular chapter on Church-Clothes!

CHAPTER III

SYMBOLS

The benignant efficacies of Silence and Secrecy. Symbols; revelations of the Infinite in the Finite: Man everywhere encompassed by them; lives and works by them. Theory of Motive-millwrights, a false account of human nature. Symbols of an extrinsic value; as Banners, Standards: Of intrinsic value; as Works of Art, Lives and Deaths of Heroic men. Religious Symbols; Christianity. Symbols hallowed by Time; but finally defaced and desecrated. Many superannuated Symbols in our time, needing removal.

PROBABLY it will elucidate the drift of these foregoing obscure utterances, if we here insert somewhat of our Professor's speculations on *Symbols.* To state his whole doctrine, indeed, were beyond our compass: nowhere is he more mysterious, impalpable, than in this of 'Fantasy being the organ of the Godlike';[2] and how 'Man thereby, though based,

[1]*Cf.* Bk. III, Ch. v.

[2]Quoted from Fr. v. Schlegel's *Ideen,* p. 5 (*Athenaeum,* Berlin, 1798–1800, 3 vols., III): "Ganz recht, die Fantasie ist das Organ des Menschen für die Gottheit."

to all seeming, on the small Visible, does nevertheless extend down into the infinite deeps of the Invisible, of which Invisible, indeed, his Life is properly the bodying forth.' Let us, omitting these high transcendental aspects of the matter, study to glean (whether from the Paper-bags or the Printed Volume) what little seems logical and practical, and cunningly arrange it into such degree of coherence as it will assume. By way of proem, take the following not injudicious remarks:

'The benignant efficacies of Concealment,' cries our Professor, 'who shall speak or sing? SILENCE and SECRECY![1] Altars might still be raised to them (were this an altar-building time) for universal worship. Silence is the element in which great things fashion themselves together; that at length they may emerge, full-formed and majestic, into the daylight of Life, which they are thenceforth to rule. Not William the Silent[2] only, but all the considerable men I have known, and the most undiplomatic and unstrategic of these, forbore to babble of what they were creating and projecting. Nay, in thy own mean perplexities, do thou thyself but *hold thy tongue for one day:* on the morrow, how much clearer are thy purposes and duties; what wreck and rubbish have those mute workmen within thee swept away, when intrusive noises were shut out! Speech is too often not, as the Frenchman defined it, the art of concealing Thought;[3] but of quite stifling and suspending Thought, so that there is none to conceal. Speech too is great, but not the greatest. As the Swiss Inscription says: *Sprechen ist silbern, Schweigen ist golden*

---

[1]An elaboration upon a passage in Carlyle's Journal for 1830, and of the chief theme in "Characteristics" (*Ess.,* III, 1 ff.), namely, that the unconscious is superior to the conscious, silent action to garrulous inactivity. Carlyle was attracted to Goethe's opinions on silence, as evident in *Wilhelm Meister,* II, 75–76: "Who knows it [art] half, speaks much, and is always wrong; who knows it wholly, inclines to act, and speaks seldom or late. . . . Words are good but they are not the best. The best is not to be explained by words." (See *Carlyle and German Thought,* pp. 187–88, 230–37.)

[2]William (1533–84), Count of Nassau and Prince of Orange, founder of the Dutch Republic; silent largely for diplomatic purposes.

[3]Attributed to Voltaire and to Talleyrand.

(Speech is silvern, Silence is golden); or as I might rather express it: Speech is of Time, Silence is of Eternity.

'Bees will not work except in darkness; Thought will not work except in Silence: neither will Virtue work except in Secrecy. Let not thy left hand know what thy right hand doeth![1] Neither shalt thou prate even to thy own heart of "those secrets known to all."[2] Is not Shame (*Schaam*) the soil of all Virtue, of all good manners and good morals? Like other plants, Virtue will not grow unless its root be hidden, buried from the eye of the sun.[3] Let the sun shine on it, nay do but look at it privily thyself, the root withers, and no flowers will glad thee. O my Friends, when we view the fair clustering flowers that overwreathe, for example, the Marriage-bower, and encircle man's life with the fragrance and hues of Heaven, what hand will not smite the foul plunderer that grubs them up by the roots, and with grinning, grunting satisfaction, shows us the dung they flourish in! Men speak much of the Printing-Press with its Newspapers: *du Himmel!* what are these to Clothes and the Tailor's Goose?'[4]

'Of kin to the so incalculable influences of Concealment, and connected with still greater things, is the wondrous agency of *Symbols*. In a Symbol there is concealment and yet revelation: here therefore, by Silence and by Speech acting together, comes a double significance. And if both the Speech be itself high, and the Silence fit and noble, how expressive will their union be! Thus in many a painted Device, or simple Seal-emblem, the commonest Truth stands out to us proclaimed with quite new emphasis.

'For it is here that Fantasy with her mystic wonderland

---

[1]Matthew, vi, 3.

[2]This quotation and the sentences which follow it are Goethean (*Wilhelm Meister,* II, 260).

[3]This thought is central with Carlyle. See the brilliant treatment of it in "Characteristics" (*Ess.,* III, 4): "Under . . . Life lies a basis of Darkness, which she benignantly conceals . . . only the fair stem with its leaves and flowers . . . shall disclose itself . . ."

[4]A tailor's iron.

plays into the small prose domain of Sense, and becomes incorporated therewith.[1] In the Symbol proper, what we can call a Symbol, there is ever, more or less distinctly and directly, some embodiment and revelation of the Infinite; the Infinite is made to blend itself with the Finite, to stand visible, and as it were, attainable there. By Symbols, accordingly, is man guided and commanded, made happy, made wretched. He everywhere finds himself encompassed with Symbols, recognised as such or not recognised: the Universe is but one vast Symbol of God; nay if thou wilt have it, what is man himself but a Symbol of God; is not all that he does symbolical; a revelation to Sense of the mystic god-given force that is in him; a "Gospel of Freedom," which he, the "Messias[2] of Nature," preaches, as he can, by act and word? Not a Hut he builds but is the visible embodiment of a Thought; but bears visible record of invisible things; but is, in the transcendental sense, symbolical as well as real.'

'Man,' says the Professor elsewhere, in quite antipodal contrast with these high-soaring delineations, which we have here cut-short on the verge of the inane, 'Man is by birth somewhat of an owl. Perhaps, too, of all the owleries that ever possessed him, the most owlish, if we consider it, is that of your actually existing Motive-Millwrights.[3] Fantastic

---

[1]See p. 141, *note* 3.—Apparently Carlyle uses "Fantasy" to mean Reason (*Vernunft,* in the German), as opposed to Understanding (*Verstand*), the mechanically logical activity of the mind. Throughout this chapter the term is employed in much the same manner as it is by Novalis and Fr. v. Schlegel, to denote imaginative insight, or Wordsworth's "Reason in her most exalted mood." (*The Prelude* [1805], xiii, 170).

[2]Greek form of Hebrew *Messiah,* "the annointed one," or Christ. Novalis thought that man is to "redeem" Nature, as Christ redeemed man; Christ proceeded from the supernatural, man from the natural. Novalis's *magischer Idealismus* enabled him to see man's spiritual force as great enough to work a miracle upon birds, beasts, and flowers comparable to the moral miracle worked by Christ upon human conduct. Whether Carlyle understood Novalis's meaning is doubtful, but he quotes Novalis's expression frequently (see *Ess.,* III, 90). It may be added that as Carlyle felt obliged to give up Biblical supernaturalism, he was forced to find a deliverance in the purely human sphere, by man himself, man thus becoming his own deliverer, a *natural* messiah, *i.e.,* the "Messias of Nature."

[3]Utilitarians. See p. 117, *note* 2, and p. 159, *note* 3.

tricks enough man has played, in his time; has fancied himself to be most things, down even to an animated heap of Glass:[1] but to fancy himself a dead Iron-Balance for weighing Pains and Pleasures on, was reserved for this his latter era. There stands he, his Universe one huge Manger, filled with hay and thistles to be weighed against each other; and looks long-eared enough.[2] Alas, poor devil! spectres are appointed to haunt him: one age he is hagridden, bewitched; the next, priestridden, befooled; in all ages, bedevilled. And now the Genius of Mechanism smothers him worse than any Nightmare did; till the Soul is nigh choked out of him, and only a kind of Digestive, Mechanic life remains. In Earth and in Heaven he can see nothing but Mechanism;[3] has fear for nothing else, hope in nothing else: the world would indeed grind him to pieces; but cannot he fathom the Doctrine of Motives, and cunningly compute these, and mechanise them to grind the other way?

'Were he not, as has been said, purblinded by enchantment, you had but to bid him open his eyes and look. In which country, in which time, was it hitherto that man's history, or the history of any man, went-on by calculated or calculable "Motives"? What make ye of your Christianities and Chivalries, and Reformations, and Marseillese Hymns,[4] and Reigns of Terror? Nay, has not perhaps the Motive-

---

[1]As in Burton's *Anatomy of Melancholy* (M.).

[2]Like the ass in the medieval fable, unable to decide which one of two bundles of hay is the more attractive. If he makes a decision he has free will; if we deny free will, then the ass must starve. Attributed to Buridan, a metaphysician of the fourteenth century, though the idea is much older. It is treated in Goethe's *Faust,* I, ll. 1830–33.

[3]In the essay on Novalis (*Ess.,* II) Carlyle quotes and elaborates upon Novalis's passage on the distinction between *Mechanic* and *Dynamic* thought. Mechanism symbolized for Carlyle all the materialism and determinism expressed in English and European thought since John Locke, especially in the works of Hartley, Hume, and Bentham. In Novalis's mysticism, in Fichte's ethical idealism, and in the Spinozistic pantheism in Goethe, he found a new basis for a belief in freedom, dynamic force, vitalism. See "Characteristics" and "Signs of the Times" (*Ess.,* II, 56 ff.; III, 1 ff.).

[4]See *French Revolution, passim.*

grinder himself been *in Love?* Did he never stand so much as a contested Election? Leave him to Time, and the medicating virtue of Nature.'

'Yes, Friends,' elsewhere observes the Professor, 'not our Logical, Mensurative faculty, but our Imaginative one is King over us; I might say, Priest and Prophet to lead us heavenward; or Magician and Wizard to lead us hellward. Nay, even for the basest Sensualist, what is Sense but the implement of Fantasy; the vessel it drinks out of? Ever in the dullest existence there is a sheen either of Inspiration or of Madness (thou partly hast it in thy choice, which of the two), that gleams-in from the circumambient Eternity, and colours with its own hues our little islet of Time. The Understanding[1] is indeed thy window, too clear thou canst not make it; but Fantasy is thy eye, with its colour-giving retina, healthy or diseased. Have not I myself known five-hundred living soldiers sabred into crows'-meat for a piece of glazed cotton, which they called their Flag; which, had you sold it at any market-cross, would not have brought above three groschen? Did not the whole Hungarian Nation rise, like some tumultuous moon-stirred Atlantic, when Kaiser Joseph pocketed their Iron Crown; an implement, as was sagaciously observed, in size and commercial value little differing from a horseshoe?[2] It is in and through *Symbols* that man, consciously or unconsciously, lives, works, and has his being: those ages, moreover, are accounted the noblest which can the best recognise symbolical worth, and prize it the highest. For is not a Symbol ever, to him who has eyes for it, some dimmer or clearer revelation of the God-like?

'Of Symbols, however, I remark farther, that they have both an extrinsic and intrinsic value; oftenest the former only. What, for instance, was in that clouted Shoe, which

---

[1]The Kantian term (*Verstand*).

[2]Joseph II (1741–90) of Austria, Emperor of Germany, refused the iron crown which had been worn but once, by the Hungarian monarchs, and had it removed to Vienna; his pronounced Germanism roused the Hungarians to the verge of armed resistance.

the Peasants bore aloft with them as ensign in their *Bauernkrieg* (Peasants' War)?[1] Or in the Wallet-and-staff round which the Netherland *Gueux,*[2] glorying in that nickname of Beggars, heroically rallied and prevailed, though against King Philip himself? Intrinsic significance these had none; only extrinsic; as the accidental Standards of multitudes more or less sacredly uniting together; in which union itself, as above noted, there is ever something mystical and borrowing of the Godlike. Under a like category, too, stand, or stood, the stupidest heraldic Coats-of-arms; military Banners everywhere; and generally all national or other sectarian Costumes and Customs: they have no intrinsic, necessary divineness, or even worth; but have acquired an extrinsic one. Nevertheless through all these there glimmers something of a Divine Idea;[3] as through military Banners themselves, the Divine Idea of Duty, of heroic Daring; in some instances of Freedom, of Right. Nay the highest ensign that men ever met and embraced under, the Cross itself, had no meaning save an accidental extrinsic one.

'Another matter it is, however, when your Symbol has intrinsic meaning, and is of itself *fit* that men should unite round it. Let but the Godlike manifest itself to Sense; let but Eternity look, more or less visibly, through the Time-Figure (*Zeitbild*)! Then is it fit that men unite there; and worship together before such Symbol; and so from day to day, and from age to age, superadd to it new divineness.

'Of this latter sort are all true Works of Art: in them (if thou know a Work of Art from a Daub of Artifice) wilt thou discern Eternity looking through Time; the Godlike rendered visible. Here too may an extrinsic value gradually superadd itself: thus certain *Iliads,* and the like, have, in three-thousand

---

[1]In 1524–25, one aspect of the Reformation.

[2]"Beggars." A term applied to the nobles and others who, in 1566 in the Netherlands, opposed the tyranny of Philip II of Spain, and wore as a symbol a leathern wallet. (See Motley's *Rise of the Dutch Republic,* Part II, Ch. vi.)

[3]See p. 209, note 2.

years, attained quite new significance. But nobler than all in this kind are the Lives of heroic god-inspired Men; for what other Work of Art is so divine? In Death too, in the Death of the Just, as the last perfection of a Work of Art, may we not discern symbolic meaning? In that divinely transfigured Sleep, as of Victory, resting over the beloved face which now knows thee no more, read (if thou canst for tears) the confluence of Time with Eternity, and some gleam of the latter peering through.

'Highest of all Symbols are those wherein the Artist or Poet has risen into Prophet, and all men can recognise a present God, and worship the same: I mean religious Symbols. Various enough have been such religious Symbols, what we call *Religions;* as men stood in this stage of culture or the other, and could worse or better body-forth the Godlike: some Symbols with a transient intrinsic worth; many with only an extrinsic. If thou ask to what height man has carried it in this manner, look on our divinest Symbol: on Jesus of Nazareth, and his Life, and his Biography, and what followed therefrom. Higher has the human Thought not yet reached: this is Christianity and Christendom; a Symbol of quite perennial, infinite character; whose significance will ever demand to be anew inquired into, and anew made manifest.

'But, on the whole, as Time adds much to the sacredness of Symbols, so likewise in his progress he at length defaces, or even desecrates them; and Symbols, like all terrestrial Garments, wax old. Homer's Epos has not ceased to be true; yet it is no longer *our* Epos, but shines in the distance, if clearer and clearer, yet also smaller and smaller, like a receding Star. It needs a scientific telescope, it needs to be reinterpreted and artificially brought near us, before we can so much as know that it *was* a Sun. So likewise a day comes when the Runic Thor, with his Eddas,[1] must withdraw into

[1]The Eddas were collections of Norse myths and hymns, in prose and poetry, describing, among other things, the deeds and exploits of the thunder-god, Thor. Runes=characters or signs in the Norse alphabet.

dimness; and many an African Mumbo-Jumbo[1] and Indian Pawaw[2] be utterly abolished. For all things, even Celestial Luminaries, much more atmospheric meteors, have their rise, their culmination, their decline.'

'Small is this which thou tellest me, that the Royal Sceptre is but a piece of gilt-wood; that the Pyx[3] has become a most foolish box, and truly, as Ancient Pistol[4] thought, "of little price." A right Conjuror might I name thee, couldst thou conjure back into these wooden tools the divine virtue they once held.'

'Of this thing, however, be certain: wouldst thou plant for Eternity, then plant into the deep infinite faculties of man, his Fantasy and Heart; wouldst thou plant for Year and Day, then plant into his shallow superficial faculties, his Self-love and Arithmetical Understanding, what will grow there. A Hierarch,[5] therefore, and Pontiff[6] of the World will we call him, the Poet and inspired Maker; who, Prometheus-like,[7] can shape new Symbols, and bring new Fire from Heaven to fix it there. Such too will not always be wanting; neither perhaps now are. Meanwhile, as the average of matters goes, we account him Legislator and wise who can so much as tell when a Symbol has grown old, and gently remove it.

'When, as the last English Coronation[8] was preparing,' concludes this wonderful Professor, 'I read in their Newspapers that the "Champion of England,"[9] he who has to offer

[1]Among the Mandingos of the western Sudan, a bogie to punish or frighten unruly women.

[2]*Pawaw* (or powwow): priest, conjurer, or medicine man, among the North American Indians.

[3]The box, case, vase, or tabernacle in which the reserved Eucharist is kept.

[4]*Henry V,* III, vi, 47.

[5]Chief of a sacred order.

[6]See p. 79, *note* 5.

[7]See p. 134, *note* 2.

[8]That of George IV. [Carlyle's note.]

[9]The Coronation official whose duty it is to challenge any one who may dispute the sovereign's right of succession; he appears in full armour. The office dates from William the Conqueror. See *Past and Present,* Bk. III, Ch. i (p. 140).

battle to the Universe for his new King, had brought it so far that he could now "mount his horse with little assistance," I said to myself: Here also we have a Symbol well-nigh superannuated. Alas, move whithersoever you may, are not the tatters and rage of superannuated worn-out Symbols (in this Ragfair of a World) dropping off everywhere, to hoodwink, to halter, to tether you; nay, if you shake them not aside, threatening to accumulate, and perhaps produce suffocation?'

CHAPTER IV

HELOTAGE

Heuschrecke's Malthusian Tract, and Teufelsdröckh's marginal notes thereon. The true workman, for daily bread, or spiritual bread, to be honoured; and no other. The real privation of the Poor not poverty or toil, but ignorance. Over-population: With a world like ours and wide as ours, can there be too many men? Emigration.

At this point we determine on adverting shortly, or rather reverting, to a certain Tract of Hofrath Heuschrecke's, entitled *Institute for the Repression of Population;* which lies, dishonourably enough (with torn leaves, and a perceptible smell of aloetic drugs), stuffed into the Bag *Pisces.* Not indeed for the sake of the Tract itself, which we admire little; but of the marginal Notes, evidently in Teufelsdröckh's hand, which rather copiously fringe it. A few of these may be in their right place here.

Into the Hofrath's *Institute,* with its extraordinary schemes, and machinery of Corresponding Boards and the like, we shall not so much as glance. Enough for us to understand that Heuschrecke is a disciple of Malthus;[1] and so zealous for

[1]Malthus, Thomas R. (1766–1834), political economist, published in 1798 his "Essay on the Principle of Population," in which he presented

the doctrine, that his zeal almost literally eats him up.[1] A deadly fear of Population possesses the Hofrath; something like a fixed-idea; undoubtedly akin to the more diluted forms of Madness. Nowhere, in that quarter of his intellectual world, is there light; nothing but a grim shadow of Hunger; open mouths opening wider and wider; a world to terminate by the frightfullest consummation: by its too dense inhabitants, famished into delirium, universally eating one another. To make air for himself in which strangulation, choking enough to a benevolent heart, the Hofrath founds, or proposes to found, this *Institute* of his, as the best he can do. It is only with our Professor's comments thereon that we concern ourselves.

First, then, remark that Teufelsdröckh, as a speculative Radical, has his own notions about human dignity; that the Zähdarm palaces[2] and courtesies have not made him forgetful of the Futteral cottages. On the blank cover of Heuschrecke's Tract we find the following indistinctly engrossed:

'Two men I honour, and no third. First, the toilworn Craftsman that with earth-made Implement laboriously conquers the Earth, and makes her man's. Venerable to me is the hard Hand; crooked, coarse; wherein notwithstanding lies a cunning virtue, indefeasibly royal, as of the Sceptre of this Planet. Venerable too is the rugged face, all weather-tanned, besoiled, with its rude intelligence; for it is the face of a Man living manlike. O, but the more venerable for thy rudeness, and even because we must pity as well as love thee! Hardly-entreated Brother! For us was thy back so bent, for us were thy straight limbs and fingers so deformed: thou wert our Conscript, on whom the lot fell, and fighting our battles

---

the theory that population increases in geometrical, and subsistence in arithmetical, proportion only, and argued the necessity of parents' limiting the number of their off-spring by "self-restraint." Emigration, which Carlyle advocates as a remedy, finds little support in Malthus. Nor was Malthus, as Barrett notes, an enemy to population.—The present chapter is largely devoted to an attack on the Malthusian doctrine.

[1]*Cf.* Psalms, lxix, 9.

[2]See p. 115, *note* 4.

wert so marred. For in thee too lay a god-created Form, but it was not to be unfolded; encrusted must it stand with the thick adhesions and defacements of Labour: and thy body, like thy soul, was not to know freedom. Yet toil on, toil on: *thou* art in thy duty, be out of it who may; thou toilest for the altogether indispensable, for daily bread.

'A second man I honour, and still more highly: Him who is seen toiling for the spiritually indispensable; not daily bread, but the bread of Life.[1] Is not he too in his duty; endeavouring towards inward Harmony; revealing this, by act or by word, through all his outward endeavours, be they high or low? Highest of all, when his outward and his inward endeavour are one; when we can name him Artist; not earthly Craftsman only, but inspired Thinker, who with heaven-made Implement conquers Heaven for us! If the poor and humble toil that we have Food, must not the high and glorious toil for him in return, that he have Light, have Guidance, Freedom, Immortality?—These two, in all their degrees, I honour: all else is chaff and dust,[2] which let the wind blow whither it listeth.[3]

'Unspeakably touching is it, however, when I find both dignities united; and he that must toil outwardly for the lowest of man's wants, is also toiling inwardly for the highest. Sublimer in this world know I nothing than a Peasant Saint,[4] could such now anywhere be met with. Such a one will take thee back to Nazareth itself; thou wilt see the splendour of Heaven spring forth from the humblest depths of Earth, like a light shining in great darkness.'

And again: 'It is not because of his toils that I lament for the poor: we must all toil, or steal (howsoever we name our stealing), which is worse; no faithful workman finds his task

---

[1] *Cf.* John, vi, 35.

[2] *Cf.* Psalms, i, 4.

[3] *Cf.* John, iii, 8.

[4] This term Carlyle liked to apply to his own father and to the father of Robert Burns. (See essay on Burns [*Ess.*, I, 312, *etc.*] and *Reminiscences,* first chapter.)

a pastime. The poor is hungry and athirst; but for him also there is food and drink: he is heavy-laden[1] and weary; but for him also the Heavens send Sleep, and of the deepest; in his smoky cribs,[2] a clear dewy heaven of Rest envelops him, and fitful glitterings of cloud-skirted Dreams. But what I do mourn over is, that the lamp of his soul should go out; that no ray of heavenly, or even of earthly knowledge, should visit him; but only, in the haggard darkness, like two spectres, Fear and Indignation bear him company. Alas, while the body stands so broad and brawny, must the Soul lie blinded, dwarfed, stupefied, almost annihilated! Alas, was this too a Breath of God;[3] bestowed in Heaven, but on earth never to be unfolded!—That there should one Man die ignorant who had capacity for Knowledge, this I call a tragedy, were it to happen more than twenty times in the minute, as by some computations it does. The miserable fraction of Science which our united Mankind, in a wide Universe of Nescience, has acquired, why is not this, with all diligence, imparted to all?'

Quite in an opposite strain is the following: 'The old Spartans had a wiser method; and went out and hunted-down their Helots, and speared and spitted them, when they grew too numerous.[4] With our improved fashions of hunting, Herr Hofrath, now after the invention of fire-arms, and standing-armies, how much easier were such a hunt! Perhaps in the most thickly-peopled country, some three days annually might suffice to shoot all the able-bodied Paupers that had accumulated within the year. Let Governments think of this. The expense were trifling: nay the very carcasses would pay it. Have them salted and barrelled;

[1]*Cf.* Matthew, xi, 28.

[2]*Cf. II Henry IV,* III, i, 9.

[3]*Cf.* Genesis, ii, 7.

[4]The original inhabitants of Laconia, who lost their independence to the Dorians, were enslaved by the Spartans for agricultural labour. They could be neither freed nor sold; when they grew too numerous they were systematically murdered in large numbers. (See Plutarch's *Life* of Lycurgus.)

could not you victual therewith, if not Army and Navy, yet richly such infirm Paupers, in workhouses and elsewhere, as enlightened Charity, dreading no evil of them, might see good to keep alive?'[1]

'And yet,' writes he farther on, 'there must be something wrong. A full-formed Horse will, in any market, bring from twenty to as high as two-hundred Friedrichs d'or:[2] such is his worth to the world. A full-formed Man is not only worth nothing to the world, but the world could afford him a round sum would he simply engage to go and hang himself. Nevertheless, which of the two was the more cunningly-devised article, even as an Engine? Good Heavens! A white European Man, standing on his two Legs, with his two five-fingered Hands at his shackle-bones, and miraculous Head on his shoulders, is worth, I should say, from fifty to a hundred Horses'!

'True, thou Gold-Hofrath,' cries the Professor elsewhere: 'too crowded indeed! Meanwhile, what portion of this inconsiderable terraqueous Globe have ye actually tilled and delved, till it will grow no more? How thick stands your Population in the Pampas and Savannas of America; round ancient Carthage, and in the interior of Africa; on both slopes of the Altaic Chain,[3] in the central Platform of Asia; in Spain, Greece, Turkey, Crim Tartary,[4] the Curragh of Kildare?[5] One man, in one year, as I have understood it, if you lend him Earth, will feed himself and nine others. Alas, where now are the Hengsts[6] and Alarics[7] of our still-glowing, still-expanding Europe; who, when their home is grown too

---

[1]Possibly an adaptation of Swift's idea in "A Modest Proposal for Preventing the Children of the Poor People from being a Burden," *etc.* (1729), in which Swift advocates the cooking and eating of the children!

[2]See p. 84, *note* 3.

[3]The Altai Mountains of Mongolia and Siberia.

[4]See p. 109, *note* 4.

[5]A plain in the county of Kildare, Ireland.

[6]See p. 22, *note* 1.

[7]Alaric, or Alric (*c.* 370–410), king of the Visigoths, took and plundered Rome, A.D. 410.

narrow, will enlist, and, like Fire-pillars,[1] guide onwards those superfluous masses of indomitable living Valour;[2] equipped, not now with the battle-axe and war-chariot, but with the steam-engine and ploughshare? Where are they?—Preserving their Game!'[3]

CHAPTER V

THE PHŒNIX[4]

Teufelsdröckh considers Society as *dead;* its soul (Religion) gone, its body (existing Institutions) going. Utilitarianism, needing little farther preaching, is now in full activity of destruction.—Teufelsdröckh would yield to the Inevitable, accounting that the best: Assurance of a fairer Living Society, arising, Phœnix-like, out of the ruins of the old dead one. Before that Phœnix death-birth is accomplished, long time, struggle, and suffering must intervene.

PUTTING which four singular Chapters together, and alongside of them numerous hints, and even direct utterances, scattered over these Writings of his, we come upon the startling yet not quite unlooked-for conclusion, that Teufelsdröckh is one of those who consider Society, properly so

[1]*Cf.* Exodus, xiii, 21.

[2]Byron, *Childe Harold,* iii, 27.

[3]See p. 94, *note* 1.

[4]A fabulous bird which, in Arabia, was said to live for at least 500 years, to be consumed in fire by its own act, and then to rise in youthful freshness from its own ashes. The legend is to be found in innumerable quarters. See Tacitus, *Annals,* vi, 28; *Samson Agonistes,* 1699 ff.; Sir Thomas Browne, *Vulgar Errors,* Bk. III, Ch. xii. It is difficult to determine to whom Carlyle is indebted for his doctrine of the World-Phoenix. The principle of perpetual renewal is of course central to the philosophies of the Post-Kantians and of Goethe. Fichte: "All death in Nature is Birth" (*Werke,* II, 317). Goethe: "No Being (*Wesen*) can fall into Nothingness (*Nichts*)" (*Werke,* II, 245). Carlyle attributes the doctrine to Johannes von Müller (*Universal History,* publ. 1810); but there is no evidence that Carlyle knew the work other than by title. (*Ess.,* I, 143–44: Müller and Zacharias Werner as sources.)

called, to be as good as extinct; and that only the gregarious feelings, and old inherited habitudes, at this juncture, hold us from Dispersion, and universal national, civil, domestic and personal war! He says expressly: 'For the last three centuries, above all for the last three quarters of a century, that same Pericardial Nervous Tissue (as we named it) of Religion, where lies the Life-essence of Society, has been smote-at and perforated, needfully and needlessly; till now it is quite rent into shreds; and Society, long pining, diabetic, consumptive, can be regarded as defunct; for those spasmodic, galvanic sprawlings are not life; neither indeed will they endure, galvanise as you may, beyond two days.'

'Call ye that a Society,' cries he again, 'where there is no longer any Social Idea extant;[1] not so much as the Idea of a common Home, but only of a common over-crowded Lodging-house? Where each, isolated, regardless of his neighbour, turned against his neighbour, clutches what he can get, and cries "Mine!" and calls it Peace,[2] because, in the cut-purse and cut-throat Scramble, no steel knives, but only a far cunninger sort, can be employed? Where Friendship, Communion, has become an incredible tradition; and your holiest Sacramental Supper is a smoking Tavern Dinner, with Cook for Evangelist? Where your Priest has no tongue but for plate-licking: and your high Guides and Governors cannot guide; but on all hands hear it passionately proclaimed: *Laissez faire;*[3] Leave us alone of *your* guidance, such light is darker than darkness; eat you your wages, and sleep!

'Thus, too,' continues he, 'does an observant eye discern everywhere that saddest spectacle: The Poor perishing, like neglected, foundered Draught-Cattle, of Hunger and Over-work; the Rich, still more wretchedly, of Idleness, Satiety,

---

[1]Expanded in "Characteristics" (*Ess.,* III, 13–14).

[2]Adapted from Tacitus, *Agricola,* 30: "solitudinem faciunt, pacem appellant."

[3]Literally, "let (people) do, or make (what they choose)"; non-interference. A term used in economics, originally by the Physiocrats, deprecating government interference in behalf of labour, commerce, *etc.,* against unscrupulous masters in economic activities.

and Over-growth. The Highest in rank, at length, without honour from the Lowest; scarcely, with a little mouth-honour, as from tavern-waiters who expect to put it in the bill. Once-sacred Symbols fluttering as empty Pageants, whereof men grudge even the expense; a World becoming dismantled: in one word, the CHURCH fallen speechless, from obesity and apoplexy; the STATE shrunken into a Police-Office, straitened to get its pay!'

We might ask, are there many 'observant eyes,' belonging to practical men in England or elsewhere, which have descried these phenomena; or is it only from the mystic elevation of a German *Wahngasse*[1] that such wonders are visible? Teufelsdröckh contends that the aspect of a 'deceased or expiring Society' fronts us everywhere, so that whoso runs may read. 'What, for example,' says he, 'is the universally-arrogated Virtue, almost the sole remaining Catholic Virtue, of these days? For some half century, it has been the thing you name "Independence."[2] Suspicion of "Servility," of reverence for Superiors, the very dogleech is anxious to disavow. Fools! Were your Superiors worthy to govern, and you worthy to obey, reverence for them were even your only possible freedom. Independence, in all kinds, is rebellion; if unjust rebellion, why parade it, and everywhere prescribe it?'

But what then? Are we returning, as Rousseau[3] prayed, to the state of Nature? 'The Soul Politic having departed,' says Teufelsdröckh, 'what can follow but that the Body Politic be decently interred, to avoid putrescence? Liberals, Economists, Utilitarians enough I see marching with its bier, and chanting loud pæans, towards the funeral-pile, where, amid wailings from some, and saturnalian revelries from the most, the venerable Corpse is to be burnt. Or, in plain words, that these men, Liberals, Utilitarians,[4] or whatsoever

---

[1]See p. 20, *note* 1.

[2]Allusion to the efforts of the Americans (1776) and of the French (1793).

[3]See p. 203, *note* 4.

[4]See p. 117, *note* 2.

they are called, will ultimately carry their point, and dissever and destroy most existing Institutions of Society, seems a thing which has some time ago ceased to be doubtful.

'Do we not see a little subdivision of the grand Utilitarian Armament come to light even in insulated England? A living nucleus, that will attract and grow, does at length appear there also; and under curious phasis; properly as the inconsiderable fag-end, and so far in the rear of the others as to fancy itself the van. Our European Mechanisers[1] are a sect of boundless diffusion, activity, and coöperative spirit: has not Utilitarianism flourished in high places of Thought, here among ourselves, and in every European country, at some time or other, within the last fifty years? If now in all countries, except perhaps England, it has ceased to flourish, or indeed to exist, among Thinkers, and sunk to Journalists and the popular mass,—who sees not that, as hereby it no longer preaches, so the reason is, it now needs no Preaching, but is in full universal Action, the doctrine everywhere known, and enthusiastically laid to heart? The fit pabulum, in these times, for a certain rugged workshop intellect and heart, nowise without their corresponding workshop strength and ferocity, it requires but to be stated in such scenes to make proselytes enough.—Admirably calculated for destroying, only not for rebuilding! It spreads like a sort of Dog-madness; till the whole World-kennel will be rabid: then woe to the Huntsmen, with or without their whips! They should have given the quadrupeds water,' adds he; 'the water, namely, of Knowledge and of Life,[2] while it was yet time.'

Thus, if Professor Teufelsdröckh can be relied on, we are at this hour in a most critical condition; beleaguered by that boundless 'Armament of Mechanisers' and Unbelievers, threatening to strip us bare! 'The World,' says he, 'as it needs must, is under a process of devastation and waste, which, whether by silent assiduous corrosion, or open quicker

---

[1]See p. 221, *note* 3.

[2]Genesis, ii, 8–10; Revelation, xxii, 17.

combustion, as the case chances, will effectually enough annihilate the past Forms of Society; replace them with what it may. For the present, it is contemplated that when man's whole Spiritual interests are once *divested,* these innumerable stript-off Garments shall mostly be burnt; but the sounder Rags among them be quilted together into one huge Irish watch-coat[1] for the defence of the Body only!'—This, we think, is but Job's-news[2] to the humane reader.

'Nevertheless,' cries Teufelsdröckh, 'who can hinder it; who is there that can clutch into the wheelspokes of Destiny, and say to the Spirit of the Time: Turn back, I command thee?—Wiser were it that we yielded to the Inevitable and Inexorable, and accounted even this the best.'

Nay, might not an attentive Editor, drawing his own inferences from what stands written, conjecture that Teufelsdröckh individually had yielded to this same 'Inevitable and Inexorable' heartily enough; and now sat waiting the issue, with his natural diabolico-angelical Indifference, if not even Placidity? Did we not hear him complain that the World was a 'huge Ragfair,' and the 'rags and tatters of old Symbols' were raining-down everywhere, like to drift him in, and suffocate him? What with those 'unhunted Helots' of his; and the uneven *sic vos non vobis*[3] pressure and hard-crashing collision he is pleased to discern in existing things; what with the so hateful 'empty Masks,'[4] full of beetles and spiders, yet glaring out on him, from their glass eyes, 'with a ghastly affectation of life,'—we feel entitled to conclude him even willing that much should be thrown to the Devil, so it were but done gently! Safe himself in that 'Pinnacle of Weissnichtwo,' he would consent, with a tragic solemnity,

---

[1]A heavy overcoat worn by a watchman, or watch officer, in heavy weather. A nautical term. *Cf.* Sterne's *History of a Watchcoat.*

[2]Bad news. *Cf.* the German, *Hiobspost,* in "Dumb Love" (*German Romance,* I, 81); Job, i, 13–19.

[3]"Thus ye labour, but not for yourselves"—from Virgil. See Donatus's *Life of Virgil.* (M.)

[4]The Church-Clothes mentioned in Bk. III, Ch. ii.

that the monster UTILITARIA, held back, indeed, and moderated by nose-rings, halters, foot-shackles, and every conceivable modification of rope, should go forth to do her work;—to tread down old ruinous Palaces and Temples with her broad hoof, till the whole were trodden down, that new and better might be built! Remarkable in this point of view are the following sentences.

'Society,' says he, 'is not dead: that Carcass, which you call dead Society, is but her mortal coil[1] which she has shuffled-off, to assume a nobler; she herself, through perpetual metamorphoses, in fairer and fairer development, has to live till Time also merge in Eternity. Wheresoever two or three Living Men are gathered together, there is Society; or there it will be, with its cunning mechanisms and stupendous structures, over-spreading this little Globe, and reaching upwards to Heaven and downwards to Gehenna:[2] for always, under one or the other figure, it has two authentic Revelations, of a God and of a Devil; the Pulpit, namely, and the Gallows.'

Indeed, we already heard him speak of 'Religion, in unnoticed nooks, weaving for herself new Vestures';—Teufelsdröckh himself being one of the loom-treadles? Elsewhere he quotes without censure that strange aphorism of Saint-Simon's,[3] concerning which and whom so much were to be said: *'L'âge d'or, qu'une aveugle tradition a placé jusqu'ici dans le passé, est devant nous;* The golden age, which a blind tradition has hitherto placed in the Past, is Before us.'—But listen again:

'When the Phœnix is fanning her funeral pyre, will there

---

[1]*Cf. Hamlet,* III, i, 67.

[2]Hell. See p. 107, *note* 1.

[3]Claude Henri, Comte de Saint-Simon (1760–1825), was the philosopher and founder of Socialism in France. The Saint-Simonians were attracted to Carlyle upon the publication of his essay, "Signs of the Times" (1829); and for a short period Carlyle viewed their doctrines with considerable enthusiasm. Goethe, however, urged him to hold himself aloof from their movement, and he delicately declined their invitation to join them. (*C.E.L.,* II, Chs. iv and vi; *G.-C. Corr.,* pp. 224–25.)

not be sparks flying! Alas, some millions of men, and among them such as a Napoleon, have already been licked into that high-eddying Flame, and like moths consumed there. Still also have we to fear that incautious beards will get singed.

'For the rest, in what year of grace such Phœnix-cremation will be completed, you need not ask. The law of Perseverance is among the deepest in man: by nature he hates change; seldom will he quit his old house till it has actually fallen about his ears. Thus have I seen Solemnities linger as Ceremonies, sacred Symbols as idle Pageants, to the extent of three-hundred years and more after all life and sacredness had evaporated out of them. And then, finally, what time the Phœnix Death-Birth itself will require, depends on unseen contingencies.—Meanwhile, would Destiny offer Mankind, that after, say two centuries of convulsion and conflagration, more or less vivid, the fire-creation should be accomplished, and we to find ourselves again in a Living Society, and no longer fighting but working,—were it not perhaps prudent in Mankind to strike the bargain?'

Thus is Teufelsdröckh content that old sick Society should be deliberately burnt (alas, with quite other fuel than spice-wood); in the faith that she is a Phœnix; and that a new heavenborn young one will rise out of her ashes! We ourselves, restricted to the duty of Indicator, shall forbear commentary. Meanwhile, will not the judicious reader shake his head, and reproachfully, yet more in sorrow than in anger,[1] say or think: From a *Doctor utriusque Juris,*[2] titular Professor in a University, and man to whom hitherto, for his services, Society, bad as she is, has given not only food and raiment (of a kind), but books, tobacco and gukguk,[3] we expected more gratitude to his benefactress; and less of a blind trust in the future, which resembles that rather of a philosophical

---

[1]*Cf. Hamlet,* I, ii, 231.

[2]Doctor of both civil and canon law.

[3]See p. 15, *note* 4.

Fatalist and Enthusiast, than of a solid householder paying scot-and-lot[1] in a Christian country.

CHAPTER VI

OLD CLOTHES

Courtesy due from all men to all men: The Body of Man a Revelation in the Flesh. Teufelsdröckh's respect for Old Clothes, as the 'Ghosts of Life.' Walk in Monmouth Street, and meditations there.

As mentioned above, Teufelsdröckh, though a sansculottist, is in practice probably the politest man extant: his whole heart and life are penetrated and informed with the spirit of politeness; a noble natural Courtesy shines through him, beautifying his vagaries; like sun-light, making a rosy-fingered, rainbow-dyed Aurora[2] out of mere aqueous clouds; nay brightening London-smoke itself into gold vapour,[3] as from the crucible of an alchemist. Hear in what earnest though fantastic wise he expresses himself on this head:

'Shall Courtesy be done only to the rich, and only by the rich? In Good-breeding, which differs, if at all, from High-breeding, only as it gracefully remembers the rights of others, rather than gracefully insists on its own rights, I discern no special connexion with wealth or birth: but rather that it lies in human nature itself, and is due from all men towards all men. Of a truth, were your Schoolmaster at his post, and worth anything when there, this, with so much else, would be reformed. Nay, each man were then also his neighbour's

[1] A parish assessment formerly laid upon subjects in Great Britain according to their ability; hence obligations of every kind regarded collectively. *Cf. scot-free* = tax-free.

[2] See *Odyssey*, ii, 1.

[3] Allusion to the alchemists' attempts to transmute base metals into gold.

schoolmaster; till at length a rude-visaged, unmannered Peasant could no more be met with, than a Peasant unacquainted with botanical Physiology, or who felt not that the clod he broke was created in Heaven.

'For whether thou bear a sceptre or a sledge-hammer, art not thou ALIVE; is not this thy brother ALIVE? "There is but one temple in the world," says Novalis, "and that temple is the Body of Man. Nothing is holier than this high Form. Bending before men is a reverence done to this Revelation in the Flesh. We touch Heaven, when we lay our hands on a human Body."[1]

'On which ground, I would fain carry it farther than most do; and whereas the English Johnson[2] only bowed to every Clergyman, or man with a shovel-hat, I would bow to every Man with any sort of hat, or with no hat whatever. Is not he a Temple, then; the visible Manifestation and Impersonation of the Divinity? And yet, alas, such indiscriminate bowing serves not. For there is a Devil dwells in man, as well as a Divinity; and too often the bow is but pocketed by the *former*. It would go to the pocket of Vanity (which is your clearest phasis of the Devil, in these times); therefore must we withhold it.

'The gladder am I, on the other hand, to do reverence to those Shells and outer Husks of the Body, wherein no devilish passion any longer lodges, but only the pure emblem and effigies of Man: I mean, to Empty, or even to Cast Clothes. Nay, is it not to Clothes that most men do reverence: to the fine frogged[3] broadcloth, nowise to the "straddling animal with bandy legs"[4] which it holds, and makes a Dignitary of?

---

[1]Quoted in Carlyle's essay on Novalis (*Ess.*, II, 39); referred to in "Goethe's Works" (*Ess.*, II, 390). *Cf.* I Corinthians, iii, 16–17.

[2]Dr. Samuel Johnson (1709–84); see Boswell's *Life of Johnson* (ed. C. B. Tinker, N. Y., 1933, p. 479): "His respect for the Hierarchy, and particularly the Dignitaries of the Church, has been more than once exhibited. . . ." There is no evidence that Johnson "bowed to *every* Clergyman."

[3]Ornamented with Braid. (P.)

[4]See p. 57, *note 2*.

Who ever saw any Lord my-lorded in tattered blanket fastened with wooden skewer? Nevertheless, I say, there is in such worship a shade of hypocrisy, a practical deception: for how often does the Body appropriate what was meant for the Cloth only! Whoso would avoid falsehood, which is the essence of all Sin, will perhaps see good to take a different course. That reverence which cannot act without obstruction and perversion when the Clothes are full, may have free course when they are empty. Even as, for Hindoo Worshippers, the Pagoda is not less sacred than the God;[1] so do I too worship the hollow cloth Garment with equal fervour, as when it contained the Man: nay, with more, for I now fear no deception, of myself or of others.

'Did not King *Toomtabard,*[2] or, in other words, John Baliol, reign long over Scotland; the man John Baliol being quite gone, and only the "Toom Tabard" (Empty Gown) remaining? What still dignity dwells in a suit of Cast Clothes! How meekly it bears its honours! No haughty looks, no scornful gesture: silent and serene, it fronts the world; neither demanding worship, nor afraid to miss it. The Hat still carries the physiognomy of its Head: but the vanity and the stupidity, and goose-speech which was the sign of these two, are gone. The Coat-arm is stretched out, but not to strike; the Breeches, in modest simplicity, depend at ease, and now at last have a graceful flow; the Waistcoat hides no evil passion, no riotous desire; hunger or thirst now dwells not in it. Thus all is purged from the grossness of sense, from the carking cares and foul vices of the World; and rides there, on its Clothes-horse; as, on a Pegasus,[3] might some skyey Messenger, or purified Apparition, visiting our low Earth.

---

[1]So in Jean Paul, "Quintus Fixlein" (*German Romance*, II, 207).

[2]Toom = empty; tabard = gown. Carlyle had been reading in Sir Walter Scott's *History of Scotland* (see *C.E.L.,* II, Ch. iv, Journal for Sept. 7, 1830).—John de Baliol (1249–1315) reigned only four years (1292–96).

[3]The winged horse of the fountain, which sprang from the blood of Medusa, when her head was struck off by Perseus; ridden by Bellerophon, who caught him with a golden bridle.

'Often, while I sojourned in that monstrous tuberosity of Civilised Life, the Capital of England; and meditated, and questioned Destiny, under that ink-sea of vapour, black, thick, and multifarious as Spartan broth;[1] and was one lone soul amid those grinding millions;—often have I turned into their Old-Clothes Market to worship. With awe-struck heart I walk through that Monmouth Street,[2] with its empty Suits, as through a Sanhedrim[3] of stainless Ghosts. Silent are they, but expressive in their silence: the past witnesses and instruments of Woe and Joy, of Passions, Virtues, Crimes, and all the fathomless tumult of Good and Evil in "the Prison men call Life."[4] Friends! trust not the heart of that man for whom Old Clothes are not venerable. Watch, too, with reverence, that bearded Jewish High-priest,[5] who with hoarse voice, like some Angel of Doom, summons them from the four winds! On his head, like the Pope, he has three Hats,—a real triple tiara;[6] on either hand are the similitude of wings, whereon the summoned Garments come to alight; and ever, as he slowly cleaves the air, sounds forth his deep fateful note, as if through a trumpet he were proclaiming: "Ghosts of Life, come to Judgment!" Reck not, ye fluttering Ghosts: he will purify you in his Purgatory, with fire and with water; and, one day, new-created ye shall reappear. O, let him in whom the flame of Devotion is ready to go out, who has never worshipped, and knows not what to worship, pace and repace, with austerest thought, the pavement of Monmouth Street,

---

[1]Such as was ordered by Lycurgus to be served to the Spartans as a safeguard against luxury. See Plutarch's *Life* of Lycurgus.

[2]Noted in the eighteenth century for its numerous old-clothes shops. Now forms a part of Shaftesbury Avenue.

[3]Chief council or tribunal of the Jews. (*Cf.* Mark, xiv, 53–55.)

[4]From Werner's *Sons of the Valley,* quoted in *Ess.,* I, 109.

[5]The beginning of a satirical passage likening the old-clothes men of Monmouth Street, with two or three hats stuck upon their heads for convenience of carriage, to the Pope with his triple tiara.

[6]The Pope's triple crown, the three crowns symbolizing his temporal, spiritual, and purgatorial sovereignty; the whole is surmounted with a globe and cross.

and say whether his heart and his eyes still continue dry. If Field Lane,[1] with its long fluttering rows of yellow handkerchiefs, be a Dionysius' Ear,[2] where, in stifled jarring hubbub, we hear the Indictment which Poverty and Vice bring against lazy Wealth, that it has left them there cast-out and trodden under foot of Want, Darkness and the Devil,—then is Monmouth Street a Mirza's Hill,[3] where, in motley vision, the whole Pageant of Existence passes awfully before us; with its wail and jubilee, mad loves and mad hatreds, church-bells and gallows-ropes, farce-tragedy, beast-godhood,[4]—the Bedlam of Creation!'

To most men, as it does to ourselves, all this will seem overcharged. We too have walked through Monmouth Street; but with little feeling of 'Devotion': probably in part because the contemplative process is so fatally broken in upon by the brood of money-changers[5] who nestle in that Church, and importune the worshipper with merely secular proposals. Whereas Teufelsdröckh might be in that happy middle state, which leaves to the Clothes-broker no hope either of sale or purchase, and so be allowed to linger there without molestation.—Something we would have given to see the little philosophical figure, with its steeple-hat and loose flowing skirts, and eyes in a fine frenzy,[6] 'pacing and repacing in austerest thought' that foolish Street; which to

[1]Near Holborn Hill, in London; in Carlyle's time, the haunt of thieves and dealers in stolen goods. See *Oliver Twist,* Ch. xxvi.

[2]Dionysius the Elder (Tyrant of Syracuse, 405–367 B.C.) made a subterranean cave, "Dionysius's Ear," from which could be heard what was said by prisoners whom he held in confinement.

[3]See Addison's "Vision of Mirza," *Spectator,* No. 159, Sept. 1, 1711.

[4]This and the preceding expressions proceed from the fundamentally dualistic and paradoxical character of Carlyle's point of view, and remind us of his ever-present Calvinism. On his sense of contradiction and paradox in the world, see "Characteristics" (*Ess.,* III, 26–28), "Boswell's Johnson" (*Id.,* III, 75, 91 ["The Contradiction which yawns wide enough in every Life, which it is the meaning and task of Life to reconcile."], *etc.*).

[5]*Cf.* John, ii, 14.

[6]*Cf. Midsummer Night's Dream,* V, i, 12.

him was a true Delphic avenue,[1] and supernatural Whispering-gallery,[2] where the 'Ghosts of Life' rounded strange secrets in his ear. O thou philosophic Teufelsdröckh, that listenest while others only gabble, and with thy quick tympanum hearest the grass grow![3]

At the same time, is it not strange that, in Paper-bag Documents destined for an English work, there exists nothing like an authentic diary of this his sojourn in London; and of his Meditations among the Clothes-shops only the obscurest emblematic shadows? Neither, in conversation (for, indeed, he was not a man to pester you with his Travels), have we heard him more than allude to the subject.

For the rest, however, it cannot be uninteresting that we here find how early the significance of Clothes had dawned on the now so distinguished Clothes-Professor. Might we but fancy it to have been even in Monmouth Street, at the bottom of our own English 'ink-sea,' that this remarkable Volume first took being, and shot forth its salient point in his soul,—as in Chaos did the Egg of Eros,[4] one day to be hatched into a Universe!

---

[1]Probably an allusion to the oracle of Apollo, at Delphi.

[2]In St. Paul's Cathedral, London. Mentioned in "Quintus Fixlein" (*German Romance,* II, 252 *n*).

[3]From a German proverb (M.); Barrett cites Heimdal, porter of the Norse Gods, who could see at night and hear the grass grow.

[4]In early Greek myths, and in the cult of Orphism, Eros was one of the principal gods, born from the cosmic egg, produced by Night (or Chaos).

CHAPTER VII

ORGANIC FILAMENTS[1]

Destruction and Creation ever proceed together; and organic filaments of the Future are even now spinning. Wonderful connection of each man with all men; and of each generation with all generations, before and after: Mankind is One. Sequence and progress of all human work, whether of creation or destruction, from age to age.—Titles, hitherto derived from Fighting, must give way to others. Kings will remain and their title. Political Freedom, not to be attained by any mechanical contrivance. Hero-worship, perennial amongst men; the cornerstone of polities in the Future. Organic filaments of the New Religion: Newspapers and Literature. Let the faithful soul take courage!

For us, who happen to live while the World-Phœnix is burning herself, and burning so slowly that, as Teufelsdröckh calculates, it were a handsome bargain would she engage to have done 'within two centuries,' there seems to lie but an ashy prospect. Not altogether so, however, does the Professor figure it. 'In the living subject,' says he, 'change is wont to be gradual: thus, while the serpent sheds its old skin, the new is already formed beneath. Little knowest thou of the burning of a World-Phœnix, who fanciest that she must first burn-out, and lie as a dead cinereous heap; and therefrom the young one start-up by miracle, and fly heavenward. Far otherwise! In that Fire-whirlwind, Creation and Destruction proceed together; ever as the ashes of the Old are blown about, do organic filaments of the New mysteriously spin themselves: and amid the rushing and the waving of the Whirlwind-

[1]The elements (new religion, new society, *etc.*) out of which a new Phoenix will arise from the ashes (old clothes, or outworn conceptions, institutions, *etc.*) of the old world. There is also in this chapter a reassertion of the mystical union of men in society. *Cf.* "Voltaire" (*Ess.*, I, 399): Society is not a "chain of causes" but "a tissue, or superficies of innumerable lines" of force.

element come tones of a melodious Deathsong, which end not but in tones of a more melodious Birthsong. Nay, look into the Fire-whirlwind with thy own eyes, and thou wilt see.' Let us actually look, then: to poor individuals, who cannot expect to live two centuries, those same organic filaments, mysteriously spinning themselves, will be the best part of the spectacle. First, therefore, this of Mankind in general:

'In vain thou deniest it,' says the Professor; 'thou *art* my Brother. Thy very Hatred, thy very Envy, those foolish Lies thou tellest of me in thy splenetic humour: what is all this but an inverted Sympathy?[1] Were I a Steam-engine, wouldst thou take the trouble to tell lies of me? Not thou! I should grind all unheeded, whether badly or well.

'Wondrous truly are the bonds that unite us one and all; whether by the soft binding of Love, or the iron chaining of Necessity, as we like to choose it. More than once have I said to myself, of some perhaps whimsically strutting Figure, such as provokes whimsical thoughts: "Wert thou, my little Brotherkin, suddenly covered-up within the largest imaginable Glass-bell,—what a thing it were, not for thyself only, but for the World! Post Letters, more or fewer, from all the four winds, impinge against thy Glass walls,[2] but have to drop unread: neither from within comes there question or response into any Postbag; thy Thoughts fall into no friendly ear or heart, thy Manufacture into no purchasing hand: thou art no longer a circulating venous-arterial Heart, that, taking and giving, circulatest through all Space and all Time: there has a Hole fallen-out in the immeasurable, universal World-tissue, which must be darned-up again!"

'Such venous-arterial circulation, of Letters, verbal Messages, paper and other Packages, going out from him and coming in, are a blood-circulation, visible to the eye: but the finer nervous circulation, by which all things, the minutest

---

[1]*Cf.* "Voltaire" (Ess., I, 424); "Goethe's Works" (*Ess.*, II, 388, 389: "Hatred itself is but an inverse love").

[2]Expanded from a short passage in *Wilhelm Meister,* I, 418; quoted in "Signs of the Times" (*Ess.,* II, 81).

that he does, minutely influence all men, and the very look of his face blesses or curses whomso it lights on, and so generates ever new blessing or new cursing: all this you cannot see, but only imagine. I say, there is not a red Indian, hunting by Lake Winnipic,[1] can quarrel with his squaw, but the whole world must smart for it: will not the price of beaver rise? It is a mathematical fact that the casting of this pebble from my hand alters the centre of gravity of the Universe.[2]

'If now an existing generation of men stand so woven together, not less indissolubly does generation with generation. Hast thou ever meditated on that word, Tradition:[3] how we inherit not Life only, but all the garniture and form of Life; and work, and speak, and even think and feel, as our Fathers, and primeval grandfathers, from the beginning, have given it us?—Who printed thee, for example, this unpretending Volume on the Philosophy of Clothes? Not the Herren Stillschweigen and Company; but Cadmus[4] of Thebes, Faust of Mentz,[5] and innumerable others whom thou knowest not. Had there been no Mœsogothic Ulfila,[6] there had been no English Shakespeare, or a different one. Simpleton! it was Tubalcain[7] that made thy very Tailor's needle, and sewed that court-suit of thine.

'Yes, truly, if Nature is one, and a living indivisible whole, much more is Mankind, the Image that reflects and creates

---

[1]Lake Winnipeg, in Canada.—See Int., Sect. V, b, on Carlyle's sense of the oneness of Nature and man.

[2]See Newton, *Principia,* Lex. III, Coroll. IV. (M.)—Carlyle's references to Newton are always based on a first-hand acquaintance with the scientist's works. See D. A. Wilson, *Carlyle till Marriage,* p. 116, *etc.*

[3]See p. 171, *note* 1.

[4]Legendary founder of Thebes who introduced into Greece from Phoenicia or Egypt an alphabet of sixteen letters.

[5]See p. 40, *note* 4.

[6]Ulfila, or Ulfilas (*c.* 311–83) was Bishop of the Arian Visigoths, "apostle of Christianity to the Gothic race, and, through his translation of the Scriptures into Gothic, the father of Teutonic literature." (*Encycl. Brit.*)—*Mœsogothic:* Moesia = mod. Serbia, Bulgaria.

[7]*Cf.* Genesis, iv, 22.

Nature, without which Nature were not. As palpable life-streams in that wondrous Individual Mankind, among so many life-streams that are not palpable, flow on those main-currents of what we call Opinion; as preserved in Institutions, Polities, Churches, above all in Books. Beautiful it is to understand and know that a Thought did never yet die; that as thou, the originator thereof, hast gathered it and created it from the whole Past, so thou wilt transmit it to the whole Future. It is thus that the heroic heart, the seeing eye of the first times, still feels and sees in us of the latest; that the Wise Man stands ever encompassed, and spiritually embraced, by a cloud of witnesses[1] and brothers; and there is a living, literal *Communion of Saints,*[2] wide as the World itself, and as the History of the World.

'Noteworthy also, and serviceable for the progress of this same Individual, wilt thou find his subdivision into Generations. Generations are as the Days of toilsome Mankind: Death and Birth are the vesper and the matin bells, that summon Mankind to sleep, and to rise refreshed for new advancement. What the Father has made, the Son can make and enjoy; but has also work of his own appointed him. Thus all things wax, and roll onwards; Arts, Establishments, Opinions, nothing is completed, but ever completing. Newton[3] has learned to see what Kepler[4] saw; but there is also a fresh heaven-derived force in Newton; he must mount to still higher points of vision. So too the Hebrew Lawgiver[5] is, in due

[1]*Cf.* Hebrews, xii, 1.

[2]Adapted from the Apostles' Creed. Goethe, however (in *Wilhelm Meister,* II, 268), presents the third Article of Meister's new faith as "an inspired Communion of Saints . . . of men in the highest degree good and wise." *Cf.* also Goethe's *Mason-Lodge,* quoted at the end of Book III of *Past and Present.*

[3]Newton, Sir Isaac (1642–1727), English mathematician and philosopher.

[4]Kepler, Johann (1571–1630). Newton continued Kepler's work, showing that the laws of planetary motion (as Kepler ascertained them) were particular consequences of the laws of motion and the law of gravitation. (B.)

[5]Moses. John, i, 17.

time, followed by an Apostle of the Gentiles.[1] In the business of Destruction, as this also is from time to time a necessary work, thou findest a like sequence and perseverance: for Luther it was as yet hot enough to stand by that burning of the Pope's Bull;[2] Voltaire[3] could not warm himself at the glimmering ashes, but required quite other fuel. Thus likewise, I note, the English Whig has, in the second generation, become an English Radical; who, in the third again, it is to be hoped, will become an English Rebuilder. Find Mankind where thou wilt, thou findest it in living movement, in progress faster or slower: the Phœnix soars aloft, hovers with outstretched wings, filling Earth with her music; or, as now, she sinks, and with spheral swan-song immolates herself in flame, that she may soar the higher and sing the clearer.'

Let the friends of social order, in such a disastrous period, lay this to heart, and derive from it any little comfort they can. We subjoin another passage, concerning Titles:

'Remark, not without surprise,' says Teufelsdröckh, 'how all high Titles of Honour come hitherto from Fighting. Your *Herzog*[4] (Duke, *Dux*) is Leader of Armies; your Earl[5] (*Jarl*) is Strong Man; your Marshal,[6] cavalry Horse-shoer. A Millennium, or reign of Peace and Wisdom, having from of old been prophesied, and becoming now daily more and more indubitable, may it not be apprehended that such Fighting-titles will cease to be palatable, and new and higher need to be devised?

'The only Title wherein I, with confidence, trace eternity,

---

[1]Paul. Romans, xi, 13.

[2]In Wittenberg, on December 10, 1520, Martin Luther (1483–1546), Augustinian friar and religious reformer, publicly burnt the papal bull, or edict, by which he was excommunicated; thus initiating the destruction of Church unity throughout Europe.

[3]See p. 193, *note* 4.

[4]German for *Duke*. *Cf.* Old English *heretoga* (army leader).

[5]Old English: *eorl* (man, noble); Old Saxon: *erl* (boy, man); Icelandic: *jarl* (nobleman, count).

[6]Old High German: *marah-scalc* (*marah*, horse + *scalc*, servant).

is that of King. *König* (King),[1] anciently *Könning,* means Ken-ning (Cunning), or which is the same thing, Can-ning. Ever must the Sovereign of Mankind be fitly entitled King.'

'Well, also,' says he elsewhere, 'was it written by Theologians: a King rules by divine right.[2] He carries in him an authority from God, or man will never give it him. Can I choose my own King? I can choose my own King Popinjay,[3] and play what farce or tragedy I may with him: but he who is to be my Ruler, whose will is to be higher than my will, was chosen for me in Heaven. Neither except in such Obedience to the Heaven-chosen is Freedom so much as conceivable.'

The Editor will here admit that, among all the wondrous provinces of Teufelsdröckh's spiritual world, there is none he walks in with such astonishment, hesitation, and even pain, as in the Political. How, with our English love of Ministry and Opposition, and that generous conflict of Parties, mind warming itself against mind in their mutual wrestle for the Public Good, by which wrestle, indeed, is our invaluable Constitution kept warm and alive; how shall we domesticate ourselves in this spectral Necropolis,[4] or rather City both of the Dead and of the Unborn, where the Present seems little other than an inconsiderable Film dividing the Past and the Future? In those dim long-drawn expanses, all is so immeasurable; much so disastrous, ghastly; your very radiances and straggling light-beams have a supernatural character. And then with such an indifference, such a prophetic peacefulness (accounting the inevitably coming as already here, to him all one whether it be distant by centuries or only by days), does he sit;—and live, you would say, rather in any other age than in his own! It is our painful duty to announce, or repeat,

[1]Carlyle's etymology is no longer held. Old English: *cyning,* belonging to a tribe, from *cynn,* tribe. *Cunning* is derived from the Old English, *cunnan,* to know, be able; *can* or *"can-ning,"* is derived from Old English *cunnan* in the sense of know, or know *how.*

[2]The hero-doctrine. *Cf. C.E.L.,* II, Ch. iv, Journal for February 7, 1831.

[3]See Scott's *Old Mortality,* Ch. ii.

[4]City of the dead; cemetery.

that, looking into this man, we discern a deep, silent, slow-burning, inextinguishable Radicalism, such as fills us with shuddering admiration.

Thus, for example, he appears to make little even of the Elective Franchise; at least so we interpret the following: 'Satisfy yourselves,' he says, 'by universal, indubitable experiment, even as ye are now doing or will do, whether FREEDOM, heavenborn and leading heavenward, and so vitally essential for us all, cannot peradventure be mechanically hatched and brought to light in that same Ballot-Box[1] of yours; or at worst, in some other discoverable or devisable Box, Edifice, or Steam-mechanism. It were a mighty convenience; and beyond all feats of manufacture witnessed hitherto.' Is Teufelsdröckh acquainted with the British Constitution, even slightly?—He says, under another figure: 'But after all, were the problem, as indeed it now everywhere is, To rebuild your old House from the top downwards[2] (since you must live in it the while), what better, what other, than the Representative Machine will serve your turn? Meanwhile, however, mock me not with the name of Free, "when you have but knit-up my chains into ornamental festoons." '[3]—Or what will any member of the Peace Society[4] make of such an assertion as this: 'The lower people everywhere desire War. Not so unwisely; there is then a demand for lower people—to be shot!'

Gladly, therefore, do we emerge from those soul-confusing labyrinths of speculative Radicalism, into somewhat clearer regions. Here, looking round, as was our hest, for 'organic filaments,' we ask, May not this, touching 'Hero-worship,' be of the number? It seems of a cheerful Character; yet so quaint, so mystical, one knows not what, or how little, may lie under it. Our readers shall look with their own eyes:

---

[1]One of the demands of the Chartists in 1838; introduced in the election of 1874, under the Ballot Act of 1872.

[2]As did Goethe's father. See Goethe's *Autobiography,* I, Bk. I (p. 7).

[3]From one of Goethe's epigrams, quoted in "Goethe's Works" (*Ess.,* II, 441).

[4]Founded in London in 1816 by the Society of Friends (Quakers). (M.)

'True is it that, in these days, man can do almost all things, only not obey. True likewise that whoso cannot obey cannot be free, still less bear rule; he that is the inferior of nothing, can be the superior of nothing, the equal of nothing. Nevertheless, believe not that man has lost his faculty of Reverence; that if it slumber in him, it has gone dead. Painful for man is that same rebellious Independence, when it has become inevitable; only in loving companionship with his fellows does he feel safe; only in reverently bowing down before the Higher does he feel himself exalted.

'Or what if the character of our so troublous Era lay even in this: that man had forever cast away Fear, which is the lower; but not yet risen into perennial Reverence, which is the higher and highest?

'Meanwhile, observe with joy, so cunningly has Nature ordered it, that whatsoever man ought to obey, he cannot but obey. Before no faintest revelation of the Godlike did he ever stand irreverent; least of all, when the Godlike showed itself revealed in his fellow-man. Thus is there a true religious Loyalty forever rooted in his heart; nay in all ages, even in ours, it manifests itself as a more or less orthodox *Hero-worship.* In which fact, that Hero-worship exists, has existed, and will forever exist, universally among Mankind, mayest thou discern the corner-stone of living-rock, whereon all Polities for the remotest time may stand secure.'

Do our readers discern any such corner-stone, or even so much as what Teufelsdröckh is looking at? He exclaims, 'Or hast thou forgotten Paris and Voltaire?[1] How the aged, withered man, though but a Sceptic, Mocker, and millinery Court-poet, yet because even he seemed the Wisest, Best, could drag mankind at his chariot-wheels, so that princes coveted a smile from him, and the loveliest of France would have laid their hair beneath his feet! All Paris was one vast Temple

[1]On February 10, 1778, after an absence of twenty-eight years, Voltaire, at the age of eighty-four, returned in triumph to Paris. See Carlyle's *French Revolution,* I, 42 (Bk. II, Ch. iv); the essay on Voltaire (*Ess.,* I, 436 ff.).

of Hero-worship; though their Divinity, moreover, was of feature too apish.

'But if such things,' continues he, 'were done in the dry tree, what will be done in the green?[1] If, in the most parched season of Man's History, in the most parched spot of Europe, when Parisian life was at best but a scientific *Hortus Siccus*,[2] bedizened with some Italian Gumflowers,[3] such virtue could come out of it; what is to be looked for when Life again waves leafy and bloomy, and your Hero-Divinity shall have nothing apelike, but be wholly human? Know that there is in man a quite indestructible Reverence for whatsoever holds of Heaven, or even plausibly counterfeits such holding. Show the dullest clodpole, show the haughtiest featherhead, that a soul higher than himself is actually here; were his knees stiffened into brass, he must down and worship.'

Organic filaments, of a more authentic sort, mysteriously spinning themselves, some will perhaps discover in the following passage:

'There is no Church, sayest thou? The voice of Prophecy has gone dumb? This is even what I dispute: but in any case, hast thou not still Preaching enough? A Preaching Friar settles himself in every village; and builds a pulpit, which he calls Newspaper.[4] Therefrom he preaches what most momentous doctrine is in him, for man's salvation; and dost not thou listen, and believe? Look well, thou seest everywhere a new Clergy of the Mendicant Orders, some barefooted, some almost bare-backed, fashion itself into shape, and teach and preach, zealously enough, for copper alms and the love of God. These break in pieces the ancient idols; and, though themselves too often reprobate, as idol-breakers are

[1] *Cf.* Luke, xxiii, 31.

[2] Dry garden; a collection of dried plants for study.

[3] Scotch for "artificial flowers."

[4] Jean Paul, "Quintus Fixlein" (*German Romance,* II, 340): "An author is the Town-chaplain of the Universe." *Cf.* "Signs of the Times" (*Ess.,* II, 77): "The true Church of England . . . lies in the Editors of its Newspapers . . ."; Fichte, *The Nature of the Scholar,* Lectures ix and x, *Characteristics of the Present Age,* Lecture v.

wont to be, mark out the sites of new Churches, where the true God-ordained, that are to follow, may find audience, and minister. Said I not, Before the old skin was shed, the new had formed itself beneath it?'

Perhaps also in the following; wherewith we now hasten to knit-up this ravelled sleeve:[1]

'But there is no Religion?'[2] reiterates the Professor. 'Fool! I tell thee, there is. Hast thou well considered all that lies in this immeasurable froth-ocean we name LITERATURE? Fragments of a genuine Church-*Homiletic* lie scattered there, which Time will assort: nay fractions even of a *Liturgy* could I point out. And knowest thou no Prophet, even in the vesture, environment, and dialect of this age? None to whom the Godlike had revealed itself, through all meanest and highest forms of the Common; and by him been again prophetically revealed: in whose inspired melody, even in these rag-gathering and rag-burning days, Man's Life again begins, were it but afar off, to be divine? Knowest thou none such? I know him, and name him—Goethe.

'But thou as yet standest in no Temple; joinest in no Psalm-worship; feelest well that, where there is no ministering Priest, the people perish?[3] Be of comfort! Thou art not alone, if thou have Faith. Spake we not of a Communion of Saints,[4] unseen, yet not unreal, accompanying and brother-like embracing thee, so thou be worthy? Their heroic Sufferings rise up melodiously together to Heaven, out of all lands, and out of all times, as a sacred *Miserere;*[5] their heroic Actions also, as a boundless everlasting Psalm of Triumph. Neither say that thou hast now no Symbol of the Godlike. Is not God's Universe a Symbol of the Godlike; is not Immensity a Temple;

---

[1] *Cf. Macbeth,* II, ii, 38.

[2] So in Novalis's *Fragmente,* (quoted in *Ess.,* II, 43); religion "has to be made and produced by the union of a number of persons."

[3] *Cf.* Proverbs, xxix, 18.

[4] See p. 247, *note* 2.

[5] The 51st Psalm: "Have mercy upon me, O God" (*Miserere mei Deus, etc.*).

is not Man's History, and Men's History, a perpetual Evangel?[1] Listen, and for organ-music thou wilt ever, as of old, hear the Morning Stars sing together.[2]

CHAPTER VIII

NATURAL SUPERNATURALISM[3]

Deep significance of Miracles. Littleness of human Science: Divine incomprehensibility of Nature. Custom blinds us to the miraculousness of daily-recurring miracles; so do Names. Space and Time, appearances only; forms of human Thought: A glimpse of Immortality. How Space hides from us the wondrousness of our commonest powers; and Time, the divinely miraculous course of human history.

IT IS in his stupendous Section, headed *Natural Supernaturalism,* that the Professor first becomes a Seer; and, after long effort, such as we have witnessed, finally subdues under his feet this refractory Clothes-Philosophy, and takes victorious possession thereof. Phantasms enough he has had to struggle with; 'Cloth-webs and Cob-webs,' of Imperial Mantles, Superannuated Symbols, and what not: yet still did he courageously

[1] *Cf.* Fichte's *The Nature of the Scholar,* Lecture ii; Novalis's *Werke,* III, 192: "Die ganze Geschichte ist Evangelium." Schiller had said that "World-history is the judgement of [on] the World" (*Resignation,* penultimate stanza); and Richter had likewise declared that we can "divine and read the Infinite Spirit" in History (Carlyle, *Ess.,* II, 113, *n*).

[2] *Cf.* Job, xxxviii, 7 (adapted). A similar passage occurs in "Quintus Fixlein" (*German Romance,* II, 226–27).

[3] Carlyle's term denoting the real character of the world as he saw it: founded on mystery, a direct symbolizing of the infinite and eternal forces of truth and goodness, beyond the reach of our logical understanding, and therefore to be regarded with wonder and reverence. The age of ecclesiastical miracles has passed away; the old supernaturalism has yielded to a *natural* supernaturalism—all nature, as the revelation of God, is now sacred, and nothing is really secular. Carlyle was haunted all his life by a "strange feeling of *supernaturalism,* of 'the fearfulness and wonderfulness' of life" (*Cf. C.E.L.,* II, Ch. xii, Journal for July 21, 1832).

pierce through. Nay, worst of all, two quite mysterious, world-embracing Phantasms, TIME and SPACE,[1] have ever hovered round him, perplexing and bewildering: but with these also he now resolutely grapples, these also he victoriously rends asunder. In a word, he has looked fixedly on Existence, till, one after the other, its earthly hulls and garnitures have all melted away; and now, to his rapt vision, the interior celestial Holy of Holies lies disclosed.

Here, therefore, properly it is that the Philosophy of Clothes attains to Transcendentalism;[2] this last leap, can we but clear it, takes us safe into the promised land,[3] where *Palingenesia,*[4] in all senses, may be considered as beginning. 'Courage, then!' may our Diogenes exclaim, with better right than Diogenes the First[5] once did. This stupendous Section we, after long painful meditation, have found not to be unintelligible; but, on the contrary, to grow clear, nay radiant, and all-illuminating. Let the reader, turning on it what utmost force of speculative intellect is in him, do his part; as we, by judicious selection and adjustment, shall study to do ours:

'Deep has been, and is, the significance of Miracles,' thus quietly begins the Professor; 'far deeper perhaps than we imagine. Meanwhile, the question of questions were: What specially is a Miracle? To that Dutch King of Siam,[6] an icicle had been a miracle; whoso had carried with him an air-pump, and vial of vitriolic ether, might have worked a miracle. To my Horse, again, who unhappily is still more unscientific, do not I work a miracle, and magical "*Open sesame!*"[7] every time

---

[1]See Bk. I, Ch. x; and Int., Sect. V, b.

[2]See p. 15; *note* 2; and Int., Sect. V, b.

[3]*Cf.* Deuteronomy, xix, 8; xxvi, 9; xxvii, 3.

[4]See p. 217, *note* 1, and Int., Sect. V, b and d.

[5]In Laertius's *Lives of the Philosophers,* Diogenes, when a tedious lecture was near the end, cried to his neighbours: "Courage, friends! I see land!" (M.)

[6]Alluded to in Hume's *Inquiry Concerning the Human Understanding,* Sect. x.

[7]The magical words which opened the door to the cavern in *Ali Baba and the Forty Thieves,* in *The Arabian Nights.*

I please to pay twopence, and open for him an impassable *Schlagbaum,* or shut Turnpike?

'"But is not a real Miracle simply a violation of the Laws of Nature?" ask several. Whom I answer by this new question: What are the Laws of Nature? To me perhaps the rising of one from the dead were no violation of these Laws, but a confirmation; were some far deeper Law, now first penetrated into, and by Spiritual Force, even as the rest have all been, brought to bear on us with its Material Force.

'Here too may some inquire, not without astonishment: On what ground shall one, that can make Iron swim,[1] come and declare that therefore he can teach Religion? To us, truly, of the Nineteenth Century, such declaration were inept enough; which nevertheless to our fathers, of the First Century, was full of meaning.

'"But is it not the deepest Law of Nature that she be constant?" cries an illuminated class: "Is not the Machine of the Universe fixed to move by unalterable rules?" Probable enough, good friends: nay I, too, must believe that the God, whom ancient inspired men assert to be "without variableness or shadow of turning,"[2] does indeed never change; that Nature, that the Universe, which no one whom it so pleases can be prevented from calling a Machine, does move by the most unalterable rules. And now of you, too, I make the old inquiry: What those same unalterable rules, forming the complete Statute-Book of Nature, may possibly be?

'They stand written in our Works of Science, say you; in the accumulated records of Man's Experience?—Was Man with his Experience present at the Creation, then, to see how it all went on? Have any deepest scientific individuals yet dived down to the foundations of the Universe, and gauged everything there? Did the Maker take them into His counsel; that they read His groundplan of the incomprehensible All; and can say, This stands marked therein, and no more

---

[1] *Cf.* II Kings, vi, 6.

[2] James, i, 17.

than this? Alas, not in anywise! These scientific individuals have been nowhere but where we also are; have seen some handbreadths deeper than we see into the Deep that is infinite, without bottom as without shore.[1]

'Laplace's Book on the Stars,[2] wherein he exhibits that certain Planets, with their Satellites, gyrate round our worthy Sun, at a rate and in a course, which, by greatest good fortune, he and the like of him have succeeded in detecting, —is to me as precious as to another. But is this what thou namest "Mechanism of the Heavens," and "System of the World"; this, wherein Sirius and the Pleiades, and all Herschel's[3] Fifteen-thousand Suns per minute,[4] being left out, some paltry handful of Moons, and inert Balls, had been—looked at, nicknamed, and marked in the Zodiacal Way-bill; so that we can now prate of their Whereabout; their How, their Why, their What, being hid from us, as in the signless Inane?

'System of Nature! To the wisest man, wide as is his vision, Nature remains of quite *infinite* depth, of quite infinite expansion; and all Experience thereof limits itself to some few computed centuries and measured square-miles. The course of Nature's phases, on this our little fraction of a Planet, is

---

[1]See the argument at the end of Job, xxxviii.—Carlyle's whole argument in the opening paragraphs of the present chapter is, to some extent, a reply to Locke and Hume on the subject of miracles; both philosophers had denied their possibility, and explained reports of them on the basis of human error and credulity. Carlyle lost his belief in Biblical and ecclesiastical miracles immediately on reading Gibbon. But he still held that human experience is so limited that what appears to be impossible may actually occur as the manifestation of laws partially or totally unknown. The answer today would be that no *miracle* can therefore occur, only a phenomenon the law of which we have yet to discover. Carlyle's natural supernaturalism makes *everything* a miracle (since the mind cannot comprehend ultimates), in which case the word ceases to have its old significance.

[2]See p. 4, *note* 1.

[3]Herschel, Sir William (1738–1822), an English astronomer, born in Hanover, became court astronomer in 1782; discovered more than two thousand nebulae, over eight hundred double-stars, *etc.*

[4]The astronomical minute, the 60th part of a degree.

partially known to us: but who knows what deeper courses these depend on; what infinitely larger Cycle (of causes) our little Epicycle[1] revolves on? To the Minnow every cranny and pebble, and quality and accident, of its little native Creek may have become familiar: but does the Minnow understand the Ocean Tides and periodic Currents, the Tradewinds, and Monsoons,[2] and Moon's Eclipses; by all which the condition of its little Creek is regulated, and may, from time to time (*un*miraculously enough), be quite overset and reversed? Such a minnow is Man; his Creek this Planet Earth; his Ocean the immeasurable All; his Monsoons and periodic Currents the mysterious Course of Providence through Æons of Æons.

'We speak of the Volume of Nature: and truly a Volume it is,—whose Author and Writer is God.[3] To read it! Dost thou, does man, so much as well know the Alphabet thereof? With its Words, Sentences, and grand descriptive Pages, poetical and philosophical, spread out through Solar Systems, and Thousands of Years, we shall not try thee. It is a Volume written in celestial hieroglyphs,[4] in the true Sacred-writing; of which even Prophets are happy that they can read here a line and there a line.[5] As for your Institutes, and Academies of Science, they strive bravely; and, from amid the thick-crowded, inextricably intertwisted hieroglyphic writing, pick out, by dextrous combination, some Letters in the vulgar Character, and therefrom put together this and the other economic Recipe, of high avail in Practice. That Nature is more than some boundless Volume of such Recipes, or huge, well-nigh inexhaustible Domestic-Cookery Book, of which the whole secret will in this manner one day evolve itself, the fewest dream.

---

[1]In Ptolemaic astronomy, a circle which moves on or around another circle.

[2]Periodic winds in the Indian Ocean.

[3]*Cf.* Hebrews, xi, 10.

[4]See p. 36, *note* 3.

[5]Adapted from Isaiah, xxviii, 10.

'Custom,' continues the Professor, 'doth make dotards of us all.[1] Consider well, thou wilt find that Custom is the greatest of Weavers; and weaves air-raiment for all the Spirits of the Universe; whereby indeed these dwell with us visibly, as ministering servants, in our houses and workshops; but their spiritual nature becomes, to the most, forever hidden. Philosophy complains that Custom has hoodwinked us, from the first; that we do everything by Custom, even Believe by it; that our very Axioms, let us boast of Free-thinking as we may, are oftenest simply such Beliefs as we have never heard questioned. Nay, what is Philosophy throughout but a continual battle against Custom; an ever-renewed effort to *transcend* the sphere of blind Custom, and so become Transcendental?

'Innumerable are the illusions and legerdemain-tricks of Custom: but of all these, perhaps the cleverest is her knack of persuading us that the Miraculous, by simple repetition, ceases to be Miraculous. True, it is by this means we live; for man must work as well as wonder: and herein is Custom so far a kind nurse, guiding him to his true benefit. But she is a fond foolish nurse, or rather we are false foolish nurselings, when, in our resting and reflecting hours, we prolong the same deception. Am I to view the Stupendous with stupid indifference, because I have seen it twice, or two-hundred, or two-million times? There is no reason in Nature or in Art why I should: unless, indeed, I am a mere Work-Machine, for whom the divine gift of Thought were no other than the terrestrial gift of Steam is to the Steam-engine; a power whereby cotton might be spun, and money and money's worth realised.

'Notable enough too, here as elsewhere, wilt thou find the

---

[1]*Cf. Hamlet,* III, i, 83: "Thus conscience does make cowards of us all."—Carlyle's whole discussion of Custom in these paragraphs may be indirectly indebted to Hume, for whom custom was the "ultimate principle" of all beliefs, reasoning, and judgement. (B.) Custom as the enemy of wonder and religion places Carlyle among his contemporaries, for whom wonder and the fresh gaze of the child were among the chief marks of the romantic point of view.

potency of Names;[1] which indeed are but one kind of such custom-woven, wonder-hiding Garments. Witchcraft, and all manner of Spectre-work, and Demonology,[2] we have now named Madness and Diseases of the Nerves. Seldom reflecting that still the new question comes upon us: What is Madness, what are Nerves? Ever, as before, does Madness remain a mysterious-terrific, altogether *infernal* boiling-up of the Nether Chaotic Deep, through this fair-painted Vision of Creation, which swims thereon, which we name the Real. Was Luther's Picture of the Devil less a Reality, whether it were formed within the bodily eye, or without it?[3] In every the wisest Soul lies a whole world of internal Madness, an authentic Demon-Empire; out of which, indeed, his world of Wisdom has been creatively built together, and now rests there, as on its dark foundations does a habitable flowery Earth-rind.

'But deepest of all illusory Appearances, for hiding Wonder, as for many other ends, are your two grand fundamental world-enveloping Appearances, SPACE and TIME.[4] These, as spun and woven for us from before Birth itself, to clothe our celestial ME for dwelling here, and yet to blind it,—lie all-embracing, as the universal canvas, or warp and woof, whereby all minor Illusions, in this Phantasm Existence, weave and paint themselves. In vain, while here on Earth, shall you endeavour to strip them off; you can, at best, but rend them asunder for moments, and look through.

'Fortunatus had a wishing Hat, which when he put on, and wished himself Anywhere, behold he was There.[5] By this means had Fortunatus triumphed over Space, he had an-

[1]See p. 87, *note* 3.

[2]Barrett notes that Scott's *Demonology and Witchcraft* (1830) was reviewed by Carlyle's brother, Dr. John Carlyle, in *Fraser's Magazine*, December, 1830, pp. 507–19.

[3]Luther threw his inkstand at the Devil, who appeared to him while he was translating the Psalms. *Cf. Heroes and Hero-Worship,* Lecture iv.

[4]See Carlyle's essay on Novalis (*Ess.,* II, 26 ff.); also Int., Sect. V, b.

[5]See p. 153, *note* 3.

nihilated Space; for him there was no Where, but all was Here. Were a Hatter to establish himself, in the Wahngasse of Weissnichtwo, and make felts of this sort for all mankind, what a world we should have of it! Still stranger, should, on the opposite side of the street, another Hatter establish himself; and, as his fellow-craftsman made Space-annihilating Hats, make Time-annihilating! Of both would I purchase, were it with my last groschen;[1] but chiefly of this latter. To clap-on your felt, and, simply by wishing that you were Any*where,* straightway to be *There!* Next to clap-on your other felt, and, simply by wishing that you were Any*when,* straightway to be *Then!* This were indeed the grander: shooting at will from the Fire-Creation of the World to its Fire-Consummation;[2] here historically present in the First Century, conversing face to face with Paul[3] and Seneca;[4] there prophetically in the Thirty-first, conversing also face to face with other Pauls and Senecas, who as yet stand hidden in the depth of that late Time!

'Or thinkest thou it were impossible, unimaginable? Is the Past annihilated, then, or only past; is the Future non-extant, or only future? Those mystic faculties of thine, Memory and Hope, already answer: already through those mystic avenues, thou the Earth-blinded summonest both Past and Future, and communest with them, though as yet darkly, and with mute beckonings. The curtains of Yesterday drop down, the curtains of Tomorrow roll up; but Yesterday and Tomorrow both *are.* Pierce through the Time-element, glance into the Eternal. Believe what thou findest written in the sanctuaries of Man's Soul, even as all Thinkers, in all ages, have devoutly read it there: that Time and Space are not God, but creations

---

[1]A German coin, worth about two cents.

[2]Possible allusion to the doctrine of Heraclitus, Greek philosopher of the fifth century, B.C., who held that "all things are exchanged for fire, and fire for all things," fire being the *essence* of all things, alternately creating and destroying.

[3]St. Paul died about A.D. 62.

[4]Lucius Annaeus Seneca (*c.* 4 B.C.–A.D. 65), Roman Stoic philosopher and dramatist. His meeting or corresponding with St. Paul is legendary.

of God; that with God as it is a universal HERE, so is it an everlasting Now.

'And seest thou therein any glimpse of IMMORTALITY?—O Heaven! Is the white Tomb of our Loved One, who died from our arms, and had to be left behind us there, which rises in the distance, like a pale, mournfully receding Milestone, to tell how many toilsome uncheered miles we have journeyed on alone,—but a pale spectral Illusion! Is the lost Friend still mysteriously Here, even as we are Here mysteriously, with God!—Know of a truth that only the Time-shadows have perished, or are perishable; that the real Being of whatever was, and whatever is, and whatever will be, *is* even now and forever. This, should it unhappily seem new, thou mayest ponder at thy leisure; for the next twenty years, or the next twenty centuries: believe it thou must; understand it thou canst not.

'That the Thought-forms, Space and Time, wherein, once for all, we are sent into this Earth to live, should condition and determine our whole Practical reasonings, conceptions, and imagings or imaginings, seems altogether fit, just, and unavoidable. But that they should, furthermore, usurp such sway over pure spiritual Meditation, and blind us to the wonder everywhere lying close on us, seems nowise so. Admit Space and Time to their due rank as Forms of Thought; nay even, if thou wilt, to their quite undue rank of Realities: and consider, then, with thyself how their thin disguises hide from us the brightest God-effulgences! Thus, were it not miraculous, could I stretch forth my hand and clutch the Sun? Yet thou seest me daily stretch forth my hand and therewith clutch many a thing, and swing it hither and thither. Art thou a grown baby, then, to fancy that the Miracle lies in miles of distance, or in pounds avoirdupois of weight; and not to see that the true inexplicable God-revealing Miracle lies in this, that I can stretch forth my hand at all; that I have free Force to clutch aught therewith? Innumerable other of this sort are the deceptions, and wonder-hiding stupefactions, which Space practices on us.

'Still worse is it with regard to Time. Your grand anti-magician, and universal wonder-hider, is this same lying Time. Had we but the Time-annihilating Hat, to put on for once only, we should see ourselves in a World of Miracles, wherein all fabled or authentic Thaumaturgy, and feats of Magic, were outdone. But unhappily we have not such a Hat; and man, poor fool that he is, can seldom and scantily help himself without one.

'Were it not wonderful, for instance, had Orpheus,[1] or Amphion,[2] built the walls of Thebes by the mere sound of his Lyre? Yet tell me, Who built these walls of Weissnichtwo; summoning out all the sandstone rocks, to dance along from the *Steinbruch*[3] (now a huge Troglodyte[4] Chasm, with frightful green-mantled pools);[5] and shape themselves into Doric and Ionic pillars, squared ashlar houses and noble streets? Was it not the still higher Orpheus, or Orpheuses, who, in past centuries, by the divine Music of Wisdom, succeeded in civilising Man? Our highest Orpheus walked in Judea, eighteen-hundred years ago: his sphere-melody,[6] flowing in wild native tones, took captive the ravished souls of men; and, being of a true sphere-melody, still flows and sounds, though now with thousandfold accompaniments, and rich symphonies, through all our hearts; and modulates, and divinely leads them. Is that a wonder, which happens in two hours; and does it cease to be wonderful if happening in two million? Not only was Thebes built by the music of an Orpheus; but without the music of some inspired Orpheus was no city ever built, no work that man glories in ever done.

---

[1]Son of Apollo, regarded by the Greeks as the most celebrated of the poets before the time of Homer; his lyre tamed wild beasts.

[2]Son of Jupiter; whose sacred lyre caused the stones to build themselves into the walls of Thebes. *Cf.* Horace, *Ars Poet.,* 391–96.

[3]German for *quarry*.

[4]Prehistoric cave-dweller.

[5]*Cf. King Lear,* III, iv, 137.

[6]Perhaps an allusion to the Pythagorean doctrine that the planets by rotating produced the "music of the spheres."

'Sweep away the Illusion of Time; glance, if thou have eyes, from the near moving-cause to its far-distant Mover: The stroke that came transmitted through a whole galaxy of elastic balls, was it less a stroke than if the last ball only had been struck, and sent flying? O, could I (with the Time-annihilating Hat) transport thee direct from the Beginnings to the Endings, how were thy eyesight unsealed, and thy heart set flaming in the Light-sea of celestial wonder! Then sawest thou that this fair Universe, were it in the meanest province thereof, is in very deed the star-domed City of God;[1] that through every star, through every grass-blade, and most through every Living Soul, the glory of a present God still beams. But Nature, which is the Time-vesture of God, and reveals Him to the wise, hides Him from the foolish.

'Again, could anything be more miraculous than an actual authentic Ghost? The English Johnson longed, all his life, to see one; but could not, though he went to Cock Lane, and thence to the church-vaults, and tapped on coffins.[2] Foolish Doctor! Did he never, with the mind's eye as well as with the body's, look round him into that full tide of human Life he so loved; did he never so much as look into Himself? The good Doctor was a Ghost, as actual and authentic as heart could wish; well-nigh a million of Ghosts were travelling the streets by his side. Once more I say, sweep away the illusion of Time; compress the threescore years into three minutes: what else was he, what else are we? Are we not Spirits, that are shaped into a body, into an Appearance; and that fade away again into air and Invisibility? This is no metaphor, it is a simple scientific *fact;* we start out of Nothingness, take figure, and are Apparitions; round us, as round the veriest spectre, is Eternity; and to Eternity min-

---

[1]The title of St. Augustine's famous work, *De Civitate Dei*. *Cf.* also Richter's *Flower, Fruit, etc.*, p. 255: "The broad heaven, with the streets of the City of God all lit with the lamps which are suns," *etc.* (B.) "Star-domed" is *star-doomed,* by misprint, in the Centenary Edition.

[2]See Boswell, year 1763 (Oxf. Stand. Ed., pp. 271–73.) The ghost proved to be a girl.

utes are as years and æons. Come there not tones of Love and Faith, as from celestial harp-strings, like the Song of beatified Souls? And again, do not we squeak and jibber[1] (in our discordant, screech-owlish[2] debatings and recriminatings); and glide bodeful, and feeble, and fearful; or uproar (*poltern*), and revel in our mad Dance of the Dead,[3]—till the scent of the morning air[4] summons us to our still Home; and dreamy Night becomes awake and Day? Where now is Alexander of Macedon:[5] does the steel Host, that yelled in fierce battle-shouts at Issus and Arbela,[6] remain behind him; or have they all vanished utterly, even as perturbed Goblins must? Napoleon too, and his Moscow Retreats and Austerlitz Campaigns![7] Was it all other than the veriest Spectre-hunt; which has now, with its howling tumult that made Night hideous,[8] flitted away?—Ghosts! There are nigh a thousand-million walking the Earth openly at noon-tide; some half-hundred have vanished from it, some half-hundred have arisen in it, ere thy watch ticks once.

'O Heaven, it is mysterious, it is awful to consider that we not only carry each a future Ghost within Him; but are, in very deed, Ghosts! These Limbs, whence had we them; this stormy Force; this life-blood with its burning Passion? They are dust and shadow;[9] a Shadow-system gathered round our

---

[1]*Cf. Hamlet,* I, i, 116. Shakespeare has "gibber."

[2]*Cf. III Henry VI,* II, vi, 56–59. (B.)

[3]Evidently an allusion to Holbein's frescoes at Basle, depicting the popular medieval allegory of Death dancing with, or leading, the living to the grave. A common expression in Jean Paul.

[4]*Cf. Hamlet,* I, i, 58.

[5]*Cf.* the *Ubi sunt?* motif in medieval and modern literature, discussed by Frederick Tupper and Clark S. Northup in *Modern Language Notes,* April, June, 1913, xxviii, 106–07, 197–98. (N.)

[6]Towns in ancient Cilicia and Assyria, respectively, where Alexander defeated Darius Codomannus in 333 and 331 B.C., leading to the overthrow of the Persian empire.

[7]See p. 54, *note* 3 and p. 208, note 4.

[8]*Cf. Hamlet,* I, iv, 54.

[9]*Pulvis et umbra.* Horace, *Odes,* IV, vii, 16.

ME; wherein, through some moments or years, the Divine Essence is to be revealed in the Flesh. That warrior on his strong war-horse, fire flashes through his eyes; force dwells in his arm and heart: but warrior and war-horse are a vision; a revealed Force, nothing more. Stately they tread the Earth, as if it were a firm substance: fool! the Earth is but a film; it cracks in twain, and warrior and war-horse sink beyond plummet's sounding.[1] Plummet's? Fantasy herself will not follow them. A little while ago, they were not; a little while, and they are not, their very ashes are not.

'So has it been from the beginning, so will it be to the end. Generation after generation takes to itself the Form of a Body; and forth-issuing from Cimmerian Night,[2] on Heaven's mission APPEARS. What Force and Fire is in each he expends: one grinding in the mill of Industry; one hunter-like climbing the giddy Alpine heights of Science; one madly dashed in pieces on the rocks of Strife, in war with his fellow:—and then the Heaven-sent is recalled; his earthly Vesture falls away, and soon even to sense becomes a vanished Shadow. Thus, like some wild-flaming, wild-thundering train of Heaven's Artillery, does this mysterious MANKIND thunder and flame, in long-drawn, quick-succeeding grandeur, through the unknown Deep. Thus, like a God-created, fire-breathing Spirit-host, we emerge from the Inane; haste stormfully across the astonished Earth;[3] then plunge again into the Inane. Earth's mountains are levelled, and her seas filled up, in our passage: can the Earth, which is but dead and a vision, resist Spirits which have reality and are alive? On the hardest adamant some footprint of us is stamped-in; the last Rear of the host will read traces of the earliest Van. But whence?—O Heaven,

---

[1] *Cf. The Tempest,* V, i, 56.

[2] The Cimmerii were a mythical people living in constant mist and darkness at the extreme western limit of the Ocean. *Odyssey,* xi, 14. Carlyle, however, is quoting his translation of a line in Goethe's *Helena* given in his essay on that work (*Ess.,* I, 178).

[3] *Cf.* Schiller, *The Death of Wallenstein,* III, xv, 1928–30 (Carlyle's *Life of Schiller,* p. 129: "We storm'd across the war-convulsed Earth.")

whither? Sense knows not; Faith knows not; only that it is through Mystery to Mystery, from God and to God.[1]

> We *are such stuff*
> As dreams are made of, and our little Life
> Is rounded with a sleep!'[2]

CHAPTER IX

CIRCUMSPECTIVE

Recapitulation. Editor congratulates the few British readers who have accompanied Teufelsdröckh through all his speculations. The true use of the *Sartor Resartus,* to exhibit the Wonder of daily life and common things; and to show that all Forms are but Clothes, and temporary. Practical inferences enough will follow.

HERE, then, arises the so momentous question: Have many British Readers actually arrived with us at the new promised country; is the Philosophy of Clothes now at last opening around them? Long and adventurous has the journey been: from those outmost vulgar, palpable Woollen Hulls of Man; through his wondrous Flesh-Garment, and his wondrous Social Garnitures; inwards to the Garments of his very Soul's Soul, to Time and Space themselves! And now does the spiritual, eternal Essence of Man, and of Mankind, bared of such wrappages, begin in any measure to reveal itself? Can many readers discern, as through a glass darkly,[3] in

---

[1]See p. 22, *notes* 3, 4.

[2]*The Tempest,* IV, i, 156–58.—These verses Carlyle first saw, as a child, on a bust of Shakespeare among the wares of an image-seller in the streets of Ecclefechan; they became a kind of motto for him throughout his life. He found them also in his other favourite reading: in the philosopher Dugald Stewart (*Works,* Edinburgh, 1854–58, V, 88), and in Jean Paul (*Wahrheit aus Jean Pauls Leben,* II, quoted in Carlyle, *Ess.,* II, 154).

[3]*Cf.* I Corinthians, xiii, 12.

huge wavering outlines, some primeval rudiments of Man's Being, what is changeable divided from what is unchangeable? Does that Earth-Spirit's speech in *Faust,*[1]—

> Tis thus at the roaring Loom of Time I ply,
> And weave for God the Garment thou see'st Him by;

or that other thousand-times repeated speech of the Magician, Shakespeare,—

> And like the baseless fabric of this vision,
> The cloudcapt Towers, the gorgeous Palaces,
> The solemn Temples, the great Globe itself,
> And all which it inherit, shall dissolve;
> And like this unsubstantial pageant faded,
> Leave not a wrack behind;[2]

begin to have some meaning for us? In a word, do we at length stand safe in the far region of Poetic Creation and Palingenesia,[3] where that Phœnix Death-Birth of Human Society, and of all Human Things, appears possible, is seen to be inevitable?

Along this most insufficient, unheard-of Bridge,[4] which the Editor, by Heaven's blessing, has now seen himself enabled to conclude if not complete, it cannot be his sober calculation, but only his fond hope, that many have travelled without accident. No firm arch, over-spanning the Impassable with paved highway, could the Editor construct; only, as was said, some zigzag series of rafts floating tumultuously thereon. Alas, and the leaps from raft to raft, were too often of a breakneck character; the darkness, the nature of the element, all was against us!

Nevertheless, may not here and there one of a thousand, provided with a discursiveness of intellect rare in our day, have cleared the passage, in spite of all? Happy few! little

---

[1]See p. 55, *note* 4.

[2]*The Tempest,* IV, i, 151–56.

[3]See p. 217, *note* 1.

[4]See p. 79, *note* 4.

band of Friends! be welcome, be of courage. By degrees, the eye grows accustomed to its new Whereabout; the hand can stretch itself forth to work there: it is in this grand and indeed highest work of Palingenesia that ye shall labour, each according to ability. New labourers will arrive; new Bridges will be built; nay, may not our own poor rope-and-raft Bridge, in your passings and repassings, be mended in many a point, till it grows quite firm, passable even for the halt?

Meanwhile, of the innumerable multitude that started with us, joyous and full of hope, where now is the innumerable remainder, whom we see no longer by our side? The most have recoiled, and stand gazing afar off, in unsympathetic astonishment, at our career: not a few, pressing forward with more courage, have missed footing, or leaped short; and now swim weltering in the Chaos-flood, some towards this shore, some towards that. To these also a helping hand should be held out; at least some word of encouragement be said.

Or, to speak without metaphor, with which mode of utterance Teufelsdröckh unhappily has somewhat infected us,—can it be hidden from the Editor that many a British reader sits reading quite bewildered in head, and afflicted rather than instructed by the present Work? Yes, long ago has many a British Reader been, as now, demanding with something like a snarl: Whereto does all this lead; or what use is in it?

In the way of replenishing thy purse, or otherwise aiding thy digestive faculty, O British Reader, it leads to nothing, and there is no use in it; but rather the reverse, for it costs thee somewhat. Nevertheless, if through this unpromising Horn-gate,[1] Teufelsdröckh, and we by means of him, have led thee into the true Land of Dreams; and through the Clothes-Screen, as through a magical *Pierre-Pertuis,*[2] thou lookest, even for moments, into the region of the Wonderful, and seest and feelest that thy daily life is girt with Wonder, and based on

---

[1]In the *Aeneid,* vi, 893 ff., the gate of Sleep, from which issue true dreams, as distinct from the "Ivory-gate," from which come false dreams.

[2]A remarkable natural opening in a great rock in the Bernese Alps, northwest of Bern, Switzerland. (M.)

Wonder, and thy very blankets and breeches are Miracles,—then art thou profited beyond money's worth; and hast a thankfulness towards our Professor; nay, perhaps in many a literary Tea-circle wilt open thy kind lips, and audibly express that same.

Nay further, art not thou too perhaps by this time made aware that all Symbols are properly Clothes; that all Forms whereby Spirit manifests itself to sense, whether outwardly or in the imagination, are Clothes; and thus not only the parchment Magna Charta,[1] which a Tailor was nigh cutting into measures, but the Pomp and Authority of Law, the sacredness of Majesty, and all inferior Worships (Worth-ships) are properly a Vesture and Raiment; and the Thirty-nine Articles themselves[2] are articles of wearing-apparel (for the Religious Idea)? In which case, must it not also be admitted that this Science of Clothes is a high one, and may with infinitely deeper study on thy part yield richer fruit: that it takes scientific rank beside Codification, and Political Economy, and the Theory of the British Constitution; nay rather, from its prophetic height looks down on all these, as on so many weaving-shops and spinning-mills, where the Vestures which *it* has to fashion, and consecrate and distribute, are, too often by haggard hungry operatives who see no farther than their nose, mechanically woven and spun?

But omitting all this, much more all that concerns Natural Supernaturalism, and indeed whatever has reference to the Ulterior or Transcendental portion of the Science, or bears never so remotely on that promised Volume of the *Palingenesie der menschlichen Gesellschaft* (Newbirth of Society),—we humbly suggest that no province of Clothes-Philosophy, even the lowest, is without its direct value, but that innumerable inferences of a practical nature may be drawn therefrom.

---

[1]The Great Charter, so called, which the English Barons forced King John to sign June 15, 1215, at Runnymede. The story is told (in Isaac Disraeli's *Curiosities of Literature* [1791], Sect. 3) how Sir Robert Cotton (1571–1631), the celebrated collector of manuscripts, rescued the document from his tailor.

[2]The statements of the tenets or doctrines of the Church of England.

To say nothing of those pregnant considerations, ethical, political, symbolical, which crowd on the Clothes-Philosopher from the very threshold of his Science; nothing even of those 'architectural ideas,'[1] which, as we have seen, lurk at the bottom of all Modes, and will one day, better unfolding themselves, lead to important revolutions,—let us glance for a moment, and with the faintest light of Clothes-Philosophy, on what may be called the Habilatory Class of our fellow-men. Here too overlooking, where so much were to be looked on, the million spinners, weavers, fullers, dyers, washers, and wringers, that puddle and muddle in their dark recesses, to make us Clothes, and die that we may live,—let us but turn the reader's attention upon two small divisions of mankind, who, like moths, may be regarded as Cloth-animals, creatures that live, move, and have their being in Cloth: we mean, Dandies and Tailors.

In regard to both which small divisions it may be asserted without scruple, that the public feeling, unenlightened by Philosophy, is at fault; and even that the dictates of humanity are violated. As will perhaps abundantly appear to readers of the two following Chapters.

---

[1]See p. 35.

CHAPTER X

THE DANDIACAL BODY

The Dandy defined. The Dandiacal Sect a new modification of the primeval superstition Self-worship: How to be distinguished. Their Sacred Books (Fashionable Novels) unreadable. Dandyism's Articles of Faith.—Brotherhood of Poor-Slaves; vowed to perpetual Poverty; worshippers of Earth; distinguished by peculiar costume and diet. Picture of a Poor-Slave Household; and of a Dandiacal. Teufelsdröckh fears these two Sects may spread, till they part all England between them, and then frightfully collide.

FIRST, touching Dandies, let us consider, with some scientific strictness, what a Dandy specially is. A Dandy is a Clothes-wearing Man, a Man whose trade, office, and existence consists in the wearing of Clothes. Every faculty of his soul, spirit, purse, and person is heroically consecrated to this one object, the wearing of Clothes wisely and well: so that as others dress to live, he lives to dress. The all-importance of Clothes, which a German Professor, of unequalled learning and acumen, writes his enormous Volume to demonstrate, has sprung up in the intellect of the Dandy without effort, like an instinct of genius; he is inspired with Cloth, a Poet of Cloth. What Teufelsdröckh would call a 'Divine Idea of Cloth'[1] is born with him; and this, like other such Ideas, will express itself outwardly, or wring his heart asunder with unutterable throes.

But, like a generous, creative enthusiast, he fearlessly makes his Idea an Action; shows himself in peculiar guise to mankind; walks forth, a witness and living Martyr to the eternal world of Clothes. We called him a Poet: is not his body the (stuffed) parchment-skin whereon he writes, with cunning Huddersfield dyes, a Sonnet to his mistress' eye-brow?[2] Say,

[1]See p. 209, *note* 2.

[2]*Cf. As You Like It*, II, vii, 140.

rather, an Epos, and *Clotha Virumque cano,*[1] to the whole world, in Macaronic verses,[2] which he that runs may read. Nay, if you grant, what seems to be admissible, that the Dandy has a Thinking-principle in him, and some notions of Time and Space, is there not in this Life-devotedness to Cloth, in this so willing sacrifice of the Immortal to the Perishable, something (though in reverse order) of that blending and identification of Eternity with Time, which, as we have seen, constitutes the Prophetic character?

And now, for all this perennial Martyrdom, and Poesy, and even Prophecy, what is it that the Dandy asks in return? Solely, we may say, that you would recognise his existence; would admit him to be a living object; or even failing this, a visual object, or thing that will reflect rays of light. Your silver or your gold (beyond what the niggardly Law has already secured him) he solicits not; simply the glance of your eyes. Understand his mystic significance, or altogether miss and misinterpret it; do but look at him, and he is contented. May we not well cry shame on an ungrateful world, which refuses even this poor boon; which will waste its optic faculty on dried Crocodiles, and Siamese Twins;[3] and over the domestic wonderful wonder of wonders,[4] a live Dandy, glance with hasty indifference, and a scarcely concealed contempt! Him no Zoölogist classes among the Mammalia, no Anatomist dissects with care:[5] when did we see any injected Preparation of the Dandy in our Museums; any specimen of him preserved in spirits? Lord Herringbone[6] may dress himself in a

---

[1]"Clothes and the man I sing." A parody on the opening line of the *Aeneid,* "Arms and the man . . ."

[2]Burlesque verses in which the vernacular words of one language are intermixed with Latin words or used with Latin terminations or constructions. Here a pun on macaroni (dandy). See p. 58, *note* 6.

[3]Chang and Eng (1811–74), born in Siam of Chinese extraction; they were joined at the breast by a thick fleshy ligament. They were exhibited in London in 1829.

[4]*Wonderful wonder: cf.* the title of one of Swift's squibs.

[5]*Cf.* Swift's *Tale of a Tub,* sect. ix; and the *Spectator,* Nos. 275, 281.

[6]A dandy; reference to the herringbone stitch.

snuff-brown suit, with snuff-brown shirt and shoes: it skills not;[1] the undiscerning public, occupied with grosser wants, passes by regardless on the other side.[2]

The age of Curiosity, like that of Chivalry, is indeed, properly speaking, gone.[3] Yet perhaps only gone to sleep: for here arises the Clothes-Philosophy to resuscitate, strangely enough, both the one and the other! Should sound views of this Science come to prevail, the essential nature of the British Dandy, and the mystic significance that lies in him, cannot always remain hidden under laughable and lamentable hallucination. The following long Extract from Professor Teufelsdröckh may set the matter, if not in its true light, yet in the way towards such. It is to be regretted, however, that here, as so often elsewhere, the Professor's keen philosophic perspicacity is somewhat marred by a certain mixture of almost owlish purblindness, or else of some perverse, ineffectual, ironic tendency; our readers shall judge which:

'In these distracted times,' writes he, 'when the Religious Principle, driven out of most Churches, either lies unseen in the hearts of good men, looking and longing and silently working there towards some new Revelation; or else wanders homeless over the world, like a disembodied soul seeking its terrestrial organisation,—into how many strange shapes, of Superstition and Fanaticism, does it not tentatively and errantly cast itself! The higher Enthusiasm of man's nature is for the while without Exponent; yet does it continue indestructible, unweariedly active, and work blindly in the great chaotic deep: thus Sect after Sect, and Church after Church, bodies itself forth, and melts again into new metamorphosis.

'Chiefly is this observable in England, which, as the wealthiest and worst-instructed of European nations, offers

---

[1]*Skills not:* matters not. An Elizabethan phrase.

[2]*Cf.* Luke, x, 32.

[3]Compare: "The age of Chivalry is gone!" (Burke's *Reflections on the French Revolution*).

precisely the elements (of Heat, namely, and of Darkness), in which such moon-calves and monstrosities are best generated. Among the newer Sects of that country, one of the most notable, and closely connected with our present subject, is that of the *Dandies;* concerning which, what little information I have been able to procure may fitly stand here.

'It is true, certain of the English Journalists, men generally without sense for the Religious Principle, or judgment for its manifestations, speak, in their brief enigmatic notices, as if this were perhaps rather a Secular Sect, and not a Religious one; nevertheless, to the psychologic eye its devotional and even sacrificial character plainly enough reveals itself. Whether it belongs to the class of Fetich-worships,[1] or of Hero-worships[2] or Polytheisms, or to what other class, may in the present state of our intelligence remain undecided (*schweben*). A certain touch of Manicheism,[3] not indeed in the Gnostic shape,[4] is discernible enough: also (for human Error walks in a cycle, and reappears at intervals) a not-inconsiderable resemblance to that Superstition of the Athos Monks,[5] who by fasting from all nourishment, and looking intensely for a length of time into their own navels, came to discern therein the true Apocalypse of Nature, and Heaven Unveiled. To my own surmise, it appears as if this Dandiacal Sect were but a new modification, adapted to the new time, of that primeval Superstition,

---

[1]See p. 156, *note* 1.

[2]Carlyle is here evidently thinking of Hume's *Natural History of Religion,* sect. v: "Various Forms of Polytheism: Allegory, Hero-Worship."

[3]The dualistic doctrine of the Manichaeans, of the third century A.D., that man's body is the product of the Kingdom of Darkness, his soul of the Kingdom of Light; eternal conflict exists between the two opposites.

[4]The Gnostics were heretics of the second century who believed in the principle of dualism or conflict between good and evil, and in the inherent evil of the material world as the creation of a rebel against God (the Demiurge). Carlyle evidently means that the dandy, while admitting the dualism of the Manichaeans, rejects the Gnostic belief that matter is evil. A somewhat laboured allusion.

[5]Of the Holy Mountain, on the coast of Macedonia. For the practices to which Carlyle refers, see Gibbon's *Decline and Fall of the Roman Empire,* Ch. lxiii.

Self-worship; which Zerdusht,[1] Quangfoutchee,[2] Mohamed,[3] and others, strove rather to subordinate and restrain than to eradicate, and which only in the purer forms of Religion has been altogether rejected. Wherefore, if any one chooses to name it revived Ahrimanism,[4] or a new figure of Demon-worship, I have, so far as is yet visible, no objection.

'For the rest, these people, animated with the zeal of a new Sect, display courage and perseverance, and what force there is in man's nature, though never so enslaved. They affect great purity and separatism; distinguish themselves by a particular costume (whereof some notices were given in the earlier part of this Volume); likewise, so far as possible, by a particular speech (apparently some broken *Lingua-franca,*[5] or English-French); and, on the whole, strive to maintain a true Nazarene[6] deportment, and keep themselves unspotted from the world.[7]

'They have their Temples, whereof the chief, as the Jewish Temple did, stands in their metropolis; and is named *Almack's,*[8] a word of uncertain etymology. They worship principally by night; and have their Highpriests and Highpriestesses, who, however, do not continue for life. The rites, by some supposed to be of the Menadic sort,[9] or perhaps with

[1]Zoroaster, or Zarathustra, founder of the ancient Persian religion, sixth century B.C.

[2]Usually spelled Confucius. Founder of the Chinese religion, sixth century B.C.

[3]Mohamed (570–632). Founder of the religion of Islam.

[4]In the ancient Parsee, or Persian, religion, the principle of evil or darkness, opposed to that of light or goodness, Ormuzd.

[5]The mixed or hybrid language, fundamentally Italian, used by the Latin races in intercourse with the Greeks and Arabs. Carlyle is punning, ridiculing the sprinkling of French words in English writing of his period.

[6]A citizen of Nazareth. Carlyle really means Nazarite (separated by *vows*). See Numbers, vi, 2–21.

[7]*Cf.* James, i, 27.

[8]An assembly-room in King Street, London, built by William Almack in 1764; famous as the scene of many aristocratic balls in the early nineteenth century.

[9]The Maenads or Bacchantes were frenzied women worshippers of Bacchus, the god of wine.

an Eleusinian or Cabiric[1] character, are held strictly secret. Nor are Sacred Books wanting to the Sect; these they call *Fashionable Novels:* however, the Canon[2] is not completed, and some are canonical and others not.

'Of such Sacred Books I, not without expense, procured myself some samples; and in hope of true insight, and with the zeal which beseems an Inquirer into Clothes, set to interpret and study them. But wholly to no purpose: that tough faculty of reading, for which the world will not refuse me credit, was here for the first time foiled and set at naught. In vain that I summoned my whole energies (*mich weidlich anstrengte*), and did my very utmost; at the end of some short space, I was uniformly seized with not so much what I can call a drumming in my ears, as a kind of infinite, unsufferable, Jew's harping and scrannel-piping[3] there; to which the frightfullest species of Magnetic Sleep[4] soon supervened. And if I strove to shake this away, and absolutely would not yield, there came a hitherto unfelt sensation, as of *Delirium Tremens,* and a melting into total deliquium: till at last, by order of the Doctor, dreading ruin to my whole intellectual and bodily faculties, and a general breaking-up of the constitution, I reluctantly but determinedly forbore. Was there some miracle at work here; like those Fire-balls,[5] and supernal and infernal prodigies, which, in the case of the Jewish Mysteries, have also more than once scared-back the Alien? Be this as it may, such failure on my part, after best efforts, must excuse the imperfection of this sketch; altogether incomplete, yet

---

[1]*Eleusinian or Cabiric:* the Eleusinians carried out secret rites in the annual festival of Ceres (goddess of agriculture), at Eleusis, near Athens. —The Cabiri were mystic divinities, of perhaps Phoenician origin, and of inferior order; they were worshipped in Egypt, Greece, and the Greek islands.

[2]The collection or list of Biblical books received as genuine and inspired.

[3]Scrannel = slight, thin. *Cf. Lycidas,* 124.

[4]Allusion to "animal magnetism," an early term for hypnotism.

[5]The balls of fire which were said to interrupt the attempts of Julian the Apostate to rebuild the Temple of Jerusalem, and thus exasperate the Christians. See Gibbon's *Decline and Fall,* Ch. xxiii.

the completest I could give of a Sect too singular to be omitted.

'Loving my own life and senses as I do, no power shall induce me, as a private individual, to open another *Fashionable Novel.* But luckily, in this dilemma, comes a hand from the clouds; whereby if not victory, deliverance is held out to me. Round one of those Book-packages, which the *Stillschweigen'sche Buchhandlung* is in the habit of importing from England, come, as is usual, various waste printed-sheets (*Maculatur-blätter*), by way of interior wrappage: into these the Clothes-Philosopher, with a certain Mohammedan reverence even for waste-paper,[1] where curious knowledge will sometimes hover, disdains not to cast his eye. Readers may judge of his astonishment when on such a defaced stray-sheet, probably the outcast fraction of some English Periodical, such as they name *Magazine,* appears something like a Dissertation on this very subject of *Fashionable Novels!* It sets out, indeed, chiefly from a Secular point of view; directing itself, not without asperity, against some to me unknown individual named *Pelham,*[2] who seems to be a Mystagogue,[3] and leading Teacher and Preacher of the Sect; so that, what indeed otherwise was not to be expected in such a fugitive fragmentary sheet, the true secret, the Religious physiognomy and physiology of the Dandiacal Body, is nowise laid fully open there. Nevertheless scattered lights do from time to time sparkle out, whereby I have endeavoured to profit. Nay, in one passage selected from the Prophecies, or Mythic Theogonies,[4] or whatever they are (for the style seems very mixed) of this Mystagogue, I find what appears to be a Confession of Faith,[5] or Whole Duty of Man,[6] according to the tenets of that Sect.

---

[1] "As not knowing but it may contain some piece of their Alcoran." *Spectator,* No. 85.

[2] Written by Bulwer, published in 1828.

[3] One who initiates or interprets religious mysteries.

[4] Genealogies of the gods.

[5] *Cf.* "The Westminster Confession of Faith" (1647), for Presbyterianism.

[6] See p. 195, *note* 4.

Which Confession of Whole Duty, therefore, as proceeding from a source so authentic, I shall here arrange under Seven distinct Articles,[1] and in very abridged shape lay before the German world; therewith taking leave of this matter. Observe also, that to avoid possibility of error, I, as far as may be, quote literally from the Original:

'Articles of Faith

'"1. Coats should have nothing of the triangle about them; at the same time, wrinkles behind should be carefully avoided.

'"2. The collar is a very important point: it should be low behind, and slightly rolled.

'"3. No licence of fashion can allow a man of delicate taste to adopt the posterial luxuriance of a Hottentot.

'"4. There is safety in a swallow-tail.

'"5. The good sense of a gentleman is nowhere more finely developed than in his rings.

'"6. It is permitted to mankind, under certain restrictions, to wear white waistcoats.

'"7. The trousers must be exceedingly tight across the hips."

'All which Propositions I, for the present, content myself with modestly but peremptorily and irrevocably denying.

'In strange contrast with this Dandiacal Body stands another British Sect, originally, as I understand, of Ireland, where its chief seat still is; but known also in the main Island, and indeed everywhere rapidly spreading. As this Sect has hitherto emitted no Canonical Books, it remains to me in the same state of obscurity as the Dandiacal, which has published Books that the unassisted human faculties are inadequate to read. The members appear to be designated by a considerable diversity of names, according to their various places of establishment: in England they are generally called the *Drudge* Sect; also, unphilosophically enough, the *White*

[1]Based on actual passages in *Pelham* which were omitted in later editions.

Negroes; and, chiefly in scorn by those of other communions, the *Ragged-Beggar* Sect. In Scotland, again, I find them entitled *Hallanshakers,*[1] or the *Stook of Duds* Sect; any individual communicant is named *Stook of Duds* (that is, Shock of Rags), in allusion, doubtless, to their professional Costume. While in Ireland, which, as mentioned, is their grand parent hive, they go by a perplexing multiplicity of designations, such as *Bogtrotters,*[2] *Redshanks,*[3] *Ribbonmen,*[4] *Cottiers,*[5] *Peep-of-Day Boys,*[6] *Babes of the Wood,*[7] *Rockites,*[8] *Poor-Slaves:* which last, however, seems to be the primary and generic name; whereto, probably enough, the others are only subsidiary species, or slight varieties; or, at most, propagated offsets from the parent stem, whose minute sub-divisions, and shades of difference, it were here loss of time to dwell on. Enough for us to understand, what seems indubitable, that the original Sect is that of the *Poor-Slaves;* whose doctrines, practices, and fundamental characteristics pervade and animate the whole Body, howsoever denominated or outwardly diversified.

'The precise speculative tenets of this Brotherhood: how the Universe, and Man, and Man's Life, picture themselves to the mind of an Irish Poor-Slave; with what feelings and opinions he looks forward on the Future, round on the Present, back on the Past, it were extremely difficult to

---

[1]Scotch for *beggars* who stood shivering at the *hallan,* or partition between the door and fireplace, shaking it for alms. (P.)

[2]Those who lived in the bogs as a refuge; applied derisively to the Irish.

[3]Having red legs; applied to the Scottish Highlanders.

[4]Members of the secret Ribbon Society of Ireland, in the early nineteenth century, hostile to the Protestant Orangemen, named for the green ribbon worn as a badge.

[5]Cottagers whose rents were determined by ruthless bidding, under the old "rack-rent system."

[6]The Irish Protestant insurgents of 1784, so called from their visiting the houses of their enemies at daybreak in search of arms.

[7]Bands of lawless Irishmen in Wicklow. (B.)

[8]Irish insurgents of 1822 who signed the fictitious name, "Captain Rock," to their revolutionary notices.

specify. Something Monastic there appears to be in their Constitution: we find them bound by the two Monastic Vows,[1] of Poverty and Obedience; which Vows, especially the former, it is said, they observe with great strictness; nay, as I have understood it, they are pledged, and be it by any solemn Nazarene[2] ordination or not, irrevocably consecrated thereto, even *before* birth. That the third Monastic Vow, of Chastity, is rigidly enforced among them, I find no ground to conjecture.

'Furthermore, they appear to imitate the Dandiacal Sect in their grand principle of wearing a peculiar Costume. Of which Irish Poor-Slave Costume no description will indeed be found in the present Volume; for this reason, that by the imperfect organ of Language it did not seem describable. Their raiment consists of innumerable skirts, lappets[3] and irregular wings, of all cloths and of all colours; through the labyrinthic intricacies of which their bodies are introduced by some unknown process. It is fastened together by a multiplex combination of buttons, thrums, and skewers; to which frequently is added a girdle of leather, of hempen or even of straw rope, round the loins. To straw rope, indeed, they seem partial, and often wear it by way of sandals. In head-dress they affect a certain freedom: hats with partial brim, without crown, or with only a loose, hinged, or valved crown; in the former case, they sometimes invert the hat, and wear it brim uppermost, like a University-cap,[4] with what view is unknown.

'The name Poor-Slaves seems to indicate a Slavonic,[5] Polish, or Russian origin: not so, however, the interior essence and spirit of their Superstition, which rather displays a

---

[1]A similar passage occurs in "Quintus Fixlein" (*German Romance,* II, 260–61). (B.)

[2]See p. 276, *note* 6.

[3]See p. 25, *note* 1.

[4]Mortar-board or flat-cap.

[5]From "slav," prisoner of war, we have apparently derived our word *slave;* hence Carlyle's use of "Poor-Sla[illegible]

Teutonic or Druidical character.[1] One might fancy them worshippers of Hertha,[2] or the Earth: for they dig and affectionately work continually in her bosom; or else, shut-up in private Oratories,[3] meditate and manipulate the substances derived from her; seldom looking-up towards the Heavenly Luminaries, and then with comparative indifference. Like the Druids, on the other hand, they live in dark dwellings; often even breaking their glass-windows, where they find such, and stuffing them up with pieces of raiment, or other opaque substances, till the fit obscurity is restored. Again, like all followers of Nature-Worship, they are liable to outbreakings of an enthusiasm rising to ferocity; and burn men, if not in wicker idols,[4] yet in sod cottages.

'In respect of diet, they have also their observances. All Poor-Slaves are Rhizophagous (or Root-eaters);[5] a few are Ichthyophagous, and use Salted Herrings: other animal food they abstain from; except indeed, with perhaps some strange inverted fragment of a Brahminical feeling,[6] such animals as die a natural death. Their universal sustenance is the root named Potato, cooked by fire alone; and generally without condiment or relish of any kind, save an unknown condiment named *Point,* into the meaning of which I have vainly inquired; the victual *Potatoes-and-Point*[7] not appearing, at least not with specific accuracy of description, in any European Cookery-Book whatever. For drink, they use, with an almost epigrammatic counterpoise of taste, Milk, which is

---

[1]The Druids were priests of the ancient Celtic religion.

[2]Or Nerthus, the Earth-goddess of Teutonic mythology. See Tacitus, *Germania,* xl.

[3]Factories and workshops.

[4]Caesar (*Gallic War,* vi, 16) tells of the Druids burning men alive in huge wicker idols.

[5]The Rhizophagi (*root-eaters*) were an Ethiopian tribe mentioned in Diodorus Siculus, who also tells of an Indian tribe of Ichthyophagi (*fish-eaters*). (B.)

[6]The Brahmins oppose all killing of animals.

[7]The Irish joke of looking at his potatoes and then merely pointing at an empty salt-cellar or at a flitch of bacon carefully saved for the future.

the mildest of liquors, and *Potheen,*[1] which is the fiercest. This latter I have tasted, as well as the English *Blue-ruin,* and the Scotch *Whisky,* analogous fluids used by the Sect in those countries: it evidently contains some form of alcohol, in the highest state of concentration, though disguised with acrid oils; and is, on the whole, the most pungent substance known to me,—indeed, a perfect liquid fire. In all their Religious Solemnities, Potheen is said to be an indispensable requisite, and largely consumed.

'An Irish Traveller, of perhaps common veracity, who presents himself under the to me unmeaning title of *The late John Bernard,*[2] offers the following sketch of a domestic establishment, the inmates whereof, though such is not stated expressly, appear to have been of that Faith. Thereby shall my German readers now behold an Irish Poor-Slave, as it were with their own eyes; and even see him at meat. Moreover, in the so precious waste-paper sheet above mentioned, I have found some corresponding picture of a Dandiacal Household, painted by that same Dandiacal Mystagogue, or Theogonist: this also, by way of counterpart and contrast, the world shall look into.

'First, therefore, of the Poor-Slave, who appears likewise to have been a species of Innkeeper. I quote from the original:

'Poor-Slave Household

' "The furniture of this Caravansera[3] consisted of a large iron Pot, two oaken Tables, two Benches, two Chairs, and a Potheen Noggin.[4] There was a Loft above (attainable by a ladder), upon which the inmates slept; and the space below was divided by a hurdle into two Apartments; the one for

[1]Illicit whiskey privately distilled by the Irish peasantry.

[2]John Bernard (1756–1828) was an English actor and writer whose *Retrospections of the Stage* appeared in 1830 in two volumes. The extract is from I, xi, 349–50.

[3]*Caravansera* (Persian): an inn.

[4]A small mug or cup.

their cow and pig, the other for themselves and guests. On entering the house we discovered the family, eleven in number, at dinner: the father sitting at the top, the mother at the bottom, the children on each side, of a large oaken Board, which was scooped-out in the middle, like a trough, to receive the contents of their Pot of Potatoes. Little holes were cut at equal distances to contain Salt; and a bowl of Milk stood on the table: all the luxuries of meat and beer, bread, knives and dishes were dispensed with." The Poor-Slave himself our Traveller found, as he says, broad-backed, black-browed, of great personal strength, and mouth from ear to ear. His Wife was a sun-browned but well-featured woman; and his young ones, bare and chubby, had the appetite of ravens.[1] Of their Philosophical or Religious tenets or observances, no notice or hint.

'But now, secondly, of the Dandiacal Household; in which, truly, that often-mentioned Mystagogue and inspired Penman himself has his abode:

'Dandiacal Household[2]

' "A Dressing-room splendidly furnished; violet-coloured curtains, chairs and ottomans of the same hue. Two full-length Mirrors are placed, one on each side of a table, which supports the luxuries of the Toilet. Several Bottles of Perfumes, arranged in a peculiar fashion, stand upon a smaller table of mother-of-pearl: opposite to these are placed the appurtenances of Lavation richly wrought in frosted silver. A Wardrobe of Buhl[3] is on the left; the doors of which, being partly open, discover a profusion of Clothes; Shoes of a singularly small size monopolise the lower shelves. Fronting the wardrobe a door ajar gives some slight glimpse of a Bath-

[1] *Cf.* Job, xxxviii, 41; Psalms, cxlvii, 9.

[2] This passage is taken almost *verbatim* from Bulwer's Introduction to *The Disowned* (1828), omitted in later editions.

[3] Cabinetwork inlaid with tortoise shell, yellow metal, white metal, *etc.*

room. Folding-doors in the background.—Enter the Author," our Theogonist in person, "obsequiously preceded by a French Valet, in white silk Jacket and cambric Apron."

'Such are the two Sects which, at this moment, divide the more unsettled portion of the British People; and agitate that ever-vexed country. To the eye of the political Seer, their mutual relation, pregnant with the elements of discord and hostility, is far from consoling. These two principles of Dandiacal Self-worship or Demon-worship, and Poor-Slavish or Drudgical Earth-worship, or whatever that same Drudgism may be, do as yet indeed manifest themselves under distant and nowise considerable shapes: nevertheless, in their roots and subterranean ramifications, they extend through the entire structure of Society, and work unweariedly in the secret depths of English national Existence; striving to separate and isolate it into two contradictory, uncommunicating masses.

'In numbers, and even individual strength, the Poor-Slaves or Drudges, it would seem, are hourly increasing. The Dandiacal, again, is by nature no proselytising Sect; but it boasts of great hereditary resources, and is strong by union; whereas the Drudges, split into parties, have as yet no rallying-point; or at best only coöperate by means of partial secret affiliations. If, indeed, there were to arise a *Communion of Drudges,* as there is already a Communion of Saints,[1] what strangest effects would follow therefrom! Dandyism as yet affects to look-down on Drudgism: but perhaps the hour of trial, when it will be practically seen which ought to look down, and which up, is not so distant.

'To me it seems probable that the two Sects will one day part England between them; each recruiting itself from the intermediate ranks, till there be none left to enlist on either side. Those Dandiacal Manicheans, with the host of Dandyising Christians, will form one body: the Drudges, gathering round them whosoever is Drudgical, be he Christian or Infidel

[1]See p. 247, *note* 2.

Pagan; sweeping-up likewise all manner of Utilitarians, Radicals, refractory Potwallopers,[1] and so forth, into their general mass, will form another. I could liken Dandyism and Drudgism to two bottomless boiling Whirlpools that had broken-out on opposite quarters of the firm land: as yet they appear only disquieted, foolishly bubbling wells, which man's art might cover-in; yet mark them, their diameter is daily widening: they are hollow Cones that boil-up from the infinite Deep, over which your firm land is but a thin crust or rind! Thus daily is the intermediate land crumbling-in, daily the empire of the two Buchan-Bullers[2] extending; till now there is but a foot-plank, a mere film of Land between them; this too is washed away: and then—we have the true Hell of Waters, and Noah's Deluge is outdeluged!

'Or better, I might call them two boundless, and indeed unexampled Electric Machines[3] (turned by the "Machinery of Society"), with batteries of opposite quality; Drudgism the Negative, Dandyism the Positive: one attracts hourly towards it and appropriates all the Positive Electricity of the nation (namely, the Money thereof); the other is equally busy with the Negative (that is to say the Hunger), which is equally potent. Hitherto you see only partial transient sparkles and sputters: but wait a little, till the entire nation is in an electric state; till your whole vital Electricity, no longer healthfully Neutral, is cut into two isolated portions of Positive and Negative (of Money and of Hunger); and stands there bottled-up in two World-Batteries! The stirring of a child's finger brings the two together; and then—What then? The Earth is but shivered into impalpable smoke by that Doom's-thunderpeal; the Sun misses one of his Planets in

[1]In certain boroughs of England, before the Reform Bill of 1832, voters secured their qualification for suffrage as householders by merely boiling (walloping, *dial.* for boiling) their own pot, *i.e.*, establishing their own household.

[2]A caldron-like place in the rocks on the coast of Buchan, Scotland, in which the water forms a violent "boiling" whirlpool.

[3]This passage is expanded from a shorter one in "Characteristics" (*Ess.*, III, 20), on wealth and poverty as "positive and negative poles."

Space, and thenceforth there are no eclipses of the Moon.—Or better still, I might liken——'

O, enough, enough of likenings and similitudes; in excess of which, truly, it is hard to say whether Teufelsdröckh or ourselves sin the more.

We have often blamed him for a habit of wire-drawing and over-refining; from of old we have been familiar with his tendency to Mysticism[1] and Religiosity, whereby in everything he was still scenting-out Religion: but never perhaps did these amaurosis-suffusions[2] so cloud and distort his otherwise most piercing vision, as in this of the *Dandiacal Body!* Or was there something of intended satire; is the Professor and Seer not quite the blinkard he affects to be? Of an ordinary mortal we should have decisively answered in the affirmative; but with a Teufelsdröckh there ever hovers some shade of doubt. In the meanwhile, if satire were actually intended, the case is little better. There are not wanting men who will answer: Does your Professor take us for simpletons? His irony has overshot itself; we see through it, and perhaps through him.

CHAPTER XI

TAILORS

Injustice done to Tailors, actual and metaphorical. Their rights and great services will one day be duly recognized.

THUS, however, has our first Practical Inference from the Clothes-Philosophy, that which respects Dandies, been sufficiently drawn; and we come now to the second, concerning Tailors. On this latter our opinion happily quite coincides with that of Teufelsdröckh himself, as expressed in the concluding page of his Volume, to whom, therefore, we willingly

---

[1]See p. 66, *note* 4.

[2]A form of blindness, from a disease of the optic nerve.

give place. Let him speak his own last words, in his own way:

'Upwards of a century,' says he, 'must elapse, and still the bleeding fight of Freedom be fought, whoso is noblest perishing in the van, and thrones be hurled on altars like Pelion on Ossa,[1] and the Moloch[2] of Iniquity have his victims, and the Michael[3] of Justice his martyrs, before Tailors can be admitted to their true prerogatives of manhood, and this last wound of suffering Humanity be closed.

'If aught in the history of the world's blindness could surprise us, here might we indeed pause and wonder. An idea has gone abroad, and fixed itself down into a wide-spreading rooted error, that Tailors are a distinct species in Physiology, not Men, but fractional Parts of a Man.[4] Call any one a *Schneider* (Cutter, Tailor), is it not, in our dislocated, hoodwinked, and indeed delirious condition of Society, equivalent to defying his perpetual fellest enmity? The epithet *schneidermässig* (tailor-like) betokens an otherwise unapproachable degree of pusillanimity: we introduce a *Tailor's-Melancholy,*[5] more opprobrious than any Leprosy, into our Books of Medicine; and fable I know not what of his generating it by living on Cabbage. Why should I speak of Hans Sachs (himself a Shoemaker, or kind of Leather-Tailor), with his *Schneider mit dem Panier?*[6] Why of Shakspeare, in his

---

[1]Mountains in ancient Thessaly. The giants tried to reach heaven by piling Pelion on Ossa. *Cf. Odyssey,* xi, 305 ff.

[2]Hebrew: Mölek, King. The idol (fire-god) of the Ammonites. *Cf.* Leviticus, xx, 1–5; I Kings, xi, 7; II Kings, xvii, 31; *Paradise Lost,* i, 392–405; ii, 43–105.

[3]The archangel. *Cf.* Daniel, xii, 1; Revelation, xii, 7; *Paradise Lost,* vi, 44. Michael led the angelic hosts against Lucifer.

[4]Alluding to the proverb: "Nine tailors make a man."

[5]See Charles Lamb's essay, *On the Melancholy of Tailors,* which quotes Burton's *Anatomy of Melancholy* as declaring that cabbage "sends up black vapours to the brain." Carlyle is punning here: cabbage = cloth filched by a tailor.

[6]Hans Sachs: a German poet and miscellaneous writer of the sixteenth century. One of his songs, *Der Schneider mit dem Panier* (The Tailor with the Banner), tells how a thievish tailor is frightened in a dream by

Taming of the Shrew,[1] and elsewhere? Does it not stand on record that the English Queen Elizabeth, receiving a deputation of Eighteen Tailors, addressed them with a "Good-morning, gentlemen both!" Did not the same virago boast that she had a Cavalry Regiment, whereof neither horse nor man could be injured; her Regiment, namely, of Tailors on Mares? Thus everywhere is the falsehood taken for granted, and acted on as an indisputable fact.

'Nevertheless, need I put the question to any Physiologist, whether it is disputable or not? Seems it not at least presumable, that, under his Clothes, the Tailor has bones and viscera, and other muscles than the sartorious?[2] Which function of manhood is the Tailor not conjectured to perform? Can he not arrest for debt? Is he not in most countries a tax-paying animal?

'To no reader of this Volume can it be doubtful which conviction is mine. Nay if the fruit of these long vigils, and almost preternatural Inquiries, is not to perish utterly, the world will have approximated towards a higher Truth; and the doctrine, which Swift,[3] with the keen forecast of genius, dimly anticipated, will stand revealed in clear light: that the Tailor is not only a Man, but something of a Creator or Divinity. Of Franklin it was said, that "he snatched the Thunder from Heaven and the Sceptre from Kings":[4] but which is greater, I would ask, he that lends, or he that snatches? For, looking away from individual cases, and how a Man is by the Tailor new-created into a Nobleman, and clothed not only with Wool but with Dignity and a Mystic

---

a banner made of pieces of cloth he has stolen. Carlyle refers to this song in his Journal. (M.)

[1]A nameless tailor figures in *The Taming of the Shrew;* Starveling is a tailor in *Midsummer Night's Dream.*

[2]The longest muscle in man, crossing the front of the thigh, and noticeably assisting in rotating the leg to the position assumed in sitting like a tailor.

[3]*Cf. A Tale of a Tub,* sect. ii, for the germ passage of *Sartor Resartus:* "They held the Universe to be a large Suit of Clothes which invests everything," *etc.*

[4]The motto by Turgot for the Picture of Franklin by Dupleiss. (M.)

Dominion,—is not the fair fabric of Society itself, with all its royal mantles and pontifical stoles, whereby, from nakedness and dismemberment, we are organised into Polities, into nations, and a whole coöperating Mankind, the creation, as has here been often irrefragably evinced, of the Tailor alone? —What too are all Poets and moral Teachers, but a species of Metaphorical Tailors? Touching which high Guild the greatest living Guild-brother has triumphantly asked us: "Nay if thou wilt have it, who but the Poet first made Gods for men; brought them down to us; and raised us up to them?"[1]

'And this is he, whom sitting downcast, on the hard basis of his Shopboard, the world treats with contumely, as the ninth part of a man! Look up, thou much-injured one, look up with the kindling eye of hope, and prophetic bodings of a noble better time. Too long hast thou sat there, on crossed legs, wearing thy ankle-joints to horn; like some sacred Anchorite,[2] or Catholic Fakir,[3] doing penance, drawing down Heaven's richest blessings, for a world that scoffed at thee. Be of hope! Already streaks of blue peer through our clouds; the thick gloom of Ignorance is rolling asunder, and it will be Day. Mankind will repay with interest their long-accumulated debt: the Anchorite that was scoffed at will be worshipped; the Fraction will become not an Integer only, but a Square and Cube. With astonishment the world will recognise that the Tailor is its Hierophant and Hierarch,[4] or even its God.

'As I stood in the Mosque of St. Sophia,[5] and looked upon these Four-and-Twenty Tailors, sewing and embroidering that rich Cloth, which the Sultan sends yearly for the Caaba[6]

[1]From *Wilhelm Meister,* I, 114.

[2]A religious recluse, renouncing the world, espousing poverty.

[3]The original fakirs were members of any sect or fraternity of Mohammedans taking a vow of poverty.

[4]An expositor, and ruler, respectively, of sacred things.

[5]The Mosque of Heavenly Wisdom, at Constantinople.

[6]The Mohammedan temple at Mecca, containing the famous stone fabled to have been changed to black by the sins of those who have touched it.

of Mecca, I thought within myself: How many other Unholies has your covering Art made holy, besides this Arabian Whinstone!

'Still more touching was it when, turning the corner of a lane, in the Scottish Town of Edinburgh, I came upon a Signpost, whereon stood written that such and such a one was "Breeches-Maker to his Majesty"; and stood painted the Effigies of a Pair of Leather Breeches, and between the knees these memorable words, SIC ITUR AD ASTRA.[1] Was not this the martyr prison-speech of a Tailor sighing indeed in bonds, yet sighing towards deliverance, and prophetically appealing to a better day? A day of justice, when the worth of Breeches would be revealed to man, and the Scissors become forever venerable.

'Neither, perhaps, may I now say, has his appeal been altogether in vain. It was in this high moment, when the soul, rent, as it were, and shed asunder, is open to inspiring influence, that I first conceived this Work on Clothes: the greatest I can ever hope to do; which has already, after long retardations, occupied, and will yet occupy, so large a section of my Life; and of which the Primary and simpler Portion may here find its conclusion.'

---

[1] "Thus one travels to the stars." *Aeneid,* ix, 641. The motto on the Canongate (Scott's *Chronicles of the Canongate,* Ch. i).

CHAPTER XII

FAREWELL

Teufelsdröckh's strange manner of speech, but resolute, truthful character: His purpose seemingly to proselytize, to unite the wakeful earnest in these dark times. Letter from Hofrath Heuschrecke announcing that Teufelsdröckh has disappeared from Weissnichtwo. Editor guesses he will appear again. Friendly Farewell.

So have we endeavoured, from the enormous, amorphous Plum-pudding, more like a Scottish Haggis,[1] which Herr Teufelsdröckh had kneaded for his fellow-mortals, to pick out the choicest Plums, and present them separately on a cover of our own. A laborious, perhaps a thankless enterprise; in which, however, something of hope has occasionally cheered us, and of which we can now wash our hands not altogether without satisfaction. If hereby, though in barbaric wise, some morsel of spiritual nourishment have been added to the scanty ration of our beloved British world, what nobler recompense could the Editor desire? If it prove otherwise, why should he murmur? Was not this a Task which Destiny, in any case, had appointed him; which having now done with, he sees his general Day's-work so much the lighter, so much the shorter?

Of Professor Teufelsdröckh it seems impossible to take leave without a mingled feeling of astonishment, gratitude, and disapproval. Who will not regret that talents, which might have profited in the higher walks of Philosophy, or in Art itself, have been so much devoted to a rummaging among lumber-rooms; nay too often to a scraping in kennels, where lost rings and diamond-necklaces[2] are nowise the sole con-

[1]A pudding made by boiling the heart, liver, and lungs in the maw of a sheep or calf, with suet, oatmeal, *etc.*

[2]Carlyle's essay, "The Diamond Necklace," was commenced, as Barrett notes, in 1833, and projected still earlier. It was published in 1837.

quests? Regret is unavoidable; yet censure were loss of time. To cure him of his mad humours British Criticism would essay in vain: enough for her if she can, by vigilance, prevent the spreading of such among ourselves. What a result, should this piebald, entangled, hyper-metaphorical style of writing, not to say of thinking, become general among our Literary men! As it might so easily do. Thus has not the Editor himself, working over Teufelsdröckh's German, lost much of his own English purity? Even as the smaller whirlpool is sucked into the larger, and made to whirl along with it, so has the lesser mind, in this instance, been forced to become portion of the greater, and, like it, see all things figuratively: which habit time and assiduous effort will be needed to eradicate.

Nevertheless, wayward as our Professor shows himself, is there any reader that can part with him in declared enmity? Let us confess, there is that in the wild, much-suffering, much-inflicting man, which almost attaches us. His attitude, we will hope and believe, is that of a man who had said to Cant,[1] Begone; and to Dilettantism,[2] Here thou canst not be; and to Truth, Be thou in place of all to me: a man who had manfully defied the 'Time-prince,' or Devil, to his face; nay perhaps, Hannibal-like, was mysteriously consecrated from birth to that warfare,[3] and now stood minded to wage the same, by all weapons, in all places, at all times. In such a cause, any soldier, were he but a Polack Scythe-man,[4] shall be welcome.

Still the question returns on us: How could a man occasionally of keen insight, not without keen sense of propriety, who had real Thoughts to communicate, resolve to emit them in a shape bordering so closely on the absurd? Which question he were wiser than the present Editor who should satisfactorily

---

[1]*Cf.* Carlyle's quotation of Dr. Johnson's "Clear your mind of Cant" in "Boswell's Life of Johnson" (*Ess.*, III, 125).

[2]See p. 70, *note* 1.

[3]Hannibal, the Carthaginian general (247–183 B.C.). At the age of nine he took an oath of eternal hostility to Rome.

[4]In 1830, the Poles, for the want of better weapons, armed themselves with scythes, under the leadership of Chlopicki. (B.)

answer. Our conjecture has sometimes been, that perhaps Necessity as well as Choice was concerned in it. Seems it not conceivable that, in a Life like our Professor's, where so much bountifully given by Nature had in Practice failed and misgone, Literature also would never rightly prosper: that striving with his characteristic vehemence to paint this and the other Picture, and ever without success, he at last desperately dashes his sponge, full of all colours, against the canvas, to try whether it will paint Foam?[1] With all his stillness, there were perhaps in Teufelsdröckh desperation enough for this.

A second conjecture we hazard with even less warranty. It is, that Teufelsdröckh is not without some touch of the universal feeling, a wish to proselytize. How often already have we paused, uncertain whether the basis of this so enigmatic nature were really Stoicism and Despair, or Love and Hope only seared into the figure of these! Remarkable, moreover, is this saying of his:[2] 'How were Friendship possible? In mutual devotedness to the Good and True: otherwise impossible; except as Armed Neutrality, or hollow Commercial League. A man, be the Heavens ever praised, is sufficient for himself; yet were ten men, united in Love, capable of being and of doing what ten thousand singly would fail in. Infinite is the help man can yield to man.' And now in conjunction therewith consider this other: 'It is the Night of the World, and still long till it be Day: we wander amid the glimmer of smoking ruins, and the Sun and the Stars of Heaven are as if blotted out for a season; and two immeasurable Phantoms, HYPOCRISY and ATHEISM, with the Gowl,[3] SENSUALITY, stalk abroad over the Earth, and call it theirs:

---

[1]As did Apelles, the Greek painter, when unable to paint the foam of a horse by studied effort. *Cf. G.-C. Corr.*, p. 285.

[2]First, that men are united in a mystic bond (as Novalis held); second, that the "Night of the World" has come (as Jean Paul remarked in the Preface to *Hesperus,* in a passage which Carlyle was fond of quoting, as in *Ess.*, II, 154), which will yield in time to an era of Light (as Goethe held, in his doctrine of the alternation of epochs of doubt and faith).

[3]Ghoul (a demon who feeds on corpses).

well at ease are the Sleepers for whom Existence is a shallow Dream.'

But what of the awestruck Wakeful who find it a Reality? Should not these unite; since even an authentic Spectre is not visible to Two?—In which case were this enormous Clothes-Volume properly an enormous Pitchpan, which our Teufelsdröckh in his lone watchtower had kindled, that it might flame far and wide through the Night, and many a disconsolately wandering spirit be guided thither to a Brother's bosom!—We say as before, with all his malign Indifference, who knows what mad Hopes this man may harbour?

Meanwhile there is one fact to be stated here, which harmonises ill with such conjecture; and, indeed, were Teufelsdröckh made like other men, might as good as altogether subvert it. Namely, that while the Beacon-fire blazed its brightest, the Watchman had quitted it; that no pilgrim could now ask him: Watchman, what of the Night?[1] Professor Teufelsdröckh, be it known, is no longer visibly present at Weissnichtwo, but again to all appearance lost in space! Some time ago, the Hofrath Heuschrecke was pleased to favour us with another copious Epistle; wherein much is said about the 'Population-Institute'; much repeated in praise of the Paper-bag Documents, the hieroglyphic nature of which our Hofrath still seems not to have surmised; and, lastly, the strangest occurrence communicated, to us for the first time, in the following paragraph:

'*Ew. Wohlgeboren*[2] will have seen from the public Prints, with what affectionate and hitherto fruitless solicitude Weissnichtwo regards the disappearance of her Sage. Might but the united voice of Germany prevail on him to return; nay could we but so much as elucidate for ourselves by what mystery he went away! But, alas, old Lieschen[3] experiences or affects the profoundest deafness, the profoundest igno-

---

[1]Isaiah, xxi, 11.

[2]Equivalent to *Your Honour.*

[3]See p. 24.

rance: in the Wahngasse[1] all lies swept, silent, sealed up; the Privy Council itself can hitherto elicit no answer.

'It had been remarked that while the agitating news of those Parisian Three Days[2] flew from mouth to mouth, and dinned every ear in Weissnichtwo, Herr Teufelsdröckh was not known, at the *Gans*[3] or elsewhere, to have spoken, for a whole week, any syllable except once these three: *Es geht an* (It is beginning).[4] Shortly after, as *Ew. Wohlgeboren* knows, was the public tranquillity here, as in Berlin, threatened by a Sedition of the Tailors. Nor did there want Evil-wishers, or perhaps mere desperate Alarmists, who asserted that the closing Chapter of the Clothes-Volume was to blame. In this appalling crisis, the serenity of our Philosopher was indescribable: nay, perhaps through one humble individual, something thereof might pass into the *Rath* (Council) itself, and so contribute to the country's deliverance. The Tailors are now entirely pacificated.—

'To neither of these two incidents can I attribute our loss; yet still comes there the shadow of a suspicion out of Paris and its Politics. For example, when the *Saint-Simonian Society*[5] transmitted its Propositions hither, and the whole *Gans* was one vast cackle of laughter, lamentation, and astonishment, our Sage sat mute; and at the end of the third evening said merely: "Here also are men who have discovered, not without amazement, that Man is still Man; of which high, long-forgotten Truth you already see them make a false application." Since then, as has been ascertained by examination of the Post-Director, there passed at least one Letter

---

[1]See p. 20, *note* 1.

[2]See p. 6, *note* 2.

[3]See p. 15, *note* 5.

[4]A rough German rendering of *Ça ira,* the catchword of the popular French Revolutionary song. By 1833–34, when *Sartor* began to run serially in *Fraser's Magazine,* Carlyle had embarked upon a voluminous course of reading in preparation for his essays on Diderot and "The Diamond Necklace," and for his *French Revolution* (1837).

[5]See p. 236, *note* 3.

with its Answer between the Messieurs Bazard-Enfantin[1] and our Professor himself; of what tenor can now only be conjectured. On the fifth night following, he was seen for the last time!

'Has this invaluable man, so obnoxious to most of the hostile Sects that convulse our Era, been spirited away by certain of their emissaries; or did he go forth voluntarily to their head-quarters to confer with them and confront them? Reason we have, at least of a negative sort, to believe the Lost still living; our widowed heart also whispers that ere long he will himself give a sign. Otherwise, indeed, his archives must, one day, be opened by Authority; where much, perhaps the *Palingenesie*[2] itself, is thought to be reposited.'

Thus far the Hofrath; who vanishes, as is his wont, too like an Ignis Fatuus, leaving the dark still darker.

So that Teufelsdröckh's public History were not done, then, or reduced to an even, unromantic tenor: nay, perhaps the better part thereof were only beginning? We stand in a region of conjectures, where substance has melted into shadow, and one cannot be distinguished from the other. May Time, which solves or suppresses all problems, throw glad light on this also! Our own private conjecture, now amounting almost to certainty, is that, safe-moored in some stillest obscurity, not to lie always still, Teufelsdröckh is actually in London!

Here, however, can the present Editor, with an ambrosial joy as of over-weariness falling into sleep, lay down his pen. Well does he know, if human testimony be worth aught, that to innumerable British readers likewise, this is a satisfying consummation; that innumerable British readers consider him, during these current months, but as an uneasy interruption to their ways of thought and digestion; and indicate so much, not without a certain irritancy and even spoken invective. For which, as for other mercies, ought not he to thank the

[1]Amand Bazard (1791–1832) and Barthélemy Prosper Enfantin (1796–1864) were followers of St.-Simon.

[2]See p. 217, *note* 1.

Upper Powers? To one and all of you, O irritated readers, he, with outstretched arms and open heart, will wave a kind farewell. Thou too, miraculous Entity, who namest thyself YORKE and OLIVER,[1] and with thy vivacities and genialities, with thy all-too Irish mirth and madness,[2] and odour of palled punch, makest such strange work, farewell; long as thou canst, fare-*well!* Have we not, in the course of Eternity, travelled some months of our Life-journey in partial sight of one another; have we not existed together, though in a state of quarrel?

---

[1]See p. 12, *note* 2.

[2]An appropriate final allusion to the reputation of *Fraser's Magazine*, in which *Sartor Resartus* should find, if anywhere, suitable presentation, but in which, nevertheless, it drew upon the magazine and the editor, Maginn, "the most unqualified disapprobation." *Cf. C.E.L.*, II, xvi–xviii.

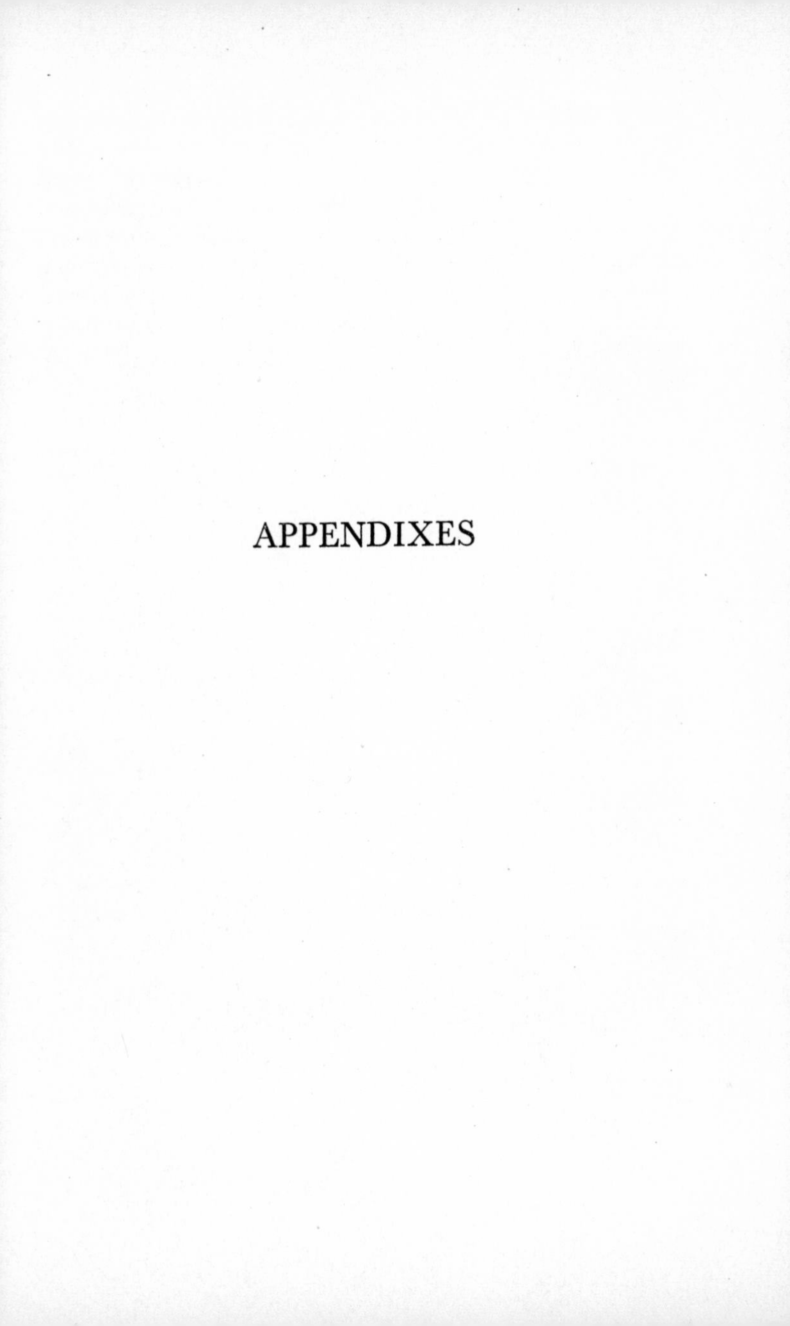

APPENDIXES

APPENDIX I

ON THE TITLE OF *SARTOR RESARTUS*

THE verses, "The Tailor Done over," referred to in Barrett's edition of *Sartor Resartus* (p. 7, *n.*), were a well known old Scottish song, sung widely in Carlyle's time and country. When he finally decided to abandon the rather awkward title, "Thoughts on Clothes: or Life and Opinions of Herr D. Teufelsdröckh," and to give his book the cryptic Latin title which was to become famous, he no doubt found the English original in the old countryside song, the first stanza of which runs as follows:

I once was a tailor, I lived with great pleasure,
I cut all my cloth to my customer's measure;
Oh, I once was so lusty they called me Bill the Rover,
But now I'm a skeleton fairly done over.
  Oh ohover oho hover, ohover ohover oho ho.

In Dyer's *Carlyle Bibliography* may be found also an interesting note from a "learned friend" who furnishes the following information:

Sartor Resartus doubtless means the "Tailor Patched," but it has, surely, also a secondary meaning, the "Clothes Volume Edited"; and thus I was pleased when I noted that the Latin word had of old been used in this secondary sense. The work in question is:

"Concilia illustrata . . . Conciliorum et colloquiorum . . . omnium . . . consessus . . . aeta et decreta . . . sistens, *etc.* J. L. Ruelius coepit, J. L. Hartmannus continuavit. 4 vols. in 3. 4⁰ Noribergae, 1675."

The 3rd volume bears the words: *"Reseratore* J. L. Hartmanno."

(See I. W. Dyer, *Carlyle Bibliography,* p. 585.)

APPENDIX II

CARLYLE'S DESCRIPTION OF *SARTOR RESARTUS*

IN A letter of May 27, 1833, to James Fraser, publisher of *Fraser's Magazine,* Carlyle has left a record of what he considered to be his methods and aims in *Sartor,* and his expectations for its future. The letter appears in Charles Eliot Norton's edition of the *Letters of Thomas Carlyle: 1826–1836* (London, 1889), pp. 364–67. As given below, the first paragraph and most of the last three have been omitted as irrelevant. From what is presented here, one may note the following points: (1) Carlyle has been told, and perhaps agrees, that the book is most profitably read "a few chapters at a time." The nature of *Sartor,* as a "kind of Didactic Novel," a "Satirical Extravaganza," is thus early seen to require of the reader a special approach, a reflective and discontinuous reading rather than a persistent effort to discover mechanical pattern. (2) Carlyle declares the book to contain the gist of all that he has hitherto thought and written; it comes from him as an original work; and it expresses at once a conservative and a "speculative-radical" point of view, allying Carlyle with none of the political parties and with no religious group. (3) This combination of critical conservatism and opposition to the *status quo* should make *Sartor,* in Carlyle's opinion, a work peculiarly suitable for *Fraser's Magazine,* noteworthy at that time for such a combination of views. (4) Carlyle is quite certain that *Sartor* will receive no quiet acceptance, but will "astonish," prove "spiritually interesting" to, or repel readers according to their disposition. The prophetic character of the work is indicated by Carlyle's statement that "the time seems come to set these little bits of Doctrine forth."

Norton notes (p. 365, *n.*) that by February, 1833, the name *Teufelsdreck* has been changed to *Teufelsdröckh,* and that by September of the same year Carlyle has decided to adopt the title, *Sartor Resartus.*

To Mr. Fraser, Publisher, London.

CRAIGENPUTTOCK, 27th May 1833.

MY DEAR SIR—

Most probably you recollect the Manuscript *Book* I had with me in London; and how during that Reform hurly-burly, which unluckily still continues and is like to continue, I failed to make any bargain about it. The Manuscript still lies in my drawer; and now after long deliberation I have determined to slit it up into strips, and send it forth in the Periodical way; for which in any case it was perhaps better adapted. The pains I took with the composition of it, truly, were greater than even I might have thought necessary, had this been foreseen: but what then? Care of that sort is never altogether thrown away; far better too much than too little. I reckon that it will be easy for the Magazine Printer to save me some thirty or forty complete copies, as he prints it; these can then be bound up and distributed among my Friends likely to profit thereby; and in the end of all we can *re*print it into a Book proper, if that seem good. Your Magazine is the first I think of for this object; and I must have got a distinct negative from you before I go any farther. Listen to me, then, and judge.

The Book is at present named "Thoughts on Clothes; or Life and Opinions of Herr D. Teufelsdröckh, D.U.J."; but perhaps we might see right to alter the title a little; for the rest, some brief Introduction could fit it handsomely enough into its new destination: it is already divided into three "Books," and farther into very short "Chapters," capable in all ways of subdivision. Nay some tell me, what perhaps is true, that taking a few chapters at a time is really the profitablest way of reading it. There may be in all some Eight sheets of *Fraser*. It is put together in the fashion of a kind of Didactic Novel; but indeed properly *like* nothing yet extant: I used to characterise it briefly as a kind of "Satirical Extravaganza on Things in General"; it contains more of my opinions on Art, Politics, Religion, Heaven, Earth and Air, than all the things I have yet written. The Creed promulgated on all these things, as you may judge, is *mine,* and firmly *believed:* for the rest, the main Actor in the business ("Editor of these Sheets," as he often calls himself) assumes a kind of Conservative (though Anti-quack) character; and would suit *Fraser* perhaps better than any other Magazine. The ultimate result, however, I need hardly premise, is a deep religious speculative-radicalism (so I call it for want of a better name), with which you are already well enough acquainted in me.

There are only five persons that have yet read this Manuscript: of whom two have expressed themselves (I mean convinced me that they *are*) considerably interested and gratified; two quite *struck,* "overwhelmed with astonishment and new hope" (this is the result I aimed at for souls worthy of hope); and one in secret discontented and displeased. William Fraser is a sixth reader, or rather half-reader; for I think he had only got half-way or so; and I never learned his opinion. With him, if you like, at this stage of the business you can consult freely about it. My own conjecture is that *Teufelsdröckh,* whenever published, will astonish most that read it, be wholly understood by very few; but to the astonishment of some will add touches of (almost the deepest) spiritual interest, with others quite the opposite feeling. I think I can practically prophesy that for some six or eight months (for it must be published without interruption), it would be apt at least to *keep the eyes* of the Public on you.

Such is all the description I can give you, in these limits: now what say you to it? Let me hear as soon as you can; for the time seems come to set these little bits of Doctrine forth. . . .

And now, in great haste, adieu! Believe me always, my dear sir, most faithfully yours,

T. Carlyle

APPENDIX III

JOHN STERLING'S CRITICISM OF *SARTOR RESARTUS,* AND CARLYLE'S REPLY

WHAT proved to be the earliest substantial criticism of *Sartor,* and the earliest also in date of printed publication, came from Carlyle's good friend, John Sterling. Writing on May 29, 1835, three months after he had resigned from his curateship at Herstmonceux, owing to ill health and to religious misgivings, Sterling writes as an unorthodox Christian who finds Carlyle's philosophy and literary method considerably at variance with his own. He is shocked at Carlyle's "pantheism," at Teufelsdröckh's disbelief in a "Personal God," at his consequent "savage isolation," even after the conversion, and at his "fierce dissatisfaction" with his times. Carlyle's sense of the mystery of man's appearance and disappearance, through birth and death, is met by Sterling's staunch declaration, "On the other hand, I affirm, we do know whence we come and whither we go!" In these criticisms, one may see a typical reaction which *Sartor* elicited from the believers of Carlyle's own day;—in this instance, from one no longer orthodox.

On the formal side of *Sartor,* Sterling speaks both as an advocate of contemporary standards and as a spokesman for subsequent readers even to the present day. (1) He is repelled by the "lawless oddity" of *Sartor's* "rhapsodico-reflective" method. While it suggests, at various points, some comparison with Rabelais, Montaigne, Sterne, and Swift, it fails nevertheless through obscurity, stylistic affectation, and caprice. (2) The language likewise is faulty. Sterling is interestingly conservative. Like Macaulay, he objects to the word "talented," also to "visualize," and "environment," words which have since become completely accepted in good usage. Sterling, like many later readers, is repelled moreover by Carlyle's mannerisms: his repetitions, over-employment of favourite expressions, and inversions of normal English syntax. (3) Nor is the *plan* successful. Philosophic truths, if presented by means of narrative, require a *simple* fable, rather than such a bewildering extravaganza as the life and opinions of an eccentric German professor. Sterling, the product of the "classical education" of Cambridge, is of course thinking of Plato in his *Dialogues,* of Bishop Berkeley in his *Siris.* Thus *Sartor,* with all its exuberance and exaggerative humour, contains so much "unprofitable surplusage" that the philosophic message underneath is lost for the majority of readers.

In the third paragraph from the end of Sterling's letter, Carlyle omits a passage which might throw light on his friend's attitude towards Goethe. Sterling shows much of the contemporary opinion of the German poet. He is repelled by "the unsympathising factitious calm of Art, which we find in Goethe. . . . At what expense is it bought? . . . He attains his inhuman ghastly calmness by reducing the Universe to a heap of material for the idea of beauty to work on."

Carlyle defends himself on two points: on his style and on the charge of pantheism. That his friend misunderstood Goethe, or attacked only the younger Goethe whom Carlyle had never followed, rather than the old Goethe of the *Wanderjahre,* Carlyle makes no mention, no doubt convinced, as he said in his lectures on Heroes, that the age was not as yet capable of estimating Goethe at his true worth. In respect to his style, Carlyle has several noteworthy things to say. (1) The imperfections arise largely, he says, from his urgent need to *act* rather than to be acutely self-critical. (2) His coinages and combinations of words are his response to the need of new words for new ideas, ideas "not hitherto uttered in English Books." (3) His style, with all its irregularities, is the product of a time which has little place for "Purism of Style," being itself anarchic and journalistic in its prose, breaking away from "Johnsonian English," and in need, above all, of truth rather than beauty or grace.—To the charge of disbelief in a "Personal God," Carlyle replies in a fashion to foreshadow a later and characteristically Victorian manner of dealing with fundamental questions. He is vague and ambiguous. Though he denies the disbelief imputed by Sterling, he leaves the question suspended with Goethe's *Wer darf ihn nennen?* He is not a pantheist, nor yet a theist; but he still denies a disbelief in a personal deity. He abhors systems and sects, complex and specific statements of belief or knowledge. Yet he rejoices that Sterling can believe. As for himself, the only creed worth insisting on is that "one has got two eyes to look with; and also a mind capable of knowing, of believing." This reply must have left Sterling considerably in the dark. It is worth our notice here, since it indicates an attitude towards final and embarrassing questions which was to develop into late-Victorian religious vagueness and rhetoric. Carlyle's God—"a formless Infinite," as Sterling called it—became more and more a mere force, a "stream of tendency not ourselves which makes for righteousness," as Arnold later phrased it, and ultimately not even a force or tendency, but "a larger hope," in which one "faintly trusted."

In their consideration of the style, plan, and purport of *Sartor,* Sterling's letter and Carlyle's reply have an interesting historical significance.

To Thomas Carlyle, Esq., Chelsea, London.[1]

HERSTMONCEUX near BATTLE, 29th May, 1835.

MY DEAR CARLYLE,—I have now read twice, with care, the wondrous account of Teufelsdröckh and his Opinions; and I need not say that it has given me much to think of. It falls in with the feelings and tastes which were, for years, the ruling ones of my life; but which you will not be angry with me when I say that I am infinitely and hourly thankful for having escaped from. Not that I think of this state of mind as one with which I have no longer any concern. The sense

[1]Carlyle published this letter in his *Life of John Sterling* (1851). See Chapter ii of Part II.

of a oneness of life and power in all existence; and of a boundless exuberance of beauty around us, to which most men are well-nigh dead, is a possession which no one that has ever enjoyed it would wish to lose. When to this we add the deep feeling of the difference between the actual and the ideal in Nature, and still more in Man; and bring in, to explain this, the principle of duty, as that which connects us with a possible Higher State, and sets us in progress towards it,—we have a cycle of thoughts which was the whole spiritual empire of the wisest Pagans, and which might well supply food for the wide speculations and richly creative fancy of Teufelsdröckh, or his prototype Jean Paul.

How then comes it, we cannot but ask, that these ideas, displayed assuredly with no want of eloquence, vivacity or earnestness, have found, unless I am much mistaken, so little acceptance among the best and most energetic minds in this country? In a country where millions read the Bible, and thousands Shakspeare; where Wordsworth circulates through book-clubs and drawing-rooms; where there are innumerable admirers of your favourite Burns; and where Coleridge, by sending from his solitude the voice of earnest spiritual instruction, came to be beloved, studied and mourned for, by no small or careless school of disciples?—To answer this question would, of course, require more thought and knowledge than I can pretend to bring to it. But there are some points on which I will venture to say a few words.

In the first place, as to the form of composition,—which may be called, I think, the Rhapsodico-Reflective. In this the *Sartor Resartus* resembles some of the master-works of human invention, which have been acknowledged as such by many generations; and especially the works of Rabelais, Montaigne, Sterne and Swift. There is nothing I know of in Antiquity like it. That which comes nearest is perhaps the Platonic Dialogue. But of this, although there is something of the playful and fanciful on the surface, there is in reality neither in the language (which is austerely determined to its end), nor in the method and progression of the work, any of that headlong self-asserting capriciousness, which, if not discernible in the plan of Teufelsdröckh's Memoirs, is yet plainly to be seen in the structure of the sentences, the lawless oddity, and strange heterogeneous combination and allusion. The principle of this difference, observable often elsewhere in modern literature (for the same thing is to be found, more or less, in many of our most genial works of imagination,—*Don Quixote,* for instance, and the writings of Jeremy Taylor), seems to be that well-known one of the predominant objectivity of the Pagan mind; while among us the subjective has risen into superiority, and brought with it in each individual a multitude of peculiar associations and relations. These, as not explicable from any one *external* principle assumed as a premiss by the ancient philosopher, were rejected from the sphere of his æsthetic creation: but to us they all have a value and meaning; being connected by the bond of our own personality, and all alike existing in that infinity which is its arena.

But however this may be, and comparing the Teufelsdröckhean Epopee only with those other modern works,—it is noticeable that Rabelais, Montaigne and Sterne have trusted for the currency of their writings, in a great degree, to the use of obscene and sensual stimulants. Rabelais, besides, was full of contemporary and personal satire; and seems to have been a champion in the great cause of his time,—as was Montaigne also,—that of the right of thought in all competent minds, unrestrained by any outward authority. Montaigne, moreover, contains more pleasant and lively gossip, and more distinct good-humoured painting of his own character and daily habits, than any other writer I know. Sterne is never obscure, and never moral; and the costume of his subjects is drawn from the familiar experience of his own time and country: and Swift, again, has the same merit of the clearest perspicuity, joined to that of the most homely, unaffected, forcible English. These points of difference seem to me the chief ones which bear against the success of the *Sartor*. On the other hand, there is in Teufelsdröckh a depth and fervour of feeling, and a power of serious eloquence, far beyond that of any of these four writers; and to which indeed there is nothing at all comparable in any of them, except perhaps now and then, and very imperfectly, in Montaigne.

Of the other points of comparison there are two which I would chiefly dwell on: and first as to the language. A good deal of this is positively barbarous. "Environment," "vestural," "stertorous," "visualized," "complected," and others to be found I think in the first twenty pages,—are words, so far as I know, without any authority; some of them contrary to analogy: and none repaying by their value the disadvantage of novelty. To these must be added new and erroneous locutions; "whole other tissues" for *all the other,* and similar uses of the word *whole;* "orients" for *pearls;* "lucid" and "lucent" employed as if they were different in meaning; "hulls" perpetually for *coverings,* it being a word hardly used, and then only for the husk of a nut; "to insure a man of misapprehension"; "talented," a mere newspaper and hustings word, invented, I believe, by O'Connell.

I must also mention the constant recurrence of some words in a quaint and queer connection, which gives a grotesque and somewhat repulsive mannerism to many sentences. Of these the commonest offender is "quite"; which appears in almost every page, and gives at first a droll kind of emphasis; but soon becomes wearisome. "Nay," "manifold," "cunning enough significance," "faculty" (meaning a man's rational or moral *power*), "special," "not without," haunt the reader as if in some uneasy dream which does not rise to the dignity of nightmare. Some of these strange mannerisms fall under the general head of a singularity peculiar, so far as I know, to Teufelsdröckh. For instance, that of the incessant use of a sort of odd superfluous qualification of his assertions; which seems to give the character of deliberateness and caution to the style, but in time sounds like mere trick or involuntary habit. "Almost" does more than yeoman's, *almost* slave's service in this way. Something similar may be remarked of the use of the double negative by way of affirmation.

Under this head, of language, may be mentioned, though not with strict grammatical accuracy, two standing characteristics of the Professor's style,—at least as rendered into English: *First,* the composition of words, such as "snow-and-rosebloom maiden": an attractive damsel doubtless in Germany, but, with all her charms, somewhat uncouth here. "Life-vision" is another example; and many more might be found. To say nothing of the innumerable cases in which the words are only intelligible as a compound term, though not distinguished by hyphens. Of course the composition of words is sometimes allowable even in English: but the habit of dealing with German seems to have produced, in the pages before us, a prodigious superabundance of this form of expression; which gives harshness and strangeness, where the matter would at all events have been surprising enough. *Secondly,* I object, with the same qualification, to the frequent use of *inversion;* which generally appears as a transposition of the two members of a clause, in a way which would not have been practised in conversation. It certainly gives emphasis and force, and often serves to point the meaning. But a style may be fatiguing and faulty precisely by being too emphatic, forcible and pointed; and so straining the attention to find its meaning, or the admiration to appreciate its beauty.

Another class of considerations connects itself with the heightened and plethoric fulness of the style: its accumulation and contrast of imagery; its occasional jerking and almost spasmodic violence;—and above all, the painful subjective excitement, which seems the element and groundwork even of every description of Nature; often taking the shape of sarcasm or broad jest, but never subsiding into calm. There is also a point which I should think worth attending to, were I planning any similar book: I mean the importance, in a work of imagination, of not too much disturbing in the reader's mind the balance of the New and Old. The former addresses itself to his active, the latter to his passive faculty; and these are mutually dependent, and must coexist in certain proportion, if you wish to combine his sympathy and progressive exertion with willingness and ease of attention. This should be taken into account in forming a style; for of course it cannot be consciously thought of in composing each sentence.

But chiefly it seems important in determining the plan of a work. If the tone of feeling, the line of speculation are out of the common way, and sure to present some difficulty to the average reader, then it would probably be desirable to select, for the circumstances, drapery and accessories of all kinds, those most familiar, or at least most attractive. A fable of the homeliest purport, and commonest every-day application, derives an interest and charm from its turning on the characters and acts of gods and genii, lions and foxes, Arabs and Affghauns. On the contrary, for philosophic inquiry and truths of awful preciousness, I would select as my personages and interlocutors beings with whose language and "whereabouts" my readers would be familar. Thus did Plato in his Dialogues, Christ in his Parables. Therefore it seems doubtful whether it was judicious to make a German Professor the hero of *Sartor*. Berkeley began his *Siris* with tar-water; but what can English readers be expected to make of *Gukguk* by way of prelibation to your nectar and tokay? The circumstances and details do not flash with living reality on the minds of your readers, but, on the contrary, themselves require some of that attention and minute speculation, the whole original stock of which, in the minds of most of them, would not be too much to enable them to follow your views of Man and Nature. In short, there is not a sufficient basis of the common to justify the amount of peculiarity in the work. In a book of science, these considerations would of course be inapplicable; but then the whole shape and colouring of the book must be altered to make it such; and a man who wishes merely to get at the philosophical result, or summary of the whole, will regard the details and illustrations as so much unprofitable surplusage.

The sense of strangeness is also awakened by the marvellous combinations, in which the work abounds to a degree that the common reader must find perfectly bewildering. This can hardly, however, be treated as a consequence of the *style;* for the style in this respect coheres with, and springs from, the whole turn and tendency of thought. The noblest images are objects of a humorous smile, in a mind which sees itself above all Nature and throned in the arms of an Almighty Necessity; while the meanest have a dignity, inasmuch as they are trivial symbols of the same one life to which the great whole belongs. And hence, as I divine, the startling whirl of incongruous juxtaposition, which of a truth must to many readers seem as amazing as if the Pythia on the tripod should have struck up a drinking-song, or Thersites had caught the prophetic strain of Cassandra.

All this, of course, appears to me true and relevant; but I cannot help feeling that it is, after all, but a poor piece of quackery to comment on a multitude of phenomena without adverting to the principle which lies at the root, and gives the true meaning to them all. Now this principle I seem to myself to find in the state of mind which is attributed to Teufelsdröckh; in his state of mind, I say, not in his opinions, though these are, in him as in all men, most important,—being one of the best indices to his state of mind. Now what distinguishes him, not merely from the greatest and best men who have been on earth for eighteen hundred years, but from the whole body of those who have been working forwards towards the good, and have been the salt and light of the world, is this: That he does not believe in a God. Do not be indignant, I am blaming no one;—but if I write my thoughts, I must write them honestly.

Teufelsdröckh does not belong to the herd of sensual and thoughtless men; because he does perceive in all Existence a unity of power; because he does believe that this is a real power external to him and dominant to a certain extent over him, and does not think that he is himself a shadow in a world of shadows. He had a deep feeling of the beautiful, the good and the true; and a faith in their final victory.

At the same time, how evident is the strong inward unrest,

the Titanic heaving of mountain on mountain; the storm-like rushing over land and sea in search of peace. He writhes and roars under his consciousness of the difference in himself between the possible and the actual, the hoped-for and the existent. He feels that duty is the highest law of his own being; and knowing how it bids the waves be stilled into an icy fixedness and grandeur, he trusts (but with a boundless inward misgiving) that there is a principle of order which will reduce all confusion to shape and clearness. But wanting peace himself, his fierce dissatisfaction fixes on all that is weak, corrupt and imperfect around him; and instead of a calm and steady co-operation with all those who are endeavouring to apply the highest ideas as remedies for the worst evils, he holds himself aloof in savage isolation; and cherishes (though he dare not own) a stern joy at the prospect of that Catastrophe which is to turn loose again the elements of man's social life, and give for a time the victory to evil;—in hopes that each new convulsion of the world must bring us nearer to the ultimate restoration of all things; fancying that each may be the last. Wanting the calm and cheerful reliance, which would be the spring of active exertion, he flatters his own distemper by persuading himself that his own age and generation are peculiarly feeble and decayed; and would even perhaps be willing to exchange the restless immaturity of our self-consciousness, and the promise of its long throe-pangs, for the unawakened undoubting simplicity of the world's childhood; of the times in which there was all the evil and horror of our day, only with the difference that conscience had not arisen to try and condemn it. In these longings, if they are Teufelsdröckh's, he seems to forget that, could we go back five thousand years, we should only have the prospect of travelling them again, and arriving at last at the same point at which we stand now.

Something of this state of mind I may say that I understand; for I have myself experienced it. And the root of the matter appears to me: A want of sympathy with the great body of those who are now endeavouring to guide and help onward their fellow-men. And in what is this alienation grounded? It is, as I believe, simply in the difference on that point: viz. the clear, deep, habitual recognition of a one Living *Personal* God, essentially good, wise, true and holy, the Author of all that exists; and a reunion with whom is the only end of all rational beings. This belief. . . [*There follow now several pages on "Personal God," and other abstruse or indeed properly unspeakable matters; these, and a general Postscript of qualifying purport, I will suppress; extracting only the following fractions, as luminous or slightly significant to us:*]

Now see the difference of Teufelsdröckh's feelings. At the end of book iii. chap. 8, I find these words: "But whence? O Heaven, whither? Sense knows not; Faith knows not; only that it is through mystery to mystery, from God to God.

We *are such stuff*
As dreams are made of, and our little life
Is rounded with a sleep."

And this tallies with the whole strain of his character. What we find everywhere, with an abundant use of the name of God, is the conception of a formless Infinite whether in time or space; of a high inscrutable Necessity, which it is the chief wisdom and virtue to submit to, which is the mysterious impersonal base of all Existence,—shows itself in the laws of every separate being's nature; and for man in the shape of duty. On the other hand, I affirm, we do know whence we come and whither we go!—

. . . And in this state of mind, as there is no true sympathy with others, just as little is there any true peace for ourselves. There is indeed possible the unsympathizing factitious calm of Art, which we find in Goethe. But at what expense is it bought? Simply, by abandoning altogether the idea of duty, which is the great witness of our personality. And he attains his inhuman ghastly calmness by reducing the Universe to a heap of material for the idea of beauty to work on!—

. . . The sum of all I have been writing as to the connection of our faith in God with our feeling towards men and our mode of action, may of course be quite erroneous: but granting its truth, it would supply the one principle which I have been seeking for, in order to explain the peculiarities of style in your account of Teufelsdröckh and his writings. . . . The life and works of Luther are the best comment I know of on this doctrine of mine.

Reading over what I have written, I find I have not nearly done justice to my own sense of the genius and moral energy of the book; but this is what you will best excuse. Believe me most sincerely and faithfully yours,

John Sterling

T. Carlyle to John Sterling, Herstmonceux, Sussex.[1]

5 Cheyne Row, Chelsea,
4th June, 1835.

My Dear Sterling,

Your objections as to phraseology and style have good grounds to stand on; many of them indeed are considerations to which I myself was not blind; which there (unluckily) were no means of doing more than nodding to as one passed. A man has but a certain strength; imperfections cling to him, which if he wait till he have brushed off entirely, he will spin forever on his axis, advancing nowhither. . . . If one has thoughts not hitherto uttered in English Books, I see nothing for it but that you must use words not found there, must *make* words,—with moderation and discretion, of course. That I have not always done it *so,* proves only that I was not strong enough. . . . With unspeakable cheerfulness I give up *"Talented":* indeed, but for the plain statement you make, I could have sworn such a word had never, except for parodistic,

[1]The first, third, and last two paragraphs of Carlyle's letter have been omitted as comparatively irrelevant. The letter has been published in the *Letters of Thomas Carlyle to John Stuart Mill, John Sterling, and Robert Browning,* edited by Alexander Carlyle, London, 1923. See pp. 191–94.

ironical purposes, risen from my inkhorn, or passed my lips. . . . But finally, do you reckon this really a time for Purism of Style; or that Style (mere dictionary Style) has much to do with the worth or unworth of a Book? I do not: with whole ragged battalions of Scott's-Novel Scotch, with Irish, German, French, and even Newspaper Cockney (when "Literature" is little other than a Newspaper) storming in on us, and the whole structure of our Johnsonian English breaking up from its foundations,—revolution *there* as visible as anywhere else! . . .

You say finally, as the key to the whole mystery, that Teufelsdröckh does not believe in a "personal God." It is frankly said, with a friendly honesty for which I love you. A grave charge nevertheless, an *awful* charge: to which, if I mistake not, the Professor, laying his hand on his heart, will reply with some gesture expressing the solemnest *denial.* In gesture, rather than in speech; for "the Highest *cannot* be spoken of in words." *"Personal,"* "impersonal," One, Three, *what* meaning can any mortal (after all) attach to them in reference to such an object? *Wer darf ihn NENNEN?*[1] I dare not, and do not. That you dare and do (to some greater extent) is a matter I am far from taking offence at: nay, with all sincerity, I can rejoice that you have a creed of that kind, which gives you happy thoughts, nerves you for good actions, brings you into readier communion with many good men; my true wish is that such creed may long hold compactly together in you. . . . Finally, assure yourself, I am neither Pagan nor Turk, not circumcised Jew, but an unfortunate Christian individual resident at Chelsea in *this* year of Grace; neither Pantheist nor Pottheist, nor any Theist or *ist* whatsoever, having the most decided contempt for all manner of Systembuilders and Sectfounders—so far as contempt may be compatible with so mild a nature; feeling well beforehand (taught by experience) that all such are and even must be *wrong.* By God's blessing, one has got two eyes to look with; and also a mind capable of

[1]"Who dare NAME Him?"

knowing, of believing: that is all the creed I will at this time insist on. . . .

I remain always,

Yours with great sincerity,

T. Carlyle

APPENDIX IV

PARALLELISMS OF *WOTTON REINFRED* AND *SARTOR RESARTUS*

"The Parallelisms of *Wotton Reinfred* and *Sartor Resartus,* given by John Davidson in the *Glasgow Herald,* April, 1908," says Dyer, . . . "by no means exhaust the subject." The paging is to *The Last Words of Thomas Carlyle* (London, 1892) and to *Sartor* as it appears in the present edition.

Wotton Reinfred	*Sartor Resartus*
pp. 6–7	pp. 147–48
p. 10	p. 155
pp. 32–35	pp. 138–42
p. 36	p. 145
p. 49	p. 149

All of these parallelisms are given in Dyer's *Carlyle Bibliography,* p. 586, except the final item, which, like a number of other, though minor, items, might well be added to the list. (See also Heinrich Kraeger, "Carlyles Deutsche Studien und der 'Wotton Reinfred,'" *Anglia Beibl.,* IX [1898], 193–219.)

APPENDIX V

TESTIMONIES OF AUTHORS

THIS questionable little book was undoubtedly written among the mountain solitudes, in 1831; but, owing to impediments natural and accidental, could not, for seven years more, appear as a Volume in England;—and had at last to clip itself in pieces, and be content to struggle out, bit by bit, in some courageous *Magazine* that offered. Whereby now, to certain idly curious readers, and even to myself till I make study, the insignificant but at last irritating question, What its real history and chronology are, is, if not insoluble, considerably involved in haze.

To the first English Edition, 1838, which an American, or two Americans had now opened the way for, there was slightingly prefixed under the title *"Testimonies of Authors,"* some straggle of real documents, which, now that I find it again, sets the matter into clear light and sequence;—and shall here, for removal of idle stumbling-blocks and nugatory guessings from the path of every reader, be reprinted as it stood. (*Author's Note of* 1868.)

I. HIGHEST CLASS, BOOKSELLER'S TASTER

Taster to Bookseller.—"The Author of *Teufelsdröckh* is a person of talent; his work displays here and there some felicity of thought and expression, considerable fancy and knowledge: but whether or not it would take with the public seems doubtful. For a *jeu d'esprit* of that kind it is too long; it would have suited better as an essay or article than as a volume. The Author has no great tact; his wit is frequently heavy; and reminds one of the German Baron who took to leaping on tables, and answered that he was learning to be lively. *Is* the work a translation?"

Bookseller to Editor.—"Allow me to say that such a writer requires only a little more tact to produce a popular as well as an able work. Directly on receiving your permission, I sent your *MS.* to a gentleman in the highest class of men of letters, and an accomplished German scholar: I now inclose you his opinion, which, you may rely upon it, is a just one; and I have too high an opinion of your good sense to" &c. &c.—*MS.* (*penes nos*), *London, 17th September 1831.*

II. Critic of the Sun

"*Fraser's Magazine* exhibits the usual brilliancy, and also the" &c. "*Sartor Resartus* is what old Dennis used to call 'a heap of clotted nonsense,' mixed however, here and there, with passages marked by thought and striking poetic vigour. But what does the writer mean by 'Baphometic fire-baptism'? Why cannot he lay aside his pedantry, and write so as to make himself generally intelligible? We quote by way of curiosity a sentence from the *Sartor Resartus;* which may be read either backwards or forwards, for it is equally intelligible either way. Indeed, by beginning at the tail, and so working up to the head, we think the reader will stand the fairest chance of getting at its meaning: 'The fire-baptised soul, long so scathed and thunder-riven, here feels its own freedom; which feeling is its Baphometic baptism: the citadel of its whole kingdom it has thus gained by assault, and will keep inexpugnable; outwards from which the remaining dominions, not indeed without hard battering, will doubtless by degrees be conquered and pacificated.' Here is a"— . . . . . —*Sun Newspaper, 1st April 1834.*

III. North-American Reviewer

. . . . . "After a careful survey of the whole ground, our belief is that no such persons as Professor Teufelsdröckh or Counsellor Heuschrecke ever existed; that the six Paper-bags, with their China-ink inscriptions and multifarious contents, are a mere figment of the brain; that the 'present editor' is the only person who has ever written upon the Philosophy of Clothes; and that the *Sartor Resartus* is the only treatise that has yet appeared upon that subject;—in short, that the whole account of the origin of the work before us, which the supposed editor relates with so much gravity, and of which we have given a brief abstract, is in plain English, a *hum*.

"Without troubling our readers at any great length with our reasons for entertaining these suspicions, we may remark, that the absence of all other information on the subject, excepting what is contained in the work, is itself a fact of a most significant character. The whole German press, as well as the particular one where the work purports to have been printed, seems to be under the control of *Stillschweigen und Co.*—Silence and Company. If the Clothes-Philosophy and its author are making so great a sensation throughout Germany as is pretended, how happens it that the only notice we have of the fact is contained in a few numbers of a monthly magazine, published at London? How happens it that no intelligence about the matter has come out directly to this country? We pique ourselves, here in New England, upon knowing at least as much of what is going on in the literary way in the old Dutch mother-land, as our brethren of the fast-anchored isle; but thus far we have no tidings whatever of the 'extensive, close-printed, close-meditated volume,' which forms the subject of this pretended commentary. Again, we would respectfully inquire of the 'present editor' upon what part of the map of Germany we are to look for the city of *Weissnichtwo,*—'Know-not-where,'—at which place the work is supposed to have been printed and the author to have resided. It has been our fortune to visit several portions of the German territory, and to examine pretty carefully, at different times and for various purposes, maps of the whole, but we have no recollection of any such place. We suspect that the city of *Know-not-where* might be called, with at least as much propriety, *Nobody-knows-where,* and is to be found in the kingdom of *Nowhere*. Again, the village of *Entepfuhl,*

—'Duck-pond,'—where the supposed author of the work is said to have passed his youth, and that of *Hinterschlag,* where he had his education, are equally foreign to our geography. Duck-ponds enough there undoubtedly are in almost every village in Germany, as the traveller in that country knows too well to his cost, but particular village denominated Duck-pond, is to us altogether *terra incognita.* The names of the personages are not less singular than those of the places. Who can refrain from a smile at the yoking together of such a pair of appellatives as Diogenes Teufelsdröckh? The supposed bearer of this strange title is represented as admitting, in his pretended autobiography, that 'he had searched to no purpose through all the Herald's books in and without the German Empire, and through all manner of Subscribers'-lists, Militia-Rolls, and other Name-Catalogues'; but had nowhere been able to find the name Teufelsdröckh, except as appended to his own person. We can readily believe this, and we doubt very much whether any Christian parent would think of condemning a son to carry through life the burden of so unpleasant a title. That of Counsellor Heuschrecke,—'Grasshopper,'—though not offensive, looks much more like a piece of fancy work than a 'fair business transaction.' The same may be said of *Blumine,*—'Flower-Goddess,'—the heroine of the fable, and so of the rest.

"In short, our private opinion is, as we have remarked, that the whole story of a correspondence with Germany, a university of Nobody-knows-where, a Professor of Things in General, a Counsellor Grasshopper, a Flower-Goddess Blumine, and so forth, has about as much foundation in truth, as the late entertaining account of Sir John Herschel's discoveries in the moon. Fictions of this kind are, however, not uncommon, and ought not, perhaps, to be condemned with too much severity; but we are not sure that we can exercise the same indulgence in regard to the attempt, which seems to be made to mislead the public as to the substance of the work before us, and its pretended German original. Both purport, as we have seen, to be upon the subject of Clothes, or dress. *Clothes, their Origin and Influence,* is the title of the supposed German treatise of Professor Teufelsdröckh, and the rather odd name of *Sartor Resartus*—the Tailor Patched,—which the present editor has affixed to his pretended commentary, seems to look the same way. But though there is a good deal of remark throughout the work in a half-serious, half-comic style upon dress, it seems to be in reality a treatise upon the great science of Things in General, which Teufelsdröckh is supposed to have professed at the university of Nobody-knows-where. Now, without intending to adopt a too rigid standard of morals, we own that we doubt a little the propriety of offering to the public a treatise on Things in General, under the name and in the form of an Essay on Dress. For ourselves, advanced as we unfortunately are in the journey of life, far beyond the period when dress is practically a matter of interest, we have no hesitation in saying, that the real subject of the work is to us more attractive than the ostensible one. But this is probably not the case with the mass of readers. To the younger portion of the community, which constitutes everywhere the very great majority, the subject of dress is one of intense and paramount importance. An author who treats it appeals, like the poet, to the young men and maidens—*virginibus puerisque,*—and calls upon them, by all the motives which habitually operate most strongly upon their feelings, to buy his book. When, after opening their purses for this purpose, they have carried home the work in triumph, expecting to find in it some particular instruction in regard to the tying of their neckcloths, or the cut of their corsets, and meet with nothing better than dissertation on Things in General, they will,—to use the mildest term—not be in very good humour. If the last improvements in legislation, which we have made in this country, should have found their way to England, the author, we think, would stand some chance of being *Lynched*. Whether his object in this piece of *supercherie* be merely pecuniary profit, or whether he takes a malicious pleasure in quizzing the Dandies, we shall not undertake to say. In the latter part of the work, he devotes a separate chapter to this class of persons, from the tenour of which we should be disposed to conclude, that he would consider any mode of divesting them of their property very much in the nature of a spoiling of the Egyptians.

"The only thing about the work, tending to prove that it is what it purports to be, a commentary on a real German treatise, is the style, which is a sort of Babylonish dialect, not destitute, it is true, of richness, vigour, and at times a sort of singular felicity of expression, but very strongly tinged throughout with the peculiar idiom of the German language. This quality in the style, however, may be a mere result of a great familiarity with German literature; and we cannot, therefore, look upon it as in itself decisive, still less as outweighing so much evidence of an opposite character."—*North-American Review, No. 89, October* 1835.

IV. New England Editors

"The Editors have been induced, by the express desire of many persons, to collect the following sheets out of the ephemeral pamphlets in which they first appeared, under the conviction that they contain in themselves the assurance of a longer date.

"The Editors have no expectation that this little Work will have a sudden and general popularity. They will not undertake, as there is no need, to justify the gay costume in which the Author delights to dress his thoughts, or the German idioms with which he has sportively sprinkled his pages. It is his humour to advance the gravest speculations upon the gravest topics in a quaint and burlesque style. If his masquerade offend any of his audience, to that degree that they will not hear what he has to say, it may chance to draw others to listen to his wisdom; and what work of imagination can hope to please all? But we will venture to remark that the distaste excited by these peculiarities in some readers is greatest at first, and is soon forgotten; and that the foreign dress and aspect of the Work are quite superficial, and cover a genuine Saxon heart. We believe, no book has been published for many years, written in a more sincere style of idiomatic English, or which discovers an equal mastery over all the riches of the language. The Author makes ample amends for the occasional eccentricity of his genius, not only by frequent bursts of pure splendour, but by the wit and sense which never fail him.

"But what will chiefly commend the Book to the discerning reader is the manifest design of the work, which is, a Criticism upon the Spirit of the Age—we had almost said, of the hour —in which we live; exhibiting in the most just and novel light the present aspects of Religion, Politics, Literature, Arts, and Social Life. Under all his gaiety the Writer has an earnest meaning, and discovers an insight into the manifold wants and tendencies of human nature, which is very rare among our popular authors. The philanthropy and the purity of moral sentiment, which inspire the work, will find their way to the heart of every lover of virtue."—*Preface to Sartor Resartus: Boston,* 1835, 1837.

SUNT, FUERUNT VEL FUERE

London, 30th June, 1838.

INDEX

INDEX

(The following Index to the Introduction, Text, Notes, and Appendixes lists all important items, and also incorporates the substance of the short Index which Carlyle added to the edition of *Sartor* which appeared as Volume I of the Library Edition, 1869.)